Adm.
15.95
N

W9-CMP-982

JK
271
.R43
1988

24,655

Remaking American
politics

DATE DUE

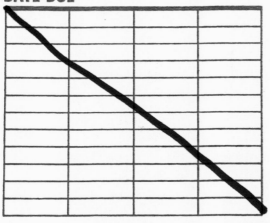

Remaking American politics
JK271.R43 1988   24655

Harris, Richard A.
VRJC/WRIGHT LIBRARY

TRANSFORMING AMERICAN POLITICS SERIES
Lawrence C. Dodd, Series Editor

Dramatic changes in political institutions and behavior over the past two decades have underscored the dynamic nature of American politics, confronting political scientists with a new and pressing intellectual agenda.

Transforming American Politics is dedicated to documenting these changes, reinterpreting conventional wisdoms, tracing historical patterns of change, and asserting new theories to clarify the direction of contemporary politics.

TITLES IN THIS SERIES

Remaking American Politics, edited by Richard A. Harris and Sidney M. Milkis

Managing the Presidency: The Eisenhower Legacy—From Kennedy to Reagan, Phillip G. Henderson

Democracies in Crisis: Public Policy Responses to the Great Depression, Kim Quaile Hill

The Congress, the President, and Public Policy: A Critical Analysis, Michael Mezey

Issues and Elections: Presidential Voting in Contemporary America, A Revisionist View, Euel Elliott

Transformations in American Political Parties, edited by L. Sandy Maisel

The Evolution of Competition in House Elections, 1946–1988, Gary C. Jacobson

Remaking American Politics

EDITED BY

Richard A. Harris
Rutgers University

Sidney M. Milkis
Brandeis University

Westview Press
BOULDER, SAN FRANCISCO, AND LONDON

TO OUR PARENTS

Transforming American Politics

All rights reserved. No part of this publication may be reproduced or transmitted in any form or by any means, electronic or mechanical, including photocopy, recording, or any information storage and retrieval system, without permission in writing from the publisher.

Copyright © 1989 by Westview Press, Inc., with the exception of Chapter 9, which is © 1989 by Jeffrey M. Berry

Published in 1989 in the United States of America by Westview Press, Inc., 5500 Central Avenue, Boulder, Colorado 80301, and in the United Kingdom by Westview Press, Inc., 13 Brunswick Centre, London WC1N 1AF, England

Library of Congress Cataloging-in-Publication Data
Remaking American politics.
  (Transforming American politics)
  Includes bibliographies and index.
  Contents: A decade of reform/Richard Harris—
Reformers of the 1960s and 1970s/Donald Brand—Dealing
Democratic honor out/Robert Eden—[etc.]
  1. United States—Politics and government—
1945–   . 2. Political participation—United States.
I. Harris, Richard A., 1951–   . II. Milkis, Sidney.
III. Series: Transforming American politics series.
JK271.R43 1989   320.973   87-12820
ISBN 0-8133-0495-4
ISBN 0-8133-0496-2 (pbk.)

Printed and bound in the United States of America

∞ The paper used in this publication meets the requirements of the American National Standard for Permanence of Paper for Printed Library Materials Z39.48-1984.

10   9   8   7   6   5   4   3   2   1

Contents

Preface   vii

INTRODUCTION

1   A Decade of Reform, *Richard A. Harris*   3

PART I
PHILOSOPHICAL FOUNDATIONS

2   Reformers of the 1960s and 1970s: Modern Anti-
    Federalists? *Donald R. Brand*   27

3   Dealing Democratic Honor Out: Reform and the
    Decline of Consensus Politics, *Robert Eden*   52

PART II
GOVERNMENTAL INSTITUTIONS

4   The Rise of the Technocratic Congress:
    Congressional Reform in the 1970s,
    Lawrence C. Dodd   89

5   Congress, Codetermination, and Arms Control,
    Edward Weisband   112

6   The Presidency, Policy Reform, and the Rise of
    Administrative Politics, *Sidney M. Milkis*   146

7   The Courts, Congress, and Programmatic Rights,
    R. Shep Melnick   188

PART III
NONGOVERNMENTAL INSTITUTIONS

8   Candidate-Centered Parties: Politics Without
    Intermediaries, *Stephen A. Salmore and Barbara G. Salmore*   215

v

9   Subgovernments, Issue Networks, and Political
    Conflict, *Jeffrey M. Berry*   239

10 Politicized Management: The Changing Face of
    Business in American Politics, *Richard A. Harris*   261

CONCLUSION

11 The Emerging Regime, *Hugh Heclo*   289

About the Contributors   321
Index   323

Preface

This project began in June 1985, when, as I was simultaneously struggling to complete a manuscript and preparing to move from Greencastle, Indiana, to Watertown, Massachusetts, I received a call from my close friend and colleague Richard Harris. Upon answering the phone, I heard Rich's voice, more excited than usual, pose a question of which through the years of our fruitful collaboration I had become suspicious: "Are you sitting down?" Since I knew that an exciting and ambitious proposal was about to be presented for my reaction, a proposal to which, I strongly suspected, I had no time to devote, I received Rich's call with the expectation of hearing him out but refusing, in the end, to take on any additional responsibilities. As usual, however, I found my good friend's enthusiasm for and commitment to scholarship (in the best sense of the term) impossible to resist, and, against my better judgment, I was enlisted as coeditor of *Remaking American Politics*. The stress of an impossible schedule has led me to have regrets from time to time over the course of the past three years for agreeing to take on this project; but I am grateful, now that this volume is complete, for having had the opportunity to participate in a shared research endeavor with a remarkably talented, patient, and cooperative group of scholars. Working with the likes of Donald Brand, Robert Eden, Jeffrey Berry, Edward Weisband, R. Shep Melnick, Stephen and Barbara Salmore, Hugh Heclo, and Lawrence Dodd was a broadening and edifying experience—an experience that reinforced my belief that the study of American politics can be a worthwhile and exciting endeavor.

This book represents an effort to document important developments in American politics that have occurred during the past two decades—developments that have been insufficiently examined by many of the basic and supplementary texts that purport to provide a comprehensive view of the American political system. In our own study of regulatory politics, Rich Harris and I had come to the conclusion that the advent of environmental and consumer protection during the late 1960s and 1970s was associated with major efforts to restructure the institutions of regulatory policy. These efforts to remake regulatory institutions, we suspected, were born of ambitious reform aspirations that sought to bring about fundamental changes in the principles and institutional arrangements of American politics. Our suspicions in this regard were strengthened by research on other institutional settings; the work of several scholars that examined changes in elections, political parties, Congress, and the Judiciary appeared to relate to our own in a systematic way. *Remaking American Politics* is the result of our effort to bring together a number of original essays that suggest a common theme: The American political system underwent a major realignment during the 1970s that can best be discerned by an exploration of the massive and profoundly important institutional developments of the past two decades.

Recent scholarship has often depicted the institutional and policy changes of the 1970s as an antinomian attack on the political organization that was the product of the New Deal, resulting in a decline of consensus and institutional fragmentation. Yet it is our contention that the wide-ranging changes highlighted by this volume are bound by common ideas about how American politics ought to operate. Together the following chapters suggest that the reforms of the 1970s resulted not so much in the degeneration of American political institutions as in the development of new institutional arrangements that were designed to accommodate a post–New Deal version of liberal politics. In effect, a new philosophy of government had emerged during the 1960s—a philosophy which held that our problems could not be solved by New Deal programs, which emphasized the public responsibility to guarantee economic security. Rather, the reforms of the 1970s were animated by a set of principles which held that our people were suffering from a sense of alienation, requiring attention to so-called quality-of-life issues that were as important to the well-to-do as they were to the poor. Thus, these reforms resulted in institutions and programs designed to foster "participatory democracy" and to expand the national government's policy responsibility in areas such as environmentalism, consumer protection, women's rights, and worker safety. These developments eventually gave rise to serious political opposition, culminating in the election of Ronald Reagan to the presidency in 1980. Yet, although the "Reagan Revolution" severely challenged many of the principles and institutions that emerged during the late 1960s and 1970s, the reforms have proven to be remarkably resilient, both shaping and circumscribing the impact of the Reagan presidency on the American political system.

The examination of recent reforms in American politics that follows encompasses a number of different perspectives. As Hugh Heclo writes in the conclusion, "It seems that not everyone writing in this book can be right." Yet the rich variety of analysis and evaluation included in this book seems appropriate, given the complex way in which our political system has been changing over the past two decades. Moreover, for all the competing and contradictory themes and evidence that this volume brings to light, some striking similarities span the chapters that follow, thus revealing the broad contours of the contemporary American political system. Even if this book does not make order out of chaos, it does suggest, we believe, that a common set of principles and an enduring pattern of institutional arrangements have evolved during the past two decades that define a *system* of governance, albeit one characterized by a disconcerting tendency toward uncertain political attachments and intractable group demands.

This volume never would have come together without the generous help of several people. Rich and I will always be grateful to the authors who agreed to write chapters for the book, and who, in spite of very demanding schedules, made such distinguished contributions. We are especially indebted to Lawrence Dodd, who not only authored a fine chapter for this volume but also had enough faith in our project to include it in his new series for Westview Press, Transforming American Politics: Studies in Intellectual and Political Change. The staff at Westview did extraordinary work in helping us get the volume into shape. Miriam Gilbert, Holly Arrow, and Jennifer Knerr displayed sensitivity and patience in supporting our editorial work, and made several helpful substantive suggestions as well. A word of thanks is also owed to Christine Arden, who did a superb copy-editing job on the book, and Beverly LeSuer, our project editor, who worked enthusiastically and skillfully to bring this volume to fruition.

In addition to our contributors and the fine staff at Westview, Rich and I are grateful to several others who supported this endeavor. The John Olin Foundation and the Rutgers University Research Council provided financial assistance that contributed to the preparation of *Remaking American Politics*. Martin Levin, director of the Gordon Public Policy Center at Brandeis University, and Jay Sigler, chair of the Graduate Department of Public Policy at Rutgers University, provided us with aid and comfort in the form of office space, research support, and a stimulating environment in which to work as we tackled the seemingly unending chores that were required to complete this book. Sandra Cheesman of the Rutgers Department of Public Policy and Lisa Carisella of the Brandeis Department of Politics helped in a number of ways in the preparation of the manuscript.

Finally, Rich and I want to express our love and gratitude to our families. With just the right mixture of compassion and impatience, Ellen, Carol, Eric, Jeffrey, Deborah, Lauren, and David watched us put this and other projects together. They encouraged us to persevere in difficult projects such as this one, while reminding us in various ways of the need to maintain a sense of perspective as we pushed our task to conclusion.

Sidney M. Milkis
Waltham, Massachusetts

Introduction

1

A Decade of Reform

RICHARD A. HARRIS

The decade of the 1970s was a decade of reform in the United States. A host of policy concerns, ranging from environmental protection to affirmative action, emerged on the national agenda and ultimately found expression in an impressive array of federal laws, regulations, and court decisions. As significant as these reforms were, however, it would be a serious error to construe the 1970s as a period in which only the substance of public policy shifted. The salience of such issues as campaign finance and control of the intelligence community demonstrated that the reform impulse encompassed the political process and policymaking institutions as well. Indeed, the central argument of this volume is that the decade of the 1970s was one in which American politics was *remade*— one in which major reforms were implemented not only in the substance of public policy but also in decisionmaking institutions and processes.

A first inkling that the reforms of the 1970s might constitute a remaking of American politics came from research on the development of environmental and consumer regulation.[1] Initially we approached this subject with the idea that environmentalists and consumer advocates were seeking institutional and process reform simply as a necessary condition for achieving their policy goals. Over time, however, it became clear that they also viewed such reforms as intrinsically worthwhile. In fact, at least with respect to environmental and consumer affairs, activist reformers consciously attempted to put in place a "new regulatory regime"—that is, a coherently structured system of new regulatory ideas and institutions as well as policies.[2] In a sense they "remade" regulatory politics. This conclusion suggested not only that the considerable activity in other areas of reform during the 1970s reflects some sort of "regime change" but also that these various reform efforts relate to one another in systematic ways.

The fact that so many changes in policy and process took place more or less contemporaneously during the 1970s was reason enough to take

3

notice. On a deeper level, though, the various reforms of the decade seemed to share an origin in the social ideals and political criticisms voiced by the New Left during the 1960s. All of the reforms, for example, appeared to be rooted both in a conviction that citizens ought to play a direct role in policy decisions that affected them and in a profound suspicion of big government and big business. This common ideological foundation provided a nexus linking the reforms at a very basic level: No matter what the specific policy objective involved, almost all of the reforms of the 1970s entailed some effort to rein in the power of what the New Left used to call the "establishment" and to open up governmental processes to the citizenry. It was in this spirit that many of the new regulatory laws mandated specific mechanisms to ensure that interested citizens could participate in administrative proceedings that previously were policy arenas insulated from public scrutiny and therefore susceptible to domination by bureaucrats and businesspeople. Of course, other reforms—such as those dealing with presidential selection, war powers, and campaign finance—were designed specifically to remake institutions and processes.

Was it possible that the activist reforms of the 1970s, articulating a coherent critique of American society, altered the institutional and procedural bases of politics as well as the substance of public policy in accord with their vision? And, if they had succeeded, what would be the long-run implications of these changes?

In an effort to address these questions, we have assembled outstanding examples of research on the reforms of the 1970s. Moreover, these individual works may be viewed as elements of a larger whole that, when pieced together, shows that American politics was indeed *remade*. In part, the changes in institutions and process were a means to an end. However, we believe that they were important in their own right as well, inasmuch as they represented a broad-based attempt to restructure principal political institutions and processes. By drawing together independent studies of the reforms, we hope to illustrate these arguments.

It is important to understand that the linkages across the current research of the contributors were preexisting, not contrived to conform with our notion of remaking American politics. Before this project's inception, each of the contributors was laboring on his own plot of a larger intellectual vineyard, so to speak; each had developed his interest in specific elements of the reforms and formulated ideas about institutional change. Thus, the chapters in this volume are integrated in two respects. First, they all deal with the same historical material—the reforms of the 1970s and their origins. Second, they approach the reforms from a common conceptual orientation, institutional analysis—that is, the examination of political institutions such as interest groups, branches of government, and business firms—both from an internal perspective as well as in terms of their interrelations.

Our primary task in this introductory chapter is to sketch in broad outline how American politics was remade in the 1970s and, in doing so, to illustrate the breadth and depth of the reforms in general. We also shall raise the possible implications of the reforms not only for the 1980s, but beyond. In this regard, institutional and process reforms loom larger than substantive reforms because changes in institutions and processes have the potential to affect policy decisions and the exercise of influence in the future. Finally, we will present the organization of the book, explaining the nature of the various chapters and suggesting the interconnections among them in order to help the reader see the conceptual as well as the substantive unity underlying this enterprise.

NEW POLICIES

The clearest indication that the 1970s constituted a significant period of reform activity was the tremendous expansion of the national agenda during that time. The list of major new issues in public debate was an imposing one, indeed. It included air and water pollution, strip mining, toxic waste, public health, product safety, consumer access to information, safety in the workplace, rights of the handicapped, affirmative action, abortion and birth control, campaign finance, the presidential nominating process, control over the intelligence community, and constitutional war powers. Many of these issues reflected the "quality-of-life" concerns that, according to some observers, typified postindustrial society.[3] Almost all of these issues, however, had antecedents in earlier reform periods but now reappeared under a slightly different guise and with renewed vigor. Environmental protection, for example, could be traced to the conservative movement in the Progressive Era, consumer protection to the Federal Trade Act of the Progressive Era and the Wheeler-Lea Act of the New Deal, campaign finance to the good-government movement among Progressives, and safety in the workplace to the labor struggles of the New Dealers. The reemergence of these issues in the 1970s defined that decade as one of substantial reform effort.

But the decade was one of policy achievement as well as political debate, as reformers successfully translated many of their policy concerns into governmental programs. These programs found concrete expression in new federal laws and new federal agencies. An enumeration of these laws and agencies, as shown in Tables 1.1 and 1.2, helps to convey a sense of how broad the reform effort actually was. As the tables indicate, the period from the late 1960s through the 1970s rivals the New Deal

Richard A. Harris

TABLE 1.1
Major Social Regulatory Measures Enacted Between 1969 and 1977

Law	Year
Mine Safety and Health Act	1969
National Environmental Policy Act	1969
Poison Prevention Packaging Act	1970
Clean Air Act Amendments	1970
Cigarette Advertising Act	1970
Railroad Safety Act	1970
Tire Safety Act	1970
Water Quality Improvement Act	1970
Occupational Safety and Health Act	1970
Consumer Product Safety Act	1972
Bumper Standards Act	1972
Ocean Dumping Act	1972
Pesticide Regulation Act	1972
Federal Water Pollution Control Act	1972
Noise Pollution and Control Act	1972
Safe Drinking Water Act	1973
Hazardous Materials Transportation Act	1974
Clean Air Amendments Act	1974
Federal Trade Commission Authorization	1974
Safe Drinking Water Act	1974
Seat Belt and School Bus Standards	1974
Magnuson-Moss Warranty Improvement Act	1974
Energy Policy and Conservation Act	1974
Coal Leasing Amendments Act	1974
Hart-Scott-Rodino Anti-Trust Amendments	1976
Federal Rail Safety Act	1976
Toxic Substances Control Act	1976
School Bus Safety Act	1976
Medical Devices Safety Act	1976
Department of Energy Organization Act	1977
Clean Water Act Extension	1977
Clean Air Act Amendments	1977
Safe Drinking Water Extension Act	1977
Surface Mining Control and Reclamation Act	1977
Saccharin Study and Labelling Act	1977

as a time in which many new laws were enacted and bureaucracies were created.

Yet a simple counting of federal initiatives grossly understates the impact of the reforms on American society and the economy. Like the 1930s, the later period witnessed a marked expansion of the public sector at the expense of the private sector as new issues focused national attention on areas of social and economic intercourse that custom had barred from government action. To fully appreciate the significance of

TABLE 1.2
Federal Regulatory Agencies by Date of Establishment

1932–1945	1970–1978
Federal Home Loan Bank Board (1932)	Environmental Protection Agency (1970)
Commodity Credit Corporation (1933)	Federal Railroad Administration (1970)
Federal Deposit Insurance Corporation (1933)	National Highway Traffic Safety Administration (1970)
Securities and Exchange Commission (1934)	National Oceanic and Aeronautic Administration (1970)
Federal Communications Commission (1934)	Postal Rate Commission (1970)
National Labor Relations Board (1934)	Consumer Product Safety Commission (1972)
Federal Maritime Commission (1936)	Mine Safety and Health Administration (1973)
Agricultural Marketing Service (1937)	Occupational Safety and Health Administration (1973)
Civil Aeronautics Board (1940)	Economic Regulatory Administration (1974)
	Nuclear Regulatory Commission (1975)
	Securities and Federal Grain Inspection Service (1976)
	Office of Surface Mining (1977)

the reforms of the 1970s, we must take into account not only the thousands of regulations written and administrative actions undertaken to implement the new laws but also the hundreds of court cases filed to clarify or contest them.

These activities involved vast governmental resources. Moreover, they dealt in great detail with the operations and decisions of a great many important public and private institutions. Elementary and secondary schools, universities, police and fire departments, business firms, regulatory bureaucracies, and even intelligence agencies were affected in major ways by the reform impulse of the 1970s. Many of these organizations had to devote significant resources in order to comply with federal reporting requirements on affirmative action, pollution control, and other new regulatory programs. They also had to spend tremendous sums of money to meet environmental or product-quality standards and to develop technical/scientific studies for environmental or social impact statements required under various laws. Finally, in responding to the reforms, these organizations had to change their internal operations and structures. The missions of such governmental bodies as regulatory bureaucracies and the CIA were redefined or "clarified" in the wake of the reforms. In short, political, economic, and social relations of the 1970s were profoundly influenced by reforms as the focus of political discourse shifted to new policy concerns.

The roots of this reform period lay in the turbulent politics of mobilization associated with the preceding decade. Suddenly the mainstream American values came into question. Politically, the 1960s were dominated by two issues: civil rights and the war in Vietnam. These two issues, however, served as catalysts and rallying cries for a deeper critique of American society, a critique associated with the New Left and dedicated to direct political action. The fundamental argument of New Leftists was that the individual in society was being overwhelmed and exploited by the "establishment," an unholy alliance of big government, big business, and the military. For New Leftists, the modern liberalism of the New Deal had degenerated into little more than a huge engine of oppression. Resistance to the civil rights movement and prosecution of the war in Vietnam not only offered a convenient confirmation of their critique but also propelled the United States out of the quiescent 1950s and into the tumultuous 1960s.

The 1950s were characterized by a faith in "pluralism"—that is, by a vigorous but peaceful competition among interests, primarily economic, out of which the public interest presumably was served. Pluralism, as historian Robert Wiebe has observed, promoted "a strikingly benign vision that drew a healthy, united America from the clutter of its ceaseless, petty struggles."[4] However, "the late 1960's shattered this decorum,"[5] as bitter critics inveighed against what they saw as the hypocrisy and myth of America: "Beneath official claims to a humane world mission, an egalitarian society, and a rule of law, they found a record of imperialism, racism, and oppression, a barbarous society camouflaged with shiny rhetoric."[6] Such radical attacks, of course, evoked equally strident counterattacks from officialdom and defenders of the status quo. The political and intellectual ferment of the 1960s undermined the consensus on national priorities—or the political "decorum," as Wiebe termed it. It also laid the foundation for the new national agenda and reform policies of the 1970s.

Although it would be simplistic (and untrue) to assert that the reforms of the 1970s amounted to a realization of the ideals and agenda of the New Left, the radical critiques of the 1960s did inform and shape many demands in the 1970s.[7] (This conclusion will become more apparent when we discuss institutional and process reforms.) Policy reforms dedicated to preserving the ecology, protecting the consumer, and advancing minority rights clearly reflected concerns raised in the 1960s. Thus, in the numerous reforms of the 1970s we can find echoes of the previous decade's political fervor.

The election of Ronald Reagan in 1980 testifies eloquently—if somewhat ironically—to the reform achievements of the 1970s. The essence of his presidential campaign was that we had gone too far: too far in regulating private enterprise, too far in insinuating government into peoples' personal lives, and too far in establishing federal programs to rectify past injustices. In short, we had gone too far in attempting to realize ideals expressed in the 1960s through reform policies developed in the 1970s. The accuracy of these campaign allegations notwithstanding, much of Reagan's electoral and financial support grew out of a sense that the preceeding decade of reform had indeed gone too far, that the costs of many of the reforms far outweighed the benefits, and that it was time to swing the pendulum back.

POLICY REFORM IN PERSPECTIVE

Of course, the 1970s did not mark the first time in the twentieth century that political reformers consciously attempted to institute policy reforms in American politics. As we have suggested, major reform periods in the Progressive Era and the New Deal not only preceded, but in many respects foreshadowed, the policy reforms of the 1970s. An understanding of these two antecedent efforts at reform is instructive inasmuch as they also embodied a close linkage between reform of substance and reform of process in public policy. Indeed, it is precisely this linkage of policy substance and process that accounts for the significance of all three episodes in American history.

The Progressives were associated not only with antitrust policy, child labor laws, and improved product quality but also with reform of municipal government, direct election of senators, and House reforms that sharply cut back the Speaker's near-dictatorial powers. What has led historians to view this conglomeration of reforms as a well-defined movement is a certain intellectual coherence underlying all of the reforms. That coherence is all the more evident in the process reforms because they most clearly embodied the Progressives' concerns about the viability of the political-economic order in American society. A common element in the process reforms of the Progressive Era was the belief that economic power concentrated in the hands of industrial magnates was leading to a consolidation of control over the political system by big business and the gradual disenfranchisement of the citizenry. Some Progressives, such as Louis Brandeis, expressed an "antibigness ethic" and supported vigorous reforms that would establish the national government as the guardian of small business.[8] Others, such as Theodore Roosevelt, did not oppose big business in principle but were concerned that it wielded inordinate political influence. As Roosevelt asserted in his well-known "New Nationalism" address of 1910: "The way out lies, not in attempting to prevent [industrial] combinations, but in completely controlling them in the interest of the public welfare."[9] Clearly, progressive efforts at eliminating patronage in local government and directly electing senators were measures intended not only to facilitate substantive policy changes but also to restore control over political decisions to the people.

Perhaps the most stunning example of the linkage of policy substance and policy process during the Progressive Era was the so-called House Revolt of 1910. Since the election of 1896 Republicans had controlled the House of Representatives and, hence, had elected the Speaker who, through his authority to appoint committee members and chairs, wielded almost uninhibited power. Within the Republican ranks, an archconservative group known as the "Old Guard" held sway, electing Speakers who unswervingly upheld the interests of big business and frustrated the policy aims of Progressives, Democrat and Republican alike. In 1910, the Progressive Republicans finally broke ranks on some critical votes, a move that undermined the Speakers' authority and helped to establish the current system of appointing committee members and committee chairmen on the basis of seniority. In this instance, reformation of the decisionmaking structure of the House of Representatives advanced substantive policy goals, but it also revealed a general dismay over the state of politics.

New Dealers, for their part, instituted the most far-reaching policy reforms in American history by establishing programs in welfare, social security, labor rights, and economic management. However, the court-packing fiasco of 1937 (explained below) and the governmental reorganization attempted in 1938 and enacted the following year dominated Franklin Roosevelt's second term, illustrating a deep concern with institutions and process. As in the Progressive Era, these efforts to change the policy process reflected both a frustration with the inability to achieve specific policy goals and a deep dissatisfaction with the way in which the system was operating generally. The Court-Packing episode grew out of the acrimonious confrontation between the Supreme Court and the president that occurred when the justices declared key New Deal legislation unconstitutional. In response, Franklin Roosevelt sought to increase the number of justices sitting and to appoint individuals of his own choosing in order to ensure that future laws would pass muster with the highest court. Although he did not succeed, the Court ceased to oppose New Deal legislation.

Roosevelt did, however, reform the executive branch, thereby establishing increased independence from Congress and additional mechanisms for strong White House control. The blueprint for this administrative reform was crafted by the Brownlow Commission, a blue-ribbon panel of reform-minded experts from universities and the business community. Although the commission's plan was not adopted in its entirety and Roosevelt had to compromise on certain issues, the administrative process was substantially remade and, perhaps more important, set on a course of executive branch dominance that would continue for decades to come.[10]

During both the Progressive Era and the period of the New Deal, reformers recognized that the inherent inertia of the American political system could stall a reform agenda, even one with fairly widespread popular support. In order to advance reform, the political system would inevitably have to overcome separation of powers, federalism, bicameralism, and other institutional safeguards against tyranny of the majority. Institutions and processes are central to the American political system because they create constraints that are at the essence of constitutional government, a political form dedicated primarily to limiting the role of the state. This limitation is ensured by the construction of institutional procedures that promote the pursuit of self-interest over any government-directed quest for the general welfare. Moreover, the traditional liberal values associated with constitutional government have acquired, as James Madison hoped, a sort of "transcendent" status in America; they are a part of the political culture. The double dilemma for the early reformers was how to overcome both the constitutional constraints on collective action and the cultural bias against positive government. When the twentieth-century reform advocates demanded an ever-increasing role for government in society, they necessarily confronted the principle of limited government more directly, and, as a consequence, their programs appeared more "revolutionary."

Such process changes as those embodied in the House Revolt of 1910 and the 1939 Reorganization Act were linked to the very practical problems experienced by the Progressive and New Deal reformers; but they were also justified at an abstract level. During both periods the clamor for reform was rooted in the profound belief that the policy process and political institutions, as configured at the time, were incapable of generating acceptable policy. Simply electing the right people or forging the right coalitions would not or, in the view of some reformers, could not have worked under the existing regime. Thus, process reform was sought not only as a means to specific ends but also for its own sake.

INSTITUTIONAL AND PROCESS REFORMS
IN THE 1970S

Both the Progressives and the New Dealers apparently recognized that successful policy reform ultimately depended on changing the policy process in such a way as to redistribute political influence in their favor. Precisely the same argument may be made with respect to the reformers of the 1970s, who were convinced that institutional and process changes were a necessary concomitant of major policy shifts. The 1970s, therefore, can be viewed as the latest manifestation of a twentieth-century reform tradition directed toward a reassertion of popular control over policy-making. This is not to suggest that reformers in any of the three periods articulated a coherent reform program that explicitly linked substantive and process changes, although there are individual examples to be found—Herbert Croly or Robert LaFollette among the Progressives, Rexford Tugwell or Marriner Eccles among the New Dealers, and Ralph Nader or John Gardner in the contemporary period. The fact remains that during each period, changes in both the substance and process of public policy sprang from common ideological critiques and common political aspirations of the reform tradition.

In certain respects, of course, the 1970s were very different from antecedent reform periods. Above all, the reforms of this decade embodied both a fundamental critique of American society and a deep suspicion of American government, neither of which typified earlier reforms. This extremely critical perspective derived from New Left ideas and experiences in the civil rights movement and antiwar activities of the 1960s—that is, from the vigorous attack on pluralist American society noted by Robert Wiebe.

As was the case at the turn of the century and during the 1930s, reform advocates in the 1970s sought to influence public policy by enacting new laws and establishing new federal agencies to implement those laws. Most of the new programs in this reform tradition were intended to promote the welfare of individuals and the public as a whole by regulating private economic activity and controlling the power of organized interests. In essence, the reformers perceived a gross imbalance in the exercise of influence that favored big business and restricted the representation of the public in policymaking. They tried to restore a sense of fairness and equity to pluralist competition.

The activists of the 1970s also revealed, by their demands and pronouncements, the more fundamentally critical view associated with the New Left. But this feature of their actions is problematic in that the New Left essentially rejected pluralism. The result was an apparent tension in the demands for process reform: On the one hand, there was an implicit yearning for pluralism to work, for the public simply to be represented adequately in the councils of government; on the other, there was a profound suspicion of pluralism.

The suspicion of pluralism, rooted in the strident politics of the 1960s, was given greater legitimacy by the influential work of Theodore Lowi. Lowi's work, which was known to reformers of the 1970s, echoed the New Left's view that American politics was not based on a pluralist harmony in which a multiplicity of interests competed on more or less equal terms but that *organized interests* wielded undue influence in a policy process substantially insulated from the public-at-large. Traditionally, reformers had viewed the problem of American pluralism as one of imbalance: Things could be set right if only the public interest were factored into the political debate by organizing and promoting the representation of the public interest.

Theodore Lowi, in contrast, perceived a more profound problem with pluralism. Whereas reformers historically had perceived a representational imbalance in American politics, Lowi attempted to explain the origins of that imbalance. He asserted that the emergence during the New Deal of an "administrative state," characterized by the policymaking predominance of the executive branch, fostered a new system of representation that he labeled "interest group liberalism." Interest group liberalism referred to a situation in which organized interests (again, especially business interests) predominated because key decisions were made within the narrow and insultated administrative networks of a highly balkanized policy process.

According to Lowi, the real threat was not just that a particular set of interests would almost always prevail in the policy process, but that the institutional arrangements established under the Constitution were undermined, resulting in the making of "policy without law": "Congressmen are guided in their votes, Presidents in their programs, and administrators in their discretion by whatever *organized interests* they have taken for themselves as most legitimate; and that is the measure of legitimacy of demands" (emphasis added).[11] In Lowi's view, the traditional prescription would exacerbate the problems of pluralism by fostering a proliferation of organized interests. Whether organized interests purported to represent business or the public, Lowi felt that such interests, as permanent players in a policy process shielded from the citizenry's eyes, enhanced the administrative state and denigrated democratic decisionmaking. Not surprisingly, in the second edition of *The End of Liberalism*, Lowi expresses serious misgivings about the ultimate consequences of the contemporary reforms. Indeed, for him they represent a logical outcome of interest group liberalism: "socialism for the organized, capitalism for the unorganized."[12]

Despite the implicit contradiction, reformers in the 1970s adapted Lowi's arguments to their traditional attempts at restoring a pluralist balance; both Lowi and traditional reformism expressed a hostility toward big business that the reformers enthusiastically accepted. Consistent with Lowi's critique of American politics, advocates of reform held that successful policy change had to be predicated on profound changes in the policy process—that is, on changes that would guard against the subversion of public policy through the politics of "interest group liberalism." One way to overcome the difficulties of this system of "plural elitism," reformers reasoned, was to participate in the policy process on a permanent basis.

The dilemma for reformers was how to play a permanent role in the permanent state without becoming co-opted into its policymaking system. The only way they could play this role was to operate as a sort of fifth column, subscribing to the rules of the establishment while attacking its organizing principles. This posture evinced a certain schizophrenia: Activist reformers readily accepted Lowi's scathing portrayal of American pluralism as a recipe for disenfranchising the citizenry, yet their remedies invariably entailed an expansion of administrative policymaking, which was the root cause of the problem in Lowi's analysis. They sought to invade the entrails of the governmental leviathan, without its digesting them.

A major reason for the ambivalence of the 1970s reformers toward pluralism is that, unlike the Progressives or New Dealers, they were the first to confront a mature administrative state. For them, the problem was not simply the influence of big business on government but, as the New Leftists suggested, the alliance of big business and big government in an administratively centered policy process. The mere passage of reform legislation and creation of new agencies could not ensure the general welfare under such a system, inasmuch as control over the implementation of reform policy lay in the hands of bureaucrats and businesspeople.

The reform advocates in the 1970s thus began to demonstrate a keen sensitivity to the significance of implementation in the policy process. Historically, reforms that had apparently succeeded in the enactment phase of the policy process were substantially weakened by organized interests in the implementation phase because earlier activists had not maintained a strong presence following the enactment of reform measures. The classic scenario for undermining the general welfare in this way was to be found with independent regulatory commissions—federal agencies established to control private economic activity injurious to the public. The Interstate Commerce Commission, for example, was established to prevent railroads from charging exorbitant freight rates, but it eventually became the rail industry's best friend in Washington. Similarly, in the eyes of many critics the Civil Aeronautics Board protected the rates and routes of the airline industry for decades, the Federal Communications Commission seemed to serve major broadcasters more than the public, and the Federal Trade Commission catered to business at the expense of the consumer. Over time, reformers concluded that there was politics after enactment, and that administrative institutions and processes were primary considerations if policy reform was to succeed.

With these conclusions in mind, reformers in the 1970s pursued means to ensure that their programs would be properly implemented rather than subverted by administrative institutions and processes. Along with environmental statutes, reformers insisted on and won public permitting procedures that allowed them to play a role in Environmental Protection Agency (EPA) decisions on approving business operations or construction. In environmental and consumer laws they often acquired automatic grants of standing, which allowed them to sue business firms and even federal agencies. This procedure proved to be a pivotal mechanism through which reformers could use the federal courts to ensure that bureaucrats would strictly enforce statutory preformance standards on business. Moreover, it was during the 1970s that previously closed committee and subcommittee hearings were opened to the public, thereby curtailing collusion among business people, bureaucrats, and key congressional allies. The passage of the Freedom of Information Act also served to open up administrative decisionmaking by providing reformers with access to governmental files—a valuable resource for effective participation in policymaking institutions. In fact, each of these measures was intended to build public participation into administration—indeed, to overhaul the policy process to ensure the effective implementation of reform programs.

Though not accompanied by programmatic demands, significant reforms were also instituted in the legislative, executive, and judicial branches (as well as in their interrelations). In general, these reforms were designed to check the expanding discretionary power of the presidency and bureaucratic agencies by increasing the oversight responsibilities of Congress and the courts. Persuaded that strict oversight was imperative, reformers attempted to enlist legislators and the judiciary in a grand enforcement effort. Ostensibly a challenge to the "administrative state," these efforts in fact reflected the reformers' understanding that policymaking had become largely a matter of "implementation." The renascence of Congress and the courts in the 1970s, therefore, involved these institutions extensively in the details of administration.[13] More fundamentally, modifications in administrative law and practice bound the courts, bureaucratic agencies, and congressional subcommittees into "issue networks," which short-circuited the regular legislative process and generally made policymaking institutions more hospitable to program advocates.[14]

Although the reformers' focus on process changes was intended to reshape the substance of public policy, they also perceived these changes as intrinsically worthwhile efforts to rectify the systematic injustices in American politics described by Lowi. They believed that without such efforts, reform in the areas of public health, safety, pollution control, and consumer protection would be seriously compromised by the pre-dominance of business interests in administrative processes. The social reformers of the 1970s, however, went beyond a concern with programs and policymaking per se; they articulated a broad critique of principles and institutions at the heart of American politics generally.

In surveying the 1970s, one finds major reforms in Congress, political parties, and campaign finance. Each of these reform areas was aimed at fundamentally reordering the political process, but the measures that were taken affected policies and programs only indirectly. Weakening the seniority system in Congress, selecting presidential nominees through primaries rather than party caucuses, and limiting individual campaign contributions were championed as methods of democratizing American politics—that is, of making political institutions responsive to the broad citizenry rather than just to organized socioeconomic elites.

Behind all of the reform efforts were public-lobby groups specifically designed to enable reformers to play a permanent role in every phase of the policy process. These organizations embodied both the traditional reform ambition of redressing power imbalances in pluralist competition power and an antipathy to the administrative state with its attendant problems of interest group liberalism. In fact, many of the process reforms must be seen as bold efforts to facilitate the participation of public lobbyists in the policy process.[15] In this way, they could monitor the oversight activities of the federal government that had been entrusted to administrative agencies.

As public lobbies began to play a more prominent role in the drama of public policy, private lobbyists began adopting different strategies. In particular, individual business firms increasingly found it prudent to develop their own participatory capabilities, independent of trade as-sociations and other business lobbies.[16] The newer regulation system-atically imposed benefits as well as costs on firms, thereby tending to undermine the trade associations' efforts at collective action. Although strictly speaking not the reformers' intention, this development also served to redefine the policy process as business interests became more fragmented: For their own competitive and strategic reasons, some firms tacitly or even openly supported environmental and consumer regulation. Firm-level participation also tended to emphasize more specific and technical issues in the policy process than was possible when trade associations attempted to work out common positions among their members. In this environment, firms and public lobbyists had incentives to cooperate as well as to compete in policymaking, a situation that created anxiety on both sides.

All of the changes in the policy process that occurred during the 1970s, though not part of a single, organic reform program, were all of a piece. Thus far political scientists have not systematically linked these process changes with one another. Nor have they linked them collectively with the broad policy changes of the 1970s. Nevertheless, we believe that they are tied together by both purpose and ideology; in other words, the process reforms were at once a means of ensuring the success of policy changes sought in the 1970s and reflective of the ideals and criticisms of the 1960s. All of these seemingly disparate process changes, moreover, were the result of self-conscious actions taken by political reformers who were challenging the legitimacy of prevailing policymaking institutions. As we have noted, reformers in the 1970s were as interested in ending the perceived perversion of public policy by interest group liberalism as in achieving their substantive policy goals; both aims required institutional and process reforms.

THE NEW INSTITUTIONALISM

In the 1970s, and even today, the interest of political scientists in public policy has tended to focus on the social and economic effects of policy or on interest conflict in the policy process. The question of interest conflict, or "who governs," has been an especially central concern. Indeed, Harold Lasswell's classic formulation—that politics is about "who gets what, when and how"—has preoccupied political science for a generation. However, the contemporary activists' concentration on institutions and process does not fit neatly into political analyses built around notions of self-interest and purposive behavior; if anything, such a concentration appears "irrational" in the context of interests competing for scarce resources.

One way to reconcile attention to institutions with interest-conflict models of politics is to assume that this attention has a purely rational, instrumental character; institutional and process reform is not an end in itself but a necessary condition for concrete policy goals. When actions to change policymaking institutions are undertaken for the effect such change may have on policy outcomes, political behavior is endowed with a sense of "rationality": Institutional and process reform constitute means to particular ends. This type of reasoning, though, is inconsistent with much of the reform activity that took place in the 1970s. To be sure, reformers were concerned with policy outcomes and sought to restructure institutions to promote the kinds of policies they favored. Yet, clearly, they also pursued changes because they viewed them as intrinsically worthwhile—as an antidote to the malaise of interest group liberalism. Moreover, their arguments often took the form of ideological critiques of the larger political system. Ideas and values, in addition to interests, fueled reform politics.

In an insightful article, James March and Johan Olsen took note of the theoretical problems confronting mainstream political scientists in their efforts to assess policy changes.[17] These problems were most pronounced in the field of American politics. Models of interest conflict grounded on assumptions of "rational" political behavior simply did not account for the energy and passion that reformers had devoted to critiquing institutions and processes. March and Olsen observe that political scientists, as a consequence, have demonstrated a rekindled interest in institutions and processes during the 1970s. One reason for this renewed interest was the growing disenchantment with interest-based theories in political science; these theories seemed unable to account for many interesting phenomena. Another important reason, though, was that the decade of the 1970s was one of profound change in political institutions, during which reform efforts were appearing on nearly every front.

Studying these reforms logically entailed a focus on institutions. Younger scholars especially (though not exclusively) who had come of age politically in the 1960s and early 1970s were attuned to the importance of institutions and processes. Yet March and Olsen do not advocate a complete rejection of interest-based theory. On the contrary, what they recommend is an effort to reintegrate the study of institutions into the study of politics. That reintegration is what is meant by the "new institutionalism."

Of course, an emphasis on institution and process is hardly an unprecedented approach to the study of American politics; indeed, it can be traced to the founding. In his well-known essay on factions, James Madison acknowledged the primacy of self-interest and economic position in accounting for political behavior, but insisted that such behavior could be controlled and channeled by means of institutions and processes embodied in the proposed constitution.[18] Similarly, twentieth-century reformers beginning with Woodrow Wilson have argued that political actions were shaped largely by political institutions.[19] A focus on political institutions has long been important to the study of American government because such institutions are the practical manifestation of liberal principles. But what does a focus on institutions mean? And how does it change political analysis?

In the second half of the twentieth century, an institutionalist perspective naturally means a focus on the role of organizations in policymaking (as March and Olsen suggest in their title). Political organizations include congressional committees and subcommittees, the White House, bureaucratic agencies, the courts, and public and private lobby groups. Clearly the institutional and process reforms of the 1970s changed the structure and operation of many of these entities. Some, such as the public-lobby groups, new agencies, and new business lobby organizations, were wholly new organizational actors. The concept of political institution, however, also encompasses the formal and informal relationships among such organizations as well as the more or less stable processes through which these organizations and their members interact. The new institutionalism refers to a research emphasis on what goes on among as well as within organizations.

From a theoretical standpoint, the new institutionalism in political analysis means that institutions and processes are treated as critical explanatory variables. Institutions cannot be regarded as simply the locus or the product of political behavior. Nor can the assumption that political behavior is rooted solely in the rational pursuit of material interests be sustained. Rather, the new institutionalism asserts what March and Olsen term the "autonomy" of political institutions. Institutional analyses treat institutions and processes as both independent and dependent variables: They affect as well as reflect society. For example, the institutional reforms of the 1970s explain a good deal about the frustrations President Reagan confronted in his efforts to deregulate the economy during his first term. They also may help us understand the increasingly prominent role played by the courts in the administrative state in the 1970s and 1980s, not to mention their implications for policymaking in the 1990s.

Another important theoretical implication of the new institutionalism, consistent with the relaxation of assumptions about rationality and self-interest, is that much political behavior is value-oriented or symbolic. To the extent that ideas and values of reform underlie institutional arrangements, political behavior is at least partially a function of those ideas and values. Institutional analyses suggest that politics may reflect a preoccupation with rights and legitimacy of action rather than policy outcomes. In other words, means matter as much as ends. As March and Olsen put it, "Potential participants seem to care as much for the right to participate as for the fact of participation; participants recall the features of the process more easily and vividly than they do its outcomes."[20]

As a result of this overwhelming concern about participation, decision procedures publicly defended in instrumental terms may take on a ritualistic or symbolic cast. In fact, Aaron Wildavsky argues that the environmental reforms of the 1970s were characterized by just such symbolically based behavior. He claims that environmental policy has come to entail a "ritual of purification" in which an adherence to the appropriate implementation procedures eclipsed the goal of a cleaner environment as a measure of successful policy.[21] This view, in turn, suggests the possibility that political institutions embody the prevailing

VERNON REGIONAL
JUNIOR COLLEGE LIBRARY

cultural values of society and, more important for our purposes, that historical shifts in those values may be registered through institutional reform. One reason for the seemingly inflexible demands that business follow the letter of the law is the deep suspicion of big government and big business bred among activists in the 1960s and carried over into the 1970s.

ORGANIZATION

This book is divided into three main parts. Appropriately, we begin with chapters by Donald Brand and Robert Eden regarding the ideas and values of reformers. Brand examines the evolution of public philosophy and its institutional implications. His point of departure is Theodore Lowi's influential depiction of American politics since the New Deal as constituting a "second republic." He argues that the New Deal was predicated on a conception of pragmatism that departed from the "rule of law" embodied in the traditional public philosophy. Brand also illustrates how, in the 1970s, attempts to translate Lowi's critique of interest group liberalism into institutional reality were predicated on a new public philosophy, one at odds not only with the pragmatism of the New Deal but also, ironically, with the "rule of law" principle on which Lowi attacked the second republic. In a provocative argument, he suggests that the contemporary reformers find themselves in this uncomfortable position because they hold a vision of society much like the one advanced by the Anti-Federalists at the founding, and hence, they face the same basic dilemmas in trying to realize that vision. Reformers of the 1960s and 1970s, Brand asserts, were genuinely interested in empowering citizens and restraining the autonomy of the central government. Yet, as he also points out, such goals can undermine the government's capacity to realize important public-policy goals. Ultimately, Brand suggests, these recent reformers (like the Anti-Federalists before them) ended up tilting at windmills: They were following an impossible dream of a decentralized state that could provide vigorous policy leadership.

Robert Eden's analysis demonstrates that the public philosophy was indeed altered, but in a decidedly undemocratic direction. In this sense, he departs from Brand, who offers a much more sympathetic portrayal of the activist reformers. At the heart of Eden's challenging thesis is an application of Alexis de Tocqueville's concept of "democratic honor." As Eden explains, this concept was rooted in the fearless and vigorous individualism of commercial endeavor, but the New Deal irrevocably changed that scenario, substituting a notion of honor that paid homage to the courageous pursuit and management of collective enterprise. Under

VERNON REGIONAL
JUNIOR COLLEGE LIBRARY

FDR, though, democratic honor continued to underlie a public consensus on societal values. The contemporary period of reform, however, replaced even the New Deal consensus with a "politics of organized minorities." Eden somewhat pessimistically asserts that the politics of the 1960s and 1970s put in place a series of competing notions of democratic honor, and that politics and policy are the poorer for it.

From this ideological and philosophical discussion we move to a consideration of specific reforms as reflected in our governmental institutions. In the first of the chapters on this subject, Lawrence Dodd analyzes the numerous congressional reforms of the 1970s against the backdrop of a cyclical theory of institutional change in Congress. He then delineates the institutional form ("technocratic government" as he terms it) associated with these reforms. His characterization of technocratic government, with its emphasis on interactions with the executive branch and subgovernmental politics, bears a remarkable resemblance to Eden's description of the politics of organized minorities. He extends this analysis to explain the executive/legislative wrangling over the federal budget during the Reagan administration and finally suggests implications for the future.

Whereas Dodd focuses on the congressional role in domestic policy, Edward Weisband examines the impact of institutional reforms on Congress's role in foreign policy. Specifically, he explores the relationship between congressional reforms and the increasingly prominent role of the legislature in arms-control policy. He contends that Congress has attempted to pursue a strategy of "co-determination" with the White House in this crucial area of foreign policy, and that this strategy carries over into other realms of foreign policy as indicated by recent controversies surrounding the Iran-contra investigation and the congressional involvement in Central American peace initiatives. Much like Dodd, he argues that specialization and increased technical expertise in Congress have promoted this more activist posture among legislators.

Sidney Milkis's contribution focuses on the contemporary institutional transformation of the executive branch. This transformation, argues Milkis, can be traced partly to the New Deal. He maintains that Roosevelt attempted to shield substantive policy reforms from the uncertainties of regular political conflict by cultivating a central role for administrative decisionmaking in the policy process. In this respect, Milkis's chapter stands somewhere between those of Brand and Eden. Like Brand, he asserts that the contemporary reforms are qualitatively different from those of the New Deal in that they embody an effort to infuse public policymaking with an element of meaningful citizen participation. Like Eden, however, he raises questions about the democratic character of an administratively based policy process.

In the final chapter on governmental institutions, R. Shep Melnick illustrates how the federal courts have become a part of the new institutional arrangements. Indeed, the implication of his analysis is that the courts ought to be viewed as regular participants in the subgovernmental networks that comprise "technocratic government" (to use Dodd's term). The courts, according to Melnick, have been called upon to accept the role of arbiter for the disputes arising from the implementation of reform policies—a role they have willingly accepted. More important, contends Melnick, the courts will likely continue to play a key role in promoting and expanding the central government's role in reform.

The third part of the book deals with nongovernmental institutions. First, in their discussion of party reform, Stephen and Barbara Salmore broadly investigates the party reforms that were effected at all levels during the 1970s. Beginning with the impact of the McGovern-Fraser Commission on presidential selection, but carrying through to changes in the role and functioning of parties generally, they argue that these reforms substantially weakened party organization in favor of candidate-centered organizations and issue activists. Yet they also point to significant factors, such as the "institutionalization" of the parties' national committees, that suggest a renewal of party strength. In fact, the decline of the traditional party system, based on patronage practices and organized primarily at the state and local levels, has made possible the rise of a "new American party system" in which programmatic commitment and national organization are prominent factors. The Salmores remain skeptical, however, about the long-term prospects of this party renewal. In the final analysis, they see the changes in elections and governance during the 1970s as having established an enduring institutional legacy that is inhospitable to partisan politics and organization.

Next, Jeffrey Berry takes up the critical question of interest representation. He describes how the reforms of the 1970s were accompanied by a shift in interest group politics—that is, by a shift from traditionally insulated subgovernments to issue networks that "come closer to fulfilling the pluralist prescription for democratic politics." This conclusion contrasts with the dire analysis provided by Robert Eden; it also adopts a more positive perspective than that of Donald Brand regarding the broadening of interest representation in issue networks. Especially in light of the decline of political parties, the greater scope of interest representation in issue networks has provided an alternative vehicle for citizen participation. A key question, though, is the extent to which the issue networks have served that function. Or have they simply become part of what Morris Fiorina has called the "Washington establishment"? Berry, in fact, views the politics of issue networks quite positively, arguing that these networks have led to policy outcomes more representative of the citizenry as a whole.

In the final chapter on nongovernmental institutions, Richard Harris examines the organizational responses of business to the reforms. He shows how the process reforms of the 1970s provided incentives for individual business firms to play an increasing role in almost all aspects of policymaking. Politics and social responsibility have become key decision factors in strategic planning for many firms. The institutional significance of this fact is that trade associations and other business lobbies now share their role with firms that have developed their own lobbying bases in Washington. In adapting, the firms have changed their institutional structures and outlooks; by participating, they have also changed the institutional relationships in electoral, legislative, and issue network politics. While not entirely at ease about the nature of these changes, Harris indicates that they may hold the promise of greater cooperation among competing interests in national politics.

In the concluding chapter, Hugh Heclo assesses the extent to which the shift in public philosophy has been translated into institutional and process reforms, which in turn have amounted to a remaking of American politics. Because the reforms were both wide-ranging and linked by a common ideological orientation, it is likely that their impact was not simply encapsulated in particular policy spheres but, indeed, was felt systematically throughout American politics. It is also likely that the reforms will continue to shape American politics in the future. Such insight is facilitated by the reemergence of institutional analyses in the study of American politics. This volume reflects that reemergence as much as it reflects an interest in the reforms themselves.

NOTES

1. R. Harris and S. Milkis, "Deregulating the Public Lobby Regime: A Tale of Two Agencies," prepared for the annual meeting of the American Political Science Association, Chicago, Illinois (1983).

2. Ibid.

3. See, for example, D. Bell, *The End of Ideology* (Glencoe, Ill.: Free Press, 1960); C. Reich, *The Greening of America* (New York: Random House, 1970); and R. Inglehart, *The Silent Revolution: Changing Values and Political Style Among Western Publics* (Princeton, N.J.: Princeton University Press, 1977).

4. R. H. Wiebe, *The Segmented Society: An Introduction to the Meaning of America* (New York: Oxford University Press, 1974), p. 5.

5. Ibid., p. 7.

6. Ibid., p. 11.

7. M. McCann, *Taking Reform Seriously: Perspectives on Public Interest Liberalism* (Ithaca, N.Y.: Cornell University Press, 1986); S. Rothman and R. Lichter, "Elite

Ideology and Risk Perception in Nuclear Energy Policy," *American Political Science Review* (June 1987); and S. Beer, "In Search of a New Public Philosophy," in A. King, ed., *The New American Political System* (Washington, D.C.: American Enterprise Institute, 1978).

8. T. McGraw, *Prophets of Regulation* (Cambridge, Mass.: Harvard University Press, 1984).

9. T. Roosevelt, *The Works of Theodore Roosevelt*, vol. 18 (New York: Da Capo Press, 1926), p. 12.

10. S. Milkis, "The Presidency and Political Parties," in M. Nelson, ed., *The Presidency and the Political System*, 2nd ed. (Washington, D.C.: Congressional Quarterly Press, 1987).

11. T. J. Lowi, *The End of Liberalism* (New York, W. W. Norton, 1979), p. 72.

12. Ibid., p. 279.

13. A. Schick, "Congress and the Details of Administration," *Public Administration Review* (September/October 1976); J. Rabkin, "The Judiciary in the Administrative State," *The Public Interest* (Spring 1983); and J. A. Wettergreen, "Constitutional Problems of American Bureaucracy in INS v. Chadha," prepared for the annual meeting of the American Political Science Association, New Orleans, Louisiana (1985).

14. R. S. Melnick, "The Politics of Partnership: Institutional Coalitions and Statutory Rights," Occasional Paper No. 84-3, Center for American Political Studies, Harvard University (1985).

15. B. Ackerman and W. Hassler, *Clean Coal/Dirty Air* (New Haven, Conn.: Yale University Press, 1981).

16. J. Pfeffer and G. Salancik, *The External Control of Organizations* (New York: Harper and Row, 1978); J. Post, *Corporate Behavior and Social Change* (Reston, Va.: Reston Publishing Company, 1978); and R. Harris, *Coal Firms Under the New Social Regulation* (Durham, N.C.: Duke University Press, 1985).

17. J. March and J. Olsen, "The New Institutionalism: Organizational Factors in Political Life," *American Political Science Review* (September 1984).

18. C. Rossiter, ed., *Federalist Papers*, no. 10 (New York: New American Library, 1961).

19. W. Wilson, "The Study of Administration," *Political Science Quarterly* (June 1887).

20. March and Olsen, "The New Institutionalism," p. 741.

21. A. Wildavsky, *Speaking Truth to Power: The Art and Craft of Policy Analysis* (Boston, Mass.: Little, Brown, 1978), chapter 8.

PART I

Philosophical Foundations

2

Reformers of the 1960s and 1970s: Modern Anti-Federalists?

DONALD R. BRAND

The 1960s and 1970s were years of dramatic political change. Participation in politics was expanded, institutions were restructured, and new regulatory, welfare, and civil rights programs were established. Reformers, noting the progress achieved in many areas, have defended these reforms and hope to extend them. But critics have noted other consequences of the reforms, many of them unintended, which they believe now pose a serious threat to the vitality of our political institutions. This contemporary debate is reminiscent of a much earlier debate between the Federalists and the Anti-Federalists concerning the fate of the proposed Federalist Constitution; viewing the current debate through this historical perspective will shed some light on the respective merits of the arguments of reformers and their critics.

Animating the dizzying array of reforms in the 1960s and 1970s were certain common ideals that permeated the reform culture. The reformers of this period were intensely democratic, often seeking to complement or even displace *representative democracy* with a more radical *participatory democracy*. This emphasis on participatory democracy led to a renewed interest in territorial and functional decentralization. The reformers were also liberals, emphasizing the themes of rights and law, the twin pillars of classical liberal political thought. These liberal values shaped the reformers' skepticism of bureaucrats and of their capacity to exercise discretionary powers, a skepticism that led them to insist on greater legal formalism in government. Finally, the reformers were united by their suspicion of capitalism and of a pluralist politics based on self-interest, tendencies that have always been associated with reform movements but have rarely become as radical as they were in the 1960s and 1970s. Participatory democracy, liberal formalism, suspicion of capitalism and pluralism—these were the unifying themes of the 1960s and 1970s.

These reform themes were initially developed and elaborated by intellectuals who were criticizing aspects of the American political and economic system and the thought that "rationalized" them. One of the most influential political scientists of the late 1960s and early 1970s, Theodore Lowi, wove together a commitment to legal formalism and a suspicion of capitalism and interest group politics in *The End of Liberalism*, a damning survey of the post–New Deal American state.[1] Robert Dahl, in a striking repudiation of his more conservative views of the 1950s, became increasingly critical of modern capitalism during the 1970s. He transformed participatory democracy from the rallying cry of the New Left fringe into a fashionable mainstream position when he suggested that participatory economic institutions might provide an alternative to firms dominated by management.[2] John Hart Ely's criticisms of a strict interpretation of the Constitution also elevated participatory democracy to constitutional respectability with his "participation-oriented, repre-sentation-reinforcing approach to judicial review."[3] John Rawls and Ronald Dworkin made prominent contributions to the revival of liberal formalism through their respective revivals of rights-based theories.[4] Mancur Olson's devastating criticisms of pluralism effectively undermined the dominant pluralist paradigm in political science and shifted the discipline toward an increasingly critical posture toward interest group politics.[5] Finally, suspicion of capitalism is one of the dominant motifs of Charles Lindblom's highly critical analysis of democratic capitalism, *Politics and Markets*.[6]

A HISTORICAL ANALOGY

One of the most important tasks of contemporary political science is to examine the relationship between ideas and institutions in the 1960s and 1970s and to evaluate the consequences of the extensive reforms of this era. A starting point for that analysis is to recognize that the configuration of political ideals that inspired those reforms was by no means unprecedented. It bears a strong resemblance to the ideals held by the Anti-Federalists in the early years of the American republic.[7] The Anti-Federalists opposed the Constitution proposed by the Federalists and defended a looser confederation of state governments because they believed that genuine republican government was viable only on a smaller scale, a scale that encouraged far more democratic participation than would have been possible under the Federalists' Constitution. The Anti-Federalists also believed that the states provided a foundation for liberal government, a government by laws that secured rights, whereas the Federalists' Constitution proposed a powerful executive that might set itself above the law and use its discretion to undermine rights. Finally, those Anti-Federalists who had thought through their fundamental principles most clearly favored agrarian capitalism over industrial capitalism and a homogeneous polity over a pluralistic one, believing that such conditions were more conducive to republican virtue, which they believed was an indispensable prerequisite of republican government.

As we turn from principles to applications, we find that there are naturally important differences between the Anti-Federalists' attempt to preserve a looser confederation of states and the 1960s and 1970s reformers' attempt to reform the modern administrative state. The Anti-Federalists were the conservatives of their day, seeking to preserve as much of the Articles of Confederation as was possible against the more radical proposals for reform of their Federalist counterparts. The Anti-Federalists fought for states' rights, whereas the more radical of the 1960s and 1970s reformers have generally favored a revitalization of local communities and functional associations.[8] The Anti-Federalists were hostile to the creation of a powerful federal judiciary. They did not believe that an active judiciary would protect rights and uphold due process of law, a suspicion that was reinforced after the Constitution was ratified and Federalists like John Marshall came to dominate the court. In contrast, reformers in the 1960s and 1970s have provided powerful political support for an activist judiciary and have viewed the courts as their most loyal institutional ally. If these differences, however, are less fundamental than the similarities, as the language of principle and application suggests, then the analogy between the Anti-Federalists and the 1960s and 1970s reformers may be valid—and if this analogy is persuasive, it raises a number of questions concerning the ultimate viability of the modern reformers' enterprise.

In describing reform in the 1960s and 1970s as a revival of Anti-Federalism, I am not suggesting that the modern reformers learned their principles from the writings of the Anti-Federalists. Although it might be possible for diligent intellectual historians to show that Anti-Federalism constitutes a genuine, unbroken tradition in American political thought and to trace the history of Anti-Federalist thought from the Founding to the 1960s and 1970s, I am more modestly describing analogies in the reformers' and Anti-Federalists' principles. It is nevertheless interesting to note that during this period a new school of thought regarding the American Founding arose; its most illustrious members were J.G.A. Pocock, Bernard Bailyn, and Gordon Wood, and it emphasized the centrality of a republican tradition in early American political thought.[9] The republican tradition identified by these historians is more closely linked to the Anti-Federalists than it is to the Federalists. The plausibility of a connection between the Anti-Federalists and the reformers of the 1960s and 1970s is enhanced by the emergence of a historical school during the latter era that has revived interest in and sympathy for Anti-Federalist thought.

THE REFORMERS OF THE 1960S AND 1970S

Each of the four themes that unified reformers in the 1960s and 1970s were reflected in the institutional and procedural changes initiated during this era.

Democratization

As has generally been the case with American reform movements, the reformers of the 1960s and 1970s wanted to democratize our political system. The era began with the civil rights movement and a systematic attack on barriers to the participation of blacks in politics. Abuses in the use of literacy tests were curbed, the poll tax was abolished (by the 24th Amendment, in 1964), and federal examiners were stationed in the southern states with records of discrimination to assist blacks in registering.[10] As the momentum for democratization increased, a uniform 18-year-old voting age was established for federal elections by the 26th Amendment, in 1971. A 1970 federal law prohibited residency requirements of more than thirty days for presidential elections. In 1972, the courts assisted these developments by imposing similar limitations on the use of residency requirements in state and local elections.[11] Not only was the electorate expanded, but new steps were taken to ensure that legislatures reflected those electorates. In landmark cases such as *Baker v. Carr* and *Reynolds v. Sims,* the Supreme Court developed the principle of one man/one vote and embarked on a sweeping campaign to reapportion state legislatures.[12]

Political parties were also democratized in the 1960s and 1970s. The most dramatic reforms came in the wake of the tension-filled 1968 Democratic party convention, where a grass-roots movement to repudiate Hubert Humphrey for his complicity in the Vietnam War was frustrated by the party establishment. Party elites seeking to heal the wounds of the 1968 campaign established the McGovern-Fraser Committee to consider reforms in the party that would make its nomination procedures more open and democratic. The McGovern-Fraser reforms, adopted by the Democratic party for the 1972 elections, imposed central party discipline on state party organizations and compelled them to take steps to ensure that the composition of delegations included "minority groups, young people and women in reasonable relationship to their presence in the population of the State" and either to adopt a "participatory convention" mode of delegate selection (an open caucus) or to hold a primary election.[13] The most dramatic consequence of party reform during this era has been a rapid rise in the number of presidential primaries, a consequence that has also altered the character of the Republican party even though Republican party reforms were far less extensive than those of the Democratic party. In the period from 1968 to 1980, the proportion of delegates chosen in primaries rose from 40 percent to more than 70 percent in both parties. Under the new system, the power of party elites was significantly eroded as a new class of activist amateurs and media specialists arose to run candidate campaigns in states with primaries.[14]

Democratization was also the dominant theme in the sweeping institutional changes that restructured Congress during the 1970s. Attacking the decentralized, committee-centered system that dominated Congress in the 1950s and 1960s, congressional reformers in the 1970s opened committee meetings to the public and humbled the once all-powerful committee chairs. Seniority no longer guaranteed representatives in the majority party the right to chair committees. Electoral mechanisms were devised that allowed party majorities to depose chairs who had proved particularly unresponsive to their agenda, and the demotion of three autocratic committee chairs in 1975 notably enhanced the responsiveness of the chairs who retained their offices. The reformers expanded and equalized opportunities for participation in the legislative process by devolving more power onto subcommittees, limiting the number of chairmanships of committees and subcommittees that could be held by individuals, and ensuring even freshmen legislators places on important committees. The role of the caucus, the majoritarian voice of the party in Congress, was expanded and invigorated.[15]

These congressional reforms, and many other reforms in the era, were intended to democratize our system of representation—that is, to make it more accountable and better suited to reflect the genuine will of the people. Of particular significance for understanding the fundamental principles of reformers in this era, however, were the reforms introduced to enhance direct participation in politics. As reformers generally did not draw a sharp distinction between participatory democracy and representative democracy, the two goals sometimes appeared in conjunction. Some of those who played an important role in party reform in the 1970s valued participation in politics for its own sake; others saw party reform as a means of achieving a more responsible party system. But in still other cases, particularly in the area of administrative reform, the participatory thrust of the reform agenda during this era was unmistakable.

One of the first programs that incorporated citizen participation as a fundamental component of its administrative strategy was the Com-

munity Action Program (CAP) in President Johnson's War on Poverty.
In response to the claim that poverty was a political problem as well
as an economic one, and that poor people needed to develop a sense
of community and a sense of their own potential power, Congress
included a provision in the Economic Opportunity Act which required
that local CAPs "be developed and administered with the maximum
feasible participation of the members of the groups and residents of the
area served."[16] The Office of Economic Opportunity, the federal organization overseeing the Community Action Program, established guidelines requiring local Community Action agencies to reserve at least one-
third of the seats on their policymaking bodies for representatives of
the poor. Local activists seized the opportunity that had been provided
for them and quickly established local citizens' groups, demanding
representation in (and, in some cases, control of) these policymaking
bodies.[17]

In many cases CAP participatory democracy was ephemeral. Conflicts
between these citizens' groups and local governments soon ensued as
the local governments belatedly discovered that the new participatory
organizations posed a threat to their own power. By the early 1970s,
President Nixon's opposition to the participatory thrust of the Community
Action Program was helping local governments to regain control over
the program.[18] But despite this initial setback for participatory democracy,
institutional reforms to secure greater participation in the administration
of other government programs accelerated during the late 1960s and
early 1970s. Congress began to require and subsidize (through intervenor
funding—that is, federal reimbursements for legal expenses of private
groups engaged in public-interest litigation) public participation in agency
deliberations in new regulatory statutes, and the courts began to discover
the implicit right to participate in a variety of statutes and in the due-
process clause of the Constitution.[19]

The Magnuson-Moss Act, which shored up Federal Trade Commission
(FTC) rulemaking authority, exemplified the new congressional commitment to public participation in administrative deliberations. The act
required the FTC to hold public hearings before issuing trade regulation
rules and provided procedural safeguards to assure participants an
effective voice in the process.[20] The Magnuson-Moss Act is of particular
interest because in this case public participation sometimes benefited
the business interests that would be subject to FTC regulations, posing
a conflict for reformers torn between their hostility to capitalism and
their enthusiasm for participatory administration.[21] The depth of the
reformers' commitment to participatory democracy was demonstrated by
their willingness to apply their principles even in this case, although
with notably less enthusiasm than they had shown in cases where

participation clearly served their interests.[22] The reformers valued participation for its own sake, not just instrumentally as a means to the other ends they pursued.

Office of Communication of the United Church of Christ v. FCC[23] exemplified the commitment of the courts to public participation. In this case the courts upheld the right of an organization representing listeners to participate in adjudication proceedings involving a license renewal. The courts rejected the idea that merely allowing listeners to file statements or to appear as informal witnesses provided sufficient public input into agency decisionmaking, and they insisted upon a formal hearing with an "unrestricted" opportunity to be heard. In cases that followed *Church of Christ*, the courts have extended the logic of that case in some particulars and limited it in others; but the general trend of decisions has facilitated public participation in diverse proceedings ranging from Federal Power Commission and Nuclear Regulatory Commission power plant licensing cases to Department of Transportation hearings on highway planning and location. The courts have also opened up a whole new judicial avenue for public participation by relaxing traditional requirements for standing and granting public-interest groups the right to sue federal agencies based on little more than a general interest in securing vigorous enforcement of the laws.[24]

Liberalism

Many reformers of the 1960s and 1970s fashioned themselves as radical critics of the American regime, a perception that their conservative critics have been all too willing to endorse. The New Left origins of their participatory democracy ideas, their suspicion of capitalism and pluralism (see subsequent sections for further discussion), and the strident rhetoric and combative posture of their public spokespersons have all contributed to the impression that their agenda for political reform is a radical one. Indeed, this image may seem accurate if we confine our attention to particular aspects of reform during this era. As a characterization of the reform movement as a whole, however, the image is a distortion. Reformers in the 1960s and 1970s were far more traditional than might have been supposed, and their links to tradition are nowhere more apparent than in their commitments to individual rights and to the rule of law. In searching for an intellectual framework that would justify their reform agenda, they were far more likely to turn to John Rawls than to Karl Marx.

The liberalism of the 1960s and 1970s reformers was evident in the civil rights movement, the movement that launched this reform era. This movement appealed to the conscience of America, a conscience infused with liberal principles, in its efforts to secure equal rights for black Americans. Although black activists in the late 1960s generally framed their demands in terms of black power rather than black rights, it was ultimately the language of rights that struck a more responsive chord and provided the basis for reform initiatives in other areas. Soon, the demand for welfare rights, consumer rights, and the right to a safe work environment had become commonplace. Environmentalists even toyed with such concepts as animal rights and the rights of trees, but they ultimately found that their cause was more effectively served by a focus on the right of environmentalists to participate in the administrative arenas where important environmental decisions were being made. The upshot, in any event, was a rights explosion in the 1960s and 1970s.

This dramatic expansion in the scope of rights-based claims was also fueled by a reform-minded and activist judiciary. Through its reinterpretations of traditional rights, its unacknowledged revival of substantive due process, and its new conception of equal protection, the judiciary extended the sphere of rights to encompass virtually unlimited free speech, zones of privacy, and claims for individual dignity. To a considerable extent the history of constitutional law during this era had its own logic, but its broad affinities with the political thrust of the reform movement is clear. In the area of civil rights the courts led the way with *Brown* v. *Board of Education* and then became the most trusted institutional ally of civil rights activists in the 1960s and 1970s.[25] In varying degrees the courts subsequently allied themselves with the causes of environmentalists, consumer advocates, and welfare-reform activists by providing a legal environment in which organizationally disadvantaged constituencies could more effectively pursue their interests. This alliance between the judiciary and the reform activists ultimately produced a unique phenomenon in the history of American reform—a litigation-oriented reform movement.

The emphasis on rights in the reforms of the 1960s and 1970s has also led to a corresponding emphasis on the rule of law. Accepting the liberal argument that rights are jeopardized by discretionary authority and protected when public officials confine themselves to governance through general rules impartially applied, the reformers of these two decades inaugurated a "due-process" revolution that significantly altered the manner in which many government programs are administered.[26] Bureaucratic discretion has been the dominant concern—in part, no doubt, because bureaucrats are unelected public officials; yet the extraordinary scope of judicial discretion, which has generally worked to the benefit of reformers, has rarely evoked similar concerns. Bureaucratic discretion has been suspect less because administrators have imperiously used their discretion to tyrannize over citizens (although such charges were not uncommon with regard to the administrators of the welfare state) than because those administrators entrusted with discretionary powers in the regulatory state were presumed to have been particularly vulnerable to capture by the interests they were charged with regulating.[27]

Reformers have responded to the challenge of dealing with administrative discretion in a variety of ways, but the most characteristic responses have been to expand participation in the administrative process (as discussed above) and to make administration more formal by emphasizing rules, principles, and standards. Under prodding from reformers in Congress, the courts, and the academic establishment, administrative agencies have increasingly relied upon their rulemaking powers. According to Antonin Scalia:

> The 1970s have been aptly described by expert observers of the federal administrative process as the "era of rulemaking." To an astonishing degree, a system which previously had established law and policy through case-by-case adjudication involving individual parties—whether in licensing, rate-making, or enforcement proceedings—began setting its general prescriptions in rules, leaving little to be decided in subsequent adjudications beyond the factual issue of compliance or noncompliance with the rules.[28]

At the same time, rulemaking procedures were becoming more formal. Much of the flexibility of rulemaking under the Administrative Procedures Act was lost when Congress and the courts required some agencies to observe many of the same procedural safeguards that were previously associated with adjudication. Some agencies have been required to publish studies that form the basis for agency policy and to receive and respond to public comments on those studies. Others have been compelled to hold hearings before they issue rules, to allow parties to the hearings to cross-examine and rebut witnesses, and to base final rules on the evidence developed through these procedures. Courts began reviewing agency rulemaking more stringently, demanding that decisions be made on the record to facilitate judicial review and that "adequate consideration" be given to competing objectives.[29]

In more extreme cases, reform-minded members of Congress, distrusting the bureaucracy, have not been willing to allow agencies the discretion to formulate their own rules governing agency action, insisting that rulemaking or standard setting was a job for Congress. The Clean Air Act Amendments of 1970, for instance, included extraordinarily detailed standards to guide administrative discretion and precise deadlines for meeting regulatory goals, standards, and deadlines that often proved unrealistic or counterproductive.[30] Even in those cases where Congress permits agency rulemaking, it has frequently demanded a second look at the rules developed through legislative veto provisions. The extent to which these reforms have succeeded in circumscribing bureaucratic discretion is disputable, but they do reveal the degree to which reformers have been committed to a formalistic conception of the rule of law.

Capitalism

Reformers of the 1960s and 1970s rarely embraced socialism as a comprehensive alternative to capitalism, but they were nevertheless deeply suspicious of capitalism and of the quintessential capitalist institution, the large modern corporation. Many of the most important reforms of the era were either regulatory reforms constraining the self-interested profit seeking of capitalists or redistributive reforms that implicitly or explicitly repudiated the distribution of wealth produced by capitalism in favor of a more equalitarian distribution of wealth. The conflict between capitalists and reformers, which pervades almost every aspect of this reform era, is paradigmatically exemplified by the environmental movement.[31] Environmentalists criticized corporations for polluting and plundering our natural environment and usually framed such criticisms as attacks upon a system rather than upon the corruption of particular individuals. They sometimes advocated a zero-growth option, which was inconsistent with the fundamental commitment of capitalism to economic growth.

An elaborate case could be made for considering the reformers of the 1960s and 1970s to be critics of capitalism, but this case has already been very effectively made by the neoconservative opponents of reform. Indeed, the neoconservatives, borrowing heavily from the work of Joseph Schumpeter, have identified hostility to capitalism as *the* fundamental characteristic of reformers. According to Irving Kristol, although the "new class" of reformers in the 1960s and 1970s

> continue to speak the language of "progressive reform," in actuality they are acting upon a hidden agenda: to propel the nation from that modified version of capitalism we call "the welfare state" toward an economic system so stringently regulated in detail as to fulfill many of the traditional anti-capitalist aspirations of the Left.[32]

My own analysis accepts many of the conclusions of this neoconservative criticism of reform in the 1960s and 1970s, but it is distinguished from neoconservatism by its emphasis on the multifaceted and liberal character of reform. The reformers must be understood in terms of what they were for, participatory democracy and liberal formalism, as well as what they were against, unfettered capitalism *and* interest group politics.[33]

Special Interests

No theme was more pervasive in the reform circles of the 1960s and 1970s than hostility to special interests and their influence in the legislative and administrative process. Reformers have considered themselves partisans of the public interest. Insisting that the public interest is more than an aggregation of heterogeneous private interests, they have searched for a new form of politics that would rise above the brokered interest group politics of the 1950s. Mistrustful of government institutions and their capacity to speak for the public interest, largely because these institutions were tainted by their accommodations to interest group politics, reformers established their own pristine organizations to defend the public interest against narrow, self-interested claims.[34] Public-interest groups (and public-interest law firms) have provided the organizational infrastructure for many of the most important reform initiatives of this era.

In choosing public-interest groups as the vehicle for pursuing their goals, the reformers of the 1960s and 1970s demonstrated a capacity for political pragmatism that complemented their moral idealism. The combination proved extraordinarily successful. Adopting the tactics of established interest groups, public-interest groups lobbied legislators on issues ranging from consumerism to the Vietnam War. They developed new techniques for bringing constituency pressure to bear on legislators. To combat the tendency of regulatory agencies to serve rather than regulate business interests, reformers monitored and participated in the administrative process as well as the legislative process. Actively pursuing a strategy of litigation, they were frequently able to use victories in the courts as leverage for securing the political outcomes they desired.[35]

At times, political pragmatism did succumb to moral idealism. Some excessively zealous Naderites, for example, became too self-righteous and too unwilling to compromise—characteristics that only served to alienate the power brokers of Washington. When reformers were able to gain control of government agencies, as they did during the Carter years, they could overextend themselves. For instance, Michael Pertchuk's efforts to regulate unfair advertising provoked a congressional reaction that jeopardized the autonomy of the FTC. On the whole, however, the pragmatic propensities of reformers, reinforced by socialization to the political norms governing Washington, imposed a salutary discipline on moral idealism.

In examining the brief history of public-interest groups, however, we face the danger that the forest will get lost in the trees. Even though public-interest groups immersed themselves in interest group politics, even though they often acted very much like other interest groups in the system, they were never simply one more set of actors in the system. Public-interest groups sprang from a reform movement that was hostile to interest group politics, and their membership and financial viability depend upon sustained moral enthusiasm for reform. If they became too much like interest-based groups, they would jeopardize their own existence. It is highly likely, for instance, that public-interest groups will always be more combative than their interest-based counterparts because conflict generates publicity and allows public-interest groups to mobilize their constituents. As public-interest groups have one foot inside the interest group system and one foot outside of it, it is essential to keep this ambivalence in mind in trying to understand the reformers of the 1960s and 1970s.

Common Cause, the public-interest group that has focused its reform energies on the political process and its institutions rather than on a particular substantive cause, embodies the reformers' hostility to interest group politics more clearly than any other public-interest group. Common Cause has attacked interest group politics by favoring public financing of electoral campaigns, a change that was intended to undermine the influence of interest groups by preventing political officials from incurring debts to the interest groups that had traditionally helped to finance their campaigns privately. It achieved at least a partial victory for its proposals in the Campaign Finance Act of 1974, which introduced some public financing into presidential campaigns and imposed limits on Political Action Committee (PAC) and individual contributions to all candidates. Common Cause has also successfully lobbied for reforms intended to open up the political process, to expose it to greater public scrutiny, and to minimize the influence of interest groups by depriving them of the "behind the scenes" arena in which they have operated so successfully. With a similar intention in mind, Common Cause unsuccessfully pushed for reforms in the 1946 Federal Regulation of Lobbying Act, seeking to close some of the loopholes in that act and to make it enforceable.[36] Although many other public-interest lobbyists opposed this reform, fearing that its stringent provisions would jeopardize their own activities, Common Cause had the higher ground in this dispute with political allies, for it was countering their pragmatic concerns with an appeal to fundamental principles.

THE ANTI-FEDERALISTS

When the four principles that animated reform in the 1960s and 1970s were combined, they impelled reformers beyond narrowly conceived piecemeal reforms. Indeed, the conjunction of direct democracy, legal formalism, suspicion of capitalism, and suspicion of interest group politics posits a fundamentally different political system than that established by the American framers in 1789. To understand how these principles can be linked, however, we must turn from the twentieth century to the eighteenth century. Rousseau's *The Social Contract* provided the most systematic theoretical synthesis during that earlier century, and the American Anti-Federalists subsequently appealed to a similar combination of principles in opposing the Constitution proposed by the Federalists.[37] What distinguishes earlier proponents of a regime based on this combination of principles from the reformers of the 1960s and 1970s was that the former proponents of such a regime had always argued that those principles could be realized only in a small republic. Thus the foremost argument of the Anti-Federalists against the Constitution was that republican government was viable only in relatively small states, and that the Federalists' attempt to create "a more perfect union" would inevitably lead to monarchical or tyrannical government. Small states could join together in a confederation to better secure their collective defense, but sovereignty had to remain with the states.[38]

Although the fundamental logic of the Anti-Federalist position was a defense of small republics, the Anti-Federalists were willing to accept practical departures from the strict demands of their theory. For instance, some of the Anti-Federalists went so far as to accept the need for a federal rather than a confederal government, objecting only to specific features of the proposed Constitution rather than to its federal design. Even in these cases, however, the kinds of modifications being proposed reflected the influence of the small-republic theory. Departures from the sound principles of the small-republic theory were necessary, they argued, but those departures needed to be minimized. This reasoning can be sharply contrasted with that of the Federalists; expressed most coherently in *The Federalist* the latter argument asserted that the small-republic theory was inapplicable to the large republic that would be created by ratification of the Constitution.

The Anti-Federalists preferred a small republic to a large republic because small republics had a more homogeneous citizenry. According to Brutus,

> In a republic, the manners, sentiments, and interests of the people should be similar. If this be not the case, there will be a constant clashing of opinions; and the representative of one part will be continually striving against those of the other. This will retard the operations of government, and prevent such conclusions as will promote the public good. If we apply this remark to the condition of the United States we shall be convinced that it forbids that we shall be one government.[39]

James Madison's arguments for a pluralistic, heterogeneous republic in *The Federalist* (no. 10) were rejected by the Anti-Federalists because they were concerned that diversity would undermine the fellow-feeling that provided a basis for public spiritedness. This hostility to pluralism was also the source of the Anti-Federalists' fear that foreign immigration would corrupt republican virtue—a fear that led Agrippa, a prominent Anti-Federalist, to oppose giving the federal government the power to naturalize aliens.[40]

The Anti-Federalists' reservations concerning a commercial or capitalistic economy were rooted in similar considerations. Capitalism would lead to greater diversity of interests in a republic and, for that reason, was encouraged by the Federalists.[41] The Anti-Federalists, on the other hand, feared that diversity, particularly the diversity in the distribution of property that would be opened up. Industrial capitalism would promote inequality; it would provide wealth for a few and impose poverty on many others, neither condition being conducive to republican virtue. On the contrary, as Centinel has noted, "a republican, or free government, can only exist where the body of the people are virtuous, and where property is pretty equally divided."[42] Hence the Anti-Federalists rested their hopes on "those in middling circumstance," "the substantial yeomanry of the country."[43] Jefferson, who was not an Anti-Federalist but whose ideas had powerful affinities with those of the Anti-Federalists, drew the radical, but logical, conclusion to this line of reasoning when he argued that the United States should remain an agrarian republic and leave manufacturing, with all of its corrupting tendencies, to the decadent Europeans.

The Anti-Federalists' conception of democracy also reveals striking parallels to the conception of democracy held by reformers in the 1960s and 1970s. In its classic form, as presented by Rousseau, the argument for a small republic was an argument for a type of participatory democracy. Such a democracy, Rousseau argued, would, to the extent possible, inhibit the emergence of a distinction between rulers and ruled—a differentiation that had had baneful consequences for regimes. Although the Anti-Federalists were using this tradition to defend the smaller states and their confederation against an attempt to create a large republic, even the small states defended by the Anti-Federalists were too large for a direct or participatory democracy. The Anti-Federalists therefore turned to what could be considered a second-best alternative within a participatory framework, an alternative that maximized democratic accountability.

If the people could not legislate themselves, the second-best alternative was that the legislature be a mirror of the people. The Anti-Federalist Federal Farmer argued that "a full and equal representation, is that which possesses the same interests, feelings, opinions, and views the people themselves would were they all assembled";[44] he then concluded that the qualities which should be esteemed in representatives were not the "brilliant talents" of the "natural aristocracy" but "a sameness, as to residence and interests, between the representative and his constituents."[45] To ensure that the national legislature would accurately represent the diverse interests and views of the people of the United States, House electoral districts had to be relatively small and homogeneous, a characteristic that ultimately compelled representatives to act as spokespersons for their constituents. If districts were to be small, then the legislature would have to be large, composed of numerous representatives; and one of the most frequent Anti-Federalist objections to the proposed Constitution was that the House had too few members. Furthermore, since representatives were to be spokespersons for their districts, short terms and frequent elections were praised as means to intensify accountability and reinforce identification with the home district. Thus the Anti-Federalists objected to two-year terms for House members, arguing in favor of one-year terms. The lengths to which the Anti-Federalists would go to ensure democratic responsiveness were extreme even by the standards of reformers in the 1960s and 1970s.

The participatory foundations of the Anti-Federalists' arguments were even more evident in their discussions of the role of juries in the judicial system. A frequent Anti-Federalist objection to the proposed Constitution was that it did not require juries in civil trials and would therefore tend to undermine or destroy this vitally important institution. One Anti-Federalist went so far as to argue that the jury was a more indispensable bulwark of republican government than representation in the legislature because "those usurpations, which silently undermine the spirit of liberty, under the sanction of law, are more dangerous than direct and open legislative attacks."[46] The Anti-Federalists conceived of juries as participatory institutions that "are the means by which the people are let into the knowledge of public affairs" and that "secure to the people at large, their just and rightful control in the judicial department"—a particularly important consideration given that many of the responsibilities currently entrusted to administrative agencies were in those days handled by the courts.[47] Herbert Storing, the most astute student of Anti-Federalist thought, concluded from his study of this issue that, as important as juries were for the Anti-Federalists in protecting the people against a potentially tyrannical judiciary, they were even more important in protecting "the role of the people in the *administration* of government" (original emphasis).[48]

Finally, the Anti-Federalists were the liberal formalists of their day, although this characteristic does not emerge so clearly in the debates over ratification of the Constitution. Like their Federalist opponents, the Anti-Federalists were liberals who believed that the aim of government was to protect rights and that the most effective means for doing so was to institute a government of laws, not of men. Unlike the Federalists, however, the Anti-Federalists had a relatively rigid conception of the rule of law, a conception far less congenial than the Federalists' notion of the rule of law to the vesting of important discretionary powers in government officials.

In the debates over the Constitution, this issue emerged most prominently with regard to the executive branch. The Federalist proposal for a unitary and powerful executive with important discretionary powers was viewed with suspicion by many Anti-Federalists, who tended to prefer a weaker executive whose primary responsibility was to enforce the laws duly enacted by Congress.[49] Some of the most astute Anti-Federalists, however, conceded that a strong executive was indispensable in a nation the size of the United States, so the issue did not reflect the differences between the principles of the Federalists and those of the Anti-Federalists as clearly as certain later issues would.

After the Constitution was ratified, many of the specific issues that had divided the Federalists and the Anti-Federalists were definitively resolved. Partisan differences were further dampened as Washington assumed the presidency, for he was widely esteemed by Federalists and Anti-Federalists alike. Differences of principle remained, however, and those differences laid the foundations for the subsequent split between the Federalists and the Jeffersonian Republicans, the heirs of the Anti-Federalists. The Jeffersonians defended the states against the encroachments of the federal government, the legislature against the usurpations of the executive branch, and the people against the growing power of a thoroughly Federalist judiciary. The latter two issues were particularly revealing concerning the status of legal formalism in Jeffersonian thought.

After the Federalists passed the Alien and Sedition acts and attempted to use them to stifle the criticisms of the Jeffersonian press, Jeffersonian criticism of executive power once again became vociferous. In his 1799 Virginia Resolutions, Madison, who by this time had apparently abandoned his earlier Federalist position,[50] argued that "Executive prerogative" in conjunction with "excessive augmentation of the offices, honors and emoluments, depending on the Executive will," would transform "the republican system of the United States into a monarchy."[51] His description of the method by which executive prerogative would grow is particularly interesting:

> In proportion as the objects of legislative care might be multiplied, would time allowed for each be diminished, and the difficulty of providing uniform

and particular regulations for all be increased. From these sources would necessarily ensue a greater latitude to the agency of that department which is always in existence, and which could best mold regulations of a general nature so as to suit them to the diversity of particular situations. And it is in this latitude, as a supplement to the deficiency of the laws, that the degree of Executive prerogative materially consists.[52]

This line of argument clearly prepared the ground for the development of a restrictive nondelegation principle, which would attempt to confine executive (and bureaucratic) discretion within the boundaries of the rule of law—an argument that Theodore Lowi, a prominent 1960s and 1970s reformer, would eventually pursue in *The End of Liberalism.*

The Jeffersonians' struggle against the Federalist Judiciary reveals similar legal formalist propensities. Jefferson himself had long been skeptical of the power of judges, arguing as early as 1776 that judges should be a "mere machine" without the power to set aside the laws in the name of equity.[53] His followers soon radicalized his suspicions of judicial power and discretion by turning against the common law, one of the foundations of judicial power in the new republic. Jeffersonian suspicion of the Common Law was fueled by the fact that the Common Law was encrusted with feudal anachronisms, lingering vestiges of the aristocratic age in which it had developed. But rather than allow the Federalist judiciary to proceed with its gradual, case-by-case adaptation of the Common Law to a republican regime, the Jeffersonians insisted that lawmaking was the exclusive prerogative of the legislature in a republic; hence they attempted to confine judges to the role of applying statutory law to individual cases. These Jeffersonian tendencies culminated in a widespread and powerful movement to codify state laws in the 1830s. It is interesting to note that codification, which is an attempt to formalize the law by reducing it to clearly defined rules, was also advocated by Theodore Lowi in *The End of Liberalism.*

CONCLUSION

If the reformers of the 1960s and 1970s revived the fundamental principles of the Anti-Federalists, then an analysis of the Anti-Federalist position and of the debate between the Federalists and the Anti-Federalists may provide a basis for understanding what is problematic in this more recent reform movement. Herbert Storing has persuasively argued that the Federalists triumphed over the Anti-Federalists in the ratification debates not simply because they were more organized or more skilled politically, but because they had the better argument. The Anti-Federalist argument ultimately foundered on an irreconcilable contradiction. The

Anti-Federalists were defending a confederational system of government for the existing thirteen states, although they were often willing to concede the need for a somewhat stronger confederation, on the basis of a small-republic theory. Such a defense was defective because the existing states were not small republics. Such states as Virginia and New York did not even approximate the city-states envisioned by Rousseau in his classic elaboration of the small-republic theory.

Moreover, to argue, as the Anti-Federalists did, that a confederation of states would have come closer than the Federalists' Constitution to realizing the small-republic ideal was clearly inadequate. This was a situation in which merely being closer to that ideal was not enough. Unless the Anti-Federalists had been prepared to go further, to the point of breaking down the existing states into a system of city-states that would allow direct citizen participation in governance and imposing far more severe constraints on commercialism, they would have been tolerating conditions that would have undermined the form of republican government they had aspired to. Yet the Anti-Federalists were not prepared to go the extra mile. They were already too enamored of the benefits of a larger and more commercial republic to want to return fully to stern republican virtue.

The reformers of the 1960s and 1970s were vulnerable to the same objections. These modern reformers were generally not as aware as the Anti-Federalists had been that the ideals of participatory democracy and strict legal formalism are inextricably linked to the ideal of a small republic. Yet participatory democracy is clearly not a plausible ideal for the governance of a nation of 200 million people. Similarly, strict governance by rules (the epitome of legal formalism) may be plausible for a small homogeneous republic in which the rules will constrain similar individuals in similar ways, but it is certain to impose unacceptable injustices in a large and heterogeneous nation where the uniform rule will constrain individuals in very different circumstances in very different ways. How can a large and complex industrial society be effectively and justly governed if it does not entrust discretionary authority to its rulers? How can we repudiate capitalism and continue to enjoy its fruits, such as national wealth and individual material comforts? How can we design a modern industrial society that allows political freedom and yet escape a pluralistic interest group politics driven by "ignoble" self-interest? These were the unanswered questions of the 1960s and 1970s— unanswered, one suspects, because they have no answer.

The small-republic ideals of modern reformers inspired reforms that have seriously weakened American political institutions. The impact of their reforms on political parties has been particularly striking. The democratization of political parties during this era, which has led to a greater reliance on primaries, has sapped the power of party elites. Parties have found it more difficult to act as brokers unifying their disparate coalitions. As their influence over candidate selection has declined, inexperienced and more ideologically extreme candidates have found it easier to win the nomination of a major party.

Similarly, the internal democratization of Congress dispersed power among so many members that the formation of Congressional majorities needed to push a measure through Congress became increasingly difficult. Ironically, as the institutional mechanisms for coalition building decayed, opportunities for special interests to influence a more ad hoc, decentralized congressional process increased. Reforms intended to enhance democratic participation in the administrative state have also sometimes seriously disrupted the efficient administration of government programs. The Consumer Products Safety Commission's initial rulemaking process had allowed any person to petition the agency for a rule establishing a product's safety standard, but this participatory device undermined the capacity of the agency to set its own priorities and compelled it to waste resources in unproductive investigations.[54]

The pursuit of liberal formalism, when carried to extremes by many reformers of the 1960s and 1970s, has also impaired the effectiveness of our political institutions. Rulemaking, especially when circumscribed by extensive due-process protections, can become an excessively conflictual and time-consuming affair with little reward to show for great effort. Under many conditions, negotiation and bargaining among private parties and between government and private parties are far more productive forms of conflict resolution.[55] Furthermore, a legalistically oriented administration can easily become blinded to its overriding goal or purpose in its quest for a legally correct solution. The history of the Environmental Protection Agency is replete with examples of regulators pursuing irrational policies because the agency itself was excessively focused on statutory interpretation or trying to anticipate the legal concerns of the courts.[56]

These reservations concerning the institutional and procedural innovations of the reformers do not necessarily impugn the specific substantive goals they have fought for. Certainly a comprehensive evaluation of the modern reform era would also have to do justice to the causes it has advanced—among them environmental and consumer protection, humanitarian aid to the poor, and the fight against racial injustice. Even with regard to institutional and procedural innovations, these debits must be weighed against the gains. To cite only one example: Congressional reform in the 1970s may have made coalition building more onerous, but it has also made it more difficult for minorities to frustrate the clear will of the majority (as well-situated southern representatives did with regard to civil rights legislation in the pre-reform Congress). An evaluation of the specific reforms of this era would have to proceed on a case-by-case basis, a task that is undertaken, in fact, by some of the other authors in this volume. Some of the institutional and procedural reforms of the era (or modifications thereof) are defensible, but not *simply* on the grounds offered by the reformers and their intellectual counterparts.

The analogy between the reformers of the 1960s and 1970s and the Anti-Federalists reveals the fundamental problems associated with the reformers' principles, but it also points to an important strength. Herbert Storing reminds us in his classic analysis of the Anti-Federalists that there is a dignity and a power in the principles of the Anti-Federalists that transcend the defects of their arguments against the Constitution. Storing concludes that, although the Federalists had the better argument with regard to the Constitution, their own principles were not beyond challenge. One of the most serious problems with the Federalists' principles concerned the character of the citizenry in the regime that they were founding. In building a regime based fundamentally on the pursuit of self-interest, the Federalists had nevertheless recognized, or had been forced by the Anti-Federalists to recognize, that the regime would not be viable unless a modicum of public virtue was preserved. Yet they made no provision for maintaining that level of public spiritedness. It was here that the Federalists were most vulnerable to Anti-Federalist criticism, and most in need of correction.

The reforms best suited to correct the framers' design, however, were ultimately supplied, at least in theory, by Alexis de Tocqueville rather than by the Anti-Federalists. Tocqueville, drawing upon the Rousseauian logic that had also shaped Anti-Federalist principles, noted that participation in local politics was a particularly valuable vehicle for widening the horizons of narrow self-interested man, teaching him first to pursue an enlightened, long-term self-interest (i.e., one more compatible with the interests of others) and ultimately inculcating a weak but indispensable public spiritedness.[57] Tocqueville thus provided a rationale for participatory democracy, albeit one primarily at the local level and therefore of a far more limited kind than that envisioned by either the Anti-Federalists or the reformers of the 1960s and 1970s. Never suggesting that these participatory principles were applicable to the national government, Tocqueville generally approved of the Federalists' Constitution, with its provisions for representative government and a strong executive exercising discretionary powers at the national level.[58] Nor did he repudiate America's emerging industrial capitalism and its pluralist interest group politics, believing that a society based on self-interest inevitably accompanied the principle of equality, which was becoming dominant in the modern world. Generally, Tocqueville sought only to moderate or soften the logic of self-interest, not to displace it altogether. He promoted a politics of enlightened self-interest, the kind of self-interest likely to be fostered by participation in local government.[59]

Had the reformers of the 1960s and 1970s adopted Tocqueville's approach to reform, strengthening the regime of the Federalists by supplementing it, their legacy would have been impressive indeed. Instead, they chose a more radical project of reconstruction—one that has been undermining our political institutions for the sake of an ideal that can only be considered romantic in our contemporary circumstances. Regrettably, they chose to repeat the errors of their Anti-Federalist predecessors.

NOTES

1. Theodore Lowi, *The End of Liberalism* (New York: W. W. Norton and Co., 1969).

2. Robert Dahl, *Dilemmas of Pluralist Democracy: Autonomy Vs. Control* (New Haven, Conn.: Yale University Press, 1982).

3. John Hart Ely, *Democracy and Distrust: A Theory of Judicial Review* (Cambridge: Harvard University Press, 1982), p. 87.

4. John Rawls, *A Theory of Justice* (Cambridge: Harvard University Press, 1971); Ronald Dworkin, *Taking Rights Seriously* (Cambridge, Mass.: Harvard University Press, 1977).

5. Mancur Olson, *The Logic of Collective Action* (Cambridge: Harvard University Press, 1971).

6. Charles Lindblom, *Politics and Markets* (New York: Basic Books, 1977).

7. William Shambra noted the affinities between the 1960s and 1970s reformers and the Anti-Federalists in "The Roots of the American Public Philosophy," *The Public Interest*, no. 67 (Spring 1982).

8. The revitalization of federalism and the devolution of authority onto state governments have generally been conservative issues during the recent era. Nevertheless, the emergence of new federalism as a conservative theme is not without significance. Conservatives were on the intellectual defensive during this era, and they sometimes borrowed the principles of the reformers—except that they applied them in different ways. Whereas the reformers can be analogized to the Anti-Federalists, conservatives cannot in all cases be analogized to the Federalists.

9. J.G.A. Pocock, *The Machiavellian Moment: Florentine Political Thought and the Atlantic Republican Tradition* (Princeton, N.J.: Princeton University Press, 1975); Bernard Bailyn, *The Ideological Origins of the American Revolution* (Cambridge: Harvard University Press, 1967); Gordon S. Wood *The Creation of the American Republic, 1776–1787* (New York: W. W. Norton and Company, 1969).

10. James Q. Wilson, *American Government: Institutions and Policies* (Lexington, Mass.: D. C. Heath and Company, 1980), pp. 508–539.

11. Ibid., p. 196; see also *Dunn* v. *Blumstein* (405 U.S. 330, 1972).

12. *Baker* v. *Carr* (369 U.S. 186, 1962); *Reynolds* v. *Sims* (377 U.S. 533, 1964).

13. Nelson W. Polsby, *Consequences of Party Reform* (Oxford: Oxford University Press, 1983), p. 35.

14. James Ceaser, *Reforming the Reforms* (Cambridge: Ballinger Publishing Co., 1982), pp. 31–76.

15. James Sundquist, *The Decline and Resurgence of Congress* (Washington, D.C.: Brookings Institution, 1981), pp. 367–414.

16. J. David Greenstone and Paul E. Peterson, *Race and Authority in Urban Politics* (Chicago: University of Chicago Press, 1975), pp. 4–5.

17. Ibid., pp. 19–49.

18. Donald Horowitz, *The Courts and Social Policy* (Washington, D.C.: Brookings Institution, 1977), pp. 68–105.

19. Richard B. Stewart, "The Reformation of American Administrative Law," *Harvard Law Review*, vol. 88 (1975), p. 1667; Jerry Mashaw, *Due Process in the Administrative State* (New Haven, Conn.: Yale University Press, 1985).

20. William West, *Administrative Rulemaking: Politics and Process* (Westport, Conn.: Greenwood Press, 1985), pp. 109–143.

21. Ibid., pp. 124–133, 166–171.

22. Congressman Bob Eckhardt, a consumer advocate, was a key figure in paving the way for the Magnuson-Moss Act. He appears to have supported its participatory provisions because of a principled commitment to participation, a commitment shared by the foremost consumer advocate of the early 1970s, Ralph Nader. The reformers' willingness to accept the procedural requirements of Magnuson-Moss was not just a concession made to secure other provisions of the bill desired by the reformers (specifically, enhanced FTC rule-making authority); indeed, the courts were on the verge of granting that authority to the FTC without additional legislation.

23. 359 F.2nd 994 (D.C. Cir. 1966), id., 425 F.2nd 543 (D.C. Cir. 1969).

24. Stewart, "The Reformation"; Mashaw, *Due Process*; R. Shep Melnick, *Regulation and the Courts: The Case of the Clean Air Act* (Washington, D.C.: Brookings Institution, 1983), pp. 9–13.

25. Henry Abraham, *Freedom and the Court*, 3rd ed. (New York: Oxford University Press, 1977).

26. Mashaw, *Due Process*.

27. Lowi, *The End of Liberalism*.

28. Antonin Scalia, "Back to Basics: Making Law Without Making Rules," *Regulation Magazine* (July-August 1981), p. 25.

29. Melnick, *Regulation*, p. 11.

30. Alfred Marcus, "Environmental Protection Agency," in James Q. Wilson, ed., *The Politics of Regulation* (New York: Basic Books, 1980), pp. 269–274; Bruce Ackerman and William Hassler, *Clean Coal, Dirty Air* (New Haven, Conn.: Yale University Press, 1981), pp. 7–12, 104–115.

31. At this point, the objection might be raised that a detailed examination of the political coalitions formed in the struggle over particular regulatory measures would reveal a far more complex structure than the case of environ-

mentalists versus capitalists. Characteristically, these coalitions have pitted reformers and particular firms or industries against other firms and industries. In some instances, not only capitalists but reformers as well would be found on each side of the opposing coalitions. These facts should not be allowed to obscure the broader picture, however. Coalitions between particular business groups and reformers were often temporary and based on narrow convergences of interest. They illustrate the time-honored political maxim that politics often makes strange bedfellows. The fundamental cleavages were those defined by ideology, which shaped perceptions of long-term interests and provided general strategic guidance in coalition building; and capitalists and reformers generally were divided along ideological lines.

32. Irving Kristol, *Two Cheers for Capitalism* (New York: Mentor, 1978), p. 14.

33. My analysis of the 1960s and 1970s reformers also differs from that of the neoconservatives in its reluctance to turn to psychological and sociological explanations of the reform phenomena. The neoconservatives have made a powerful case for the superior economic efficiency of capitalism and have thus been encouraged to emphasize the irrational aspects of reform, aspects that call for psychological or sociological explanations. However useful these explanations may be in explaining the excesses of the reformers, they do not do justice to the rational foundations of the reformers' argument, a matter I will turn to in the conclusion of this chapter.

34. The only government institution that has been held in high esteem by the reformer—the court system—is also the institution most removed from interest group politics.

35. Melnick, *Regulation,* pp. 113–154.

36. Andrew S. McFarland, *Common Cause: Lobbying in the Public Interest* (Chatham, N.J.: Chatham House Publishers, 1984), pp. 9–11.

37. In Rousseau's ideal republic, the people were sovereign; moreover, that sovereignty could not be delegated to a representative assembly but had to be exercised directly. In this sense Rousseau's republic could be characterized as participatory. Rousseau also referred to the authentic voice of the people as the general will, a will that could retain its essential character only if it remained general or universal, governing through law rather than through ad hoc commands. As Rousseau's *Social Contract* envisioned an equalitarian republic populated with public-spirited citizens, it was intrinsically antagonistic to capitalism, an economic system that fosters inequality and self-interest. Finally, Rousseau's republicanism was suspicious of interest group politics. Rousseau's general will was most likely to emerge when *individuals* deliberated on proposed laws independent of one another. He warned of the danger of factions: "But if groups, sectional associations are formed at the expense of the larger association, the will of each of these groups will become general in relation to its own members and private in relation to the state." See Jean Jacques Rousseau, *The Social Contract,* translated by Maurice Cranston (Baltimore: Penguin Books, 1968), p. 73.

38. The interpretation of Anti-Federalist thought provided in this section is fundamentally indebted to Herbert Storing's *What the Anti-Federalists Were For* (Chicago: University of Chicago Press, 1981).

39. "Essays of Brutus," in Herbert Storing and Murray Dry, eds., *The Anti-Federalists* (Chicago: University of Chicago Press, 1981), p. 114. Just as Madison, Hamilton, and Jay published *The Federalist* using the pseudonym Publius, so the Anti-Federalists published under a variety of pseudonyms. Those referred to in this chapter include Brutus, Centinel, Federal Farmer, and Maryland Farmer.

40. See Storing, *What the Anti-Federalists Were For*, p. 20. The Anti-Federalist argument for a homogeneous republic is far more radical than the 1960s and 1970s reformers' argument for a politics free from special-interest influence. Although the modern reformers did not reject societal pluralism (except in situations where pluralism was rooted in variations in income), is it not the case that a homogeneous society would be far more conducive to the public-interest politics affirmed by these reformers? The more homogeneous the society, the fewer the special interests to begin with. In such a society there are fewer temptations to subordinate the public good to private interests. Republican virtue is supported by interest, not at war with it. If the goal is a public-interest politics, then the problem with the reformers of the 1960s and 1970s is not that they were too radical, but that they were not radical enough.

41. See *The Federalist*, no. 12.

42. Centinel, "Letter I," in Storing and Dry, *The Anti-Federalists*, p. 16.

43. Melancton Smith, quoted in Storing, *What the Anti-Federalists Were For*, p. 18.

44. Federal Farmer, "Letter II," in Storing and Dry, *The Anti-Federalists*, p. 39.

45. Federal Farmer, quoted in Storing, *What the Anti-Federalists Were For*, p. 17.

46. A Maryland Farmer, quoted in Storing, *What the Anti-Federalists Were For*, p. 19.

47. Ibid.

48. Ibid.

49. The 1960s and 1970s also produced a sustained reassertion of congressional power vis-à-vis the president, a reassertion that was endorsed by many reformers. The analogy between the reformers of this era and the Anti-Federalists would suggest that reform hostility to the executive is not a transient reaction to a president such as Richard Nixon but, rather, is rooted in fundamental principles.

50. Madison's intellectual about-face from the time when he co-authored *The Federalist Papers* to the time when he wrote pieces more Anti-Federalist in spirit (e.g., the "Letters of Helvidicus" and the "Virginia Resolutions") remains one of the most perplexing episodes in the American founding period.

51. See Gaillard Hunt, ed., *The Writings of James Madison*, vol. 6 (New York: G. P. Putnam's, 1906), p. 358. I am indebted to Sidney Milkis and Richard Harris for pointing this paragraph out to me. See "Programatic Liberalism, the Administrative State, and the Constitution," a paper presented at the 1986 annual meeting of the American Political Science Association.

52. Hunt, *The Writings of James Madison*, vol. 6.

53. Gary McDowell, *Equity and the Constitution* (Chicago: University of Chicago Press, 1982), p. 55.

54. Mashaw, *Due Process,* pp. 261–263.

55. Peter Schuck, "Litigation, Bargaining, and Regulation," *Regulation Magazine* (July-August, 1979).

56. Melnick, *Regulation.*

57. Alexis de Tocqueville, *Democracy in America* (Garden City, N.Y.: Doubleday & Co., 1969), pp. 235–237.

58. Tocqueville explicitly distinguishes between the principles of government that apply to small states and those that apply to large states in "Advantages of the Federal System in General and Its Special Usefulness in America," *Democracy in America,* vol. 1, pt. 1, ch. 8. He argues that our federal system, which combined a national government and vigorous executive leadership with participatory local institutions, had achieved a felicitous mixture: "The Union is free and happy like a small nation, glorious and strong like a great one." See *Democracy in America,* pp. 158–163.

59. Ibid., pp. 525–528.

3

Dealing Democratic Honor Out: Reform and the Decline of Consensus Politics

ROBERT EDEN

THE AMERICAN CONSENSUS ON BASIC VALUES

"In the 1960s," according to Samuel Huntington, "the American consensus on basic values did not come apart; it came alive."[1] What kind of consensus did Huntington have in mind? He sought to challenge the pluralist tradition in American political science and the authority of "the consensual school," going back to Tocqueville. According to these interpreters, American politics was characterized by a broad agreement on fundamentals (or what the pluralists called "basic values") that supported political moderation and promoted compromise. From the consensualist perspective, the activism of the 1960s and 1970s appeared to reflect a dramatic decline of consensus politics. In both foreign and domestic affairs, the spirit of compromise and bipartisanship gave way to sharp confrontation and adversarial proceedings.

Huntington did not question the doctrine of values implied in the pluralist view that consensus politics depended upon sharing "basic values." He did challenge the more limited claim that agreement on fundamentals had regularly supported political compromise. In the long historical perspective that Huntington unfolded in his work, pluralist interest group politics appeared as the quiet commercial interval between more turbulent episodes in an extended political cycle.[2] The pluralists were mistaken about the nature of the American consensus. As Huntington explicated it, that consensus was predicated upon commitment to critical ideals, or "basic values," perpetually at war with American institutions.[3] Enacting the American creed therefore meant confrontation, not compromise.[4]

In the course of explaining how consensus on basic values could lead to conflict that undermined the routines of interest group politics,

Huntington reached a startling reassessment: What had looked like a dramatic decline of "consensus politics" during the 1960s and 1970s was actually a liberation of the American consensus from habitual inertia and artificial inhibitions.[5]

Thus, for Huntington, the traditional meanings of "consensus" became suspect residues of political lethargy and prior constraint. He acknowledged the weight of the observations of the "consensual school" regarding the exceptional moderation of democratic politics in America; those observations held good for long seasons of inertia in American public life. But he also argued that these seasons should be recognized as funks.[6] When Americans tire of serious citizenship and ignore the demands of their creed, they relapse into interest group politics: Pluralist practice is founded not upon an actively shared consensus but upon apathy. Authentic consensus politics is confrontational and revolutionary. During episodes of creedal passion, the American "nation of shopkeepers" suddenly turns into a "nation of prophets" demanding conformity to the egalitarian American consensus.[7]

Huntington's essay seems misleading to me because the new politics of the 1960s and 1970s was not so indiscriminately hostile to institutions as he contends.[8] Nor are American institutions antithetical to the politics of creedal passion (especially when it resembles the passion of the American Revolution). Perhaps for these reasons, the members of "the movement" generation were never required to abandon their political passions. Instead, they settled into various establishments, in law faculties, universities, church hierarchies, foundations, law firms, lobbies, a multitude of voluntary associations, political parties, and every branch of government. This happened with relative ease because the distinctive antinomian impulse of the revolt was never simply inimical to institutions as such—and because American institutions in particular proved highly accommodating.

Huntington's critique of the pluralists for ignoring conflict and crisis in American political history is well-founded. Yet he seems to share with them a neglect and depreciation of statesmanship and citizenship. His understanding of consensus politics suffers from this neglect, as I shall explain after I demonstrate the way in which the American consensus did come apart in the 1960s and 1970s.

To understand how American politics was remade in the wake of the revolt, and why the new politics needed so many institutional instruments, one must consider what the reformers were trying to combat. Their animus against institutions and laws was selective; it was directed most of all against an unwritten law or ruling ethos, which Tocqueville had described as the "American idea of honor." I shall dwell at some length on Tocqueville's account of the ruling ethos of Jacksonian democracy, because it was the principal target of the new politics. This animosity to the "American idea of honor" helps to explain why no consensus embracing American institutions as a whole has emerged since the dissolution of the old consensus politics of the 1950s, and why a more spirited anticonsensual politics has taken its place. I refer here to a group politics that cannot embrace American institutions as a whole or defend them as a matter of honor.

In previous crises, a working political consensus was dissolved by appeal to the principles of the American creed; but a new consensus was soon forged again on those principles. What most obviously distinguishes the present episode is that a working consensus has not again taken form.[9]

To point up this difference, I shall compare the new politics with the New Deal, approaching the latter from an unfamiliar angle and drawing attention to Roosevelt's effort to establish a new standard of American honor. In this respect especially, the New Deal contrasts sharply with the new politics. The New Deal attacked the ethos of rugged individualism but offered an alternative standard of honor on which a new consensus could rally. The new politics is more radical not only because it attacks the New Deal understanding of democratic honor but also because it is hostile to any majoritarian standard of honor on which consensus politics could be based. By discussing Roosevelt from this perspective, I hope to illuminate the unwritten law or ethos against which the new-politics generation rebelled. An account of what this generation has been attacking may help us to comprehend the institutions it has adapted to this purpose.

How does the "reform" effort of recent decades compare with Franklin Roosevelt's attempt to remake American politics? In Huntington's view, the new politics differs in being more idealistically concerned with the gap between American ideals and institutions.[10] Of course, FDR did not ignore this gap. He led a liberal reform effort to close it, with considerable success. However, Roosevelt did not suppose that the consensus to be reached would be primarily a conformity between ideals and institutions. His pragmatism on this score harks back less to the doctrine of William James or John Dewey than to the pragmata of Aristotleian politics.[11] Roosevelt thought seriously about the preconditions of concerted action in an extended and diversified democracy. He concluded that one could not sever the American consensus from ideas of honor and habitual constraint, without undermining the possibility of concerted action. As Roosevelt saw it, the most important consensus was an agreement between citizens about ruling and being ruled in turn—an agreement, in other words, that defined who was eligible to be entrusted with public offices.[12]

The form of such a consensus is visible in the kind of men and women we elect and honor. But this is not the sort of consensus Huntington had in mind. At the level of common sense, he would almost surely agree that since the 1960s no consensus has been reached on a standard of democratic honor, on who is eligible to be entrusted with social and political responsibility. He would say that "categorical representation" of women by women, blacks by blacks, or Hispanics by Hispanics spells the abandonment of any attempt to achieve such a standard.[13] At the level of political science, however, Huntington follows a tradition that regards honor as arbitrary or unintelligible—a modern tradition that begins with Hobbes and Machiavelli.[14] To understand why no consensus on a shared standard of honor has been reachable in recent decades, one must attain a certain detachment from this modern tradition in political science.[15] Toward that end, I recommend Tocqueville, whose detachment is evident both in his argument that honor is neither arbitrary nor unintelligible and in his sustained effort to explain how democratic honor and consensus politics are connected.[16]

DEALING DEMOCRATIC HONOR IN

The New Deal mounted a sustained challenge to the ruling ethos of the preceding Republican era.[17] Roosevelt reshaped the Democratic party by equating entrepreneurial individualism with economic royalism: The party of Jefferson had to choose once and for all between hatred of arbitrary executives and love for free and solitary enterprise; it had to choose against the old Jeffersonian public philosophy for the New Deal.[18] In foreign affairs, Roosevelt did not have to transfigure the party of Woodrow Wilson to make it the party of open diplomacy and disarmament; but he did have to persuade the electorate that a party hostile to the tough realism and imperial activism of Theodore Roosevelt could be entrusted with the direction of American foreign policy.[19] He had to make the Democratic party the standard-bearer of an American ruling ethos and the guardian of American democratic honor.

Roosevelt attempted to turn the electorate against the Republican ruling ethos by beginning at the top, identifying the devastation of the Crash and the Depression with the ethos that previous presidents had embodied.[20] He turned plebiscites on the economic crisis into critical elections that sealed the political fate of Herbert Hoover's conception of administrative excellence and Calvin Coolidge's ideal of limited government.[21] These revaluations not only distinguished his presidency, making Roosevelt the focus of new expectations; they also signaled a much broader changing of the guard. They announced that public honors, and a high place in public counsels, could now be won by a type of men and women who had never been in the running before. Roosevelt encouraged new patterns of recruitment to civil service and political office, patterns that often circumvented party channels.[22] Washington suddenly became a magnet for social activists, for a new breed of political lawyers and administrator-politicians.

In challenging the majority party's ruling ethos, and in bringing a sudden influx of new actors into national politics, Roosevelt provided a model that Eugene McCarthy, George McGovern, and Jimmy Carter were later to imitate. The influx of the "amateurs" into Democratic party politics during the 1960s and 1970s was a second wave imitating the first wave that broke into Democratic politics during the early days of the New Deal.[23]

Roosevelt also set several precedents by losing battles in order to win the war for a new ruling ethos. Two of his most memorable defeats fall into this category. When the Supreme Court declined to follow the election returns after Roosevelt's great victory in 1936, he proposed legislation that would have enabled him, with the support of a Democratic Congress, to create new positions on the Court. But the Court-packing plan was a setback for Roosevelt's assertion of presidential prerogative.[24] The natural course of events soon yielded several appointments to the Court, so to the extent that the aim had been to prompt the judiciary to accept the constitutionality of New Deal legislation, packing the Court proved unnecessary—and the effort to bring this about only made things worse.[25]

But Roosevelt had another purpose that he could not have achieved through timely retirements. He required an occasion to challenge the ideal of judgment and the ruling ethos that the hostile Court had upheld.[26] His brazen affront to the judiciary signaled to the legal fraternity what Roosevelt admired and how much he was willing to suffer to get it. It dramatized the choice that aspiring judges would henceforth face, a partisan choice between the tradition of Justice McReynolds and the liberal jurisprudence of Holmes and Brandeis—or, more broadly, between the old "rights industry" and the new.[27] Roosevelt's very defeat was dramatic proof of the seriousness with which he regarded the choice between these traditions. And the fact that an unusually astute, politically circumspect president was willing to risk serious political losses in order to redirect the legal profession was a political education not likely to be lost on ambitious lawyers.[28]

Roosevelt's attempt in the off-year elections of 1938 to purge the Democratic party and remake it in a more liberal image was similarly a failure on the battlefield but a success in clarifying the nature of the political war and carrying it to the enemy. As a practical initiative it failed to achieve its purpose and taught future presidents not to meddle in the congressional primaries of their own party.[29] Roosevelt was rebuffed in his choice of means, but the rebuff served to memorialize his purpose—namely, to purge the majority party in order to make it a more effective vehicle of liberalism and social change. The transformation of a political party is long work for many hands; party loyalty and solidarity raise powerful obstacles against it. By means of his attempted purge, Roosevelt made it a test of honor for liberals to challenge party solidarity and party conceptions of democratic honor. He set an example of principled disloyalty by his willingness to attempt to purge, and he thus sharpened and clarified the choice that future liberal Democrats might have to make. This lesson the McGovern Democrats embraced with a vengeance; by comparison to Roosevelt's efforts in 1938, the 1970 insurgency (which I shall describe more fully below) was a spectacularly successful purge.[30]

The New Deal also set precedent by asserting a ruling ethos that was newly inclusive, granting legitimacy and respectability to types of social leaders who had not previously been honored. Union organizing, social work, ethnic-group leadership, legal defense of minority rights—all these vocations acquired a more serious claim to public esteem during the New Deal. It was not merely that Democratic administrations were eager to work with a new coalition of interest groups. Roosevelt understood that he was engaged in a comprehensive struggle over standards of honor, that the ruling ethos of a commercial society cuts across the line between private and public or between social and governmental leadership. The attack on laissez-faire individualism meant lowering the prestige of successful financial and industrial entrepreneurs; but as prestige is always relative, the New Deal revaluation necessarily entailed raising the prestige of other types of social leadership.

Roosevelt thus initiated a many-pronged attack on an established ruling ethos, on the standard of virtue and democratic honor that had prevailed during the era of laissez-faire and had provided much of the poetry of everyday American life prior to the Depression. Although it would be foolhardy to claim that he was entirely circumspect, or that he foresaw defeat in the cases I have cited, it is not unreasonable to say that Roosevelt was occasionally willing to wage his war about standards of democratic honor by losing battles; indeed, he was even willing to risk the weakening or decline of the Democratic party for the sake of a clear division on this issue.

Moreover, Roosevelt grasped the importance of organizational rules in the war over democratic honors; Rules can redefine the game so as to give a decided advantage to certain players. He perceived that changing the rules could put a generation of public officers out to pasture and smooth the way to advancement for new cadres of political activists.[31] In all these respects, the legacy of the New Deal was a heritage of waging war against an idea of democratic honor that was at its meridian in the 1920s.

To understand how Roosevelt modified that idea and shaped a new consensus politics, let us begin with the original notion, by recalling Tocqueville's memorable account of American honor.[32]

I have shown that the Americans form an almost exclusively industrial and commercial association, the principal object of which is to exploit an immense new country. . . . All the peaceable virtues which tend to give a semblance of order to the social body and to favor trade should therefore be especially honored among this people, and to neglect those virtues will be to incur public contempt.

All the turbulent virtues, which may bring a society éclat, but more often bring it trouble, occupy on the contrary a subaltern rank in the opinion of this same people. One can neglect such virtues without losing the esteem of one's fellow citizens, and one risks losing esteem by acquiring them.

The Americans make a no less arbitrary distinction among vices. . . .

To clear, till and transform this vast uninhabited continent which is his domain, the American needs the daily support of an energetic passion. That passion can be no other than love of wealth. The passion for wealth is therefore not stigmatized in America, and provided that it does not overreach the limits that public order assigns it, it is honored. . . .

In the United States, fortunes are lost and regained without difficulty. The country is boundless and full of inexhaustible resources. The nation has all the needs and appetites of a growing being, and for all its efforts, it is always surrounded by more goods than it is capable of grasping. What is to be feared by such a people is not the ruin of some individuals, which may be soon repaired, but the inactivity and indolence of all. Audacity in industrial enterprises is the primary cause of its rapid progress, its force, its grandeur. Industry is for it like a vast lottery where a small number lose each day, but where the state gains continuously. Such a people ought thus to honor and look with favor on audacity in industrial pursuits. Now, every audacious enterprise endangers the fortune of the entrepreneur and of all those who put their trust in him. The Americans, who make of commercial temerity a kind of virtue, have no right to brand those who practice it with disgrace. . . .

In America, all the vices which corrupt the purity of morals and destroy the conjugal bond are treated with a severity unknown in the rest of the world. Public opinion in the United States only mildly reproaches love of wealth, which serves the industrial greatness and prosperity of the nation; and it particularly condemns bad morals, which distract the human spirit from the pursuit of well-being and trouble the domestic order of the family, which is so necessary for business success. To be esteemed by their peers, Americans are thus constrained to bend themselves to regular habits. In this sense one can say they make it a matter of honor to live chastely.

American honor accords with the ancient honor of Europe on one point: it places courage at the head of the virtues, and makes it the greatest of moral necessities for a man; but it does not picture courage in the same way.

Martial valor is little prized in the United States. The courage they know best and esteem most emboldens a man to defy the fury of the ocean to arrive sooner in port, bear without complaint the miseries of the desert, and of solitude, crueler than all miseries. It is the courage that makes one almost insensible to the sudden loss of a fortune painfully won, and instantly prompts fresh exertions to build a new one. Courage of this kind is primarily necessary for the sustenance and prosperity of the American association, and is particularly honored and glorified by it. One cannot betray want of such courage without dishonor.[33]

Roosevelt transformed this deeply rooted conception of democratic honor in at least three ways. First, he dramatized a kind of courage that was neither martial valor nor entrepreneurial guts. Roosevelt's epithet for Al Smith, "the happy warrior," was a sobriquet that came to stand for Roosevelt himself. It conveyed something more than the panache, combativeness, and confidence that Teddy Roosevelt had brought into presidential politics.[34] Because Franklin Roosevelt had chosen a collectivizing task, there was nothing individualistic in either the happiness or the combativeness of "the happy warrior." The alternatives for which it came to stand were rather between undertaking collective enterprises joyfully and conducting them with élan (FDR), or leaving them to grim technicians (Hoover) and modest nightwatchmen (Coolidge) who would undertake them stoically, minimally, and unobtrusively.[35] Roosevelt's civil or social courage in guiding complex collective enterprises was not entirely new to the American political tradition, but his cheerful demeanor made such courage more fetching and infectious—and thus perhaps more social—than Lincoln's tragic melancholy.[36]

Second, Roosevelt reinterpreted the task of subduing nature as a cooperative task in which the main actors were not individual entrepreneurs but, rather, organized groups. The corporatist side of the New Deal welfare state and its strategy of distributing governmental tasks to business, labor, and agriculture need to be understood in this light.[37] These delegations of power habituated Americans to think of the Baconian conquest of nature as a civilized and social work. As Tocqueville argued, democracies are like other societies in making virtues out of the most necessary vices. Democratic honor substitutes the subjugation of nature through science, technology, and hard work for the domination of a subject class; but like aristocratic honor, its standard of praise and blame is decidedly social.[38] Under Roosevelt and his successors, the vices of large organizations and of those who make them work (not merely the occasional entrepreneur-founder or robber-baron) came to be excused and praised as virtues because they were qualities of character that made America great. The war against want or, more broadly, the campaign against nature for the relief of man's estate became a war in which Americans shared not so much through lonely efforts whose only effective reward was wealth as through collective efforts in which honors and other social incentives (such as professional prestige) played a constant part. This revaluing of the typical vices of organizational leaders meant that party politicians, union officials, farm association representatives, as well as corporate executives began to see themselves, and to garner recognition, as major actors in the continuing American conquest of nature.

Third, Roosevelt sought to make the president, both as party leader and as chief executive, the guardian and the embodiment of American democratic honor. In Tocqueville's portrait, which is in this respect true to the earlier American tradition, the presidency plays no role. When Americans thought of democracy, of the needs of society as a whole, they did not envision their association as having a head in the presidency: Hamilton had lost to Jefferson on this point of honor.[39] Roosevelt worked assiduously to change this persuasion. Following Woodrow Wilson and Theodore Roosevelt, he agreed that only the presidency could overcome the centrifugal tendencies of American federalism and the separation of powers. He found a more effective strategy for enhancing the office than his precedessors had imagined. They had advocated making the presidency the spokesman for the majority, appealing to the electorate over the heads of Congressmen and governors. FDR greatly expanded the rhetorical presidency, but he managed as well to bind the organized electorate to the national government directly, through their interests in the presidency as a source of programmatic action. Instead of merely appealing to the electorate over the heads of Congress, he brought the organized electorate to their members of Congress with new demands requiring executive cooperation and leadership. In sum, Roosevelt deflected the American notion of democratic honor from its established path, advancing a new image of courage while identifying the prosperity of the country and American greatness with the presidency and with collaborative organizational leadership in business, labor, and agriculture.

The New Deal legacy was thus both a rejection and a rebirth of American democratic honor. On the one hand, it broached an attack on an established and deeply rooted ruling ethos. On the other hand, by modifying and redirecting the American conception of democratic honor, it revitalized and refined it, arguably making it immeasurably stronger by linking it to great concentrations of organizational power (above all, to the national government). The New Deal brought about a transformation in the American notion of democratic honor through critical elections in 1932 and 1936. Roosevelt's reinterpretation of democratic honor carried the nation, and like the "American notion of honor" described by Tocqueville, it came to be identified with the moral authority of the "American association" as a whole.[40]

No such consensus embracing the American polity and its basic institutions emerged after the 1960s. What took the place of the consensus politics that Roosevelt had shaped was a group politics of organized minorities. The politics of minority identity resembled the first act of Roosevelt's struggle, insofar as it continued and radicalized his attack on the idea of American honor that prevailed before 1936. But there the resemblance stopped. Roosevelt's critique ensured that the New Deal would try to restore American morale without returning to the ruling ethos of the Republican era. But the new morale that Roosevelt represented was emphatically the morale of a political majority. By contrast, the new-politics critique of the American idea of honor was peculiarly, and perhaps quixotically, directed toward building the morale of minorities. That goal was thought to require the weakening of majority morale. To deal minorities in, a series of separate but equal standards of honor had to be established in constitutional law and public opinion—hence the animus against any majoritarian standard such as the shared standard of honor made visible by Tocqueville's account.

We now turn to what Huntington calls the "ascendancy of the new politics" in the Democratic party and its contribution to the remaking of American political institutions.[41] To anticipate: It institutionalized a truncated politics of honor, centered upon what Justice Stone (in a famous footnote), had called "discrete and insular minorities."[42] Instead of clearing the way for a new ruling ethos that could be shared by and win the allegiance of a majority, the attack upon the received idea of democratic honor became perpetual. What had been the *terminus a quo* of Roosevelt's work thus became a *terminus ad quem* for the new politics. Institutional forms and new "constitutional" judge-made rights were introduced to perpetuate the attack. On the domestic front, however, this reorientation was subtler and in certain respects less visible to the public.[43] I shall therefore begin with foreign policy, where both the ends and means of remaking American politics were more obvious.

THE DECLINE OF CONSENSUS IN FOREIGN POLICY

The new regime within the Democratic party began with a falling out over foreign policy during the Vietnam War.[44] The power of Lyndon Johnson rested on two different foundations, which the new Democrats tried subsequently to undermine: the institutional powers of the presidency, and the disciplinary resources of the majority party leader.[45] As president, Johnson capitalized on the postwar tradition of bipartisanship in foreign policy to prosecute the war in Indochina.[46] But although he abhorred Woodrow Wilson's fate and sought to avoid anything like Wilson's public conflict with Lodge over the League of Nations Treaty,[47] Johnson failed to prevent Senator Fulbright from restoring the Senate Foreign Relations Committee to prominence as a center of public criticism.[48] One purpose of the McGovern insurgency was to consolidate and perpetuate such adversarial relationships between Congress and the executive in order to make future Vietnams impracticable.[49]

The congressional reforms of the early 1970s served exactly that purpose. The abandonment of the seniority system prevented full-committee chairs from controlling appointments to subcommittees, thereby leaving subcommittee chairs free to focus public attention on their preferred criticisms of the executive, or to impede the implementation of foreign policy.[50] Congress thereby became a co-partner in the formulation of policy as well as the overseer of its implementation. By multiplying formal procedures whereby policy could be challenged before and during its execution, these initiatives multiplied the occasions for debate and conflict between Congress and the executive in foreign policy.[51] These congressional reforms followed upon the reforms in the Democratic party and helped to realize their purpose: In one respect, party reform looked promising to the insurgents, because it was a way to put an end to bipartisan foreign policy as a check upon congressional dissent. The insurgents sought permanent institutional barriers to reinforce adversarial practices that had initially been sanctioned primarily as emergency measures.

Had the Democratic party remained as it was, these crisis tactics might well have receded from view as exceptional departures from norms and practices governing the legislature's role in foreign policy that had been cultivated by both major parties for a generation.[52] The insurgents concluded that new and permanent adversarial norms for foreign policy debate were necessary, in addition to new or revived institutional barriers, in order to check the freedom of maneuver that President Johnson had enjoyed, and to deny future presidents that range of discretion.[53] Restraints on criticism from within the administration party were to be removed. Foreign policy would henceforth be conducted under continuous public scrutiny of a new kind.[54]

This relaxation of bipartisan norms and the elevation of an adversarial code transformed informal practices as dramatically as they strengthened Congress's formal role in foreign policymaking. Under the aegis of the public's right to know, "leaks" and even more serious breaches of confidentiality in the executive branch would be revalued; they would be converted from shocking emergency tactics into standard operating procedure. Pressure was similarly exerted on the courts to make adversarial legal proceedings in foreign policy cases a matter of routine.

New norms more congenial to partisanship in foreign policy were a fitting objective for reform (in the first instance) because the task was not merely to give a new thrust to the separation of powers or renewed weight to the checks and balances of the formal constitution. The goal was also to create a new informal "working constitution," by changing the constraints upon politicians affiliated with the parties, especially the majority party.[55] The combined effect of the formal and informal innovations was to institutionalize highly public and dramatic dissent competing for centerstage with the president in foreign policy—in part by removing the obstacles of party loyalty and previously established foreign policy, and in part by giving new vitality to old institutional obstacles to executive action.[56]

In these respects, the reforms had the look of liberalism, relying on institutions and procedures to shape public conduct. This familiar look disarmed many Democrats, who mistook those institutions and procedures for just another set of impartial rules. The Fraser Commission proposals, for example, were more substantive than they appeared at first; they constituted a system for advancing a new type of foreign policy activist to prominence within the Democratic party.[57] The McGovern reforms reflected a preceding struggle between the modern plebiscitarian presidency on the one hand and a challenging opinion leadership on the other.[58] Under the new regulations, Democratic party institutions were remade to give more scope to independent opinion leaders and the public-interest organizations that they led.[59] The reformers sought to give oppositional opinion leadership, many new institutional footholds within the majority party and, subsequently, within all branches of government.[60] They made such footholds easier to secure by making it hard for party leaders to discourage the foreign policy initiatives of independent opinion leaders loosely affiliated with the Democratic party.[61] Thus the toleration accorded Jesse Jackson's sallies into public diplomacy by other Democratic candidates and party leaders, throughout the 1984 primary season and presidential campaign, was in a sense the logical outcome of the reformers' determination to permanently diminish the role of party in constraining open partisan conflict over foreign policy.[62]

This blurring of the line between party leaders and affiliated but independent opinion leaders helps to explain why changing the norms of the majority party had wider consequences in loosening the restraints upon opinion leadership in the media. Political parties stand on the borderline between formal, or constitutional, orders of representative government and more informal modes of representation. Like the parties, the media can advance a claim to "represent" the people, unofficially or informally; but the claim of the long-established parties was more deeply rooted, of longer standing, and on the whole more credible because parties were largely composed of candidates accountable to the people at very short electoral intervals.[63] By reshaping the norms of the Democratic party to give greater scope and respectability to independent opinion leaders, treating their spokesmanship as informal representation roughly on a par with party representation, the reformers deliberately closed the previously visible gap between political parties collectively accountable to the electorate, on the one hand, and unelected opinion leaders, in the media and in the public-interest lobbies, on the other. An expanded role for both public-interest lobbies and the media in American foreign policy was thus a pronounced and distinctive feature of the new working Constitution.[64]

Taken as a whole, these new dispositions meant that foreign policy would be kept in the public eye by adversarial proceedings. They inaugurated a new relationship between the legislature and the executive, between the two major parties, and between elected representatives and independent opinion leadership in the media and in public-interest organizations.[65] In short, they introduced a new formal and informal "constitutionalism," in which private and public bureaucracies were to collaborate on new terms in providing (or not) for the common defense.[66]

The reforms seemed to reflect the theory that programmatic competition between parties would produce better conduct in foreign policy (just as it was said to produce better government in domestic policy) by keeping clear alternatives before the electorate and fostering a more informed and more critical public. In the new dispensation this was not, however, a theory that the electorate could refute by turning away from McGovern, Carter, or Mondale at the polls. The reformers do not seem to have entertained the possibility that the best informed and most critical public might well prefer to judge both parties by impartial or bipartisan norms, especially where performance in foreign policy was concerned. That preference had been grounded, at least since *The Federalist*, in the argument or observation that rationality in public deliberations on foreign affairs seldom if ever results from a liberation of ambitious partisans and independent opinion leaders.[67] It was not this kind of rational clarity that the reform Democrats sought, however; what they sought was a rhetorical clarity that principled or committed opposition promotes, regardless of its rational content.

Keeping fundamental foreign policy alternatives intransigently and outspokenly before the electorate required the reform Democrats to transform the electorate's standards of judgment, by weaning them away from impartial bipartisan or antipartisan norms in the domain of foreign policy. Given this objective, the insurgents had to be willing to go down in defeat in presidential elections in order to reach their goal. For the habits of a large electorate are always slow to change.[68]

REFORM AND CONSENSUS
IN DOMESTIC POLICY

The McGovern reforms brought new personnel into the Washington community as well as prominence to members of the foreign policy establishment who advocated a new U.S. posture and new constraints on the executive; the reformers thus imparted some of the impetus of the antiwar movement to the making of American foreign policy.[69] Similarly, in domestic policy, the success of the insurgents reinvigorated the civil rights movement and institutionalized it, both within the Democratic party and in all branches of government.[70] Perhaps the most important result for domestic policy was that the majority party officially moved away from the national consensus embodied in the 1964 Civil Rights Act and the 1965 Voting Rights Act, a consensus based on the doctrine of equal opportunity secured by a color-blind Constitution.[71] In its place the reformers advocated a new doctrine of equality, featuring group compensation for past injustices committed by the white majority against "discrete and insular minorities."[72]

Informed readers may balk at my suggestion that this policy was adopted in order to clarify American politics on the issue of racial justice, inasmuch as the constitutional and moral basis of affirmative action remains murky and candor has hardly characterized the implementation of the new equality of compensatory privilege.[73] The reform strategy seems to have been designed to bring peculiar clarity into American politics by making at least one of the two major parties keep the issue of racial justice at the center of its program and, even more significant, in the administrative actions of its adherents.[74]

In foreign policy, open opposition by the new politics liberals, in Congress and in the media, was primarily designed to influence the government and professional politicians. Influencing the electorate was necessary, as I have suggested, only insofar as a change in their expectations about partisanship in foreign policy debate was required. But opinion leaders sought a different role for themselves (and then for government or administration) in the sphere of race relations.

Here the task of opinion leaders was primarily to influence or restrain the electoral majority while advancing the causes of minorities. Only in this way, it was thought, could the cause of civil rights be prosecuted effectively in the North—that is, under circumstances in which government action was not what kept blacks in a state of second-class citizenship.[75] The McGovern reforms in effect compelled the majority party to identify itself as closely as possible with the aspirations of politically organized racial and sexual minorities. The point of the racial and sexual quotas in state party delegations (which the McGovern rules mandated) was neither to seat token members of minority groups nor to make the party's nominating convention a microcosm of the country.[76] Rather, the objective of the policy of affirmative action adopted by the new Democrats was to speed up the momentum of social change by putting opinion leaders, the movers and shakers, where they could get the most attention from Congress, the judiciary, and executive agencies—where they could put their views forward with the greatest political effect and thereby stymie the counterefforts of spokesmen for (what was henceforth presumed to be) a racially and sexually prejudiced majority.[77]

Group compensation and quotas make tortured constitutional doctrine and in this respect do nothing to promote clear thinking about racial justice. But they have undoubtedly kept race relations near the center of regional and national attention. Since the New Deal, Democrats had commonly understood social change in terms of quantifiable economic goods, and affirmative action seemed to be in this tradition because it focused attention on such goods. But to understand the novelty of the new Democratic policy, one must appreciate that affirmative action was intended to use such goods, and the debate over the distribution of goods, to reshape the habits and prejudices of the governed.[78]

To be sure, it was a kind of party patronage to secure congressional seats, administrative positions, entrance to careers, and lucrative contracts for members of minority groups. But the new Democrats expected, and on the whole received, something other than gratitude for being so patronizing. They saw quite correctly that organized minorities and their leaders had a stake in political clarity of a kind, that their raison d'être was to keep the concerns of their constituencies in the forefront of public attention. Beyond securing jobs and tangible benefits, their task was to speak out against damaging prejudices and for more advantageous beliefs. By embracing group compensation and the new equality, the new Democrats sought to make the party a vehicle for reshaping racial prejudices and habits through partisan politics. Because the party was rapidly declining in importance, other institutions, too, were adapted to the purposes of this new politics; and, of course, race was not the only category under which groups claimed compensation and redress.

With respect to democratic honor, the most important norm of Rooseveltian consensus politics that the new politics attacked was the agreement on the American work ethic. The moral indignation of New Dealers had been largely directed against policies that made a mockery of the work ethic, by wiping out savings and tolerating the unemployment of millions of hard-working Americans who had lost their jobs because of the Depression. Roosevelt spoke for a majority thoroughly imbued with the work ethic. In this respect, the New Deal was "social conservative" and "bourgeois." It upheld the principle that those who could work should not be eligible for welfare. Similarly, what Tocqueville observed about fidelity and the stability of marriage remained essentially true for the American idea of honor that Roosevelt consolidated. The attempt that began in the 1960s, to remove moral criteria from the administration of welfare programs like Aid to Families with Dependent Children, required a sea change in public opinion precisely because the New Deal consensus on social policy supported these moral criteria.[79]

To challenge the New Deal legacy in such matters of stigma and honor, the reform movement had to weaken the moral constraints of Rooseveltian consensus politics. Under the New Deal party system, civil rights policy had been governed by norms of consensus comparable to the norms of bipartisanship that had limited the scope of partisan initiatives in foreign policy. The leadership of the Democratic party from Harry Truman to Lyndon Johnson had been committed to bipartisanship in foreign policy with all it entailed, and to equality of opportunity under the protection of a color-blind Constitution. Despite the accomplishments that this policy was able to show by 1968, tension between the civil rights leadership and the professional politicians produced bitter objections similar to those we have noted in the antiwar movement.[80]

The rules produced by the Fraser and Hughes commissions were intended to break the power of party professionals like Lyndon Johnson, George Meany, and Richard Daley; to produce a new alliance with the civil rights leadership and women's organizations; and thereby to institutionalize adversarial confrontation among branches of government and between the parties over compensation to disadvantaged minorities. They succeeded in attaining all these objectives.

DOING WITHOUT COMMON HONOR

I have tried in this sketch to delineate some of the major elements of the comprehensive change in public policy—in the institutional forms and norms of public conduct—that the reform Democrats have tried to bring about since 1968. The war they were trying to win was a struggle to introduce a new kind of clarity into American politics, featuring sharp conflict in which committed opposition spokesmen, always a minority, would have new resources, new powers, and a new position of legitimacy on offense as well as on defense. The reforms ostensibly meant that candidates who could never have contended in the past for the presidency could now be nominated by the majority party. To what degree they have had this result remains disputable.[81] The presidential nomination was not, however, the real prize. Rather, the presidency was the symbolic focus of a struggle to redefine the scope of acceptable partisanship and the kinds of citizens who could be considered respectable contenders for public honors.[82] The effect of the rules on the state party organizations and Congress was arguably more profound than that on the presidential contest, because the rules, taken together with the new Democratic program, very nearly removed the Democrats from contention. The presidency ceased to be the end of party politics. Presidential primaries became a means of redefining what kind of candidate for public office was respectable or tolerable: As I have tried to explain, the real war was over the democratic standard of honor—the ruling ethos of the American polity.

If the New Deal set a precedent for the McGovernite purge in the Democratic party, it was also very much the target of that purge. From the viewpoint of the reformers, the ultimate cause of American involvement in Vietnam was precisely the New Deal legacy of American greatness and democratic honor; the imperial presidency as the embodiment of majority will and a majoritarian ruling ethos was a formidable obstacle to minority progress and minority will. The work ethic was an especially stubborn element of this majoritarian ruling ethos. The reformers made it their business to dismantle this obstacle.[83]

If we refer again to Tocqueville's account, we can see that the reformed Democratic party has become with increasing consistency the antithesis of what Tocqueville termed the "American honor in our day." It is hard to locate a common interest or much shared ground on which the new Democrats can stand together, but such unity as they have is provided by common enmity and the determination to keep this American notion of democratic honor on the defensive or to uproot it altogether. From their viewpoint, Roosevelt not only compromised with a conception of democratic honor they found insufferable as a basis for policy; even worse, his politics fortified that standard with knowledge and organizational skill, making it a magnet for the best and the brightest and therefore most resourceful and dangerous.

The reform Democrats thus institutionalized an attack upon the New Deal legacy of democratic honor and sought to put that legacy on the defensive in the routine conduct of every branch of government. The new politics made it respectable and legitimate to oppose any possible majoritarian consensus on democratic honor, in the name of minority honor, dignity, or rights. It thus decreased the authority of democratic honor generally, without replacing the New Deal consensus on standards of honor with any comparable majoritarian standard. In matters of honor, the United States became a Pandemonium. By making routine a challenge that Roosevelt had framed as a momentous and extraordinary decision to be resolved by the American people almost at one stroke, the McGovernites' pursuit of routine and continuous conflict over democratic honor and the American ruling ethos had the effect of indefinitely postponing any practical resolution of the argument between contending notions of honor. To articulate the implications of this suspension of judgment, I offer some reflections suggested by Tocqueville's chapter on honor.[84]

Democratic honor is both positively and negatively significant for Tocqueville. Positively, it is the necessary though not sufficient condition for common action: Without shared standards of honor or the same opinions about virtue and vice, citizens cannot act in concert.[85] Honor is a matter of morals and manners, and today we think of these matters as a function of arbitrary choice by adopting the language of "values."[86] Tocqueville rejects that perspective on principle and advances an argument against it: He demonstrates that neither aristocratic nor democratic honor is arbitrary or bizarre; in other words, neither is merely a medley of invidious discriminations and vanities.[87] Tocqueville argues that the moral habit made possible by shared opinions concerning democratic honor is the habit of judging the actions and speech of others by a standard of the common good, of evaluating their virtues and vices in the perspective of the needs of "the association" as a whole.[88] Thus even the entrepreneurial ethos that Tocqueville describes was at base not simply individualistic: It was a highly social notion of honor that taught democratic citizens how to think about the connection between their virtues and the accomplishment of the common good. It did not lead them into metaphysics about invisible hands but, rather, focused their energies on the highly visible work of their own hands.

By sanctioning the infinite multiplication of competing standards of democratic honor and by promoting rivalry and contestation between deeply opposed claims to honor, the Democratic party since 1970 has, from this perspective, undermined the conditions for cooperative action on a national scale. Its policy is one that suppresses the habit of judging oneself and others by any comprehensive standard for the "association as a whole." American parties are the main associations for common action and a partisan approximation of the "association as a whole." They are not the whole, but prior to 1970 they never lost touch with the whole for long. Roosevelt attempted to make the Democratic party a party to end all parties in the sense that it would eliminate partisanship about certain paramount issues.[89] The McGovern insurgency made the Democratic party a party to end all parties in the very different sense that it would work to erode the foundation of common action by undermining any sharable standard of democratic honor. The reform Democrats have curiously made it a point of honor to convert their party (and, indeed, every significant institution they could convert) into a machine for effacing the habits of judging that make political parties, but also liberal polities, possible.

The negative side of honor, for Tocqueville, is that it provides a powerful alternative and hence opposition to the police or to administrative supervision. As we would say in contemporary lingo, a standard of honor is nothing if it is not "internalized," meaning that we identify it as our own and defend it as a matter of honor. A code of honor is a moral substitute for external supervision. More precisely, when one is on one's honor, one is alone and then submits to the approbation or disapproval of society. And knowing the standard of honor, one can ignore many possible objections and grounds for blame. As Tocqueville notes, every particular society is distinctive, though not arbitrary, in what it sanctions and what it singles out for praise. In principle, then, its solid citizens are always vulnerable to moral objections based on a comprehensive understanding of what is good for man as man, rather than on a parochial knowledge of what is good for the citizens of a given polity. The moral authority of the association secures its honorable men by suppressing those inconvenient objections. A self-respecting democracy is not, then, altogether respectful of the universal opinion of mankind or of the universal standards by which man as man is to be judged. Instead, its authority supports all citizens who live by the democratic honor code, refusing to dishonor them for certain vices and ensuring that they will be honored for certain vitures. This authority can buttress our own civil courage or spiritedness in defending our right to act on our honor—that is, without direct supervision by the police, the courts, or government agencies. It thus creates a powerful moral obstacle to the expansion of administrative supervision over the details of every citizen's life.

But the division of Americans into opposed troops with rival conceptions of democratic honor not only makes citizens unfit for common action on behalf of the common good and removes a formidable obstacle to the expansion of administrative meddling in every sphere of live. It also sweeps away trust and confidence in other citizens' self-restraint. If we do not share roughly the same notion of democratic honor, it hardly makes sense for you to try to influence my conduct by appealing to my sense of honor. On the contrary, if you are convinced beforehand that my sense of honor is not democratic, you have no alternative but to hound me with the courts, the police, or an administrative agency. Not only is an obstacle removed, therefore, but a powerful incentive for the expansion of administrative and judicial supervision is created as well. Worse yet, when contending groups of citizens are thrown back upon their own resources to defend themselves against such intrusive supervision, the inevitable result is to divert their political energies into highly focused interest groups and single-issue organizations.[90] The urgent need to defend oneself through such limited associations reinforces our narrowest interests and leaves less time for citizens to associate in political parties or to act and deliberate with the "association as a whole" in view.[91]

CONCLUSION

I have tried to indicate the connection between democratic honor and consensus politics by showing how Roosevelt connected them. I have also tried to explain the ambiguity of Roosevelt's consensus politics by considering how recent reformers selectively imitated his example in their attempts to remake American institutions. Like FDR, they sharply challenged a traditional notion of democratic honor. But they not only repudiated the notion of American honor that Roosevelt shaped; they also turned away from majority honor more fundamentally. It is not coincidental that their reforms have made it difficult for Americans as a majority to share any idea of honor together and in public. The reforms have simultaneously made consensus politics newly problematic. The reformers' partial imitation of FDR's example not only stopped short of his moderate consensus politics but impelled others to stop short as well. An essential ambiguity that Roosevelt had preserved was thereby removed from American politics. It seemed that the American creed could no longer be embodied in a working political consensus; for long periods in the past, by contrast, the terms of consensus politics and the principles of the creed had been ambiguously identified with each other.

This ambiguity would not arise if the creed were an ideal and the working consensus a mere institution or set of practices. Oddly enough, Huntington's attempt to explain consensus politics along these lines breaks down and confounds the ambiguity, specifically because he forgets himself, the political scientist. Huntington overlooks the practical import of political science, which is neither an ideal nor a set of practices but a way of thinking about both. Roosevelt seems to have understood better than Huntington the practical implications of the fact that political science has played a formative, architectonic role in American public affairs from the founding. The ambiguity I have noted in consensus politics arises because the public creed adumbrates a comprehensive and difficult political science, only a part of which ever becomes active and popular as a working consensus. Consensus politics is ambiguous because it sets a political science to work by way of opinion. The *Federalist* persuasion, to take the clearest case, was only a shadow of *The Federalist*.[92] The persuasion was a creed and, for a time, a working consensus.[93] The political science on which Madison and Hamilton drew in writing *The Federalist* was neither. Although such knowledge cannot be translated into opinion without considerable abridgement and significant omission, it remains the last resort for judgment and our northstar in assessing reform and realignment. For a new consensus to be built, an old consensus must be undermined; yet both old and new point toward principles by which every consensus may be judged—that is, toward a matrix or measure of the American consensus. Political science is the path reason must follow to apprehend those principles.[94]

Huntington's essay reflects this ambiguity of consensus politics, but without adequately explaining it. His formulation is paradoxical and dramatic because it repudiates established or traditional meanings of consensus. If these residual meanings no longer held some sway in American public discourse, his argument would neither electrify nor edify. It does both, in somewhat Socratic fashion, insofar as it compels us to articulate essential received opinions and to ask whether they are merely opinion. Huntington prompts us to do so most pointedly by challenging the beliefs of the consensual school. What makes traditional consensus politics moderate, according to Huntington, is lethargy and apathy, a surrender to inertia and despair. He categorically denies that consensus politics as we have known it was informed by the principles of the American consensus.[95]

In reply, I have tried to recall the spirited dimension of the New Deal realignment and to identify the role of democratic honor in majoritarian consensus politics. It is proper to begin with such a recollection if we wish to understand the institutions described in the contributions to this volume. For (as I have argued) the end to which they are means is an animus against an idea of honor. As means to liberate us from the authority of this idea and from the habits it has encouraged, these institutional instruments are unintelligible apart from their object. They play a counterpoint to once-respected opinions—now held guilty by association with dishonorable prejudices—whose authority they systematically combat. To make these instruments intelligible, one must bring their original purpose to view by articulating the opinions they delegitimate.

Giving challenged opinions a voice, however, is only a beginning. The next task, which I will mention only briefly in closing, is to try to ascend from these evident opinions to the truths they adumbrate. Because the opinions that inform every durable consensus in American politics point beyond opinion, they can be periodically challenged, dissolved, and a new consensus reconstituted. The Declaration of Independence

**VERNON REGIONAL
JUNIOR COLLEGE LIBRARY**

incites us to think that beyond those opinions lie not only truths but self-evident truths.[96] It is for this reason that a promise of disharmony and profound conflict is embedded in American politics, not because the American creed is inherently antinomian or hostile to institutions. Despite Roosevelt's equivocation about the American idea of honor, political science should cleave to the New Deal as a paradigm of such disharmony (as Huntington does not).[97] For the New Deal illustrates a cardinal fact: Political realignments define a new consensus and a new common horizon for comprehensive public deliberations. They do not merely raise an argument about the democratic ethos and democratic honor; they settle the argument as a political matter and consolidate the resolution in practice.

But they cannot settle it as a matter for inquiry, or consolidate the resolution in theory. There will always be a disproportion between opinion and reason, between what busy citizens take to be settled beyond dispute and what reason reveals to be profoundly disputable. At his best, Roosevelt understood this condition of freedom.[98] One cannot long expect thoughtful citizens to honor a political settlement that is merely opinional, that does not point beyond "prejudice." Nor can we reach a settlement that will long endure if we repudiate opinion as the medium of political life and as a choiceworthy approximation of the truths adumbrated in the Declaration of Independence. These limitations circumscribe an arena for statesmanship that does not accommodate every ambition. Such a consensus politics is practicable only for those who hold these truths, and hence the opinions of citizens in whom they are imperfectly reflected, to be worthy of honor.

NOTES

1. Samuel P. Huntington, *American Politics: The Promise of Disharmony* (Cambridge: Harvard University Press, 1981), p. 172.

2. Ibid., pp. 6–9, 11–12, 30, 85–167. According to Huntington, "America has been spared class conflicts in order to have moral convulsions" (ibid., p. 11).

3. Ibid., pp. 7–12, 30–60.

4. Ibid., pp. 138–166.

5. Ibid., pp. 1–4, 167–195.

6. Ibid., pp. 6–7, 112–129, 139–140.

7. Ibid., pp. 154, 122–129, 214–220, and 231–232. Can there be a principled politics of compromise? By placing hostility to power (i.e., an "anti-power ethic") at the center of American consensus, Huntington gives the impression that moderate statesmanship cannot be principled, or at least cannot appeal to the authority of consensual principles. Because the statesman cannot appeal to principle, his task is to disguise power (ibid., pp. 75, 78–84, 112, 188, 190–196, 217, 219). We are thus led to ask what is disguised in Huntington's claim that

"vigorous and responsible national leadership requires a network of petty tyrants" (ibid., p. 219). Is responsibility the mask for tyranny, or is tyranny merely responsibility "misliked" (to paraphrase Hobbes)?

8. See, for example, M. Kent Jennings, "Residues of a Movement: The Aging of the American Protest Generation," *American Political Science Review*, vol. 81 (June 1987), p. 381.

9. See Samuel P. Huntington, "The Visions of the Democratic Party," *The Public Interest*, vol. 78 (Spring 1985), pp. 63–78. Huntington, *American Politics*, pp. 196–220.

10. Huntington's account of the New Deal is among the weakest passages in his work; see *American Politics*, especially pp. 87, 90–91, 129, 139, and 215. FDR is mentioned, but not discussed, at pp. 38 and 104. These omissions point to a major difficulty in Huntington's account: his seeming inability to distinguish between political bungling and abuse of authority. The absence of any standard of political accomplishment makes *American Politics* read curiously like a catalogue of excuses for incompetence, inasmuch as accomplishment (according to Huntington) depends wholly on whether one happens to arrive at a time of creedal passion or political exhaustion.

11. The Greek term *pragma* is in part a term of distinction: It connotes a thing right or fit to be done. The Aristotleian understanding of practical wisdom is bound up with the view that in politics the capacity to do what is fit to be done is the capacity for natural right. It concludes taking men's measure. FDR is usually considered a pragmatist by those who forget (or never understood) his ability to remind Americans of their measure—and their limits. Compare Russell L. Hanson's account of the New Deal as "consumerism," in *The Democratic Imagination in America: Conversations with Our Past* (Princeton, N.J.: Princeton University Press, 1985), pp. 257–292.

12. If Huntington were right, such a consensus would be ruled out by the basic values of American political culture: We could have Jeffersonianism, but not a Jefferson. See "A Concert of Action" (April 18, 1932), in *The Public Papers and Addresses of Franklin D. Roosevelt*, vol. 1 (New York: Random House, 1938), pp. 627–639.

13. See Huntington, "The Visions of the Democratic Party," pp. 67–69.

14. If one inquires as to why liberal political science has such difficulty in taking the study of public honors or ruling ethos seriously, one is led back to the classic works of liberal political philosophy. Montesquieu, for example, accepted Hobbes's view that honor was something essentially conventional and arbitrary. It is beyond the scope of this chapter, however, to explore Tocqueville's rejection of previous liberal thought on this topic.

15. See Ralph C. Hancock, "The Theory and Practice of American Democracy According to de Tocqueville," paper presented to the annual meeting of the American Political Science Association, New Orleans (September 1985).

16. Compare Robert Eden, "Tocqueville on Political Realignment and Constitutional Forms," *Review of Politics*, vol. 48 (Summer 1986), pp. 349–373.

17. The documentary sources differ widely in their sensitivity to this issue. I have relied heavily on *Roosevelt and Frankfurter: Their Correspondence 1928–*

1945, annotated by Max Freedman (Boston: Little, Brown, 1967), because Frankfurter appears to have been a perceptive observer of Roosevelt, as well as a contributor to his outlook, on the question of office holding and public honors. This work will hereafter be cited as *RFC*.

18. Elliot A. Rosen, *Hoover, Roosevelt, and the Brains Trust: From Depression to New Deal* (New York: Columbia University Press, 1977), especially pp. 38–65.

19. Ibid., pp. 95–114. Roosevelt had to steer a course between the internationalist legacy of progressivism, as exemplified in his chief rival for the nomination for 1932, Newton D. Baker, and the isolationist faction headed by William Randolph Hearst. He was able to do so successfully not because he was a trimmer, but because he sought to combine the best of Woodrow Wilson and Theodore Roosevelt in his foreign policy. See Alonzo Hamby, *Liberalism and Its Challengers: FDR to Reagan* (New York: Oxford University Press, 1973), pp. 12–51; John Milton Cooper, Jr., *The Warrior and the Priest: Woodrow Wilson and Theodore Roosevelt* (Cambridge: Harvard University Press, 1983); and Robert Dallek, *Franklin D. Roosevelt and American Foreign Policy, 1932–1945* (New York: Oxford University Press, 1979).

20. *RFC*, May 31, 1932: "The behavior of those who determined the standards of society during the mad years preceding the October crash was bound to be followed by the long course of wreckage through which we are now living. Seeing life, as I do, so largely through the effects of men and measures upon the minds of generous, able and ambitious youth, I could see, as though it were a visible object, the directions in which they were pushed by those who set directions for them—those who are conventionally recognized and esteemed as the most successful in our society. 'We live by symbols,' says Holmes. The symbols for these lads here during the post-war period were the Coolidges and the Mellons, the Hoovers and the Hugheses, the Youngs and Bakers. And I ask you in all sadness of heart what directions and standards did these men set for the young? What examples of courage in speech and action did these men set before them, what criteria of 'success' did they represent?" (*RFC*, pp. 63–64).

21. It should be emphasized that both Hoover's unpopularity and the economic crisis led many Democrats to the conclusion that a normal campaign would defeat him. Hoover was initially delighted at the nomination of Roosevelt, regarding him as the weakest of the Democratic contenders. That there would be a critical election and a realignment in 1932 was by no means predetermined. It was the result of a conscious gamble that Roosevelt and his advisers had chosen to take. A realignment of political parties was proposed in a memo by Raymond Moley on May 19, 1932. Moley recognized what Kristi Anderson has documented—that the Democratic Party could become a majority party by including a previously ignored electorate: "Constant references in the 'Forgotten Man' speech, the memoranda and drafts of the St. Paul Address, and again in the Moley memo . . . to the nation's 'economic infantry' cannot be dismissed as a cliché. As Al Smith had discerned, Roosevelt was determined to shift the party's orientation to the laboring class, the farmer, and the small businessman."

See Rosen, *Hoover, Roosevelt, and the Brains Trust*, p. 141. Indeed, the scope was even wider than Rosen suggests. See also Kristi Andersen, *The Creation of a Democratic Majority, 1928–1936* (Chicago: University of Chicago Press, 1979); and James E. Campbell, "Sources of the New Deal Realignment: The Contributions of Conversion and Mobilization to Partisan Change," *Western Political Quarterly*, vol. 38, no. 3 (September 1985), pp. 357–376.

22. Rosen, *Hoover, Roosevelt, and the Brains Trust*; Katie Louchheim, ed., *The Making of the New Deal: The Insiders Speak* (Cambridge: Harvard University Press, 1983); Nancy J. Weiss, "The Black Cabinet," *Farewell to the Party of Lincoln: Black Politics in the Age of FDR* (Princeton, N.J.: Princeton University Press, 1983); Sidney M. Milkis, "The New Deal, Administrative Reform, and the Transcendence of Partisan Politics," *Administration and Society*, vol. 18 (February 1987), pp. 433–472; and Milkis, "Franklin D. Roosevelt and the Transcendence of Partisan Politics," *Political Science Quarterly*, vol. 100 (Fall 1985), pp. 479–504. See also Frankfurter to Roosevelt, January 18, 1937: "How to build up a passionate, devoted, capable, fighting personnel for national administration has been the one subject about which I have been continuously thinking for thirty years. I hope, therefore, there will be a chance of talking with you about all this in your good time" (*RCF*, p. 378). In addition, see Jerold S. Auerbach, "Lawyers and Social Change in the Depression Decade," in John Braeman, Robert H. Bremner, and David Brody, eds., *The New Deal*, vol. 1 (Columbus: Ohio State University Press, 1975), pp. 133–169; and John A. Salmond, "Aubrey Williams: Atypical New Dealer?" in *The New Deal*, pp. 218–245. Southern politicians were particularly incensed by this aspect of the New Deal. Compare with Robert A. Garson, *The Democratic Party and the Politics of Sectionalism, 1941–1948* (Baton Rouge: Louisiana State University Press and London School of Economics, 1974).

23. Jerold S. Auerbach, "New Deal, Old Deal, or Raw Deal: Some Thoughts on New Left Historiography," *Journal of Southern History*, vol. 35 (1969), pp. 17–30; Louchheim, *The Making of the New Deal*, pp. xi–xviii; and Byron E. Shafer, *Quiet Revolution: The Struggle for the Democratic Party and the Shaping of Post-Reform Politics* (New York: Russell Sage Foundation, 1983).

24. William E. Leuchtenberg, "Franklin D. Roosevelt's Court 'Packing' Plan," in Harold M. Hollingsworth and William F. Holmes, eds., *Essays on the New Deal* (Austin: University of Texas Press, 1969), pp. 69–115, especially pp. 109–115.

25. See Garson, *The Democratic Party.*

26. Consider Frankfurter's reasons for backing Roosevelt's shock tactics: "It was clear that some major operation was necessary. Any major action to the body politic, no less than to the body physical, involves some shock. But I have, as you know, deep faith in your instinct to make the wise choice—the choice that will carry intact the motley aggregation that constitutes the progressive army toward the goal of present-day needs. . . . I have a deep conviction that the problem is essentially an educational one—to make the country understand what the real function of the Supreme Court is and how, for a long stretch of years, it has been exercising it" (*RFC*, p. 383).

27. Decisive evidence on this point is FDR's reasoning for going ahead without accepting compromise, after it had become clear that he might suffer a serious defeat. C. C. Burlingham wrote urging a compromise. Roosevelt replied that "I do not in the least object to what you have written but may I put it this way: *I think you are looking a day or a week or a year ahead, while I am trying to look a generation ahead.* For exactly thirty years I have been watching, as a lawyer, the processes of American justice. I have attended Bar Association meetings of many kinds. I have read Law Journals and Reviews. I have met, liked and *given honor* to many great lawyers and many great judges. But the net result is this— neither the American Bar nor the American Bench in that whole period [has] been responsible for any major improvement in the processes of justice. And on the other side of the picture, the American Bar and the American Bench have encouraged bad morals and bad ethics on the part of American non-lawyer citizens. It is, therefore, not to be wondered that a large majority of the lawyers and judges of the country would prefer to see nothing done in regard to reforming the Federal Courts—to say nothing of state and local courts" (*RFC*, p. 400, May 27, 1937, my emphasis). I draw the term *rights industry* from Richard E. Morgan, *Disabling America: The "Rights Industry" in Our Time* (New York: Basic Books, 1984).

28. Precisely because he sought to frame such a character-forming political choice, Roosevelt was dismayed when Brandeis refused his support. Leuchtenberg repeats the judgment of contemporary journalists that Senator Robinson's death was the end of the fight for Roosevelt. See Joseph Alsop and Turner Catledge, *The 168 Days* (Garden City, N.Y.: Doubleday, 1938), pp. 274–276; and Leuchtenberg, "Franklin D. Roosevelt's Court 'Packing' Plan," pp. 105–107. To Max Freedman, it appears instead that Roosevelt was determined to continue the fight. What ended it was the desertion of one of his principal spokesmen and supporters, Governor Herbert Lehman of New York (see *RFC*, pp. 403–404). Frankfurter proposed that FDR quote Theodore Roosevelt to frame this choice: "For the peaceful progress of our people during the twentieth century we shall owe most to those judges who hold to a twentieth century economic and social philosophy, and not to a long outgrown philosophy, which was itself the product of primitive economic conditions" (*RCF*, p. 384).

29. See Sidney M. Milkis, "Presidents and Party Purges: With Special Emphasis on the Lessons of 1938," in Robert Harmel, ed., *Presidents and Their Parties* (New York: Praeger Publishers, 1986), pp. 151–175.

30. Shafer, *Quiet Revolution*, pp. 523–539; David Vogel, "The Public Interest Movement and the American Reform Tradition," *Political Science Quarterly* (Winter 1980-1981), pp. 607–628; and Huntington, "Visions of the Democratic Party."

31. Most obviously, Roosevelt initiated the change to a simple majority rule for presidential nominations in the Democratic party convention, breaking the veto-power that the two-thirds requirement had given the South. See Garson, *The Democratic Party*, pp. 1–31; Milkis, "Presidents and Party Purges," pp. 151–175; and Milkis, "The New Deal, Administrative Reform and the Transcendence of Partisan Politics." The substantive effect of procedural changes is a major theme of Shafer's *The Quiet Revolution*.

32. Tocqueville's chapter on honor is part of a sequence of chapters that begins by taking a second look at individualism. When viewed from the perspective of Book 2, individualism appeared primarily as it formed the habits of the heart and might in turn be transformed by them: Book 2 is on sentiment. In Book 3, Tocqueville; returns to the subject in the context of a debate over human spiritedness or defensiveness. Some believe, he says, that democrats will be wholly public or merge their lives into the life of the community. But to think this is to entertain what Tocqueville calls "a gross and tyrannical idea of democracy." It is tyrannical because it requires overriding that spiritedness which leads men to hold firm by what distinguishes them from others. Here individualism reappears not as a calculating self-interest that isolates but as a spirited choice that binds one to others. Spiritedness is social, so the same division of democrats into small groups that had excited Tocqueville's anxieties in Book 2 now evokes his admiration: He comes spiritedly to the defense of the choosiness that keeps democrats apart—one that reflects a more refined and less tyrannical idea of democracy. This is Tocqueville's introduction to "commitment" and engagement in political undertakings; it introduces his account of American gravity, vanity, honor, and ambition—themes regrettably ignored in the joint study by Robert N. Bellah, Richard Madsen, William M. Sullivan, Ann Swidler, and Steven M. Tipton, *Habits of the Heart: Individualism and Commitment in American Life* (Berkeley): University of California Press, 1985).

33. Alexis de Tocqueville, *Democracy in America*, vol. 2, bk. 3, ch. 18. See the translation by George Lawrence, edited by J. P. Mayer (Garden City, N.Y.: Doubleday, 1969), pp. 621–623. The translation here is my own and more literal than Lawrence's.

34. Franklin D. Roosevelt, *The Happy Warrior, Alfred E. Smith: A Study of a Public Servant* (Boston: Houghton Mifflin, 1928). Bradley Gilman's book on TR, *Roosevelt: The Happy Warrior* (Boston: Little, Brown, 1923), gave FDR his cue in choosing a title.

35. Consider Frankfurter's remarks to Walter Lippmann, June 22, 1930: "You perform an important educational task in making clear once again that government is not business, that government is quite an art in itself. Hoover may unwittingly render a great service in driving home that truth by his very failures. For, as you point out, there was a peculiarly favorable conjunction of man and circumstances in putting the engineering and business theory of politics to the test through Hoover's presidency. The professionalism of politics was one of my themes in one of the Dodge lectures and I am very much delighted to have your own illuminating analysis of the matter. Reiteration is the essence of political education"(*RCF,* p. 45). Frankfurter framed a statement that Roosevelt had made just before he took the oath of office on March 4, 1933: "The quality of National politics, viewed as a science which is capable of affecting for the better the lives of the average man and woman in America, is the concern of National leadership" (*RFC,* p. 37).

36. One of Frankfurter's anecdotes sums up well the peculiarly infectious character of Roosevelt's courage: "From the time he was a boy, according to his mother, he had the self-sufficiency and strength that come from a reserved

inner life. Thus, while to outward view he was usually debonair and had a gaiety at times easily taken for jauntiness, he had a will of steel well-sheathed by a captivating smile. For too many people optimism is an evasion, a Micawber's hope that something will turn up. In Roosevelt, optimism was not an anodyne, it was an energy—an energy to spur his resourcefulness, a force that gave creative energy to others. An official not given to idolatry was once heard to say, 'After talking with the President for an hour, I could eat bricks for lunch'" (*RFC*, p. 748).

37. The corporatist dimension of the arrangements Roosevelt pioneered is shown in Grant McConnell, *Private Power and American Democracy* (New York: Vintage Books, 1966). For an interpretation linking Progressive thought with these arrangements, see R. Jeffrey Lustig, *Corporate Liberalism: The Origins of Modern American Political Theory, 1890–1920* (Berkeley: University of California Press, 1982).

38. Tocqueville, *Democracy in America*, pp. 616–626.

39. Forrest McDonald, *Alexander Hamilton: A Biography* (New York: W. W. Norton, 1979).

40. Tocqueville, *Democracy in America*, pp. 616–626.

41. Huntington, "Visions of the Democratic Party," p. 66.

42. See the trenchant analysis of the Carolene Products doctrine by Edward J. Erler, "Equal Protection and Personal Rights: The Regime of the 'Discrete and Insular Minority,'" *Georgia Law Review*, vol. 16 (Winter 1982), pp. 407–444.

43. See John Adams Wettergreen, "Origin of Affirmative Action," paper prepared for the annual meeting of the American Political Science Association, Chicago (September 1987).

44. What follows is in part a reflection on Byron E. Shafer's fine political history of this episode, *Quiet Revolution: The Struggle for the Democratic Party and the Shaping of Post-Reform Politics* (New York: Russell Sage Foundation, 1983). To my knowledge, there is no single study that undertakes to deal with the comprehensive change in policy the new Democrats have attempted to bring about; Shafer devotes his last chapter to a very tentative account (see pp. 523–539). His caveats (p. 603, note 6) about the difficulty of moving from an account of the party reform to later developments apply to my attempt here. The closest approximation of an account of the comprehensive change I have in view is Ole R. Holsti and James N. Rosenau, *American Leadership in World Affairs: Vietnam and the Breakdown of Consensus* (Boston: Allen and Unwin, 1984). Their findings suggest the scope of the change that has come about, but they abstract from how it happened: "Discussion of the processes whereby the values and beliefs of leaders are aggregated—through public pressures, lobbying, polls, leadership interactions, policy-making processes and the like—and thereby transformed into the broader patterns and institutions through which foreign policy is framed and executed, is deferred for another time" (p. xiv).

45. In certain respects, the rules change of 1970 can be considered a countercoup, because Lyndon Johnson was an outsider to the *presidential* Democratic party: he probably could not have been nominated under the old primary system, as demonstrated by his hapless run against John Kennedy in 1960. Once in the

presidency, however, Johnson was a formidable incumbent, indeed—but precisely for the reasons that had made him unpalatable to the presidential selection party. See Alonzo L. Hamby, *Liberalism and Its Challengers: FDR to Reagan* (New York: Oxford University Press, 1985), pp. 231–281.

46. Anna Kasten Nelson, "John Foster Dulles and the Bipartisan Congress, *Political Science Quarterly,* vol. 102 (Spring 1987), pp. 43–64; Leslie H. Gelb, "Vietnam: The System Worked," originally in *Foreign Policy,* vol. 3 (Summer 1971), reprinted in Robert W. Tucker and William Watts, *Beyond Containment: U.S. Foreign Policy in Transition* (Washington, D.C.: Potomac Associates, 1973), pp. 48–49; and Seyom Brown, "The Disintegration of the Foreign Policy Consensus," in his *The Faces of Power: Constancy and Change in United States Foreign Policy from Truman to Reagan* (New York: Columbia University Press, 1983), pp. 306–317.

47. See Lyndon Baines Johnson, *The Vantage Point: Perspectives of the Presidency 1963–1969* (New York: Holt, Rinehart and Winston, 1971), pp. 152, 323, and especially 531: "Throughout those years of crucial decisions I was sustained by the memory of my predecessors who had also borne the most painful duty of a President—to lead our country in a time of war. I recalled often the words of one of those men, Woodrow Wilson, who in the dark days of 1917 said: 'It is a fearful thing to lead this great peaceful people into war. . . . But the right is more precious than peace.'" Doris Kearns describes Johnson's morbid fear of Wilson's fate in *Lyndon Johnson and the American Dream* (New York: Harper and Row, 1976).

48. See the account of the August 1964 meetings prior to the Gulf of Tonkin Resolution in Johnson, *The Vantage Point,* pp. 55, 116–119. Relations with the Senate Foreign Relations Committee were strained by the United States' intervention in the Dominican Republic nine months later (April 29, 1965); Fulbright in particular was highly critical of the Johnson administration policy. Johnson's gathering of the bipartisan precedents for his policy in Vietnam was not a retrospective rationale but, rather, a recrimination against the opposition for breaking faith with previous norms (see *The Vantage Point,* pp. 48–62, and note the substantial concurrence of Gelb, "Vietnam.")

49. See the debates in Richard M. Pfeffer, ed., *No More Vietnams? The War and the Future of American Foreign Policy* (New York: Harper and Row, 1968). One shortcoming of Shafer's study is his tendency to ignore foreign policy considerations as a driving motive of the insurgency.

50. Roger H. Davidson, "Two Avenues of Change: House and Senate Committee Reorganization," in Lawrence C. Dodd and Bruce I. Oppenheimer, eds., *Congress Reconsidered* (Washington D.C.: Congressional Quarterly Press, 1982), pp. 107–133; and Roger H. Davidson, "Subcommittee Government: New Channels for Policy Making," pp. 99–133, and Charles O. Jones, "Congress and the Presidency," pp. 134–177, both in Thomas E. Mann and Norman J. Ornstein, eds., *The New Congress* (Washington, D.C.: American Enterprise Institute, 1981).

51. Edward A. Kolodziej, "Formulating Foreign Policy," in Richard M. Pious, *The Power to Govern: Assessing Reform in the United States* (New York: The Academy of Political Science, 1981), pp. 174–189; and I. M. Destler, "Executive-

Congressional Conflict in Foreign Policy: Explaining It; Coping with It," in Dodd and Oppenheimer, eds., *Congress Reconsidered*, pp. 296–316.

52. This point will be controversial because there were many "factors" working against the continuation of these older norms and practices. I am aware that this is so.

53. See Pfeffer, ed., *No More Vietnams?*; Joshua Muravchik, "Why the Democrats Lost," *Commentary*, vol. 79 (January 1985), pp. 15–26; and Carl Gershman, "The Rise and Fall of the New Foreign Policy Establishment," *Commentary*, vol. 70, no. 1 (July 1980), pp. 13–24.

54. See I. M. Destler, Leslie H. Gelb, and Anthony Lake, *Our Own Worst Enemy: The Unmaking of American Foreign Policy* (New York: Simon and Schuster, 1984), especially pp. 129–162.

55. According to Harvey C. Mansfield, Jr., "The public constitution is the arrangement of rule which appears to the public and is taught in the schools; the private constitution is the way in which the regime 'really works' behind the scenes." See Mansfield, Jr., *Statesmanship and Party Government* (Chicago: University of Chicago Press, 1967), p. 3.

56. Destler et al., *Our Own Worst Enemy*, pp. 127–162; and Holsti and Rosenau, *American Leadership in World Affairs*.

57. That the reforms were substantive and intended to advance a new type of activist is Shafer's main theme, but he is reserved about the foreign policy dimension. See Shafer, *Quiet Revolution*, pp. 3–10, 74–75, 128–130, 235–236, 425–427, 503–504, and 523–529. See also the brief paragraph on foreign policy attitudes, p. 536.

58. The terms *plebiscitarian presidency* and *opinion leadership* are explained in more detail in Joseph M. Bessette, Jeffrey Tulis, Glenn Thurow, and James W. Ceaser, "The Rise of the Rhetorical Presidency," *Presidential Studies Quarterly*, vol. 11 (Summer 1981), pp. 158–171; Jeffrey Tulis, "Public Policy and the Rhetorical Presidency," paper presented at the annual meeting of the American Political Science Association, New York City (September 1981); Robert Eden, "Opinion Leadership and the Liberal Cause," in Eden, *Political Leadership and Nihilism: A Study of Weber and Nietzsche* (Gainesville: University of South Florida Press, 1984), pp. 1–35; and James W. Ceaser, *Presidential Selection: Theory and Development* (Princeton, N.J.: Princeton University Press, 1979).

59. Shafer, *Quiet Revolution*, pp. 74–75, 131, 317–318, 523–539.

60. See Jeffrey M. Berry, *The Interest Group Society* (Boston: Little, Brown, 1984), especially pp. 51–53; Hugh Heclo, "Issue Networks and the Executive Establishment," in Anthony King, ed., *The New American Political System* (Washington, D.C.: American Enterprise Institute, 1976), pp. 87–124.

61. Shafer, *Quiet Revolution*, pp. 524–525; Destler et al., *Our Own Worst Enemy*, pp. 127–162.

62. See Muravchik, "Why the Democrats Lost."

63. Harvey C. Mansfield, Jr., "The Media World and Democratic Representation," *Government and Opposition*, vol. 14 (Summer 1979), pp. 318–384.

64. One effect of the change described by Destler et al. in *Our Own Worst Enemy*, pp. 91–126 and 129–162, from "establishment" to "professional elite,"

is that in addition to the two foreign policy establishments identified with the major parties, we now have a wide array of organized professional factions: Every persuasion of opinion leaders has its associated cadre of experts to put before the media and congressional committees.

65. In addition to the works cited in Notes 46, 49, and 50, see Leslie H. Gelb, "Domestic Change and National Security Policy," in Henry Owen, ed., *The Next Phase in Foreign Policy* (Washington, D.C.: Brookings Institution, 1973), pp. 249–280.

66. I. M. Destler, "The Constitution and Foreign Affairs," *News for Teachers of Political Science,* vol. 45 (Spring 1985), pp. 14–16, 23. This article is curiously reserved in contrast to *Our Own Worst Enemy,* and oddly silent about the crisis outlined in that work. Conpare with Berry's remark on the tremendous change since the second edition of Raymond A. Bauer, Ithiel de Sola Pool, and Lewis Anthony Dexter's *American Business and Public Policy,* in Berry, *The Interest Group Society,* pp. 44–45. On the formal constitutional side, see Robet Scigliano, "The War Powers Resolution and the War Powers," in Joseph M. Bessette and Jeffrey Tulis, *The Presidency in the Constitutional Order* (Baton Rouge: Louisiana State University Press, 1981), pp. 115–153; and in the same volume, Gary J. Schmitt, "Executive Privilege: Presidential Power to Withhold Information from Congress," pp. 154–194.

67. In "Opinion Leadership and the Liberal Cause," Eden argues that modern liberalism inherited a new esteem for opinion leadership from Woodrow Wilson, and that *The Federalist* viewed such leadership with suspicion (pp. 1–15). See also Harvey C. Mansfield, Jr. "Rationality and Representation in Burke's 'Bristol Speech'" in C. J. Friedrich, ed., *Nomos VII: Rational Decision* (New York: Prentice-Hall, 1964), pp. 197–216. The bearing of such arguments on American foreign policy, as an alternative to the present state of deliberations between Congress and the executive, is perhaps best explained by Hadley Arkes, in *Bureaucracy, The Marshall Plan, and the National Interest* (Princeton, N.J.: Princeton University Press, 1972).

68. One evil of the arduous plebiscitary selection procedure now in place is that no candidate who entertains doubts about winning can stay the course. The reforms have exacted a high spiritual price for aspiring to the presidency, as one must sacrifice the intellect beyond what was formerly required of politicians. Thus it is unlikely that Democratic campaigners will admit to themselves that their party has dealt itself and them out of the presidential game. Perhaps it is only fair that, to balance accounts, Democratic party candidates should make similar demands on the electorate.

69. Muravchik, "Why the Democrats Lost"; and Gershman, "The Rise and Fall of the New Foreign Policy Establishment."

70. Berry, *The Interest Group Society,* pp. 26–28; and Crotty, *Decision for the Democrats,* pp. 136–137. In *Quiet Revolution,* Shafer emphasizes the contradiction between the ideology of participatory democracy that moved many of the reformers and the quota policy that the new rules imposed; his evidence supports the view that it was not civil rights groups or elected black leaders who pressed the quota policy but, rather, the representatives of the women's movement (see

pp. 119–120, 129–130, 169–175, 206–207, 462–470, and 532). Although he recognizes that the rules broke the hold of the party regulars and gave new scope for groups like the NAACP, Shafer is perhaps more sure than the civil rights leaders were that the regular or orthodox coalition provided adequate scope for them. For a partial corrective, see Hamby, "Martin Luther King, Jr.," in his *Liberalism and Its Challengers: FDR to Reagan,* pp. 139–182. Compare Wettergreen, "Origin of Affirmative Action."

71. This consensus also found expression in the Immigration Act of 1965. Its passage, as Glazer says, "marked the disappearance from Federal law of crucial distinctions on the basis of race and national origin. The nation agreed with this act that there would be no effort to control the future ethnic and racial character of the American population and rejected the claim that some racial and ethnic groups were more suited to be Americans than others." See Nathan Glazer, *Affirmative Discrimination: Ethnic Inequality and Public Policy* (New York: Basic Books, 1975), p. 4. On the new racial justice, see Herman Belz, *Affirmative Action from Kennedy to Reagan: Redefining American Equality* (Washington, D.C.: Washingon Legal Foundation, 1984); and Terry Eastland and William J. Bennett, *Counting by Race: Equality from the Founding Fathers to Bakke and Weber* (New York: Basic Books, 1979).

72. Edward J. Erler, "Equal Protection and Personal Rights: The Regime of the 'Discrete and Insular Minority,'" *Georgia Law Review,* vol. 16 (Winter 1982), pp. 407–444. On the importance of white guilt in the later thought of Martin Luther King, see Hamby, *Liberalism and Its Challengers.*

73. Harvey C. Mansfield, Jr., "The Underhandedness of Affirmative Action," *National Review* (May 4, 1984), pp. 26–32.

74. See the discussion of administration in John A. Wettergreen, "Constitutional Problems of American Bureaucracy in *I.N.S.* v. *Chadha,*" paper prepared for presentation at the annual meeting of the American Political Science Association, New Orleans, Louisiana (September 1985).

75. See Allen J. Matusow, *The Unraveling of America: A History of Liberalism in the 1960s* (New York: Harper and Row, 1984), pp. 180–216.

76. Crotty, *Decision for the Democrats,* p. 284, note 4; Shafer, *Quiet Revolution,* pp. 206–207; and Muravchik, "Why the Democrats Lost."

77. The term *institutional racism* was devised as a way of establishing the existence of racism without the existence of racists, allowing administrators and opinion leaders to wage war on prejudice without having to relieve anyone of it.

78. To remind oneself of the magnitude of this change, compare Nancy J. Weiss, "Why Blacks Became Democrats," *Farewell to the Party of Lincoln: Black Politics in the Age of FDR* (Princeton, N.J.: Princeton University Press, 1983), pp. 209–235, with Matusow, *The Unraveling of America.*

79. Charles Murray, *Losing Ground: American Social Policy 1950–1980* (New York: Basic Books, 1984), pp. 15–25, 32–33, 41–46, and 178–191.

80. Prior to the civil and voting rights legislation of 1964 and 1965 and their vigorous enforcement, civil rights leaders had grounds for doubting that this commitment was substantial. Johnson's legislation made it clear that equal

opportunity could be made law with teeth in it. See James C. Harvey, *Black Civil Rights During the Johnson Administration* (Jackson: University and College Press of Mississippi, 1973), for an assessment of the strengths and weaknesses of Johnson's commitment by the old criterion. By 1970, when the Democratic party rewrote its rules, commitment to equal opportunity had been rejected as insufficient; compensation for past injustice became the test of the liberalism of public policy.

81. The pattern described by William R. Keech and Donald R. Matthews still describes recent presidential nominations remarkably well—particularly for the cases of Carter in 1980 and Mondale in 1984, although in Mondale's case it is probably because he adopted the strategy of success appropriate to the new primary system, as modeled by John H. Aldritch. It is true that Carter would not have been the Democratic nominee in 1976 under the old rules. See Shafer, *Quiet Revolution*, p. 523 ff. and compare William R. Keech and Donald R. Matthews, *The Party's Choice* (Washington, D.C.: Brookings Institution, 1976) with John H. Aldritch, *Before the Convention: A Theory of Presidential Nominating Campaigns* (Chicago: University of Chicago Press, 1980).

82. See Jeane J. Kirkpatrick, *The New Presidential Elite* (New York: Russell Sage Foundation and Twentieth Century Fund, 1976). See also Shafer, *Quiet Revolution:* "The continuing result was nothing less than the transformation of the elite stratum in presidential politics, that collection of specialized political actors who mount campaigns and who staff the presidential administrations which follow" (p. 533).

83. Murray, *Losing Ground.*

84. See Delba Winthrop, "Rights: A Point of Honor," paper presented at the Claremont Institute Conference, *Tocqueville Observes the New Order* (January 24–26, 1985); and William Kristol, "Liberty, Equality, Honor," *Social Philosophy and Policy*, vol. 2 (Autumn 1984), pp. 125–140.

85. This conclusion can be inferred by reference to the chapter on honor in conjunction with *Democracy in America*, vol. 2, bk. 2, ch. 2.

86. See Joseph Cropsey, "Liberalism, Nature and Convention," *Independent Journal of Philosophy*, vol. 4 (1983), pp. 21–27.

87. See Tocqueville, *Democracy in America*, p. 616. Tocqueville goes on to say that "I think that [honor] can be explained by reasons other than the caprice of particular individuals or nations, which has been the reason given hitherto."

88. As Tocqueville further notes, "It is chiefly courage of this sort which is needed to maintain the American association and make it prosper, and it is held by them in particular esteem and honor. To betray a lack of it brings certain shame" (ibid., p. 622).

89. Milkis, "The New Deal, Administrative Reform, and the Transcendence of Partisan Politics."

90. Berry, *The Interest Group Society*, pp. 26–41.

91. Ibid., pp. 46–66; see also Wettergreen, "Constitutional Problems of American Bureaucracy in *I.N.S. v. Chadha.*"

92. John Zvesper contends that the party of Jefferson had a "persuasion" and a powerful rhetoric, whereas the Federalists had a political science only. In

doing so, he neglects the subtle but crucial differences between federalism as a body of shared opinions and the political science upon which Madison and Hamilton drew. His evidence, taken largely from sermons preached by Federalist ministers, indicates how in practice federalism became inseparable from religious inclinations. In the light of this evidence, it seems necessary to speak of federalism as a persuasion and creed. See John Zvesper, *Political Philosophy and Rhetoric: A Study of the Origins of American Party Politics* (Cambridge, England: Cambridge University Press, 1977).

93. Martin Van Buren, *Inquiry into the Origin and Course of Political Parties in the United States* (New York: Hurd and Houghton, 1867), pp. 46–57, 62.

94. Tocqueville, *Democracy in America*, vol. 1, pt. 2, ch. 7; and vol. 2, pt. 1, ch. 10. For an account of the relationship between the modern science of representative government and consensus politics in Britain, see Harvey C. Mansfield, Jr., "Party Government and the Settlement of 1688," *American Political Science Review*, vol. 70 (December 1964), pp. 933–946.

95. See Note 7 above.

96. Michael P. Zuckert, "Self-Evident Truth and the Declaration of Independence," *Review of Politics*, vol. 49 (Summer 1987), pp. 319–339.

97. To some degree this equivocation may have reflected Roosevelt's uncertain adherence to the principles of the Declaration. See the analysis of Roosevelt's Commonwealth Club address by Charles R. Kesler, "The Public Philosophy of the New Freedom and the New Deal," in Robert Eden, ed., *The New Deal and Its Legacy: Defense, Critique, Reappraisal* (Westview, Conn.: Greenwood Press, forthcoming).

98. "The issue of Government has always been whether individual men and women will have to serve some system of Government or economics, or whether a system of Government and economics exists to serve individual men and women. This question has persistently dominated the discussion of government for many generations. On questions relating to these things men have differed, and for time immemorial it is probable that honest men will continue to differ." See Roosevelt's Commonwealth Club address, (September 23, 1932), reprinted in *The Public Papers and Addresses of Franklin D. Roosevelt*, 1932 volume, pp. 734–744.

PART II

Governmental Institutions

4

The Rise of the Technocratic Congress: Congressional Reform in the 1970s

LAWRENCE C. DODD

The 1970s witnessed one of the greatest efforts at institutional transformation in the history of the Congress. For more than sixty years its members had allowed the executive branch to gradually usurp the policymaking powers granted to Congress in the Constitution. But confronted by a war in Vietnam that Congress had never declared yet was unable to stop, by deficit spending that it seemed unable to control, and by a president who ignored the laws Congress had passed, its members decided that they had to find a better way to make policy decisions. They needed a new structure that would allow Congress to faithfully represent the diverse and conflicting policy interests of the nation; yet they also needed a structure that would allow Congress to choose among the conflicting policy arguments and make decisions in an authoritative and decisive manner: a decisionmaking process that would enable Congress to make hard political decisions in a way that would be respected and honored by the citizenry—and the president.[1]

The creation of the new structure preoccupied members of Congress throughout the early and mid-1970s, establishing the policymaking processes that govern Congress today. The story of the reform process is complex and intriguing, and critical to any assessment of the contemporary Congress. Thus I will outline it in some detail. But the real story involves more than an understanding of the events of the 1970s. It involves an awareness of the historical dynamics that gave rise to the recent reforms.

My central argument is that both the great difficulties of the twentieth-century Congress and the extensiveness of the recent reforms resulted from the rise during the late nineteenth century of a Congress that the founding fathers failed to foresee—a Congress composed of careerist legislators. Unlike the citizen legislators of the earlier nineteenth century, the sort of legislators the founding fathers presumed Congress would attract, the careerist legislators wanted to obtain long-term personal power in Congress. In the effort to gain such power, the careerist legislators eventually overthrew the system of party government that they found in Congress and instituted a new system—committee government—in which power resided in the hands of the senior members of the majority party on each congressional committee.

Committee government and the norm of seniority succeeded in spreading power more widely in Congress, with the justification that the new system provided better expert policy guidance in Congress. Yet, although the new system did increase policy expertise, and although it simultaneously aided the careers of individual legislators, it created problems for Congress. First, the reliance on committee policymaking and committee seniority meant that decisions in particular policy areas often did not reflect the wishes of Congress as a whole, thus creating a crisis of representation; second, the existence of the new system meant that Congress often had a difficult time leading and coordinating actions across policy areas, thus creating a crisis of institutional governance.

Congress has struggled with the crises of representation and institutional governance throughout the twentieth century, with the reforms of the 1970s being only the latest and most concentrated effort to address these problems. What is distinctive about the recent reforms, aside from their extensiveness, is that they seem to have moved Congress away from committee government and the norm of seniority, a development earlier reforms had avoided. In place of committee government Congress has instituted a new technocratic government, with technical expertise replacing, or at least joining, the norm of committee seniority as a means for justifying the exercise of congressional power. This development, should it solidify and persist, will constitute a major shift in the governance of Congress. Not yet clear is whether such a development would adequately address the problems of representation and institutional governance that arose with the emergence of a careerist Congress. True reform of Congress ultimately may require constitutional revision. To understand why this may be so, we shall look first at the creation and evolution of Congress, then discuss how the modern reforms address the problems of representation and institutional governance, and conclude with an assessment of the effectiveness of these reforms.

THE EVOLUTION OF CONGRESS

The U.S. Congress was created out of the attempt by the American colonialists to find a system of government that would both allow for adequate representation of the citizenry and provide an authoritative government for the new nation. The founding fathers gave to Congress a set of clearly enumerated powers: taxing and spending authority for the nation, the authority to raise an army and to regulate interstate and foreign commerce, and a mandate to ensure the people's general welfare.[2] In light of the eighteenth-century fear of a central government, this was a strong grant of power, a grant that the founding fathers believed would help ensure the governing capacity of the new national government. Yet the founding fathers also feared that Congress, endowed with such powers, might play too strong a role in national life, leading the nation toward political tyranny.

The fear of Congress arose in large part out of the expectations that the founding fathers held about the way Congress would operate. Given an agrarian society with poor communication and transportation, and localized economies, they believed most legislators would not spend their careers in Congress but would stay only a term or two and then return to state and local endeavors. A few individuals could thus amass congressional power and dominate the assembly, with one eventually emerging as an all-powerful leader who could use the enumerated powers to overwhelm the rest of government and undermine the liberties of any groups and individuals who opposed him. It was largely in an effort to avert this danger that the founding fathers established our separation-of-powers system and federalism, dispersing power widely to check any aggrandizing tendencies in Congress. As this danger also played a large role in their decision to establish bicameralism, the founders sought to reduce the threat posed by a unified Congress.[3]

So long as an agrarian society persisted, this constitutional design operated roughly as the founding fathers had expected. Most members of Congress did return home after a term or two, leaving long-term control of Congress in the hands of a small elite. The elite was able to assert a strong policymaking role for Congress, although it was always constrained by bicameralism and balanced by the president, the courts, and the state governments. This system changed, however, with the coming of the Civil War, Reconstruction, and the early stages of in- dustrialization. These developments increased the policy role of the national government and attracted an increasing number of careerist politicians to long-term service in Congress.[4]

The rise of careerist legislators led to pressures in Congress for a wider dispersion of power, threatening to undercut centralized leadership and to erode the governing capacity of Congress. These pressures were offset in the late nineteenth century by the expansion of standing committees and the rise of patronage politics. Standing committees provided access points for large numbers of groups seeking to influence Congress, thus aiding its representativeness; they also provided an arena in which the growing number of careerists could participate in legislative decisionmaking. Patronage politics was an arrangement that allowed the leaders of Congress to gain the support of legislators by helping provide key patronage services to district constituents. The legislators, once placed on standing committees, could then be counted on to follow the policy guidance of the party leaders in Congress.

This arrangement proved so beneficial to Congress that, by the late nineteenth century, it had reached the high point of its power in our constitutional system.[5] Congress had seemingly found an arrangement that allowed it to function as an effective legislative assembly, even as turnover continued to decline. At its pinnacle of power, however, Congress faced two problems—a representational crisis and an institutional crisis— that threatened to undercut its governing arrangement.

As women were excluded from voting in most states and the Senate remained a largely nonelective chamber, progressive reformers were concerned that Congress was not sufficiently representative. The system's reliance on party leaders and patronage politics also undercut the ability of the legislators, however broadly based their elections might have been, to function as true representatives of the people. Party leaders could always use their patronage power, together with their control of committee assignments and floor deliberations, to silence those legislators whom they opposed. This misuse of power was viewed as a particular problem inasmuch as the party leaders themselves were often seen as out of touch on many issues with majority sentiment in Congress. Selected only by a majority vote of the governing caucus, these leaders pushed the policy positions of their supporters even when those positions were opposed by a congressional majority composed of dissidents in their own caucus and members of the opposition party. By contrast, the minority of the governing caucus, together with the members of the minority party, often made up a majority of Congress and were actually in closer agreement on policies with one another than with the Speaker and majority leader. This representational crisis grew to powerful pro-portions in the early twentieth century as the progressive movement united many members of both major parties against the old-guard Republican leaders who controlled Congress.

Congress also faced an institutional crisis—a crisis in its governing structure. Although the strong party leadership coordinated policymaking and provided a national voice for Congress, the leaders lacked specialized policy expertise. Nevertheless, they often ramrodded policies through committees, ignoring the advice of specialists and producing inept policy decisions. In addition, their strong patronage powers left the party leaders feeling that they and their partisan supporters were immune from defeat and thus had no need to attend to issues that did not directly concern them. Congress was consequently led to overlook issues of major concern to the nation, such as conservation, child labor, consumer protection, and trust-busting legislation, thus producing the widespread view that Congress was governed by a corrupt system that undercut both its legitimacy and its authority in national governance. Even if the leaders had truly represented the majority of Congress, a governing system based on patronage and arbitrary power was seen as too corrupt and inept to produce authoritative policy decisions.

The congressional crises of the early 1900s took on special significance when they coincided with the vast alterations taking place in the external environment of Congress—developments (particularly those giving rise to a growing number of careerist legislators) that it had never been designed to handle.[6] Congress was therefore faced not only with the need to improve its representativeness and its governing mechanisms. It simultaneously had to adjust to a new environment—to an industrial-era society that placed a large number of new policymaking demands on Congress while producing careerist legislators whose personal inclination, unless constrained by some device such as patronage, was to disperse power, thus breaking apart the party leadership structure that provided policy leadership and coordination.

The early twentieth-century Congress thus faced a serious challenge—the need to adapt to an era of careerist legislators while reforming its representative and governing processes in ways that would allow it to play a strong role in governing an industrial nation.[7] The legislators met this challenge by reforming the leadership structure of Congress. In 1910, in perhaps the greatest political upheaval in congressional history, progressive Republicans who were unhappy with the policies and patronage politics of their Republican colleague, Speaker Joseph Cannon, united with House Democrats to strip the speakership of most of its power.[8] Prior to the insurgent movement, the Speaker had served as presiding officer and, simultaneously, controlled committee appointments, the Rules Committee, private and minor House business, the Special Calendar, and the party caucus. After the insurgency, although Cannon remained Speaker, the office itself was stripped of all major duties except the constitutional role of presiding officer—and even that role was narrowed by rules limiting the Speaker's discretionary parliamentary prerogatives. This progressive revolt also destroyed the underpinnings of party government in the Senate.

A new order—committee government—emerged in the wake of these reforms and came to dominate both the House and the Senate after 1920. Committees had existed throughout the nineteenth century as forums in which hearings were held and legislation was drafted, but they had normally served as arms of the elected party leadership. After the party leaders were stripped of power (and following a short flirtation with caucus rule in the House), committee members, particularly the chairs, moved rapidly to assert their prerogatives as the masters of legislation. Each committee became virtually autonomous in its own area of jurisdiction. The committees and their leaders held their hearings and wrote their legislation behind closed doors. Because the party leadership could neither threaten their committee assignments, which were determined largely by congressional seniority, nor threaten removal of committee chairs, who were selected on the basis of committee seniority within the majority party, committee members and leaders were generally free to follow their own heads rather than look to central leaders or the party for guidance.

Committee government and the seniority system had several fundamental attributes to recommend them as efficient, rational procedures for organizing and conducting congressional business. The new arrangement provided a system of specialized expert advice within Congress that could be used in assessing policy problems but could not be arbitrarily ignored by powerful party leaders. Through the seniority system, it also provided security to committee members who wanted to plan long-term careers within particular committees without fear of removal by an arbitrary leader. Put simply, the new order appeared to provide a natural structure within which careerist legislators could supervise and control the emerging administrative state. But these appearances were deceiving.

Although the new order did provide considerable benefits to careerist legislators, in reality it failed to solve either the crisis of representation or the crisis of institutional governance.[9] From the standpoint of governing capacity, the new system provided no system of leadership that could coordinate policies across the various committees, guide policies through floor deliberations, or provide a unified voice for Congress in debates with the executive over policy directions. And from the standpoint of representation, the new system actually made matters worse in several respects. Under party government, party leaders were ultimately subject to removal; hence, if they arbitrarily treated a particular group unfairly (especially a united majority), they could always be removed. But the leaders of the new system, the committee chairs, were protected by the norm of seniority and could never be removed or seriously disciplined. Moreover, as they held their major meetings in secret, they could deny real access to the minority groups they opposed and, if they felt so inclined, could thwart the policy views of a dominant congressional majority.

Ultimately, the new system survived not because it solved the representational and governing crises within Congress but because it met the political needs of the careerist legislators. Congress itself began a long and gradual decline as a policymaking body, coming to rely increasingly on the president and the bureaucracy not only for policy leadership and coordination but also for help in breaking the internal deadlocks that undermined effective representation. These problems surfaced during the Great Depression of the 1930s, when Congress had to rely extensively on Roosevelt and the bureaucratic agencies for policy guidance and leadership. The congressional decline was exacerbated by World War II; indeed, wartime pressures led the president to exert ever greater discretionary authority. By the mid-1940s, members of Congress had begun to fear that the executive was on the verge of consummating a dramatic shift in the policymaking power granted the institutions in the Constitution. Their response was to undertake a new set of reforms.

The 1946 Legislative Reorganization Act, though ambitious in its original scope, proved inadequate in addressing the key problems faced by Congress.[10] In an effort to provide new central governing mechanisms, the act proposed both the creation of party policy committees to provide leadership for each party in each house and the establishment of a new Joint Committee on the Budget to provide fiscal coordination. The House defeated the former proposal as the members feared that such parties committees might limit the power of standing committees; and the new Joint Budget Committee, composed of all members of appropriations and revenue committee (an arrangement intended to protect the power of those committees), proved too large to be effective and was soon discarded. As the act made no effort to address the problems associated either with seniority or with the filibuster in the Senate, it failed to remove some of the primary obstacles to greater accountability and responsiveness. The success it did have in reducing the number of standing committees and subcommittees and in clarifying committee jurisdiction ultimately improved the orderliness of congressional proceedings. The act also set in motion the modern staff system and authorized committees to exercise "continuous watchfulness" over executive agencies, both of which were designed to improve the ability of Congress to maintain its independence from executive dominance.

In the final analysis, the 1946 Legislative Reorganization Act did not replace the old order of committee government with a new order better designed to ensure representativeness and governing capacity; it simply refurbished the old order and removed some of its most glaring shortcomings while leaving committee government intact and strengthened. The new committees, by virtue of their broader jurisdictions and increased staff resources, were actually stronger than before, and the committee chairs (whose prerogatives had not been reduced) emerged as even more powerful figures. The postwar system of committee government thus retained all of the fundamental problems of the prior era. The 1946 act, moreover, contributed to the isolation of most members from congressional power. In streamlining the committee system, the act left a relatively small number of autonomous positions that carried with them real power and status. The reform effort thus provided neither the benefits of decentralization (widespread expertise and policy innovation) nor the benefits of centralization (leadership and coordination). The careerist legislators, fearful that centralized party leadership or limitations on the rule of seniority might jeopardize their chances of long-term career advancement in Congress, simply avoided those reforms that might have addressed the problems of representation and governance.

Congress thus entered the postwar years with a system of internal policymaking that, if anything, decreased its long-term capacity to play a strong, responsive, and independent role in national governance. This problem was exacerbated by the 1946 elections, in which northern Democrats were defeated en masse whereas southern Democrats maintained their seats. As a result, in 1948, when the Democrats regained control of Congress, and throughout the coming postwar years, the southern minority within the Democratic party possessed rights of seniority and thus controlled the committee system. Throughout the 1950s and 1960s, as the nation and the Democratic party became more liberal, and more concerned with such issues as civil rights and social welfare, this southern minority was in a position to thwart moderate and liberal elements pushing for new social programs. Congress became not only increasingly out of touch with the policy views of the nation but also increasingly embroiled in a new and highly visible crisis of representation. Underlying this development was the reality that even if Congress had been able to resolve its representational crisis and to adequately reflect the nation's policy views in its key committees, it ultimately lacked the governing capacity to ensure that these policy views could be enacted and enforced in an authoritative, coordinated, and effective manner. Thus the dilemmas that led to the reforms of the 1970s were rooted in the historic evolution of Congress, particularly as it was shaped by the reforms of the 1910s and 1940s.[11]

THE REPRESENTATIONAL CRISIS
AND CONGRESSIONAL REFORM

The postwar representational crisis began to emerge clearly in the late 1950s. The essence of the problem was that conservatives from the noncompetitive south dominated major committee chairs in Congress while making up only a minority of the membership of Congress. This was a problem in both the House and the Senate, but particularly in the House because the committee chairs there were all-powerful. Their dominance was particularly upsetting to liberal House Democrats because, after the 1958 elections, they made up a majority of the House Democratic party—the governing party—but could do very little to turn the liberal majority into a liberal government. These liberals, committed to a new domestic social agenda—including civil rights for minorities, medical care for the aged, federal assistance to education, and an expanded social welfare system—were frustrated by the entrenched power of committee government, much as the progressives at the turn of the century had been frustrated by party government. The postwar frustration of House Democratic liberals over the unrepresentative and unresponsive nature of the existing power structure set in motion a variety of actions that led to reforms in the early 1970s—reforms that subsequently spread to the Senate.

Spreading Power in the House

The frustration of liberal House Democrats proceeded from the fact that committee government had denied them the quantity of leadership positions, and the policy control, that their numbers in the party seemed to justify. Although they held the majority of positions in the Democratic party, the southern conservatives enjoyed greater seniority and thus won the committee chairmanships. Moderate and liberal Democrats did press for the creation of subcommittees that would consider the topics that moderates and liberals saw as important, and they pressed to be chosen as subcommittee chairs. But even if the liberals had gained a subcommittee chair, the standing committee chairs still had various discretionary powers (often including control of subcommittee staffmembers) that they could have used to control the subcommittees.

This circumstance led the liberal Democrats to search for a more effective strategy to broaden the representative nature of congressional leadership and strengthen their impact on House policymaking. The strategy they adopted was to organize themselves into a united liberal subcaucus within the House Democratic party, a subcaucus that could then plan various ways to reform the House and to increase liberal influence on public policy. Thus, in 1958, liberal Democrats created the House Democratic Study Group (DSG), a liberal coterie within the House Democratic caucus devoted to lessening the power of the conservative committee chairs and to spreading that power more widely among all Democrats, particularly the liberal majority. They focused their reform efforts both on the formal rules of the House and on the informal rules, such as the norm of seniority, that dominated the Democratic party.[12]

During the 1960s the liberals in the DSG worked primarily on changing the formal House rules. Toward this end they often allied with another group of outsiders—the House Republicans. The joint efforts of these two groups produced the 1970s Legislative Reorganization Act, which reformed parliamentary procedure at both the committee and the House floor levels. The committee-level changes constrained the authority of committee chairs by making it more difficult for them to rush legislation through an unsupportive committee or to bottle up legislation within a committee that actually supported it. Changes in floor procedure limited the ability of committee chairs to push legislation through a floor vote without prior notice, debate, or amendment. As committee chairs lost the opportunity to arbitrarily control committee or floor deliberations in their jurisdictional area, they were forced to work more closely with their liberal Democratic colleagues. This situation gave the liberals increased leverage over the committee chairs both within the committee and on the floor.

As these changes in the formal rules of the House approached passage, the DSG shifted its attention to the rules and norms of the Democratic caucus. The liberals' first major success was to enact a party rule in January 1969 stating that a caucus meeting could be held each month if fifty members demanded the meeting in writing; a petition to the chair of the caucus would outline the proposed agenda for the meeting. The creation of the new party rule opened the caucus to reform-oriented Democrats and brought it to the fore as an instrument of change in the House. In March 1970, liberal Democrats used the rule to propose to the caucus that it create a committee to study reform. The caucus approved the proposal, and Representative Julia Butler Hansen (D.-Wash.) became chair of the committee, which operated through 1974.

The first result of the Hansen reforms was to spread power from committees and committee chairs to subcommittees and subcommittee chairs. By the end of the Hansen reform era, all committees composed of more than fifteen members were required to have at least four subcommittees. The power to select subcommittee chairs was placed in the Democratic membership of each standing committee. Moreover, each committee member was given the right to at least one "choice" subcommittee assignment, and subcommittees were provided fixed jurisdiction, authorization to meet and hold hearings on their own, adequate budgets, and staff selected by subcommittee chairs. These new rules of the Democratic caucus clearly encouraged the preeminence of subcommittees over committees.

The second major result of the Hansen reforms was the democratization of the process whereby committee chairs were chosen. As noted earlier, the House had followed committee seniority for sixty years in selecting its committee chairs. The Hansen reforms moved decisively to change the method of selecting these chairs by creating a new voting process that virtually guaranteed secret ballots on the voting for each committee chair election, making the enforcement of the seniority norm virtually impossible and allowing members to vote for the candidate of their choice. In January 1975, liberals used these new rules to challenge the renomination of a variety of sitting committee chairs and defeated three of them for reelection. These defeats marked the first clear-cut and premeditated violation of seniority by the party caucus since the progressive era; they also symbolized the end of the age of committee chairs.

A third consequence of the Hansen reforms was the effort made to improve the jurisdictional breakdown of the standing committees, bringing them more in line with the real issues facing the Congress. Initially proposed by a committee headed by Richard Bolling (known as the Bolling Committee), these reforms were later revised by the Hansen Committee and eventually passed in watered-down form by the full House. The reforms strengthened the ability of Congress to deal with questions of transportation, science and technology, and health policy, but they left the controversial areas of energy and environmental policy as scattered and uncoordinated as ever.

Additional efforts to make the House more representative were made in conjunction with attempts to open up congressional processes through sunshine legislation and new lobby regulations, all of which were fueled in part by the concern for openness that emerged in the midst of the Watergate scandal and Nixon's secret invasion of Cambodia. The sunshine legislation was designed to open up the operation of committee and subcommittee sessions to public purview, thus hindering the ability of a few lobby groups to dominate committee activity. Thus, in 1973, all committee sessions (with certain narrow exceptions) were required to be open to the public unless a majority of committee members voted by roll call to close a given particular meeting. The rule led to dramatic decreases in the number of closed hearings, which dropped from 44 percent in 1972 to less than 3 percent in 1975. In addition, the new campaign finance laws of 1974 and the extensive review of lobbyist regulations and congressional ethics legislation were met with attempts to reduce the role of powerful lobbyists.

Reforms in the Senate

Similar reform efforts, though less dramatic and extensive, took place in the Senate.[13] One such move came in 1970, when a rule was adopted in the Senate limiting members to service on only one of the Senate's top four committees (Appropriations, Armed Services, Finance, and Foreign Relations). Between 1973 and 1975, both Republican and Democratic caucuses in the Senate established rules altering the procedure for selecting their ranking committee members. In the case of the Democratic party (the majority party during this time), the new procedure allowed secret votes by the Democratic caucus on any chair nominee if one-fifth of the Democratic senators so requested. In 1975, the junior members decided that staff assignments were biased in favor of senior senators and called for reform. The Senate then adopted a plan allowing junior members to have additional legislative staff.

Reform efforts to spread senatorial power gathered momentum in 1976 and 1977. In 1976, a temporary committee headed by Senator Adlai Stevenson investigated the Senate committee system and suggested numerous proposals for change. The Stevenson Committee succeeded in establishing the rule that each senator could chair only one committee and only two subcommittees, thus forcing a dispersal of exiting committee and subcommittee chairs. It also realigned committee jurisdictions somewhat, making fundamental changes primarily in the area of energy policy.

In 1975, three years following a similar action by the House, the Senate moved to bring sunshine into its committee rooms. It also adopted rules requiring that most markup (bill-drafting) sessions be opened to the press and public. This set of rules, too, required open-conference committee meetings—a change that the House adopted in 1975.

Finally, the Senate reforms included efforts to address the filibuster problem.[14] For decades many analysts had argued that the cloture rule, which required an extraordinary majority of two-thirds of those present and voting to close debate, allowed a minority of one-third plus one to obstruct the Senate and hinder its responsiveness to national policy sentiments by undertaking filibusters. In 1975, liberal senators led by then-Senator Walter Mondale succeeded in overcoming a filibuster against changing the cloture rule and instituted a new and less stringent rule. Under the new rule, sixty senators are required to support a cloture vote on legislative matters in order to close debate and allow a vote on the legislation. The old cloture rule of two-thirds present and voting still applied to votes on rules changes, including future changes in the cloture rule.

The Democratization of Congress

By the mid-1970s, both the House and Senate had instituted major reforms designed to break up the power and insulation of committee chairs and spread power more widely. These reforms were presented as a democratization of Congress—that is, as an effort to make Congress more accountable to its "real" majority, less insulated from the public, and more truly representative in its internal distribution of power as well as in its electoral process. The reforms also served to bring significant policymaking power to those policy specialists at the subcommittee level who possessed the greatest technical expertise in the subject matter. This spread of power—particularly the spread of power to subcommittees—had a cost, however. Although more members gained access to positions of influence as a result of the subcommittee reforms, and although the overall ideological distribution of power positions more accurately reflected the real majority of Congress, the expansion in the number of legislators with power also rendered the leadership and coordination of Congress much more difficult. An aggressive executive could now play an increasingly dominant role in national policymaking, usurping the constitutional power of Congress. As Congress moved to disperse power, this is precisely what happened.

THE GOVERNING CRISIS
AND CONGRESSIONAL REFORM

With the dispersion of power within Congress, only the president had a truly national view; only he could respond rapidly to domestic and international crises and plan long-term policy in a coordinated manner. The spread of power positions within Congress among numerous individual members meant that there was no central figure within Congress who enjoyed allegiance from numerous factions and had the ability to act rapidly and authoritatively for Congress. Rather, each of the many committee and subcommittee chairs had a regional and committee constituency, with no strong incentive to be national in focus. And as many committees and subcommittee chairs had jurisdictional influence in overlapping policy areas, rapid agreement in response to crises was difficult to achieve. Leadership in handling such issues as civil rights, urban violence, or an international crisis was expected to come primarily from the president, the Executive Office, or the bureaucracy.

This pattern emerged in foreign and much of domestic policy and had a devastating effect on the role of Congress in national politics. By the 1970s, the presidency was again ascendant in American politics, as it had been during the administration of Franklin Roosevelt; and, again, it was undertaking political actions in excess of its constitutional role. As Arthur Schlesinger put it, "constitutional comity" between Congress and the president had broken down.[15] Vietnam, the invasion of Cambodia, and Watergate were obvious symptoms. But the most serious and direct assault on Congress came with Richard Nixon's attempts to impound appropriated funds. That crisis stimulated Congress to undertake a series of reforms designed to strengthen internal fiscal coordination, policy leadership, and executive oversight—reforms that represented a significant attempt to reassert the governing capacity of Congress.

Budget Reform

Ideally, it is the level and nature of expenditures of the national government in a particular year, and the level and type of revenue collected, that prompt the government to stimulate or restrain the economy in a rational, planned, and foresightful fashion.[16] But because Congress lacked a central budget process to coordinate authorizations, appropriations, and revenue decisions during the era of committee government, no internal mechanism existed whereby Congress or some component of it could plan for a specific mix of spending and taxing. This inability to design economic policy and to control fiscal policy led during the postwar years to a second problem—an unplanned rise in both federal spending and federal deficits. As Congress began to decentralize in the late 1950s, its problems of fiscal coordination mounted. Spending increased dramatically and deficits expanded, with the federal debt more than doubling between 1956 and 1976.

The situation was primed for confrontation between the president and Congress. So long as their ideological orientations were similar, Congress could rely on the president's budget as a guide for its decisions. And to the extent that congressional decisions went beyond the president's proposals, liberal presidents normally found it politically infeasible to challenge congressional spending. But the combination of a conservative president and a liberal Congress was another matter. Each had different priorities, with neither willing to follow the other's lead.

The conflict broke into the open with Nixon's ascent to the presidency—particularly during his second term, when he was not facing reelection and thus did not have to worry about raising campaign funds from large, established lobby groups. Nixon was at loggerheads with Congress, determined to use the existing situation as a justification for imposing his conservative policy priorities on the nation at large. His strategy was to impound funds duly appropriated by Congress to run the government. His impoundments, while unconstitutional, were considered politically defensible to taxpayers who saw Congress as a fiscally irresponsible body. To many it appeared that Nixon was on the verge of consummating a major shift in the balance of power between Congress and the presidency.

In response to these pressures and in an effort to gain control over fiscal matters, Congress moved in 1973 and 1974 to reform its budgetary procedures. The reform took two directions. On the one hand, Congress established a procedure for reviewing and controlling Executive impoundments, the first such procedure ever instituted by the nation. On the other, the Congress sought to put its own house in order by creating a more responsible procedure for making budgetary decisions. In doing so, it left the committee system intact and created a new budgetary process to overlay it. At the heart of the congressional budgetary process, Congress created two new committees: a House Budget Committee and a Senate Budget Committee. These two committees are responsible for planning congressional budgets and for guiding the Congress in serving their passage.

As an aid in planning and implementing the budget, Congress outlined a timetable to be followed each year, specifying the dates by which key budgetary decisions must be made. The Congress and the budget committees are assisted in meeting this timetable and making budget decisions by a newly created Congressional Budget Office. This office, somewhat analogous to the Office of Management and Budget in the executive branch, provides a full-time staff to the budget committees and Congress—a staff capable of undertaking sophisticated analyses of economic trends, agency spending patterns, and so forth. In order to help make the new process work, Congress changed the beginning of the federal government's fiscal year from July to October. This change was important because Congress, which goes into session in January, cannot be expected to design and enact a budget in five months. A period of nine months is a much more reasonable length of time in which to create a budget and pass supporting legislation.

The new budget-making structure provided a much more orderly process than the one it replaced. It also provided Congress a body of technical experts in budget making (i.e., elected members as well as staffers) that it previously had lacked. These budget experts possessed a real opportunity to shape a congressional budget and to have their technical expertise, rather than issues of seniority, play a role in budget and policy deliberations. But the new process also left a number of problems unsolved.

First, the new process left the existing committee structure intact and simply enacted the new budgetary process on top of that structure. From the outset, therefore, the new budget committees were in conflict with the other committees, particularly those dealing with appropriations and revenue, over the nature of jurisdictional authority. A second problem with the new process was its dichotomization between the House and Senate, inasmuch as separate committees were operating in the two houses. By separating the process in this way, the two houses generated highly dissimilar budget resolutions that were difficult to reconcile.

A third problem with the new budget process was the inherent difficulty in finding a majority in favor of any one budget. Even if there were no structural problems associated with the new process, there would be some difficulty in making it work well. Members of Congress come from vastly different constituencies and have widely differing ideologies. These differences are often quite genuine. Among other things, they may reflect the geographical origin of representation in Congress, such that every member wants to represent the interests of his or her district or state to the fullest extent possible. The ultimate success of the new budget process, and the governing capacity of Congress, may thus depend on the existence of mechanisms that can encourage compromise among legislators and assist the budget committees in building majority support for their budget resolutions. In searching for such mechanisms, the members of Congress have turned to reform of the political parties.

Party Government in Congress

Throughout most of the twentieth century, starting with the progressive movement of the early 1900s, the impetus of congressional change has been away from reliance on strong parties in Congress. Strong parties have been seen as an unnecessary threat to the power of individual legislators and to their ability to exercise personal policy judgments. In addition, strong parties have been viewed as a threat to electoral security: A party that forced a member to support a controversial issue that was unpopular at home could cost that member's reelection.

In the 1970s, the perspective on political parties began to come full circle. Members of Congress came to realize that their power ultimately depended on the power of Congress as an institution. For Congress to be powerful it needed some means for internal leadership and coordination, for interest aggregation and compromise. In their search for such mechanisms, the members of Congress turned to the issue of political party reform, with a focus on strengthening the leadership role of the Speaker of the House.

The move toward a strong speakership came in two waves. The initial effort, which accompanied the Hansen reforms of 1973, placed the Speaker, as well as the majority leader and caucus chair, on the Committee on Committees that made committee nominations. This move gave the Speaker a role in the selection of committee members and committee chairs. The 1973 reforms also created a new Steering and Policy Committee to replace the dormant Steering Committee. The role of the new committee was to help devise and direct party strategy in the House. The Speaker was made the chair of the committee. In addition, the Speaker had a dominant role in selecting the members of the committees.

The second wave in strengthening the Speaker came at the end of 1974 and in early 1975. During this period the House strengthened the Speaker by giving him considerable control over the referral of bills. The Democratic caucus also gave the Speaker the power within the party to nominate the Democratic members and the chairperson of the House Rules Committee, thus bringing the committee more clearly under the control of the Speaker and the party. In addition, the caucus took the role of Committee on Committees away from Ways and Means Democrats and placed it in the Steering and Policy Committee. This measure considerably increased the role of the party leadership in selecting committee members and committee chairs.

While these two stages of party reforms were taking place, an additional set of changes occurred that served the party leadership. First, through the 1970s, the financial and staff resources of the party whip office were increased and the number of whips appointed by the party leadership was increased.[17] The end product was a stronger, more active, and more expert whip system at the disposal of the party leadership in efforts to pass legislation. Second, as Bruce Oppenheimer has shown, the Speaker was gaining control of the Rules Committee.[18] Third, the creation of the new budgetary process provided mechanisms through which a skillful party leadership could control budgetary matters and coordinate decisionmaking by house committees. The Speaker's potential influence over the House budgetary process resulted from his appointment (in conjunction with the Senate's president pro tem) of the director of the Congressional Budget Office, the leadership's appointment of one of its lieutenants to the House Budget Committee, and the ability of the Speaker, as chair of the Steering and Policy Committee, to oversee appointments of Democrats to the Budget Committee.

Executive Oversight

The strengthening of House party leadership, together with the new budget processes, improved the governing capacity of Congress; but a key problem remained: the need for better mechanisms of control and oversight of the executive. Perhaps the most visible effort to address this issue was the War Powers Act, which established new procedures that a president had to follow when using military troops abroad—procedures that Congress hoped would give it greater control over military action. Less visible, but no less important, were the efforts to restructure the procedures that Congress used to oversee bureaucratic implementation of public policy.

Congressional oversight of the executive, along with jurisdictional reforms, was a major concern of the Bolling Committee. Following extensive hearings by the Bolling Committee and review by the Hansen Committee, the House gave the Government Operations Committee authority to prepare extensive oversight reports, authority to investigate subject areas despite the existence of similar investigations by other committees, and authority to have its oversight findings presented in the relevant reports of other committees. Aside from these proposals, the House supported efforts to strengthen the oversight function of other committees, including authorization of special oversight subcommittees and the designation of seven committees as having a "special oversight" function.

These various efforts to improve oversight through committee reforms were joined by several other efforts. In the late 1960s and 1970s, for example, Congress began to develop the use of computers on Capitol Hill as a means of information processing; it created and expanded the role of telecommunications and telecommunications facilities, a development that was expanded in the 1980s with televised coverage of House and Senate debates; and continued the expansion of congressional staff, including leadership staff. Finally, it developed new resource agencies to help in its policymaking and oversight activities, creating not only the Congressional Budget Office but also a new Office of Technology Assessment; and it expanded the resources of its traditional resource agencies, the Congressional Research Service and the General Accounting Office. These various developments vastly increased the technical means available for Congress to oversee executive action. Together with the new budget process and the renewed authority of the Speaker, the oversight reforms gave Congress a more systematic set of centralized governing mechanisms than at any time since the turn of the century.

CONCLUSION

The enactment of new central governing mechanisms brought to a close the concentrated effort to reform Congress. In their wake the reforms left a new governing structure unlike any that Congress had ever possessed before. Policymaking power, which throughout previous decades had been centered in the standing committees and committee chairs, had spread downward to subcommittees and individual members and upward to the party leaders, central budget committees, and expanded resource agencies. The one thread that seemed to run through these reforms was the growing reliance on technical expertise—from expert policy specialists at the subcommittee level to expert planning specialists at the level of budget making to coalition-building specialists in the party leadership to oversight specialists in the committees and resource agencies. In essence, the reforms put in place a new technocratic government in Congress, with power passing increasingly to technical experts, including both elected members and nonelected staffers.[19]

The decade since the passage of the reforms has witnessed continued refinements in these arrangements. Both the Senate and the House have moved to televise floor debates, thus increasing the ability of the citizenry to follow the actions of Congress and, hence, to hold it accountable for policy decisions. The House Democratic caucus decided in the mid-1980s to make the position of party whip an elective one, rather than a position appointed by the party leadership, thus increasing the control of the party membership over the direction of party affairs. And in one of its most controversial acts, the Congress passed the Gramm-Rudman-Hollings legislation, designed to redress some of the problems of the new budget process by providing explicit incentives and procedures for balancing the federal budget. Although significant parts of this legislation were declared unconstitutional, it did manage to demonstrate the continued concern of Congress with the development of mechanisms that will improve the capacity to control budget making. In relying on automatic budget cuts made by outside bureaucrats, the act also reflected the continued efforts being made to find technocratic solutions to the policymaking problems of Congress.

At this point it is difficult to assess the full impact of the new congressional reforms. They do seem to have addressed the major structural problems of the twentieth-century Congress. The institution itself appears more open and accessible now than twenty years ago, as a result of the spread of power to subcommittees, the constraints on the filibuster, the renewed ability of partisan majorities to select key leaders irrespective of seniority, and the greater openness of congressional hearings. Congress likewise appears to have more effective governing mechanisms and better procedures for controlling the executive, as witnessed in the new budget processes, the strengthened speakership, the new oversight procedures, and the War Powers Act. This new Congress—which is more representative and yet possessed of stronger governing procedures—can, indeed, boast of certain accomplishments, including the energy policies of the late 1970s, the tax reductions and reforms of the early and mid-1980s, and a decade free from extensive military involvements.

Despite this record, however, there appear to be real limits to the effectiveness of the new reforms. The public continues to express widespread support for a balanced national budget; economists are voicing grave concern over the effects of large budget deficits; Congress has a budget process designed to help it control spending; and yet the period since the enactment of the new budget process has witnessed the greatest increase in deficit spending in the nation's history. Likewise, despite widespread opposition to U.S. involvement in Central America, the Reagan administration was able to provide extensive covert support for the Nicaraguan contras. Obviously, serious problems still exist in the ability of Congress to make decisions that are responsive to the public and authoritative in their policy impact.

These problems may be exacerbated over the long term by two additional issues. First, to the extent that the new congressional structure is technocratic in nature (i.e., to the extent that it relies on technical expertise in policymaking), it ultimately undermines the representativeness of Congress, inasmuch as policy problems and policy solutions are determined not by attention to public opinion but by the opinion of policy experts. In essence, such a Congress would be a body of elected bureaucrats and would lose its distinctive role and legitimacy as representative of the policy concerns of the citizenry. Second, to the extent that policy expertise has become the new source of personal power and legitimacy in Congress, careerist legislators have a new justification for dispersing policymaking power and constraining the authority of central governing mechanisms. The norm of policy expertise, in other words, may simply replace the old norm of seniority, in which case yet another move to a highly dispersed and uncoordinated system of policymaking becomes rationalized, such that central policy planning and leadership can be overruled by the united opposition of specialized policy experts. In short, central policy guidance would become virtually impossible in Congress.

The new structure of Congress, then, may ultimately be prone to the same sorts of problems that beset Congress at the beginning of the twentieth century. So long as careerist legislators proliferate in Congress, and so long as there are no external incentives that facilitate cooperation among careerist legislators (such as the patronage rewards of the nineteenth century or the existence of great crises that require collective action), careerist legislators can find persuasive rationales with which to fragment policymaking power in ways that serve their personal career interests, albeit at the long-term cost of effective congressional governance.

In sum, although the reforms of the early 1970s were impressive in their recognition of the need for an effective balance between representation and governance, they did nothing to address the central problem of the twentieth-century Congress—the rise of a careerist legislature. The key problem, of course, is not the existence of careerist legislators. As informed experts whose understanding of societal problems is often crucial to effective policymaking and to effective control of the executive, such individuals are capable of providing a great boost to Congress. The key problem is how to facilitate cooperation and institutional support among careerist legislators, all of whom are necessarily concerned with their own survival and career advancement as well as with their particular policy specialties.

Such cooperation requires the existence of an incentive structure that enables career legislators to see common interests and to work together collectively. In the late nineteenth century, patronage politics provided such an arrangement; but this system was ultimately discarded because it undermined the responsiveness and legitimacy of Congress. Executive usurpation of congressional power has, at least in periods of extreme crises, provided twentieth-century legislators an incentive to unite and protect the institution.

The dilemma faced by the new Congress is that its very success in addressing and defusing the policy crises and executive interventions of the 1960s and 1970s removed the primary incentive that encouraged careerist members to work together and support the new governing procedures—that incentive being the desire to protect their own power by protecting the power of Congress. The central governing mechanisms in Congress—the budget process and the strengthened speakership—probably survived as well as they have because of the divided government that has existed during the Reagan years, all of which have seen a Democratic House facing a Republican president. This situation has provided a continuation of the sort of adversarial tension that seems necessary for the modern Congress, particularly the House, to sustain its central governing mechanisms. But should the country enter a period of united government (particularly one of close ideological congruence and cooperation between Congress and the president), the lessening of the adversarial tension could release the fragmenting tendencies contained in a careerist Congress and wreak havoc with the new congressional system.

The survival of Congress as an effective governing institution rests on the development of a long-term incentive structure that facilitates support for central governing mechanisms within Congress while simultaneously ensuring that Congress will be an open and responsive institution. Ultimately, the creation of such a structure may be impossible for a careerist Congress to undertake, as, by their very nature, careerist legislators tend to evaluate all reforms from the standpoint of the impact of reforms on their careers. Hence we may yet have to consider constitutional provisions that impose central governing mechanisms on Congress. Should the new congressional system falter badly, the primary way to save Congress may be found through constitutional reforms, including efforts to reassert the war-making power of Congress, to require some sort of balanced budget, and to strengthen the power of congressional leaders. In short, the most effective way to reform Congress may yet be through constitutional change.[20]

NOTES

1. James L. Sundquist, *The Decline and Resurgence of Congress* (Washington, D.C.: Brookings Institution, 1981).
2. Bob Eckardt and Charles L. Black, Jr., *The Tides of Power: Conversations on the American Constitution* (New Haven, Conn.: Yale University Press, 1976).
3. Edward G. Carmines and Lawrence C. Dodd, "Bicameralism in Congress: The Changing Partnership," in Lawrence C. Dodd and Bruce I. Oppenheimer, eds., *Congress Reconsidered*, 3rd ed. (Washington, D.C.: Congressional Quarterly Press, 1985), pp. 414–436.
4. On the decline in turnover, see H. Douglas Price, "Congress and the Evolution of Legislative 'Professionalism,'" and Morris P. Fiorina, David W. Rohde, and Peter Wissel, "Historical Change in House Turnover," both in Norman J. Ornstein, ed., *Congress in Change* (New York: Praeger Publishers, 1975); see also Nelson Polsby, "The Institutionalization of the House of Representatives," *American Political Science Review* (*APSR*), vol. 62 (1968), pp. 144–169.
5. Woodrow Wilson, *Congressional Government* (Gloucester, Mass.: Peter Smith, 1885, 1973).
6. Lawrence C. Dodd, "Congress and the Quest for Power," in Dodd and Oppenheimer, eds., *Congress Reconsidered*, 1st ed.; and Lawrence C. Dodd, "Congress, the Constitution, and the Crisis of Legitimation," in *Congress Reconsidered*, 2nd ed.
7. See Joseph Cooper and David W. Brady. "Organization Theory and Congressional Structure," paper delivered at the annual meeting of the American Political Science Association, New Orleans, Louisiana (September 4–8, 1973); see also Samuel Huntington, "Congressional Responses to the Twentieth Century," in David B. Truman, ed., *The Congress and America's Future* (Englewood Cliffs, N.J.: Prentice-Hall, 1965).
8. See Kenneth W. Hechler, *Insurgency: Personalities and Politics in the Taft Era* (New York: Columbia University Press, 1940); and John D. Baker, "The Character of the Congressional Revolution of 1910," *Journal of American History*, vol. 60 (1973), pp. 679–691.
9. George R. Brown, *The Leadership of Congress* (Indianapolis: Bobbs-Merrill, 1922).
10. George B. Galloway, "The Operation of the Legislative Reorganization Act of 1946," *APSR*, vol. 45 (March 1951), pp. 41–68; Charles W. Shull, "The Legislative Reorganization Act of 1964," *Temple Law Review* (January 1947), pp. 375–395.
11. My discussion of the congressional reforms relies particularly on Chapters 5 and 6 of Lawrence C. Dodd and Richard L. Schott, *Congress and the Administrative State* (New York: John Wiley and Sons, 1979). See also Roger H. Davidson and Walter J. Oleszek, *Congress Against Itself* (Bloomington: Indiana University Press, 1977); Lawrence C. Dodd and Bruce I. Oppenheimer, "The House in Transition: Partisanship and Opposition," in Dodd and Oppenheimer, eds., *Congress Reconsidered*, 3rd ed.; Leroy N. Rieselbach, *Congressional Reform* (Washington, D.C.:

Congressional Quarterly, Inc., 1986); and James L. Sundquist, *The Decline and Resurgence of Congress*, (Washington, D.C.: Brookings Institution, 1981).

12. On the DSG, see Mark F. Ferber, "The Formation of the Democratic Study Group," in Nelson W. Polsby, ed., *Congressional Behavior* (New York: Random House, 1971).

13. Norman J. Ornstein, Robert L. Peabody, and David W. Rohde, "The Changing Senate: From the 1950s to the 1970s," in Dodd and Oppenheimer, eds., *Congress Reconsidered*, 1st ed.

14. Bruce I. Oppenheimer, "Changing Time Constraints on Congress: Historical Perspectives on the Use of Cloture," in Dodd and Oppenheimer, eds., *Congress Reconsidered*, 3rd ed.

15. Arthur M. Schlesinger, Jr., *The Imperial Presidency* (New York: Popular Library, 1973), p. 298.

16. On fiscal policy and budget reform, see, in particular, John W. Ellwood and James A. Thurber, "The New Congressional Budget Process: The Hows and Whys of House-Senate Differences," in Dodd and Oppenheimer, eds., *Congress Reconsidered*, 1st ed.; Louis Fisher, *Presidential Spending Power* (Princeton, N.J.: Princeton University Press, 1975), pp. 148–176; Allen Schick, *Congress and Money* (Washington, D.C.: Urban Institute Press, 1980); and John W. Ellwood, "The Great Exception: The Congressional Budget Process in an Age of Decentralization," in *Congress Reconsidered*, 3rd ed.

17. Lawrence C. Dodd, "The Expanded Roles of the House Democratic Whip System," *Congressional Studies*, vol. 6 (1979).

18. Bruce I. Oppenheimer, "The Rules Committee: New Arm of Leadership in a Decentralized House," in Dodd and Oppenheimer, eds., *Congress Reconsidered*, 1st ed.

19. Lawrence C. Dodd, "A Theory of Congressional Change," in Gerald C. Wright, Jr., Leroy N. Rieselbach, and Lawrence C. Dodd, eds., *Congress and Policy Change* (New York: Agathon, 1986).

20. Lloyd Cutler, "To Form a Government—On the Defects of Separation of Powers," *Foreign Affairs* (Fall 1980).

5

Congress, Codetermination, and Arms Control

EDWARD WEISBAND

IN SEARCH OF A CODETERMINATIVE CONGRESS

Rarely in American history has such a strong impulse toward revision of policymaking institutions reverberated through Washington as that which developed in the immediate aftermath of the U.S. military debacle in Southeast Asia and the Watergate scandal. The focus of concern during this period of reform was the general lack of accountability with which the executive branch had been able to make policy and implement it. America's unceremonious departure from Vietnam and the revelations that emerged from Watergate seemed to confirm the criticisms of the 1960s that national policymaking, to an alarming degree, had become detached from the people and concentrated in the White House. For those who deplored this situation, a natural avenue of redress lay in a reassertion of Congress's constitutional role. Not only was the legislature the logical institution through which citizens could hold government accountable, but under the Constitution it also shared the prerogative of policymaking with the executive. Indeed, the founders envisioned a spirited competition between the two branches in making public policy. As we have seen in the preceding chapter, major reforms altered the way Congress operated procedurally and, perhaps more important, remade the institutional arrangements through which the legislature and the executive interact.

This chapter examines the impact of these reforms on foreign policy-making—particularly on arms-control policy. Using reformist procedures and statutes as its main weapons, Congress in the 1970s sought a reinvigorated relationship with the president in foreign policy—a relationship guaranteeing its constitutionally derived powers, even in areas where the presidency in recent history has tended to reign supreme. Thus, in the 1970s, Congress forcefully asserted a "codeterminative" role in diplomacy, national security, and iternational economics. To this day, codetermination of foreign policy reflects both American political expectations and legislative practice.[1]

The same sense of mistrust and disillusionment with the presidency that brought Congress into a more activist posture regarding foreign policy overall also propelled it into a codeterminative role in arms control. Legislative intervention in arms control is especially significant inasmuch as presidents have demanded a free hand in this field perhaps more than any other, contending, with some justification, that such negotiations require the secrecy, delicacy, and bipartisan support that a heavy legislative hand might preclude. Congress, nevertheless, has intervened continually during both the Carter and Reagan administrations to modify and influence executive arms-control policies.

While codetermination was a signal feature of American foreign policymaking in the mid-1970s, an examination of the legislature's role in arms-control policy during the Reagan years provides an important illustration of the long-term impacts of the reforms in congressional institutions and processes. No policy realm is more sensitive, complex, or central to American national interest; in short, it is difficult to imagine a field of policymaking more ideally suited to clear-cut executive domination. Yet, the very ease with which Congress has insinuated itself into the arms-control process during the 1980s reflects the extent to which the reforms of the 1970s have taken hold, establishing codetermination as a continuing feature of foreign policymaking.

Codetermination has tended to assume one of two forms: *policy innovation* or *policy evaluation*. In the former case, Congress initiates proposals; in the latter, Congress scrutinizes policies previously articulated by the executive branch. The reform movement of the 1970s strengthened congressional capacities to perform both policy innovation and evaluation—but in different ways. The internal or procedural reforms of legislative operations (see Chapter 4 of this volume) allowed Congress to become more innovative in highly technical and complex policy areas such as arms control. Reforms of the external, or liaison, processes involving the executive, on the other hand, enabled Congress to evaluate presidential arms-control policies more effectively, thus fostering greater executive accountability. Dual-branch codetermination has resulted from this vibrant transformation in policymaking, as illustrated quite clearly by examples of both congressional innovation and evaluation in arms-control policy.

Codetermination, however, should not be misconstrued as "congressional arms control" or overly obtrusive "micro-management," to use the current jargon. Defense policy by Congress is not about to happen, nor should it. The precept of president as commander-in-chief is etched too clearly in the Constitution and entrenched too deeply in our political traditions to be erased in favor of a congressional defense policy. But this is a fraudulent issue, a canard raised by those who see in renewed congressional activism a threat to the constitutionally ordained roles set down for legislators and presidents. Codetermination, on the contrary, signifies a renewed emphasis both on the constitutional separation of powers as a general doctrine and on Congress's specific responsibilities in the field of foreign policy. Congress rightfully ought to play a role in arms-control policy, albeit one consistent with its basic institutional and constitutional functions.

The executive and Congress, then, jointly determine arms-control policy, but *how* they do so must differ in keeping with their respective constitutional mandates. Herein lies the significance of codetermination as a body of reform aimed at revitalizing American politics. As Arthur Maass writes:

> The Legislature plays a role in both policy and administration, in both the legislative process and in the administrative process. The same is true of the Executive. . . . There is no basis for distinguishing the President from Congress if one considers the processes of government in which they participate, but a solid basis for distinction can be found in the roles that they play in these processes. *The Executive's role is leadership—to initiate and impel; the Congress', control—to oversee and to improve, reject, or amend* (emphasis added).[2]

This capacity to "oversee and to improve, reject, or amend" outlines the basis of codetermination as it relates to a policy-evaluation role in arms control.

However, an activist Congress, fully cognizant of its codeterminative responsibilities, will undertake to do more than merely respond to presidential initiatives. To cite Maass again, "For subjects that the President elects not to initiate, for subjects that are not on the President's program, Congress can and sometimes does take the lead. On these occasions there is a leadership reserve in the Congress, and it is one of the main strengths of the American system of government, one that is not to be found in any other major parliamentary government in the world."[3] The development of this "leadership reserve" is crucial to the assertion of congressional codetermination and relates directly, as we shall see, to the reforms that facilitated a policy-innovation role for Congress in arms control.

Ultimately, codetermination is about leadership as well as accountability in foreign policymaking. Advocates of codeterminative reform have sought to "remake American politics" by creating new institutions and processes that combine presidential prerogative with the full force of legislative authority. Codetermination, of course, has its passionate detractors as well—critics who see it not as a set of salutary measures but, rather, as an unwarranted intrusion upon executive authority and a dangerous step toward political fragmentation. Both proponents and opponents agree, however, that foreign policymaking has changed considerably since the beginning of the 1970s. Moreover, the area of arms control well illustrates both the benefits and the possible costs of codetermination.

CODETERMINATION IN PERSPECTIVE

Traditionally, interpretations of congressional forays into foreign affairs and defense policy have held that the influence of the legislative branch has waxed and waned, creating a pattern of historical oscillations sometimes in favor of the president, sometimes in favor of Congress. Codetermination, however, should not be likened to the swing of a great political pendulum. On the contrary, codetermination actually restricted the arc through which all future swings between presidential and congressional influence may move. Codeterminative reform constrained the swings between presidential and congressional influence in two ways: first, by statutorily mandating congressional involvement in foreign policy decisions on a continuing basis; and, second, by helping to create a new climate of expectations grounded in the belief that Congress is intrinsically part of the foreign and defense policymaking. In this sense, codetermination was an effort to reaffirm the system of separated powers, but shared responsibility, set forth in the Constitution.

The codeterminative reforms of the 1970s, however, implied more than merely a return to pristine constitutional theory. They went much further, recasting the relationship between Congress and the executive to ensure a greater *variety of policy perspectives* as well as a *greater degree of accountability* in foreign policymaking. This latter objective was especially important with respect to highly complex and technical issues that the founding generation could not have foreseen and that, in the later twentieth century, have served to enhance the executive at the expense of Congress; arms control is one such contemporary issue. Thus, in the 1970s, the legislature engaged in a historically unprecedented effort not only to secure its rightful constitutional role in the realm of foreign affairs and institutionalize that role through statute and procedural reform but also to develop its own resources and expertise in order to operate as a coequal of the modern presidency, thereby ensuring alternative perspectives and accountability in foreign policymaking.

In this context, the Iran-contra hearings conducted by a joint Senate-House committee in the summer of 1987, and televised worldwide, testified to Congress's ongoing commitment to ensure that alternative views are introduced into U.S. foreign policy decisionmaking and that the executive branch conforms to basic constitutional principles of presidential accountability.

In the 1970s, Congress made these commitments through codeterminative reform. First, institutional reforms restructured internal legislative procedures in ways that permitted Congress to participate more extensively than ever before in policy innovation. Congressional capacity for policy innovation was perceived as crucial to the quest for a variety of perspectives in U.S. foreign and defense policies, and it was a consistent goal of codeterminative reform that such a variety of policy perspectives be sustained.

If internal reforms promoted codetermination by enhancing Congress's policy-innovation capacity, reforms focusing on external relations and congressional-executive liaison enhanced Congress's ability to evaluate foreign policy.[4] Concern over the rise of a so-called imperial presidency in the late 1960s and early 1970s underlay those aspects of codetermination aimed at a more vigorous and robust evaluation role for the legislature in foreign policy. The precise historical context of these concerns was, of course, the escalation of the war in Vietnam and the post-Watergate revelations of CIA and FBI activity. Both of these phenomena indicated that policymaking, especially in the field of foreign policy, was becoming severed from its political base and dangerously devoid of congressional input. Many feared that legislative oversight and evaluation of executive policy were on the verge of becoming moribund. To reformers in the 1970s, then, codetermination also meant invigorating congressional abilities to evaluate foreign policy more effectively and earlier in the decisionmaking process. The inextricable linkage between congressional oversight and evaluation on the one hand and executive accountability on the other became all too clear in the 1970s; moreover, it helped to generate codeterminative reform.

Indeed, the Iran-contra affair of the late 1980s would not have taken on the proportions of a major assault on the Constitution as well as an affront to Congress and the public were it not for the codeterminative reforms put in place during the 1970s. At the center of the crisis over the sale of arms to Iran and the diversion of profits from those sales to the contra resistance in Nicaragua was the calculated effort by high-ranking members of the executive branch to circumvent the codeterminative reforms of the 1970s, especially those pertaining to liaison between the two branches. And as the scandal unfolded, the connection between congressional policy evaluation and executive accountability was highlighted. To the extent that the Reagan administration attempted to avoid the critical assessment of Congress in making and implementing foreign policy, it violated the system of codetermination and, for many legislators, raised the specter of a return to the bad old days of the Vietnam era.

The political crisis provoked by the Iran-contra excesses seemed to confirm the basic premise of codetermination—namely, that the introduction of a variety of viewpoints and greater accountability by making Congress an integral part of foreign policymaking can minimize the possibility of major international blunders. Attempts to deny Congress a role in policy innovation and to sharply circumscribe its evaluation activities jeopardize not only the understandings worked out through codeterminative reform in the 1970s but also, in the view of many, the very structure of federal policymaking established by the Constitution. Codetermination requires that legislators play a role before, during, and after policies are executed by the president.

Before examining the codeterminative reforms themselves, we will find it useful to explore briefly the nature of Congress as an institution. This background is necessary if we are to appreciate the character of the reforms and the extent of change they introduced into the process of making foreign policy in general and arms-control policy in particular. A convenient approach to understanding the Congress as an institution is to ask what functions the legislature performs and how it performs them. This is the task we turn to now.

THE FUNCTIONS OF CONGRESS

What Congress does and how it can best perform its role are questions that have preoccupied many officials of the federal government in their efforts to disentangle what the Constitution so effectively intertwined. Similarly, students of Congress have rarely been able to agree upon the precise standing of the legislature in the politics of policymaking. In a well-known examination of conflicting views on the Congress, Roger H. Davidson, David Kovenok, and Michael K. O'Leary have summarized this analytical debate by defining six traditional functions performed by the legislature.[5]

These functions, arranged in descending order from the most inherently political to those most purely technical in nature, provide a convenient framework for discussing the codeterminative reforms of the 1970s.[6] In their ideal form, political functions deal with broad questions of leadership and governance, whereas technical functions deal with questions of implementation and accountability. Put in terms of our discussion of codetermination, the more political the function, the more closely associated it is with Congress's role as policy innovator; and the more

FIGURE 5.1
Functions of Congress from Political to Policy Oriented (in Descending Order)

- Representation, Interest Articulation, or Education

- Consensus Building, Interest Aggregation, or Pluralist Bargaining

- Policy Clarification or Legislative Debates

- Legitimation or Policy Validation

- Oversight or Policy Investigation

- Lawmaking or Legislative Framing

Source: Adapted from Roger H. Davidson, David M. Kovenok, and Michael K. O'Leary,
Congress in Crisis: Politics and Congressional Reform (Belmont, Calif.: Wadsworth Publishing
Co., 1966), p. 35.

technical the function, the more closely associated it is with Congress's role as policy evaluator.

Representation, interest articulation, or education, in the words of Davidson, Kovenok, and O'Leary, "is the process of articulating the demands or interests of geographic, economic, religious, ethnic, and professional constituencies."[7] A diverse nation requires an institution through which it can express its diversity. Accordingly, one important function of Congress is to represent the broad range of particularistic interests, perspectives, and philosophies that emerge within American politics. Congress translates these various demands into a national policy whole. Representation often involves activities designed to sway, influence, or educate the public by means of distributing information on constituency concerns or convictions—hence the constitutionally protected role of lobbying in American politics. Representation, then, is about policy, but from a thoroughly contentious, self-interested, and political standpoint.

Consensus building, interest aggregation, or pluralist bargaining points to the pluralist tradition in American democracy by assigning to Congress the essential function of organizing the distribution of social benefits and costs.[8] Along with representation, it is a function that is most essentially political in character. Consensus building may involve attempts to achieve distribution or redistribution through a myriad of bargains, but its overall purpose is to aggregate political interests in such a way as to ensure that no coalition or political alliance so distorts the distributive bargains that national unity becomes chronically weakened, and to guarantee that a great many interests share in the gains at least some of the time.

In contrast to the representation function, the consensus-building function is about seeking political accommodation and, as such, reflects the other face of pluralist bargaining. Whereas representation veers in the direction of political conflict, consensus building works toward the resolution of conflict and the promotion of national harmony.

Policy clarification (i.e., legislative debate) is the public, political side of policy deliberation.[9] Chaotic and discursive though they often appear, debates are more effective in focusing the thoughts of legislators than most other activities on their agendas. The great irony and the great strength of democratic debates over public policy is that their confused form often produces clarity of content. Such debates, whether political or technical, drive the process through which representative government creates a collective will.

Legitimation (i.e., policy validation) involves "the ratification of a measure or policy in such a way that it seems appropriate, acceptable, and authoritative."[10] Legitimation, in other words, is the imprimatur that Congress bestows upon presidential action. It is easy, in outlining patterns of congressional-executive relations, to overemphasize a distinction in roles and an adversarial relationship—but it is unwise. The president must execute the laws, and Congress must allow him to do so. The presidential voice, however strong or persuasive, often requires the chorus of Congress to validate its policy pronouncements. Hence there are times when it becomes necessary for the administration of any president to receive confirmation of its policies—confirmation that only Congress can bestow. The logic of legitimation as a function of Congress is that legislative politics plays a part in executive policymaking, specifically by combining the technical with the political.

Oversight (i.e., policy investigation) requires congressional review and evaluation of government agencies, policies, and programs to ensure high standards of performance.[11] It is through a variety of means—including authorization, appropriation, committee hearings, investigations, and select committees—that Congress performs its oversight function. It receives assistance in this endeavor from a variety of administrative agencies under its putative control: the General Accounting Office, the Congressional Budget Office, the Congressional Research Service, and the Office of Technology Assessment.

Just as representation and consensus building are opposite sides of the coin (one fostering policy conflict and the other resolving it), oversight may be viewed as the conflictual counterpoint to legitimation. It is central to congressional-executive relations, but it often sets the branches against one another as each musters its resources and energies to assert branch prerogatives in the policy process. Oversight tends to involve Congress directly in technical and specialized details of policy, concerns ordinarily regarded by the executive branch as falling within its purview.

The final function identified by Davidson, Kovenok, and O'Leary is that of lawmaking, "the traditional task of deliberating, often at a technical level, the actual content of policies."[12] The framing of laws, whether it involves the search for proper governmental mechanisms or proper statutory language, is the ultimate purpose of legislative activity. The essential business of Congress is to make laws that give statutory expression to the public will as worked out through representation and consensus building. Despite the connection with these loftier political functions, lawmaking remains, along with oversight, a highly technical and specific undertaking. As we shall see, a major impact of codeterminative reform was to make these technical functions, especially oversight, more political.

CODETERMINATIVE REFORM IN CONGRESS

What any major political institution such as Congress contributes to society appears constant over time, but how that contribution is made must, on occasion, give way to reform. More specifically, satisfactory performance of the *functions* for which Congress was created will require changes in the *procedures* by which it operates and relates to other policymaking institutions. Inadequate performance may result from new economic and social demands, political events, or new cultural attitudes. Congressional reform, then, refers to an explicit attempt to bolster the legislature's capacity to perform its functions in the light of challenging developments in the polity. Codeterminative reform, for example, was a response to the challenge of the Vietnam debacle and the climate of change during the late 1960s and early 1970s. But what were the codeterminative reforms, and how did they rejuvenate Congress in the performance of its functions relating to foreign policy?

A difficulty in addressing these questions is finding agreement on what exactly are the congressional functions relating to foreign policy. A number of leading contributors to the literature on Congress have wrestled with this problem. Walter J. Oleszek, for example, writes that "a key problem in defining reform is contemporary uncertainty with respect to Congress' role in the polity. Without a clear notion of Congress' place in the larger political system, it is difficult to know whether the legislative branch is functioning as it should."[13] He also contends that perhaps the most we can say about the congressional reform efforts of the 1970s is that they share a common aim: "to restore Congress as a co-equal partner in the federal system."[14] His conclusion, however, tells

TABLE 5.1
Reforms in the Nixon-Era

Type of Reform
Electoral
Regulating campaign finance
Procedural
Increasing subcommittee autonomy, changing committee jurisdiction, introducing multiple referral of bills
Political
Increasing the Speaker's power, changing committee appointments and seniority system
Analytical
Creating support agencies (OTA, CBO, CRS); increasing committee and personal staffs[1]
Jurisdictional
Checking presidential war powers, developing budget process
Ethical
Disclosing and limiting outside income

[1]OTA=Office of Technology Assessment; CBO=Congressional Budget Office; CRS=Congressional Research Office.

Source: Adapted from Charles O. Jones, "Congress and the Presidency," in Thomas E. Mann and Norman J. Ornstein, *The New Congress* (Washington, D.C.: American Enterprise Institute for PublicPolicy Research, 1981), p. 235.

us very little about what role Congress should play or what would constitute adequate performance. In a similar vein, Leroy N. Rieselbach laments that "promoters of legislative change do not always articulate their visions."[15] As a consequence, he notes, "Legislative reform, however current and fashionable, remains in a muddled condition."[16]

Charles O. Jones, though, has developed a taxonomy of reform that promises to lend at least some order to our inquiry.[17] The classification scheme proposed by Jones will enable us to see how codeterminative reforms relate to Congress's performance of the six basic functions we have enumerated. (Consult Chapter 4 in this volume for a discussion of some of the specific reforms.)

Jones identifies six kinds of reforms that have transformed the capacity of Congress to participate in policymaking (see Table 5.1). Although he expresses strong reservations about the prudence of legislators who assume "the pretentious role of initiating comprehensive policies," he concedes that "many members of Congress believe that the reforms of the past decade have increased their competence . . . to *expand their involvement in program development and evaluation,* foreign and domestic," and to act accordingly (emphasis added).[18]

These reforms have allowed Congress to codetermine arms-control policy, not by means of "comprehensive policy initiation" but through *periodic policy innovation* and *systematic policy evaluation*.[19] Codeterminative reforms have altered, first, the internal system of Congress through which policy innovation is generated. They have also changed the external relations between Congress and the executive in ways that foster more vigorous and detailed policy evaluation. Relating these reforms to the six legislative functions, we can begin by noting that certain reforms were more likely to alter those functions that are most exclusively political, while others tended to affect the more technical ones. Specifically, the electoral, ethical, procedural, and political reforms predominantly affected the broad political functions of representation and consensus building, thus enhancing Congress's policy-innovation role. The analytical and jurisdictional reforms, meanwhile, had the greatest impact on the more technical functions of oversight, thereby enhancing Congress's policy-evaluation role. Policy clarification and legitimation, inasmuch as they had both political and technical aspects, do not fall neatly into one group or the other. Finally, lawmaking was affected almost exclusively by jurisdictional and analytical reform.

Taken together, the codeterminative reforms of the 1970s injected into the internal legislative process greater degrees of political autonomy at lower levels of organization—that is, at the committee and subcommittee levels.[20] They also introduced into congressional-executive interactions a heightened capacity on the part of the legislature and its administrative subunits to handle complex information and hence, to better evaluate executive decisions on an independent basis. In particular, Congress is now in a much stronger position to use the budgetary process as a vehicle for questioning administration policy; arms control, as we shall see, offers a nice illustration of how legislators can use the budgetary process to gain access to policymaking when the president would prefer they did not. Codeterminative reforms, then, have strengthened not only the internal processes on which Congress's innovation role is based but also the external relations on which its evaluation role is based. It is thus not surprising that for all the complaints about codetermination, both inside and outside of Congress, no one is seriously proposing a return to the pre-reform era.

THE IMPACT OF REFORM:
BENEFITS AND COSTS

The codeterminative reforms of the 1970s went beyond the normal bounds of system change that sometimes naturally occurs as governments adjust to new circumstances or altered environments. In particular, they remade American politics by strengthening the capacity of Congress to handle complex issues of public policy and by increasing the autonomy of congressional members and subcommittees. Autonomy and complexity thus represent the two fundamental measures of reform impact; yet they also offer the prospect of costs as well as benefits.

By beefing up Congress's policy innovation and evaluation capabilities, the reforms offer the benefits of greater representativeness and executive accountability in foreign as well as domestic policy. But promoting the autonomy of the legislative subunits, taken to the extreme, may culminate in institutional paralysis, and increasing the complexity of data may produce information overloads. Paralysis and overload are the dangers that have grown out of codeterminative reform—dangers made all the more threatening since the relations between Congress and the executive branch have become so tightly interwoven. Although we must not underestimate the significance of better representativeness in policy-making or improvements in Congress's policy innovation role, it is in the realm of policy evaluation that the greatest benefits as well as the greatest costs are to be found.

Codeterminative reforms have permitted Congress to evaluate executive policies sooner, more expeditiously, and more thoroughly than was previously the case. Major revisions in oversight and budgetary procedures, combined with additional staff and administrative resources, now enable Congress to sift through the reams of information that accumulate in any particular policy area. In policy evaluation, complexity is the name of the game; and this is especially true of arms-control policy. In the absence of the institutional capacity to handle complex information and to bring it to bear quickly upon executive actions, Congress cannot responsibly fulfill its critical functional obligations of legitimation and oversight. The analytical and jurisdictional reforms implemented during the 1970s have sharpened the budgetary knives and appropriations scalpels of Congress. Regardless of whether it chooses to use them, they have added new teeth to congressional oversight capabilities at all levels of organization. As a result, Congress can perform its legitimation and oversight functions with greater analytical acuity than perhaps ever before.

Traditionally, oversight has involved a search for corruption, malfeasance, or incompetence, and was aimed at the middle-echelon bureaucracy. Codeterminative reform, however, has spawned a more radical version of congressional oversight. Legislative review of executive policymaking now entails careful oversight of senior administrators, involvement of the Congress in policy formulation, and a clear congressional role in policy implementation. The new oversight, then, is oriented toward *present and future* as well as *past* policymaking. Herein lies its true importance: By projecting Congress into all phases of policymaking, the new oversight enhances not only the performance of Congress's legitimation and evaluation functions but also the performance of its more political functions, by affording legislators the means and opportunity for policy innovation.

The new oversight, therefore, is an important feature in the remaking of American politics. It has changed the institutional relationship between the two policymaking branches of government. Legislators intent on improving representativeness and presidential accountability have been encouraged to employ the new means of "anticipatory oversight" available to them. The practice of codetermination, however, has raised some concerns about its overall impact on policymaking—concerns that are difficult to overlook.

First, anticipatory oversight has depended on technical proficiency in specific policy areas, such as arms control, and codeterminative reform has created the institutional mechanisms and rewards for legislators to become less a set of political generalists than a cluster of policy specialists. They have learned how to engage on a regular basis those officials most directly involved in executive decisionmaking. In turn, though, the executive branch officials have found themselves more and more a party to the give and take of congressional politics. The institutional membranes separating administration from legislation have thus become more permeable than ever.

Codetermination therefore constitutes an important element in the overall trend toward a *politicization of administration* in American politics. Congress now can and frequently does intervene in the formulation as well as the implementation of policy. As the distinctions between politics and administration are further eroded by the new oversight, the distinctions between the political and technical functions of Congress are likewise blurred. This is an inevitable by-product of codetermination.

Second, codetermination has led to legislative specialization. On the one hand, this means that Congress's ability to handle detail and complexity allows it to respond more effectively in the face of the executive's vast organizational resources. On the other hand, accelerating specialization dictates accelerating division of labor among legislative subcommittees: No fewer than 150 subcommittees were established in the 1970s, each chaired by a legislator normally intent on using subcommittee resources to further a specific set of interests.[21]

Two consequences flowed from this devolution of authority. Congress ran the risk of tripping over itself as the enhanced autonomy of institutional subunits caused it to veer toward fragmentation and paralysis. At the same time, executive officials found themselves responding to an increasing number of subcommittees and congressional agencies as they

FIGURE 5.2
The Relationship Between Codeterminative Reforms and Congressional Functions

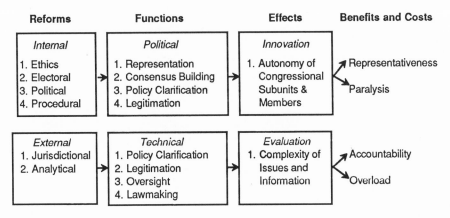

sought to participate in policymaking on behalf of their constituencies. In addition, the devolution of authority meant that the relations between Congress and the executive would increasingly be characterized by routinized contact at lower levels. Ironically, Congress must thus deal with even more information in even more detail, thereby, generating an institutional "need" for still greater complexity. In turn, this complexity presses Congress to specialize still further, and even more devolution of authority is generated as a result.

Figure 5.2 summarizes the relationships among codeterminative reforms, congressional functions, the impacts of reform, and the costs and benefits involved.

By all accounts, codeterminative reforms have inflated the workload pumped through the legislative system, as reflected in the number of days Congress remains in session, the number of bills introduced, the numbers of laws enacted, the number of committee and subcommittee meetings conducted, the number of recorded votes held, the volume of mail processed, and so on. The cycle of expanded autonomy and accelerating complexity thus often moves with what appears to be a self-perpetuating momentum.

The dividing line between those reforms that have affected the internal operations of Congress and those that have homed in on external or liaison relations among the branches must be assayed against this light. Congress increased its capacity to handle specialized materials of increasing complexity in order to respond more effectively to vastly improved organizational resources in the executive branch. Accelerating specialization, however, often indicates accelerating forms of division of labor in the sense of an increasing diffusion of subunit tasks or individual responsibilities. Such was true in the case of codeterminative reform. To meet the requirements of specialization and informational complexity, Congress spawned a series of reforms that divided legislative responsibilities into smaller and smaller committee units and substantive packages.

Thus, the procedural or legislative reforms affecting the ways in which Congress operated internally as an institution (specifically, in terms of enhanced subunit autonomy) transformed the liaison process between the branches in favor of increasing and routinized contact at lower and lower levels of organization. And such changes in the external relationship between the branches mandated that Congress expand its capacity to sift through the mounds of information generated by the executive branch. In short, the reforms of codetermination reinforced one another and seemed to render the entire battery of reforms, internal or external, legislative or liaison, all the more valid and necessary. Yet, reforms, like good intentions, may not always pave the road to heaven. What reformers wish, providence does not always provide. Codeterminative reforms have had a pronounced impact upon the way Congress conducts its business—but often with unforeseen consequences. Like the appetite that grows with the eating, a capacity for autonomous action or for evaluation of complex information feeds upon itself: More autonomous subcommittees can handle more complex material, but the more information that becomes available across the policy spectrum, the more it generates the need for autonomous subcommittees to examine it. Herein may be found the seed of congressional undoing.

Hence there arises a problem of overload—one that, on occasion, has seriously debilitated the Congress and its subagencies during the past decade. The tyranny of any member's appointment calendar, moreover, often seems to threaten suffocation as that member runs from meeting to meeting, always behind, and all too often uninformed of the full complement of considerations pertaining to any issue. A final report of the House Select Committee on Committees, published in 1980, estimated that the severity of scheduling conflicts created by overlapping committee and subcommittee meetings had reached a crisis point. "Failure to address this critical matter," the report warned, "may result in an erosion of the efficiency and productivity of the House in working its will in the legislative process."[22]

The shift from "committee government" to "subcommittee government,"[23] as evidenced by the expanding role, authority, and autonomy of congressional subcommittees, has led to excessive "jurisdictional overlaps" among the subcommittees regarding legislation and oversight. Attempts over the years to define the jurisdictional boundaries of committees and subcommittees appear to have led only to the current proliferation of subcommittees—the very cause aggravating much jurisdictional confrontation in the contemporary Congress.[24]

Turf wars over foreign, defense, and arms-control issues thus have been and undoubtedly will continue to be a feature of congressional codetermination. In part, subcommittee and even committee conflict resulting from jurisdictional overlap may derive from the inevitable complexities of modern public-policy issues. Perhaps new ways and methods will have to be developed to introduce greater degrees of flexibility in handling complex problems overlapping the provinces of numerous committees and subcommittees.

Authority has devolved not simply from the committee to the subcommittee levels but also from the subcommittees to the lower ranks of Congress, emboldening junior members and leading to a crisis in democracy at the very core of the congressional system. The crisis is one of leadership. Its source lies in the enhanced independence of junior members from senior members, from congressional party institutions, and from national political organizations that have traditionally provided election support.

Indeed, codeterminative reform represents a victory for junior members as reflected (1) in the altered and more influential patterns of committee assignments they receive, (2) in their increased participation in floor debates, (3) in their sponsorship of amendments, and (4) in the establishment of organizations intended to serve exclusively the needs and interests of freshmen or junior members. The "New Members' Caucus," for example, has actually taken upon itself the right to interview prospective committee chairs.

In addition, reforms favoring "juniority" might not have had so great an impact as they did in the late 1970s and early 1980s if it were not for the fact that the membership of Congress changed considerably during this period. This conclusion is evidenced by (1) the enlarged proportion of newly elected members, (2) the significant decreases in the average age of members, (3) increases in the numbers of women members, and (4) the greater numbers of blacks chairing important congressional committees.

The significance of these changes in membership for codetermination of arms control has been dramatic, inasmuch as greater independence for individual legislators means that congressional views now tend to be guided by individual judgment and personal political ideology. One symptom of this tendency is the emergence of ad hoc bipartisan and sometimes even bicameral groups. The number of such groups seeking to assert "surrogate legislative leadership" has multiplied with the institutionalization of codeterminative reforms and currently number in the dozens.

The nature of the surrogate legislative leadership introduced by such groups varies. One such leadership group, the "gang of six," came (as we shall discuss below) to play a crucial role in the controversy over "build-down" and the MX; but it disbanded once certain goals had been achieved. Other groups exist on a continuing basis but for the most part appear to enjoy less immediate or visible impact; note, for example, the Congress for Peace Through Law, which was formed in 1966 just prior to the emergence of a movement favoring codeterminative reforms.

In its own way, this phenomenon of surrogate legislative leadership reveals the manner in which the greater complexity of issues and increased autonomy available to individual members have manifested themselves in the modern Congress. First, such ad hoc formations allow members to identify with or focus upon single issues such as Vietnam-veteran affairs, textiles, oceans policy, and seaports, and to concentrate upon regional (especially economic and environmental) issues. One response to the complexity of issues across the range of public policymaking has thus been heightened selectivity based, no doubt, upon constituent interests or personal concerns; but this selectivity also creates the need for a broader range of surrogate legislative networks and groupings not necessarily linked to partisanship. Second, such groups represent a vehicle for members to demonstrate autonomy with respect to party leadership by encouraging nonpartisan collaboration on an unprecedented number of issues. The overall result, as previously suggested, has been maximization of the representativeness of Congress, which at times wreaks havoc with the established leadership. Codetermination therefore places major new obstacles in the way of congressional party leadership as it attempts to galvanize congressional resources for purposes of legislative decisionmaking.

The problems faced by leadership in Congress have been exacerbated, furthermore, by the changing norms of Congress since the advent of codetermination. One result of these important developments is the difficulty faced by party whips in rounding up votes. Erosion of the seniority system has been accompanied by a deterioration in the ability of national party organizations to serve as predominant political bases for any member's career. Weakened national party loyalties have had an inevitable impact upon party leadership within Congress, as a result of the leadership's attempts to muster the votes and energies of members who have loosely been indoctrinated into the norms of apprenticeship typical of the bygone days of "seniority." The desire to serve district and constituent interests in as highly visible a manner as possible, and perhaps to move beyond the House or Senate in terms of one's career, have produced a degree of individualism on the part of members within the delivery system of Congress that makes it a more representative institution but one in which it is increasingly difficult to achieve consensus over legislative policy.

Herein, for example, arises a contradiction in the attempt to revitalize the House Democratic Caucus. The Caucus has become the repository of a vastly extended set of responsibilities designed to ensure that the House legislative and oversight delivery system remain while higher levels of member, subcommittee, and committee autonomy are sustained. As its title suggests, however, the Democratic Caucus is the articulation of a national party, and thus its ability to lead and to mobilize support depends, at least in some measure, upon the strength and vitality of party consensus. A party caucus cannot be stronger than the solidarity of its members. Yet, neither party consensus regarding issues nor loyalty with respect to party affiliation provides the keys to the legislative behaviors of members in the reformed and codeterminative Congress. Indeed, considerable evidence suggests that the House Democratic Caucus was looked to for a greater leadership role within Congress as a whole, but just at the point when the political hold of the party over its members in Congress became weakest.

Even the oversight responsibilities of Congress appear threatened by the sheer weight of new responsibilities created by Congress in its press toward activism, combined with an emerging tendency on the part of some members to pursue the most visible issues or only those retaining direct constituent interest. The drive toward "new oversight" discussed earlier may be the result simply of the need for members to appear on television and in the media for the folks back home. There is certainly a crisis in systematic investigatory oversight, as suggested by Dante B. Fascell (D.-Fla.), chairman of the House Foreign Affairs Committee, who recently declared, "Oversight is meaningless, let's face it. We go through almost a charade in the Congress in exercising our oversight responsibilities."[25] But the will to intervene in arms-control policymaking, through oversight and evaluation as well as by means of policy innovation, represents another measure of the impact of codeterminative reform upon congressional executive liaison and policymaking. Despite the overload of congressional-policy delivery capacity brought on by accelerating member and subcommittee autonomy and increasing issue complexity, members of Congress have seen fit to identify a number of ways to intervene effectively in arms-control policymaking to assert their codeterminative responsibilities.

CONGRESSIONAL CODETERMINATION OF ARMS-CONTROL POLICIES

In November 1985, when the Senate Armed Services Committee asked Defense Secretary Caspar Weinberger to provide evidence of his department's responsiveness to congressional information requests, he declared: "In the last year we've received 123,130 written inquiries, we have 25,306 pages in budget justification books, I personally spent 55 hours last year, 38 hours this, in testimony and we've had 555 different witnesses in other hearings giving 1,434 hours of testimony." Weinberger hastened to add, "Now, Mr. Chairman, none of this is to say that we resent this."[26] Whatever the level of resentment that may or may not exist within the Pentagon, the White House, the National Security Council staff, and related agencies of the executive branch as a result of codetermination, congressional executive relations in matters pertaining to arms-control policy are intense and multifarious as never before.

In a previous attempt to evaluate the role of Congress in determining arms-control policy, Alton Frye wrote of the need to examine this "many-faceted relationship" from "a variety of perspectives." Arms control, "like love," Frye observed, is "a many-splendored thing. Intellectuals enamored of complexity, are fond of arms control. Politicians, driven by reality, also find themselves frequently embracing the subject."[27] But, as Frye concluded, arms control, on account of its complexity, was for many members of Congress "the object of a love-hate relationship."[28] Congress, given its constitutional powers and traditional functions, has for many years struggled to identify an appropriate institutional approach. As arms control is too important to be ignored, yet too resistant against easy solution, the result has been successive waves of indifference alternating with periods of intense interest. The question of how to define and delimit the functions of Congress with respect to arms-control policy thus has been a cause of considerable debate and consternation among policy practitioners and scholars of congressional decisionmaking alike.

It is revealing to examine congressional initiatives in arms control and to assess the efficacy of such initiatives in the context of a presidential administration that is generally given high marks for leadership in the game of legislative politics—as was the case with Reagan's administration, at least prior to the Iran-contra scandal. How and to what degree has congressional codetermination manifested itself in the realm of arms control since SALT II, and with what impacts? How significant has the congressional codetermination been since the advent of the Reagan administration? What role or set of roles has Congress played in arms control? Under what set of constraints—institutional, political, or constitutional—has it operated? These and similar questions have become especially pertinent during the current phase of Strategic Arms Reduction Talks (START) as well as in the arms-control negotiations between the United States and the Soviet Union, which appear increasingly affected by star-wars images of militarized space and ultraphysical weapons.

The congressional record in the field of arms control, since the failure of the SALT II accord, reflects a variety of legislative approaches, methods, techniques, values, and concerns. In terms of the political spectrum, they run the gamut from liberal efforts (as in the case of the nuclear freeze proposal) to more conservative attempts (such as those being made to establish nuclear risk-reduction centers and modernization of the Hotline).

The politics of each legislative or codeterminative initiative in arms control has varied in terms of the intensity with which the relevant issues were debated, the heat each generated, and the duration and effort each required—not to mention the publicity each received. By no means can the importance of any particular codeterminative initiative be measured by the attention devoted to it by the media or the public. On the contrary, a number of codeterminative arms-control initiatives that attracted considerable attention at the time, such as "build-down," seem in retrospect to have warranted much less acclaim than originally assumed.

In general, the administration was able to preside over the legislative decisionmaking process through a series of proposals that kept the Congress preoccupied and, occasionally, overloaded. But Congress was able to perform its basic functions and to render an important contribution to arms control.

A survey of major efforts at congressional codetermination of arms-control policy reveal a basic cluster of ten initiatives, not including more recent attempts to exercise some degree of policy evaluation with respect to the Strategic Defense Initiative (SDI). A brief listing of these ten initiatives suggests the ways in which congressional codetermination manifested itself during the Reagan administration.

1. Freezing a Hot Arms Race in the Cold War

The SALT II negotiations began in 1972, the same year the antiballistic missile (ABM) treaty took effect, and continued until June 1979, when President Carter and General-Secretary Brezhnev signed the most elaborate arms-control agreement ever undertaken by the two states in relation to each other. The eventual failure of this treaty to muster sufficient political support to carry it into formal ratification led indirectly to the circumstances in which a public call for a freeze on the testing, development, production, and deployment of strategic weaponry arose throughout the United States.

The very public nature of the freeze debate required many in Congress to comment openly upon it. The ferment generated within Congress by the freeze proposal came to a boiling point between May and October

1983. On May 4, 1983, the House, after forty-two hours of debate lasting seven weeks, passed a much-amended and attenuated nuclear freeze resolution by a vote of 278 to 149.[29] The resolution called upon the president to propose to the Soviet Union that a mutual and verifiable freeze on the testing, production, and deployment of all nuclear weapons be negotiated by the two countries. The resolution barely amounted to an actual requirement legally incumbent upon the executive. It declared simply that the president should seek to negotiate a freeze, but that he should also scrupulously avoid language that would have rendered this outcome mandatory.

The nuclear freeze resolution, which passed the House, thus remained advisory. The Senate, however, rejected this measure of action. On October 31, 1983, by a vote of 58 to 40, the Senate tabled a nuclear freeze resolution proposed by Senator Edward M. Kennedy (D.-Mass.).[30] Despite the considerable support in the Senate that had arisen for such an approach, the president was saved the trouble of what, almost certainly, would have been a veto.

2. Building Up for Build-Down: How to START?

A major arms-control proposal generated from within the Congress during the first Reagan term of office concerned build-down, a success story in codetermination that ultimately failed.

The basic aim of build-down was to encourage both sides to exchange gradual modernization of strategic weapons for a reduced number of weapons actually deployed. The opening position, eventually presented by the U.S. START delegation, included a ballpark figure of 5,000 warheads as the number each side would be allowed to maintain within their respective arsenals. The build-down program would have involved not only the reciprocated retirement of older weapons for those more modern but also mandated yearly cutbacks to ensure that negotiated reduction levels were introduced according to schedule—regardless of each country's modernization program.

Crosscutting conflicts and mounting pressures generated by the build-down proposal within Congress helped to bring about the emergence of a small bipartisan and bicameral group that quickly assumed (or, more correctly, was allowed to assume) a leadership role. This group, branded by the media as the "gang of six," included Senators William S. Cohen (R.-Maine), Sam Nunn (D.-Ga.), and Charles H. Percy (R.-Ill.) and Representatives Albert Gore, Jr. (D.-Tenn.), Norman D. Dicks (D.-Wash.), and Les Aspin (D.-Wisc.). Collectively, they succeeded in encouraging the administration to adopt build-down as their price for any future willingness to deliver congressional support on the MX missile.

On September 21, 1983, they presented a detailed outline of the principles intended to guide administration thinking with regard to build-down. On October 4, 1983, their efforts met with success when the president announced that the United States would present a new arms-control proposal to the START talks in Geneva based upon a build-down framework. Senator Cohen was jubilant, declaring that "this is the first time in recent history, if not recorded history, when a President of the United States has accepted Members of Congress as a working partner in formulating an arms control policy."[31] On the floor of the House, Representative Gore detailed no fewer than fifteen changes wrought by the "gang of six" upon administration arms-control and defense policies. Other members were less sanguine. Les AuCoin referred to build-down as "Hollywood arms control."[32] In retrospect, the administration does seem to have obtained the best of the bargain: Build-down came to naught because the Soviet government rejected it, whereas the MX became a reality.

3. Bargaining over the MX Bargaining Chip

Few legislative battles in recent memory have been waged with greater intensity than that over the MX. Few have left more members dissatisfied. No side ever received the half-loaf they had really wanted, although the administration appears to have obtained more than its political adversaries did.

The MX, along with the build-down proposal, helped to create the political circumstances within the Congress that gave rise to the "gang of six." It was the central issue in the establishment of the Scowcroft Commission. And it was certainly the focus of a compromise worked out by then Senate Majority Leader Howard Baker (R.-Tenn.) and then Speaker of the House Thomas P. O'Neill, Jr., not to mention the sore point in several Senate-House conference committees.

As for "bottom-line" legislative results, the omnibus continuing resolution for fiscal year 1985 contains the compromise figure of $2.5 billion toward production of the 21 MX missiles previously authorized in 1983 and procurement of the 21 additional MX missiles authorized for 1984. Funds for this second set of missiles were, in effect, "fenced off" until March 1, 1985, and could be spent only if the president submitted a report to the Congress in fulfillment of certain conditions. These conditions included the need to certify that the additional set of 21 missiles was congruent with arms-control efforts and programs. Congressional conditions also required detailed executive assessment of the basing mode to be used in the case of the MX, along with an evaluation of the effect the MX would have regarding the future vulnerability of the U.S. ICBM force.[33] The Senate-House conference committee working on the Department of Defense Authorization Act for fiscal year 1986 brought the final number of missiles authorized for deployment to 50.

The administration had campaigned long and hard for the deployment of 100 MXs, along with 132 for purposes of testing. By every account, it pulled out all the lobbying stops on this issue—a formidable array, indeed. Some half-hearted attempts were made by administration spokesmen to represent the figure of 50 as a mere pause toward the full 100. But Les Aspin, who had recently been installed as chairman of the House Armed Services Committee and was instrumental in forging the final compromise, ruled that out. "There's no way we're ever going to build more than 50 MX's for deployment," he declared. "It's over. It's done."[34]

4. Resolutions Not to "Undercut" SALT II Limitations

There is an irony associated with endeavors to achieve arms control by means of maintaining the aggregate ceiling levels established by the SALT II agreement: The United States government had rejected SALT II but until recently had adhered to its limitations. One of the major restrictions established by the treaty, for example, was a limit of 1,200 launchers designed to carry MIRVed missiles with multiple warheads. It became apparent in late 1983 and early 1984 that deployment of the Trident II–class submarine, equipped with 24 such missiles, might take the United States over this limitation, if the administration were not prepared to retire one or several of the older Poseidon class submarines or a number of the land-based Minuteman-3 missiles.[35] Congressional attempts to encourage the Reagan administration "not to undercut" the negotiated restrictions established by the SALT II accord therefore reflected concern over the imminent demise of efforts by both the United States and the Soviet Union to maintain the SALT II "caps." Thus the Senate proceeded to pass resolutions on a number of occasions calling upon the administration to adhere to the SALT II limits, as long as the Soviets did so as well.

On June 19, 1984, for example, Senator Dale L. Bumpers (D.-Ark.) successfully attached an amendment to the Department of Defense Authorization Act expressing the sense of the Senate that the United States should continue, on a reciprocal basis, to abide by the 1979 levels. The Bumpers resolution passed by a vote of 82 to 17,[36] a symbolic gesture consistent with the concept of codetermination.

One year later, the Senate reaffirmed its position on not undercutting SALT II. On June 5, 1985, by a decisive vote of 90 to 5, it urged the Reagan administration to protect the integrity of SALT II restrictions.

The Bumpers resolution contained explicit language permitting the administration to execute "proportionate responses" to Soviet violations, thus assuring the president a certain flexibility in countering any Soviet incursion against the treaty and, hence, satisfying the growing concern within the Senate on this issue. In the end, however, the efforts of reciprocal restraint failed. The SALT II limits became, in the words of the Reagan administration, "a dead letter." Yet as recently as April 1987, the Congress displayed conviction in expressing its sense that the SALT II limits should not be unilaterally abrogated.

5. The Senate Arms-Control Observer Group Delegation at START

The Constitution grants the Senate the authority to exercise advice and consent with respect to all treaties negotiated by the executive branch. In recent years, however, actual practice has involved significantly more "consent" than "advice." Concern over this imbalance in the era of codetermination led to the establishment of the bipartisan Senate Arms Control Observer Group on the first day of the 99th Congress, January 3, 1985.

Although the enabling legislation of the Senate Arms Control Observer Group specifically proscribes any attempt to conduct negotiations with Soviet representatives, the terms by which this senatorial group was created permit—indeed, encourage—its members to consult with and advise the U.S. START negotiating team, as well as to monitor and report to the Senate on the progress and development of the START talks.[37] The overriding hope was and remains that, contrary to past performance, the Senate would keep abreast of negotiations as they proceeded, thereby allowing its members to stay cognizant of the central issues and, most important, of the salient disputes. By means of the Observer Group, the Senate is now able to participate in the *journey* toward an agreement in addition to being in on its *arrival*. Experience suggests that the original expectations of Robert J. Dole (R.-Kans.), then majority leader, and Robert C. Byrd (D.-W.V.), then minority leader, both of whom proposed creation of the Observer Group, are being realized. The ten-member delegation has met regularly with the U.S. START negotiating team in Geneva. The formation of this body therefore holds out the promise of better informed and more expeditious senatorial execution of its advice and consent authority.

6. Proposals to Ratify the Threshold Test Ban Treaty and the Peaceful Nuclear Explosions Treaty and to Resume Negotiations on a Comprehensive Nuclear Test Ban Treaty

A durable symbol of arms control is that of nuclear test ban treaties, favored by many kinds of arms-control advocates. Senators Kennedy and Mathias, who joined forces across party aisles in June 1984, were able, with the assistance of Senator Sam Nunn, to muster sufficient votes for a sense of the Senate resolution calling for the ratification of two major test ban treaties that had previously been signed by the United States and the Soviet Union.

The first, the so-called Threshold Test Ban Treaty (TTBT), negotiated in 1974, prohibits all underground military tests of nuclear devices with yields greater than 150 kilotons. An additional agreement (PNET), signed by the two superpowers in 1976, imposes a similar test ban upon peaceful nuclear explosions with yields of more than 150 kilotons. Neither the TTBT nor the PNET has ever been formally ratified by the Senate.

This matter of preventing underground nuclear testing promises to remain an abiding concern within Congress and may even extend to debates over resolutions urging the president to negotiate a Comprehensive Nuclear Test Ban Treaty (CTBT) with the Soviet Union. For example, the recent ratification of TTBT and PNET was clearly linked to requests for talks leading to a CTBT. On January 3, 1985, a resolution (H.J. Res. 3) introduced by Representatives Berkley Bedell (D.-Iowa), Jim Leach (R.-Iowa), and Edward J. Markey (D.-Mass.), and co-signed by no fewer than 195 members of the House, called upon the president to request ratification of TTBT and PNET; it also requested that the president "propose to the Soviet Union the immediate resumption of negotiations toward conclusion of a verifiable comprehensive test ban treaty." The House Committee on Foreign Affairs, which reported out the resolution to the floor on July 24, 1985, focused directly upon the crucial sticking point: *verification.* The report argued that both the TTBT and PNET were verifiable and that the PNET contained, for the first time, agreement by the Soviet Union of a verification process involving on-site inspection.[38] A minority report, signed by the Republican members of the committee, took note of the unresolved problem presented by inadequate technologies of verification in order to argue for an abeyance in efforts toward CTBT. "Regrettably," they concluded, "what we see in H.J. Res. 3 is not substantive policy, but superfluous politics."[39] The test ban issue had thus become fully politicized, even in the face of a Soviet testing moratorium and its rejection by the United States. On January 13, 1987, President Reagan requested that the Senate reconsider these treaties by granting its advice and consent pending achievement of improved verification measures. The president specifically requested that the Senate proceed to give its advice and consent to ratification of the TTBT and PNET, dependent upon presidential certification that measures have been accepted by the Soviet Union allowing for "direct, accurate yield measurements taken at the site of all appropriate nuclear detonations."[40] In its own way, this recommended procedure recognizes codetermination as a viable and effective liaison process in congressional/executive relations regarding arms control.

7. The Militarization of Space: Attempts to Proscribe or Limit Anti-Satellite Weapons Testing

The codeterminative initiatives by Congress to restrain the arms race, ranging from the freeze to the search for a comprehensive test ban treaty, all revolve around technologies with which governments are largely familiar, technologies that emphasize strategic offensive capabilities geared to the earth's atmosphere. Now a new element in the strategic equation has been introduced into the superpower arms race as a result of the development of strategic capabilities in space, capabilities that hold out the promise to some of a more secure form of stability than currently available; for others, however, they portend an increasingly fragile future. According to virtually any set of historical criteria, the successful testing on September 13, 1985, by the United States of an anti-satellite (ASAT) device against a functioning spacecraft represents a significant milestone, perhaps even a crucial turning point, along the road toward incorporating space into the strategic orbit of the nuclear powers.

To an overriding degree, negative congressional initiatives with regard to ASAT have stemmed from concern over the strategic and political implications of this system. Some members of Congress have expressed concern that ASAT would hopelessly dilute the terms and strictures of the 1972 ABM treaty, which permits the testing of anti-satellite weapons but proscribes tests involving anti-missile defenses. The distinction between these two categories of weapons systems would, some feared, become meaningless through ASAT testing. Others were concerned that the development of ASAT weapons made it more, rather than less, difficult to maintain strategic levels prescribed under SALT II. Finally, the evolution of ASAT technology seemed to some skeptics to be distorting future policy in favor of SDI.

Year after year, since 1983, authorization and funding for ASAT testing have become available only through laborious legislation reflective of the concern in Congress over the consequences of ASAT tests and arms control. Such political sentiments led to a number of legislative deadlocks blocking agreement on defense authorizations. In 1984, for example, a compromise partially worked out by Senate Majority Leader Baker and Speaker of the House O'Neill led to appropriations for no more than three ASAT tests against objects in space, none of which were to be conducted prior to March 1, 1985. Congress succeeded in imposing only a five-month moratorium on ASAT testing. Thus, a last-ditch effort to prevent the September 13th ASAT test against an actual spacecraft was made by four Democratic members of Congress. This effort took the form of judicial litigation. On September 10, 1985, Representatives George E. Brown, Jr., of California, Joe Moakley of Massachusetts, John F. Seiberling of Ohio, and Matthew F. McHugh of New York filed a petition in the U.S. District Court of the District of Columbia to request an injunction against the imminent ASAT test.[41] The grounds of this suit were based upon statutory language in the Defense Appropriations Act of 1984 requiring the president to proceed "in good faith" to negotiate a ban involving the "strictest possible limitations . . . consistent with national security" and "to avert clear and irrevocable harm to the national security." The litigants filing the suit claimed that the president and executive branch had failed to uphold these standards. The suit eventually failed. District Court Judge Norma Johnson ruled that the court could not properly intervene in a matter between the executive and legislative branches that was largely "political" in nature.[42]

Thus, the battle between the executive and the Congress over ASAT was allowed to continue. During July 1985, for example, Senate/House conferees on a fiscal 1986 defense authorization bill permitted no more than three ASAT tests against targets in space during the fiscal year. In October 1985, however, the House Appropriations Subcommittee on Defense voted to eliminate funding for future ASAT tests so long as the Soviet Union maintained its moratorium. Here was yet another case in which the autonomy of Congress at lower levels of organization combined with renewed congressional capacity to assess complex information to produce a codeterminative result in arms-control policy.

8. Modernizing the Hotline: Communications over Crisis Management

The initiative to upgrade the crisis communication links between the governments of the United States and the Soviet Union arose during 1982, when, in keeping with the impulses of codetermination, Senators Jackson, Nunn, and Warner introduced an amendment to the Department of Defense Authorization Act of 1983 requiring the Pentagon to undertake a feasibility study of several measures to reduce the risk of nuclear exchange. One of these measures involved the addition of a "high-speed facsimile capability to the Hotline" that enabled the two governments to transmit and receive a variety of graphic materials, including maps and topographical materials.[43] In April 1983, Secretary Weinberger released the results of the ensuing analysis. They indicated that the United States was prepared to propose modernization of the Hotline to the Soviets. President Reagan, in May 1983, announced the decision to proceed toward negotiations on this matter. For once, American-Soviet arms-control negotiations bore fruit rapidly. On July 17, 1984, the United States and the Soviet Union signed an agreement to introduce state-of-the-art satellite technology into the direct communications link. In short, codetermination as a process had led to another arms-control policy victory.

9. Establishing Nuclear Risk-Reduction Centers: Communications over Crisis Prevention

The 1982 nuclear risk-reduction amendment to the Defense Authorization Act of 1983 proposed by Senators Jackson, Nunn, and Warner, leading to the modernization of the Hotline, included the suggestion that nuclear risk-reduction centers be established in the United States and the Soviet Union. These centers, its advocates argued, would redress the balance between crisis prevention and crisis management by providing each of the two superpowers with strengthened capacity to head off crises before they started. The basic mission of the risk-reduction centers would be to provide around-the-clock surveillance of all incidents and situations possibly leading to nuclear confrontation or crisis.

In November 1983, a Working Group on Nuclear Risk Reduction was established under the chairmanship of Senators Nunn and Warner. This group, which included several well-known arms-control specialists, made several recommendations with regard to nuclear crisis-prevention centers that were introduced in Congress on February 1, 1984, by Senators Nunn and Warner. Their resolution, calling upon the president to proceed toward negotiations with the Soviet Union, passed the Senate on June 15, 1984, by the overwhelming vote of 82 to 0 and was eventually signed into law. After several months of "interagency deliberation," the administration announced its support of the proposal to establish nuclear risk-reduction centers in Washington and Moscow. On September 3, 1985, Senators Nunn and Warner took their proposal to Moscow and enlisted the support of General-Secretary Gorbachev, who declared that his government would give the idea careful attention. As endorsed by the administration, both centers would be headed by ambassadorial officials and each would consist of diplomatic and military personnel assigned by the host country.[44]

10. Proscriptions and Permissions Regarding Chemical Munitions

In 1982 and again in 1983, Congress rejected administration efforts to terminate a long-standing moratorium on the production of chemical and biological weapons. In both years, the Reagan administration sought permission to manufacture a new kind of binary nerve gas. (Binary munitions, composed of two liquids separately contained and stored, are combined prior to use but become lethal after release.) Proponents in favor of this technology argued, first, that production is necessary on deterrence grounds and, second, that the binary nature of these munitions renders them chemically more stable and thus safer than previous chemical weapons systems. Opponents stressed the fundamental indecency of such technologies, the need to support elaborate trans-national normative proscriptions against their use, and their irrelevance to modern tactical warfare.

Proceedings on defense authorizations for 1986 proved disappointing to those anxious to maintain the moratorium against chemical weapons, inasmuch as Congress did approve the production of binary munitions. Considerable concern has been raised in Congress, however, over the role to be played by the NATO allies in storing such weapons and the conditions placed over their deployment in Europe.

CODETERMINATION AND POLICY DELIVERY

This chapter has suggested that the aim of codeterminative reform in the 1970s was to represent diverse interests and hold the executive accountable. This goal required an enhancement of congressional capacity to sift, handle, and incorporate greater degrees of issue and informational complexity at various stages of the policy process. The chapter has also linked attempts to reform the internal, procedural, and political processes within Congress with this thrust and, furthermore, has suggested that informational complexity has helped sustain a tendency within Congress toward specialization, devolution, and decentralization. This trend toward devolution and decentralization, which is clearly the result of codeter-minative reforms, has manifested itself in the extension of greater degrees of autonomy at successively lower levels of congressional organization—from party caucuses to committees and subcommittees down to the individual members of Congress. The very real governance problem Congress has faced as a result of this trend does not belie the fact that its capacity to perform specialized tasks in relation to highly specialized policy problems has been vastly increased.

This increased capacity is demonstrated by the series of *policy in-novations* in the field of arms control generated from within the Congress during the period under investigation. Although arms control was and remains a specialized subject of considerable complexity, individual members of Congress as well as the ad hoc coalitions among them were able to propose a series of important measures that succeeded in advancing the cause of arms control in original ways. These policy innovations, generated from within Congress and reflective of codetermination, include the following: (1) the freeze, (2) build-down, (3) a Senate START observer group, (4) upgrading of the Hotline, and (5) nuclear risk-reduction centers (see Figure 5.3).

Codeterminative reform was not merely an exercise in dispassionate specialization; it also represented a serious effort to redefine the balance among the branches—in particular, the manner of policy liaison between Congress and the executive branch. The soul and spirit of codetermination bespeaks a profound concern within Congress over the need to ensure greater degrees of executive accountability, a concern recently made even more dramatic by the Iran-contra scandal and revelations concerning breaches in U.S. security. By means of codeterminative reform, Congress revamped its process of external liaison such that the executive branch now permits Congress to restrain the presidency—more effectively, immediately, and responsibly—than ever before. Despite the cumbersome, time-consuming, occasionally exhausting series of laws that emerged as a result of serious conflict between the administration and Congress, congressional efforts to ensure greater degrees of accountability through independent *policy evaluation* produced important, and perhaps even historic, results.

The major exercises in the policy evaluation of arms control introduced by the Congress during the Reagan administration in the name of liaison reform and executive accountability include (1) restraints on production and deployment of the MX and the mandated revision of its basing mode, (2) limitations on the testing of ASAT weapons, (3) conditions added to legislation permitting the production of binary chemical weapons, and (4) proposals designed to encourage the administration not to undercut the SALT II agreement.

A final set of congressional initiatives dealing with various nuclear test ban treaties and verification involves elements of both policy innovation and policy evaluation and, in turn, reflects the capacity both to use specialized information in the formulation of policy and to assert oversight over administration policies in the name of accountability.

The record of congressional involvement in arms-control policymaking since the implementation of codeterminative reform is thus secure. Some might suggest that the results remain peripheral to the main issues that separate the United States and the Soviet Union. Others might allege that codetermination has fostered a less responsible Congress, one given to fragmentation in delivery and fractiousness in deliberation. But there is no doubt that the ultimate test of congressional capacity and willingness to sustain codeterminative policy involvement in arms control over the next decade will occur with respect to the Strategic Defense Initiative. The fact remains, however, that Congress has shown that it is in the business of arms-control policymaking to stay and that the remaking of

142

FIGURE 5.3
Codetermination and Arms-Control Policy Delivery

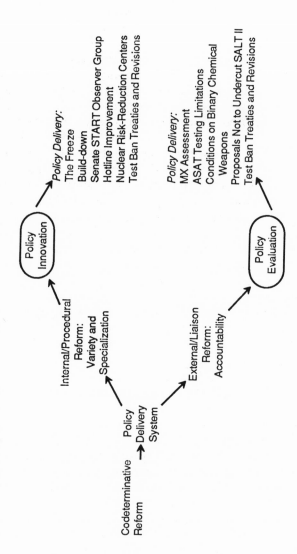

American politics must and will include the norms, principles, and rules of congressional/executive policy codetermination.

NOTES

1. Thomas M. Franck and Edward Weisband, *Foreign Policy by Congress* (New York: Oxford University Press, 1979), especially ch. 3, pp. 61–82.

2. Arthur Maass, *Congress and the Common Good* (New York: Basic Books, 1983), p. 13.

3. Ibid., p. 14.

4. Bernard Weintraub, "Power Surge By Congress," *New York Times* (September 9, 1985), pp. A1, A11.

5. Roger H. Davidson, David M. Kovenok, and Michael K. O'Leary, *Congress in Crisis: Politics and Congressional Reform* (Belmont, Calif.: Wadsworth Publishing Co., 1966), pp. 15–37.

6. This and the following discussion of the functions of Congress derive from ibid., pp. 34–37.

7. Ibid.

8. Ibid.

9. Ibid.

10. Ibid.

11. Ibid.

12. Ibid.

13. Walter J. Oleszek, "A Perspective on Congressional Reform," in Susan Welch and John G. Peters, eds., *Legislative Reform and Public Policy* (New York: Praeger Publishers, 1977), p. 5.

14. Ibid., p. 4.

15. Leroy N. Rieselbach, ed., *Legislative Reform: The Policy Impact* (Lexington, Mass.: D. C. Heath & Co., 1978); citations are from the introductory chapter entitled "Reform, Change, and Legislative Policy Making," pp. 1–7.

16. Ibid., p. 3.

17. Charles O. Jones, "Congress and the Presidency," in Thomas E. Mann and Norman J. Ornstein, eds., *The New Congress* (Washington, D.C.: American Enterprise Institute for Public Policy Research, 1981), p. 249.

18. Ibid., p. 233.

19. Ibid.

20. Ibid., p. 234.

21. David C. Kozak and John D. Macartney, eds., *Congress and Public Policy: A Source Book of Documents and Readings* (Homewood, Ill.: Dorsey Press, 1982), p. 13.

22. U.S. House of Representatives, Final Report of the House Select Committee on Committees, "Overview of Principal Legislative Developments of the 1970's," House Report No. 96-866 (Washington, D.C.: Government Printing Office, 1980, pp. 5ff.). Henceforth cited as "Overview of Principal Legislative Developments."

23. For more extensive discussion of the implications of subcommittee government in policymaking, see Lawrence C. Dodd and Bruce S. Oppenheimer,

"The House in Transition: Change and Consolidation," in Dodd and Oppenheimer, eds., *Congress Reconsidered*, 2nd ed. (Washington, D.C.: Congressional Quarterly Press, 1981), pp. 31–61; and Roger Davidson, "Breaking Up Those 'Cozy Triangles': An Impossible Dream?" in Welch and Peters, eds., *Legislative Reform*, pp. 30–53.

24. "Overview of Principal Legislative Developments," pp. 5ff.

25. U.S. House of Representatives, Committee on Foreign Affairs, Subcommittee on Arms Control, International Security and Science, *Part 1, Nuclear Arms Control: A Brief Historical Survey*, 99th Cong., 1st Sess. (May 20, 1985), p. 36.

26. Caspar Weinberger, as cited in the *New York Times* (November 23, 1985), p. A7.

27. Alton Frye, "The Congressional Resource Problem," in Alan Platt and Lawrence D. Weiler, eds., *Congress and Arms Control* (Boulder, Colo.: Westview Press, 1978), p. 19.

28. Ibid.

29. U.S. House of Representatives, Committee on Foreign Affairs, "Congress, Arms Control, and Weapons Modernization," *Congress and Foreign Policy 1983*, CP 1480 (Washington, D.C.: Government Printing Office, 1983), pp. 86–109, especially p. 91. Robert C. Gray cites then Representative Gore as observing that his colleagues in the House, because of the freeze debate, developed "some of the same sense of nuance and detail in nuclear matters that formerly was reserved for tax laws and highway construction bills." See also Albert Gore, Jr., "Beyond the Freeze," *Washington Post* (May 9, 1983), p. 11.

30. Ibid., p. 105.

31. U.S. House of Representatives, Committee on Foreign Affairs, Subcommittee on Arms Control, International Security, and Science, *Fundamentals on Nuclear Arms Control: Part III—Structuring Nuclear Arms Control Proposals and Agreements*, 99th Cong., 1st Sess. (Washington, D.C.: Government Printing Office, September 12, 1985), p. 105.

32. Ibid., p. 107.

33. For a detailed description of the legislative history during 1984, see U.S. House of Representatives, Committee on Foreign Affairs, "Congress, MX, and Arms Control, *Congress and Foreign Policy* (Washington, D.C.: Government Printing Office, 1984), pp. 48–69.

34. *Congressional Quarterly* (July 27, 1985), p. 1473.

35. *New York Times* (June 9, 1985), p. A17.

36. *Congressional Quarterly* (June 23, 1984), p. 1479.

37. U.S. Senate, Report of the Senate Arms-Control Observer Group Delegation, 99th Cong., 1st Sess., Doc. 99-7 (Washington, D.C.: Government Printing Office, March 9–12, 1985), p. III.

38. See U.S. House of Representatives, Committee on Foreign Affairs, Report 99-221, 99th Cong., 1st Sess. (July 24, 1985), H.J. Res., "To Prevent Nuclear War."

39. Ibid., p. 9.

40. U.S. Department of State, Bureau of Public Affairs, *Special Report No. 161* (January 1987); Presidential Letter to the Senate of the United States (January 13, 1987).

41. *New York Times* (September 11, 1985), p. A5.

42. *New York Times* (September 13, 1985), p. A8.

43. U.S. House of Representatives, Committee on Foreign Affairs, Subcommittee on Arms Control, International Security and Science, *Part 1, Nuclear Arms Control: A Brief Historical Survey,* 99th Cong., 1st Sess. (May 20, 1985), p. 36.

44. See Don Oberdorfer, "Reduction of Nuclear Risk Eyed," *Washington Post* (September 16, 1985), p. A10; see also "A Nuclear Risk Reduction System," report of the Nunn/Warner Working Group on Nuclear Risk Reduction (November 1983), unpublished.

6

The Presidency, Policy Reform, and the Rise of Administrative Politics

SIDNEY M. MILKIS

INTRODUCTION: THE PRESIDENCY AND
THE NEW AMERICAN POLITICAL SYSTEM

The thrust of this volume has been to suggest that the American political system underwent major change during the late 1960s and the 1970s. The purpose of this chapter is to examine the effect of this change on the presidency and the executive department. Arguably, the central concern of the reforms enacted during this period was to remake the executive department. Such a reform movement was animated by the concern that public administration had become the center of government activity after the 1930s and that much of this activity was disassociated from the understanding and control of the rank-and-file citizenry. Thus, the flurry of legislation passed during the 1970s with the purpose of curbing the abuses of the "imperial presidency" was part of a broader endeavor to restore the sense of citizenship considered lost with the development of the administrative state.[1]

The reconstruction of the executive department during the 1960s and 1970s reflected an important departure from the New Deal. The New Deal was based on the premise that the national government should become responsible for guaranteeing the economic security of the American people. Moreover, the political reforms of the 1930s resulted in institutional changes whereby primary responsibility for public policy, hitherto centered in the Congress and state legislatures, was delegated to the president and the executive agencies. Beginning with the Great Society, however, a new phase of liberalism was launched emphasizing "quality-of-life" concerns. As Harry McPherson, who served as a special counsel to Lyndon Johnson, has observed, the post–New Deal version of liberal politics:

held that our problems were more of the spirit than the flesh. People were suffering from a sense of alienation from one another, of anomie, of powerlessness. This affected the well to do as much as it did the poor. . . . What would change all this was a creative public effort: for the middle class, new parks, conservation, the removal of billboards and junk, adult education, consumer protection, better television, aid to the arts; for the poor, jobs, training, Head Start, decent housing, medical care, civil rights; for both, and for bridging the gap between them, VISTA, the Teacher Corps, the community action agencies, mass transportation, model cities.[2]

This more expansive liberal philosophy was closely related, in cause and effect, to major institutional developments that challenged the New Deal practice of delegating power to the executive department. The president and executive agencies could perhaps distribute monthly checks to indigents and sponsor public-work programs, thus contributing to income maintenance and job security. Yet many of the expressed concerns of the 1960s and 1970s had little to do with money or public management. The emphasis on community and moral development emphasized by the new liberal philosophy of government presupposed a significant departure from the institutional arrangements of the New Deal. As a result, statutes were enacted and federal court rulings were pronounced that greatly reduced the discretionary power of presidents and executive agencies. Furthermore, institutional arrangements were designed to foster "participatory democracy"—that is, to give "power at the level of immediate impact directly to those people most affected by government policy."[3] This celebration of citizen activism led not only to major changes in electoral politics but also to an extensive transformation of governing institutions. As Anthony King notes, "In the 1960s it came to be thought good for both the participating individuals and the polity that ordinary men and women should have a direct say not merely in the choice of public office holders but in the making of public policy."[4]

Recent scholarship suggests that the presidency, which had emerged since the 1930s as the center of government activity, was shorn of the institutional tools required to provide effective leadership. As Samuel Huntington observed in 1976, "Probably no development of the 1960s and 1970s has greater impact for the future of American politics than the decline in the authority, status, influence, and effectiveness of the Presidency."[5] Not only were several formal restrictions imposed on the executive during this period, but political parties, upon which presidents depended for support in the Congress and the electorate, were weakened as well. Most significant, party leaders were virtually stripped of their authority to nominate presidential candidates, and a selection process, dominated by primary elections and participatory caucuses for selecting delegates from the states to the national conventions of the Democratic and Republican parties, was established. As Donald Horowitz has noted, this weakening of political parties left presidents without any reliable basis of popular support: "A president can no longer depend on a large core of committed supporters who will stay with him through thick and thin. Likewise, with the tenuous bonds of common party across the branches loosened further by changes in the presidential nominating process, there is less restraint in Congress on benefitting from a protracted [presidential] crisis."[6]

The erosion of executive authority, it has been claimed, is accentuated by the fact that modern presidents, though deprived of institutional support, are still at the center of citizens' growing expectations about government responsibilities. Theodore Lowi describes the rise of a "personal president," who symbolizes the *only* representative of the *people*—a role that invariably tends toward failure. The evolution of the modern presidency has combined exalted rhetoric and institutional disarray, Lowi argues, resulting in inevitable disappointment and diminishing public faith in the polity.[7]

This chapter reconsiders the prevailing notion that reforms during the 1960s and 1970s are responsible for a failed presidency and a crisis of governance. Our examination necessarily begins with a reconsideration of the New Deal. The metamorphosis of the American political system was not so much the result of a revolt against the New Deal as an extension and radicalization of it. In particular, the "crisis" of the modern presidency is the result of developments that can be traced to institutional reforms during the 1930s. The limits on the power of the modern executive are closely related to the emergence of an administrative state during the New Deal that, in the final analysis, subordinated presidential authority to the establishment of programmatic rights. These rights formed the heart of an "administrative constitution," which was shielded from the uncertainties of regular political influence, including the influence of the president. The reforms of the 1960s and 1970s were intended to strengthen, rather than dismantle, this administrative constitution.

Hence the recasting of political institutions during the previous two decades was not, as is often asserted, simply an antinomian attack on the political organization that was the product of the New Deal.[8] Rather, the evolution of liberalism has been associated with an aggrandizement of executive administration that has extensively displaced those institutions, such as political parties, that were traditionally facilitative of public deliberation and choice in American politics. This condition, which began during the New Deal, was altered but not fundamentally changed by the reforms of the 1960s and 1970s. The efforts during this later period to enhance the representative character of government action ultimately did not seek to restrain administrative power but, rather, attempted to recast it as an agent of democracy. As a result, the policy responsibility of the executive was increased, but Congress, the courts, and public-interest groups became involved in the details of administration. Thus, the reforms of the 1960s and 1970s circumscribed the administrative power of the president but fixed the business of government more on administration. Consequently, the triumph of liberalism resulted in the enervation, rather than in the surge, of popular rule.

As the conclusion of this chapter suggests, it is doubtful that the politics of the 1980s has ameliorated the crisis of the liberal order. On the contrary, the rise of conservatism suggested by the results of the 1980 and 1984 elections and the policies of the Reagan administration have extended in important respects the *institutional* inheritance of reforms carried out to make possible a stronger commitment to liberal programs. Ronald Reagan asserted his intention to restore the principles of limited government, and programs such as "new federalism" and "regulatory relief" ostensibly served this purpose. Yet the conservative challenge to national administrative power has been stalled by concerns to build a strong defense, foster economic growth, and nurture "traditional" values. Thus, the Reagan years may be marked not by an effective challenge to the aggrandizement of administrative power but by a concerted effort to extend the benefits of the national polity to those who wish to make new uses of, rather than limit, the state.

THE NEW DEAL, PROGRAMMATIC LIBERALISM, AND THE RISE OF ADMINISTRATIVE POLITICS

The New Deal is often viewed as a series of ad hoc responses to the political and economic exigencies created by the Depression. But a careful examination of Franklin D. Roosevelt's presidency reveals that he was not simply, as James MacGregor Burns has claimed, a "broker" leader, whose "shiftiness" and "improvising" detracted from "hard, long range purposeful building of a strong popular movement behind a coherent political program."[9] In fact, FDR's pragmatism was linked to a coherent understanding about the need to redefine the meaning of liberalism in American politics. This reevaluation led to the emergence of a "programmatic" form of liberalism as the public philosophy of the New Deal, requiring a fundamental departure from the principles and institutions that had long governed the political system.[10] Hitherto in American politics, liberalism was associated with Jeffersonian principles, which followed the natural rights tradition of limited government. The most significant aspect of this departure from natural rights to programmatic liberalism was the association of constitutional rights with the extension, rather than the restriction, of the programmatic commitments of the national government.

The "new liberalism" expressed by the Roosevelt administration did not propose that constitutional government and natural-rights liberalism be abandoned, but that the time had come for a very different, expanded understanding of rights. As FDR put it in his revealing 1932 campaign speech at the Commonwealth Club in San Francisco, "Faith in America, faith in our tradition of personal responsibility, faith in our institutions, faith in ourselves demand that we recognize the new terms of the old social contract."[11]

In the end, these "new terms" envisioned a fundamental change in the view of the state that hitherto had prevailed in the United States. In particular, Roosevelt called for "an economic constitutional order," grounded in a commitment to guarantee a decent level of welfare for the American people. This expansion of rights, according to New Dealers, was made necessary by the ruthless and unjust turn that natural-rights liberalism underwent during the latter part of the nineteenth century. By that time, the closing of the Western frontiers and the growth of industrial combinations to the point of "uncontrolled" and "irresponsible" units within the political system had signaled the turning of the tide. The new conditions of the political economy indicated that constitutional principles were no longer being served by a reliance on individual initiative. The impetus for the national welfare now had to shift from the shoulders of the productive private citizen to the government; and the guarantee of equal opportunity now required that constitutional status be accorded a state with extensive supervisory powers:

> Clearly, all this calls for a reappraisal of values. Our task is not discovery or exploitation of national resources, or necessarily producing new goods. It is the soberer, less dramatic business of administering resources and plants already in hand, of seeking to reestablish foreign markets for our surplus production, of meeting the problem of under consumption, of adjusting production to consumption, of distributing wealth and products more equitably, of adopting existing economic organizations to the service of the people. The day of enlightened administration has come.[12]

The institutional vehicle of this departure from traditional liberalism was to be a reconstituted executive department. Since the end of the nineteenth century, progressive reformers had looked to the enhancement of national administrative capacities, feeling that such a step was necessary to infuse American constitutional government with the requisite energy for governing an industrial society. Ostensibly, this endeavor looked to establish the polity upon a more "rational" basis, thereby informing the affairs of state with the necessary expertise and stability to make the working of republican government effective. Yet, this "scientific" enterprise camouflaged a commitment to bringing about a fundamental change in the American Constitution. FDR's Commonwealth Club address expressed a long-standing understanding among progressive thinkers that the concept of limited government and constitutional mechanisms supportive of such a concept were obsolete. Given the nation's virtually religious devotion to the Constitution, however, the task was not to address its failures head on but to enhance that element of the American political framework most likely to facilitate the development of comprehensive national programs with the purpose of ameliorating the hardships and injustice of advanced capitalist society. "Progressive democracy" could be reached only through a strengthening of the presidency and executive agencies and, concomitantly, through a reduction of the institutional status of the more decentralizing institutions—Congress and the states.[13]

The commitment of progressive reformers to strengthening national administrative capacities required, in particular, that the political process be "liberated" from the unfortunate grip of partisan politics. Paradoxically, although Roosevelt was a great party leader, he viewed the American party system as a flawed political institution that had reinforced what he considered outmoded constitutional understandings and mechanisms. The party system was forged on the anvil of Jeffersonian principles, dedicated to establishing "a wall of separation" between the national government and society. Hence, from its inception in the early 1800s, it was wedded to constitutional mechanisms such as the separation of powers and federalism, which were designed to constrain state action. Beginning with Woodrow Wilson, therefore, American party politics was criticized by twentieth-century reformers as an obstacle to the development of a significant progressive program. The origins and organizing principles of the American party system had established it as a political force against the creation of a modern state; the New Deal commitment to building such a state meant that party politics had to be either reconstituted or eliminated.[14]

In effect, Roosevelt's party leadership and the institutional legacy of the New Deal both reconstituted and weakened partisanship in the United States. An understanding of this paradoxical influence of the New Deal on the political process provides a critical backdrop to the reform movement that emerged during the 1960s and 1970s. On the one hand, Roosevelt's partisan rhetoric and practices facilitated a realignment of parties whereby a sharp distinction would be drawn between a reformed Democratic party, unified on the basis of "militant liberalism," and a conservative Republican party supported by those who opposed the creation of an economic constitutional order. As Democratic leader, he sought to transform a decentralized party, responsible only to a local electorate, into an organization responsible to the will of the national party leader—the president—and the interests of a national electorate.[15]

The most dramatic aspect of this attempt to remake the Democratic party into an instrument of liberal reform was Roosevelt's celebrated "purge" campaign of 1938. This action involved the president in one gubernatorial and several congressional primary campaigns; he interceded in a dozen states in an effort to unseat entrenched House, Senate, and gubernatorial incumbents within his own party. Such intervention was not unprecedented; both William Howard Taft and Woodrow Wilson had made limited efforts to cleanse their parties of political opponents in this way. Yet FDR's campaign against those who did not support his program took place on an unprecedented scale and, unlike previous efforts, made no attempt to work through the regular party apparatus.[16]

After the 1938 campaign, the columnist Raymond Clapper noted that "no president ever has gone as far as Mr. Roosevelt in striving to stamp his policies upon his party."[17] But this push for a more liberal America did not evolve into a full-scale commitment to reconstruct the party system. First of all, such a fundamental revamping of partisan politics in the United States was deemed impractical, given the constitutional impediments to party government in the American republic. The enormity of the failure of the purge campaign reinforced a view already held by the Roosevelt administration that a substantial strengthening of the party system was not possible, given the decentralized and fragmented character of political institutions in the United States.[18] Moreover, and more fundamentally, New Dealers did not view liberal programmatic reforms as a partisan issue. Rather, we have noted, the reform program of the 1930s was conceived as a constitutional matter—as a "second bill of rights," to use Roosevelt's term—that would eliminate partisanship about the national government's obligation to provide economic security for the American people.[19]

For these reasons, the New Deal resulted not in a program to reform party politics but in an effort to reconstruct the state that would make party politics less necessary. Due to certain reforms of the progressive era, such as the direct primary and the extension of the civil service, such a development was already well under way by the 1930s—a situation that Roosevelt hoped the New Deal would advance even further.[20] Roosevelt was not willing to abandon partisanship completely. He believed that party leadership was necessary, at least for the time being, to organize public opinion into a governing coalition. Nevertheless, the program Roosevelt imposed on the Democratic party during his second term transformed it into a way-station on the road to administrative government—that is, into a centralized and bureaucratic form of democracy that focused on the president and executive agencies for the formulation and execution of public policy. Concomitantly, such a development tended to deemphasize the role of traditional party politics, Congress, and the state legislatures.[21]

This program focused on two government reorganization bills—one dealing with the judiciary, the other with the executive department—that would remake constitutional law and the executive department in the New Deal image. Both of these bills were established by FDR and the Democratic leadership in Congress as party programs; and the political controversy they aroused dominated the president's second term. Although the administration's proposals to carry out these programs were rejected by Congress, Roosevelt did finally manage to influence the development of significant changes in adjudication and public administration that fundamentally reshaped the policy process. Changes in the judiciary's personnel and doctrines during FDR's presidency eliminated "constitutional" barriers to national consolidation and to the delegation of authority to the executive department.[22] Moreover, the Executive Reorganization Act of 1939, though considerably weaker than Roosevelt's original administrative reform proposal, was an important accomplishment that not only provided authority for the creation of the White House Office and the Executive Office of the president but also enhanced the chief executive's control over bureaucratic agencies. As such, the 1939 act reflects the genesis of the modern presidency, which, to a much greater extent than was previously possible in American politics, could now exercise "extensive autonomous domestic power, through rule-making and implementation, as well as autonomous power in international affairs."[23] But, the "administrative presidency" did not begin with Franklin Roosevelt; indeed, the absence of detailed specifications of presidential powers in Article 2 of the Constitution had provided the opportunity for extensive independent presidential action throughout American history. The institutionalization of the presidency, however, established a formal organizational apparatus by which administrations could short-circuit the constraints imposed by the separation of powers, giving impetus to a significant shift of authority from the Congress and the courts to the executive department.[24]

Roosevelt's assault on the traditional Democratic party, then, was closely connected to the strengthening of administrative power. In essence, he had foisted a program on a reluctant party that eventually contributed to making party politics nearly obsolete. As the presidency came gradually to encompass an elaborate and far-reaching staff, it preempted party leaders in many of their limited, albeit significant, duties—providing a link to interest groups, staffing the executive department, contributing to policy development, and organizing campaign support.[25] Moreover, New Deal administrative reform was directed not to presidential government per se but to an imbedding of progressive principles, considered tantamount to political rights, in a bureaucratic structure that would insulate reform and reformers from electoral change.

The civil service reform carried out by the Roosevelt administration was an important part of the effort to displace partisan politics with executive administration. The original reorganization proposals of 1937 contained provisions to make administration of the civil service more subject to presidential influence and to extend the merit system. The Executive Reorganization Act passed in 1939 was shorn of this controversial feature, but Roosevelt found it possible to accomplish extensive civil service reform along these lines by means of executive order. Although the general purpose of administrative reform was to strengthen the presidency, the extension of the merit system "upward, outward, and downward" cast a New Deal hue over government machinery. As a consequence, merit protection after 1938 was extended over the personnel appointed by the Roosevelt administration during his first term, four-fifths of whom were brought into government outside of regular merit channels.[26] Civil service reform, therefore, did not replace patronage politics with professional administration ("neutral competence"); rather, it transformed the political character of public administration. Whereas previously the emphasis had been on patronage appointments, which nourished the regular party apparatus, the New Deal initiated personnel practices that emphasized the orientation of the executive department for the expansion of programmatic liberalism.[27]

Thus, New Deal administrative reform recast the executive in a way that undercut the importance of, rather than transformed, party politics. Whereas a reconstituted party system would have established stronger linkages between the executive and the legislature, the administrative program of the New Deal sought to unify governmental *policy* and executive *administration*. The president and executive agencies, therefore, would be delegated authority to govern, making unnecessary the constant cooperation of party members in Congress. The attainment of such cooperation was felt to be manifestly impractical by New Dealers, given the structure of the American Constitution and its dedication to the principle, expressed by Madison in *The Federalist Papers*, no. 51, that "ambition must be made to counteract ambition." The task, then, was to strengthen national administrative capacities in order to ameliorate the lack of energy endemic to the American political system. As the *Report of the President's Committee on Administrative Management* (the Brownlow Committee) put it, with the strengthening of the executive, "the national will [would] be expressed not merely in a brief, exultant moment of electoral decision, but in a persistent, determined, competent day-by-day administration of what the Nation has decided to do."[28]

Whereas the courts were the guardians of the rights emphasized in the pre–New Deal constitutional order, political reformers during the 1930s expected the executive to play an analogous role in protecting the rights guaranteed by an economic constitutional order. The task, then, was to develop a professional welfare state, largely insulated from the fluctuations of party politics. That the Roosevelt administration expected party politics to become less important as the welfare state grew is suggested clearly by the instructions given by Joseph Harris, the director of the research staff of the Brownlow Committee, during an initial planning session in May 1936:

> We may assume that the nature of the problems of American economic life are such as not to permit any political party for any length of time to abandon most of the collectivist functions which are now being exercised. This is true even though the details of policy programs may differ and even though the old slogans of opposition to the enlargement of governmental society will survive long after their meaning has been sucked out.[29]

In the final analysis, it can be said that the institutional legacy of the New Deal gave rise to an administrative state that established an uncertain foundation for strong presidential leadership. On the one hand, the rise of *political administration* as the center of government activity during the 1930s established the conditions for presidential government. Roosevelt's extraordinary political leadership was in a sense institutionalized with the 1939 Executive Reorganization Act, for this statute ratified a process whereby public expectations and institutional arrangements established the presidency as the center of government activity. On the other hand, the administrative presidency was conceived with the expectation that it would be an ally of programmatic liberalism. It is thus not surprising that, when this expectation was violated, serious conflict developed between the presidency and bureaucracy. Nor is it surprising that this conflict influenced the development of still another reform of administrative law, intended to insulate reform programs from presidential influence to a greater degree.

PARTICIPATORY DEMOCRACY, THE EXTENSION OF LIBERALISM, AND THE CRISES OF CITIZENSHIP

The Great Society and the Twilight of the Modern Presidency

Lyndon Johnson's aide, Harry McPherson, has noted that LBJ had the misfortune to be a defender of authority and institutions during a period of unprecedented insurgency:

Johnson was a manipulator of men when there was a rejection of power politics; he was a believer in institutions at a time when spontaneity was being celebrated; he was a paternalist when parental authority was being rejected; and he came to political authority during the 1930s when democracy was threatened by facism and communism, making him an unbending anti-communist. To the young, this experience of the 1930s might as well have happened during the Renaissance.[30]

Nevertheless, Johnson's presidency also helped to initiate the assault on prevailing institutions during the 1960s and 1970s. For in seeking to surpass the accomplishments of Franklin Roosevelt and the New Deal, LBJ unwittingly encouraged the rise of an administrative politics that extensively circumscribed the administrative power of the president. The emergence of a new version of programmatic liberalism during the Johnson presidency, inspired by a concern to depart from the New Deal, was the first cause of this fundamental change in the institutional fabric of American politics.

Most significant, the liberalism of the Great Society envisioned moving beyond the New Deal focus on economic security toward a commitment to enhance the "quality of American life." LBJ gave expression to this new philosophy in an address at the University of Michigan on May 22, 1964. In those remarks he boldly set the tone for the Great Society, viewing past reform aspirations only as a point of departure:

> The Great Society rests on abundance and liberty for all. It demands an end of poverty and racial justice, to which we are totally committed in our time. But that is just the beginning.
> The Great Society is a place where every child can find knowledge to enrich his mind and to enlarge his talents. It is a place where leisure is a welcome chance to build and reflect, not a feared cause of boredom and restlessness. It is a place where the city of man serves not only the needs of the body and the demands of commerce but the desire for beauty and hunger for communtiy.[31]

Until the latter part of 1965, this vision was a tangential concern of the Johnson administration, preoccupied as it was by civil rights and welfare policy. As one journalist noted, the initial programs of the Great Society emphasized "codifying the New Deal vision of a good society."[32] This codifying, in turn, entailed expansion of the benefits of the economic constitutional order with such programmatic commitments as medicare and, even more significant, extension of these benefits to black Americans. FDR gave clearest expression to the meaning of the economic bill of rights in his 1944 State of the Union Address, in which he called for "a new basis of security and prosperity [to] be established for all—

regardless of station, race, or creed."[33] But the New Deal offered virtually nothing in the way of a civil rights program, and the initial years of Johnson's presidency were devoted primarily to filling the gap in the New Deal left as the result of inattention to racial problems.[34]

The architects of the Great Society, however, were not content to complete the work of the New Deal. Johnson, himself, as the historian William Leuchtenburg notes, had "gargantuan aspirations," which drove him to "out-Roosevelt Roosevelt."[35] Thus, from the beginning of his presidency, Johnson committed himself to an ambitious program that would leave its mark on history not only in civil rights but in several other areas as well, thus presupposing a significant departure from the New Deal *economic* constitutional order.[36] In an August 1965 memo, White House aide Douglas Cater urged the president to demonstrate that he was "deeply concerned" with the "quality" as well as the "quantity of life in America," by "proclaim[ing] a number of specific noneconomic goals toward which [the president was] striving." Johnson approved of this idea and made it a major part of his 1966 State of the Union Address. In those remarks he declared that the Great Society must be pursued along three roads—economic growth, "justice" for all races, and, finally, "liberation," which would utilize the economic success of the nation to achieve "fulfillment of our lives":

A great people flower not from wealth and power, but from a society which spurs them to the fullness of their genius. That alone is the Great Society. . . . [S]lowly, painfully, on the edge of victory has come the knowledge that shared prosperity is not enough. In the midst of abundance modern man walks oppressed by forces which menace and confine the quality of his life, and which individual abundance alone will not over- come.[37]

In laying out the obligation of the government to ensure "the good life," Johnson proposed that the commitments of programmatic liberalism be extended to such tasks as educational opportunity, urban renewal, environmentalism, and consumer protection.[38] In effect, as presidential aide Bill Moyers noted in a memo of September 1965, this speech set the agenda for reforms that represented a conscious "turning away from considerations of quantity (except for the most poverty ridden one-fifth of the nation)" to those that aspired to advance the human condition well beyond the dominant concerns of the New Deal.[39]

Thus the presidency of Lyndon Johnson and the development of a program dedicated to forming a Great Society were significant factors in giving effect to ambitious reform aspirations during the 1960s. The efforts of the Johnson administration to advance not only the New Deal goal of economic security but also the aim of quality of American life necessarily required major changes in American political institutions. To be sure, the devastation of LBJ's presidency brought on by the national reaction to urban riots and the Vietnam War sharpened and focused reformers' criticisms of the American political system. But the foundation for the insurgency that was to challenge the modern presidency and the regular party apparatus was laid by long-developing institutional changes that came to a head during the Johnson administration. In fact, the party reforms initiated by the McGovern-Fraser Commission were the culmination of long-term, systemic developments that began during the 1930s. The national reform fostered by the New Deal shifted the focus of power away from the traditional party apparatus as well as from the more decentralizing institutions—Congress and the state governments. What emerged as a result was a politics of administration that depended primarily upon a revamped presidency for coherence and energy. The more the emergent "presidential branch of government" preempted the party organization in its limited but significant tasks, the less vital and vigilant that organization became. This trend was greatly accelerated during the creation of the Great Society and ultimately led to the creation of a fully developed political and policy network outside the regular political process. It is ironic that, by contributing so much to this development, Lyndon Johnson helped construct the road that eventually enabled insurgents to challenge his presidency successfully.

In the development of domestic policy, especially, the Johnson administration made a significant push to preempt traditional political channels. One of the most significant innovations of the Johnson presidency was the creation of several "outside" task forces, under the auspices of the White House Office and the Bureau of the Budget, intended to establish the basic blueprint of the Great Society. These working groups were made up of leading academics throughout the country who prepared reports in all areas of public policy, including government organization, environmental quality, and urban planning. Several specific proposals that came out of these meetings became public policy, forming the heart of the Great Society program. Perhaps more important, however, was the revolutionary character of the process itself. By establishing a policy process under the supervision of the presidency that was free of traditional institutional restraints, the task-force approach was able to break through what the architects of the Great Society considered the timidity and conservatism of the old system.

New Deal reforms, as noted, began to develop a policy process outside of traditional bureaucratic and partisan channels. Created during the Roosevelt presidency were the White House Office and the Executive Office of the President, which reduced the influence of party leaders and cabinet members on the development of public policy.[40] But the use the Johnson administration made of the task forces illustrated its desire to go much further than the New Deal had gone in developing a policy network that was insulated from regular political processes. The Johnson administration took great care to protect the work of these organizations from political pressures, even keeping the task-force procedure secret. Moreover, participants in this process were told to pay no attention to any "political" considerations; they were not to worry about whether their recommendations would be accountable to Congress and the party leaders.[41] As noted by James Gaither, who, as an assistant to LBJ's principal domestic policy adviser, Joseph Califano, was extensively involved in the task force effort:

> After a while, particularly after you've had a party in power for a long time, you've seen most of the ideas that the government can generate; and you really do have to go outside to try and get new ideas and new approaches and people who are not so wedded to the particular approaches you've taken over the last few years. . . . I would have to say that I regard the change [in legislative program development] as one of the most significant institutional changes of the Presidency. . . . I think it reflected in part the President's experience in the Congress as well as the Executive branch and his belief that the traditional processes were not producing the kind of innovative and imaginative new approaches that were necessary to deal with the very significant problems facing the country.[42]

Eventually, the efforts being made to circumvent traditional political channels by the Johnson administration also became prominent in staffing and campaigns, laying the foundation for the disintegration of parties that became so visible after the 1968 Democratic Convention in Chicago. As the *Wall Street Journal* reported in late 1967, these actions greatly "accelerated the breakdown of state and local Democratic machinery," placing organizations "in acute distress in nearly every large state."[43]

By the end of the 1960s, then, the stage was set for the final triumph of progressive reform over the regular party machinery. The events that took place at the 1968 Democratic Convention and the party reforms that followed in the wake of those events were the result of long-standing efforts to free the presidency from traditional partisan influences. In this respect, the expansion of presidential primaries and other changes in nomination politics initiated by the McGovern-Fraser Commission were a logical extension of the modern presidency. The fact that the "revolution" in party rules that took place during the 1970s was accomplished so "quietly" is evidence in itself that the party system had begun to falter by the end of the Johnson era. As David Truman has noted, the McGovern-Fraser reforms certainly could not have been carried out over the opposition of an alert and vigorous party leadership.[44]

As many chapters in this volume reveal, however, the reforms of the late 1960s and 1970s collectively brought about a significant departure from the institutional legacy of the New Deal and Great Society. Consistent with the tradition of modern liberalism, the reforms of the late 1960s and 1970s were associated with efforts to enhance administrative capacities as a means of expanding the programmatic responsibilities of the national government. Yet, unlike the reform pattern of the New Deal and Great Society, the liberalism of this later period, informed by the disappointments of the Johnson and Nixon administrations, was greatly suspicious of, if not hostile to, presidential power. We have noted that the modern presidency was conceived with the view that it would be an ally of programmatic reform. When this supposition was seemingly violated by the Vietnam War and subsequent developments, reformers set out to protect liberal programs from unfriendly executive administration. Thus, the recent surge of liberal reform resulted not only in the McGovern-Fraser reforms, which administered further damage to the traditional party apparatus, but also in a plethora of laws and administrative mechanisms that imbedded liberal programs in an institutional network designed to be independent of the president's influence. The new institutional coalition that displaced the modern presidency as the steward of public welfare—composed of public-interest groups, bureaucratic agencies, the courts, and congressional subcommittees—further insulated liberal programs and program advocates from the traditional operations of American politics. The legacy of the most recent variant of liberal reform, therefore, resulted not in institutional disintegration but in the formation of an "institutional partnership" designed to make public administration as enlightened as the New Deal was supposed to have been.[45]

This effort to enhance the programmatic commitment of the national government was necessarily linked to foreign policy. The modern presidency was created primarily to strengthen the national resolve in terms of progressive domestic programs, but the institutional legacy of the New Deal and Great Society also had the effect of reinforcing the chief executive's foreign policy role—one that was made potentially very strong by the Constitution. A strong executive in foreign affairs during World War II was one thing; but the continued expansion of executive discretion during the postwar years created a concern, especially after the national trauma of Vietnam, to restrain presidential power. The New Deal historian Arthur Schlesinger, long an advocate of the modern presidency, warned in his influential 1973 volume, *The Imperial Presidency*, that the Watergate scandal of the Nixon administration was symptomatic of an underlying constitutional crisis: It revealed that "the imperial presidency, created by wars abroad, was making a bold bid for power at home."[46] The Nixon presidency demonstrated all too clearly that a chief executive capable of pursuing a vigorous foreign policy threatened to undo domestic reform. During the Johnson years this threat amounted to the severe budgetary constraints confronted by his administration as a result of the war effort.[47] During the Nixon administration, however, especially in the second term, the accrued responsibilities of the modern presidency began to pose a more direct challenge to programmatic liberalism.

Thus, the protection of programmatic liberalism—and the hope of extending it further—depended upon imposing strong restraints on the executive's initiative in foreign policy. The legislation passed during the 1970s designed to accomplish this task, such as the War Powers Resolution of 1973, should be viewed only in part as an attempt to revive Congress's constitutional prerogatives; just as surely, such measures were intended to facilitate an ambitious expansion of welfare and regulatory programs.[48] Similarly, the passage of the Budget Control Act of 1974, which was designed to give Congress control over the executive budget, was intended to protect social reform from the sort of fiscal assault on social welfare programs that Nixon sought to carry out after his 1972 reelection.

It is important to realize, however, that the reform assault on the modern presidency was not simply a pragmatic adjustment of institutional arrangements meant to ensure a more strident and consistent commitment to programmatic liberalism. In fact, the restraints imposed on presidential power during the late 1960s and 1970s reflected a strong suspicion of any administrative power not open to public participation. In important respects, such suspicion was a logical outgrowth of the reform vision of the Great Society. Lyndon Johnson was a presidentialist: The thrust of his institutional approach was to strengthen the managerial tools of the presidency with a view to enhancing the programmatic vision and energy of executive agencies. Yet the vision of the Great Society presupposed a "hunger for community" that suggested the limits of "presidential government." Implicit in the philosophy of liberalism that emerged during the 1960s was the view that the problems afflicting the well-to-do and the poor could not be solved by centralized administration and federal largesse alone, but required a more creative intervention of the state that would address the underlying causes of social and political discontent: alienation, powerlessness, and the decline of community. It is not surprising, therefore, that one of the outside task forces established by the Johnson presidency to identify and seek solutions to social problems recommended that community action be made an integral part of the war on poverty. In pursuance of this proposal, the Community Action Program, governed by federal guidelines requiring "maximum

feasible participation of residents of the areas and the groups served,"
were established to administer anti-poverty policy.[49]

Such programs actually played a limited part in the Johnson administration, which in an unprecedented fashion relied on presidential politics
and governance. Yet the Community Action Program was an important
and revealing prelude to the emergence of participatory democracy as
a leading principle of the reformers who gained influence with the
demise of the modern presidency. First, the concern to involve the
"community" in the decisionmaking process that surfaced during the
Great Society suggested how an emphasis on the "quality of life" in
American society was potentially in tension with the centralization of
authority required by an extensive welfare state. Second, these programs
reveal the uneasy alliance of expertise and romanticism that characterized
reform institutions of the post–New Deal era. It is important to remember,
as Samuel Beer points out, that "the antipoverty program was not shaped
by the demands of pressure groups of the poor—there were none—but
by deliberations of government task forces acting largely on the research-
based theories of two sociologists, Professor Lloyd Ohlin and Richard
A. Cloward of the Columbia School of Social Work."[50] At least in part,
then, the communal concerns of liberal reformers were closely connected
to administrative invention.

Yet this administrative innovation was an attempt to respond to real
problems that could not readily be addressed by executive administration.
And the attempt to involve citizens, including the poor, in federal
programs was accomplished in a few cases, thereby contributing to the
success of the projects involved. For example, Head Start, which was
created as part of the Community Action Program, has employed
considerable and effective efforts to involve the parents of participating
children in the day-to-day activities of centers, thereby, according to
Peter Skerry, helping it establish a "tangible presence to ordinary citizens,"
a quality lacking in many federal programs.[51] Thus, although the efforts
to involve those affected in the shaping of federal programs were rarely
a response to public demands and have not involved a large number
of citizens in the actual running of federal programs, a genuine commitment emerged in the late 1960s to a norm of participation that
transcended concerns to check the abuses of presidential power. As a
result, the assault on the prerogatives of the modern presidency was
associated with institutional changes that expanded the national government's administrative power but tied the use of such power to
procedural safeguards designed to reconcile the administrative state and
participatory democracy.

Public Participation and the Reform
of Administrative Politics

The effort to enhance the representative character of the administrative state was most closely associated with the expansion of regulatory programs during the 1970s. The most significant of these programs were ambitious undertakings launched in the area of "social" regulation, leading to the creation of new administrative agencies and the redirection of certain existing ones to address issues such as environmentalism, consumer protection, health, and safety.[52] In part, these new developments constituted a change in the political economy that required unprecedented centralization of the national government's administrative power. Businesses found the new social regulation especially disturbing, because it empowered executive agencies to intrude into broad problem areas with detailed prescriptions for the manufacture and sale of products. As Bernard Falk of the National Electrical Manufacturers' Association noted about the expansion of the government's regulatory role in the 1970s, "In the past going back ten or fifteen years, you didn't have a consumer movement. The manufacturer controlled the make-up of his own product, and Washington could be ignored. Now we all have a new partner, the federal government."[53]

Yet, paradoxically, this government intrusion went hand in hand with changes in administrative law that reflected strong suspicion of administrative power. Hence the institutional initiatives that were linked with the social reforms of the 1970s were motivated by concerns to recast the concept of citizenship in American politics in conformity with the emergence of the administrative state.

As noted in Chapter 2, hostility to administrative power has a long tradition in the United States. In many respects, this tradition reflects the strong underlying tension between democracy and bureaucratic organization. Yet the problem of sustaining popular confidence in administrative officials has been especially difficult in the United States. Tocqueville discerned an ineluctable tendency for centralization of authority in modern democratic societies, but he noted an uncommon resistance to such a trend in the American political system. An important element of this resistance to encroachments by the central government in the American case was the extraordinary commitment to "local freedom," which created an inhospitable environment for administrative centralization. This commitment to "provincial liberties" in the United States was fortunate, according to Tocqueville, for the vitality of local institutions and administrative decentralization in American democracy fostered civic virtue, which restrained a tendency in commercial republics for individuals to become part of "a common mass."[54]

Although the New Deal eroded the American "bias" against the national government's supervision of society, the deeply ingrained distrust of administrative power continued to be a powerful influence on political life in the United States. This distrust was fueled by the fact that the expansion of administrative capacities and responsibilities in American politics after the 1930s came at the expense of the more decentralizing institutions, such as Congress, political parties, and local government, which traditionally were the primary agents of popular rule. Thus, as Barry Karl has noted, the transfer of the locus of power to the federal government and the concomitant delegation of authority to bureaucratic agencies "have threatened our sense of ourselves as citizens."[55]

The reforms of the 1960s and 1970s ostensibly sought to restore this sense of ourselves. These changes reflected the view that the New Deal, although it brought certain valued reforms, had devolved into an impersonal, bureaucratic, centralized form of governance that was dehumanizing American society.[56] Moreover, reformers during the late 1960s and 1970s believed that the procedures by which decisions were made in the administrative state were dominated by large business interests that were inattentive to public values; the prominent social problems that dominated the political agenda of the 1970s, such as the despoliation of the environment and the manipulation of consumers, were depicted by reformers as by-products of the capture of the public sector by corporate interests.

The apparent tension between the administrative state and democratic citizenship created a real dilemma within the American political system. On the one hand, as Karl writes, "local government and community control remain at the heart of our most intuitive conceptions of American democracy, even though they may also represent bastions of political corruption and locally condoned injustice."[57] On the other hand, since the New Deal, Americans had come to accept as just and inevitable the development of a strong national state, deemed necessary to protect freedom from foreign threats, limit the power of corporations, and guarantee equal protection of the law.

The reformers of the late 1960s and 1970s were not unmindful of this dilemma, and it is misleading to view them as simply hostile to administrative power. There was a strong element of this sort of hostility evident in the politics of the New Left that played an important role in the civil rights and anti–Vietnam War movements; moreover, the citizen advocacy groups of these movements became a model for the reformers who influenced policy on a whole range of issues throughout the late 1960s and 1970s—especially those reformers who worked effectively to increase the national government's responsibility to consumer rights and environmental protection. Yet, whereas the rise of the public-interest movement was influenced by the anti-establishment rhetoric of the New Left, consumer, environmental, and other citizen activists mainly concerned themselves with influencing institutions. As Jeffrey Berry has observed with respect to many of the organizations formed during the late 1960s and 1970s that had as their mission the mobilization of citizen participation in public policy, "leaders of these new groups wanted to transcend 'movement politics' with organizations that could survive beyond periods of intense emotion."[58] In a sense, the consumer and environmental reformers sought to harness the revolutionary vision and fervor of the civil rights and antiwar movements as an agent for change "within the system."

The public-interest advocates who had such a strong influence on public policy during the 1970s were committed to expanding the programmatic responsibilities of the national government and, therefore, were not predisposed toward reducing the prerogatives of executive departments and agencies per se. Consequently, it was their task to create new agencies, such as the Environmental Protection Agency, and to refurbish existing ones, such as the Federal Trade Commission, thereby creating new centers of administrative power that would not become as inefficient and unresponsive as regulatory agencies typically had become in the past. Regulatory bodies, therefore, were not to be delegated responsibility to act for the public but, instead, were to be governed by administrative mechanisms providing liberal provision for public participation, "so that agency lethargy or inefficiency could be checked by interested citizen activity."[59] The achievement of consumer and environmental regulations was deemed worthless so long as the administrative process was not opened up to direct citizen action.

This participatory idea had, and continues to have, a tremendous influence on the administrative state. As Samuel Beer notes, "it would be difficult today to find a program involving regulation or delivery of services in such fields as health, education, welfare, and the environment that does not provide for 'community input.'"[60]

An instructive example of the reformation of executive departments during the 1970s is provided by the metamorphosis of the Federal Trade Commission (FTC). With the passage of the Wheeler-Lea Act in 1938, the FTC was authorized to protect the consumer. Yet, until the 1970s this authority was mainly latent potential; the FTC's amiable relations with business and bureaucratic torpor rendered the commission notoriously inactive. Beginning in 1969, however, the FTC underwent dramatic change that transformed an agency once known to its critics as "the little old lady of Pennsylvania Avenue" into an aggressive consumer advocate. The remarkable aspect of this change is that it was independent of presidential influence. The presidency was not without influence on the FTC in the 1970s; Nixon and Carter, in particular, appointed commissioners who not only upgraded the agency's organization and personnel but also encouraged its pursuit of ambitious consumer protection. But the transition at the FTC would have been far less dramatic were it not for a loosely organized yet influential coalition of consumer advocates among Senate and House members, a talented and programmatically ambitious congressional staff, an aggressive core of investigative and advocacy journalists, and an elaborate network of consumer public-interest groups.[61] In the absence of such a coalition, which constantly prodded the FTC and brought episodic but heated public pressure upon it, the agency would probably not have followed the aggressive course that it did.

The efforts of this coalition culminated in the mid-1970s. Particularly important was the passage in 1975 of the Magnuson-Moss Act, which authorized the FTC to engage in industry-wide rulemaking. The FTC in a few cases had issued trade regulation rules prior to Magnuson-Moss; and the 1971 regulation requiring octane ratings to be posted on gasoline pumps led to the first judicial recognition of the FTC's asserted rulemaking authority.[62] Yet Congress's passage of this legislation in 1975 eliminated any lingering doubt about the legitimacy of this authority and, more important, expressed Congress's support for the commission to exercise what amounted to wide-ranging legislative power. With this authority firmly established by congressional action, the FTC became, as one former staff member put it, "the fourth most powerful body in Washington," capable of altering the structure of industry.[63]

This power, however, was accompanied by a number of procedural obligations that, in effect, restricted the administrative discretion given to the FTC. These provisions, characteristic of the legislation passed during the 1970s, required the commission to conform to procedural safeguards such as publicizing proposed rules, stating with particularity the reason for the proposed rule, and allowing interested persons to submit written data, views, and arguments, all of which were to be made public.

As a 1969 American Bar Association report on the FTC put it, the procedural obligations established by the Magnuson-Moss Act were a response to "commissioners' [having] been criticized for making themselves available to those representing respondents or potential respondents on an *ex parte,* off-the-record basis."[64] Accordingly, public procedures were crafted to allay the possibility of the agency's "capture" by the targets of its activities, as well as to facilitate the participation of public-interest groups in the rulemaking process.

The goal of enhancing the participation of public-interest advocates was addressed specifically in Magnuson-Moss with the establishment of an "intervenor funding program." This program provided funds to facilitate the participation of individuals who demonstrated

> 1) . . . [that] they represent an interest that would not otherwise be adequately represented in the preceding for which assistance is sought;
> 2) . . . that representation of this interest is necessary for a fair resolution of the proceeding;
> 3) . . . that the persons seeking funding would be unable to participate in the proceeding without it.[65]

In practice, these funds overwhelmingly went to public-interest groups supportive of the ambitious pro-consumer policies that were increasingly pursued by the FTC after the enactment of Magnuson-Moss. The list of grants made under the public intervenor program read very much like an honor role of staunch consumer advocates, including the Americans for Democratic Action (a group that received $177,000 in grants to participate in five separate rulemaking proceedings), Action for Children's Television (which received $84,614 to participate in a children's advertisement proceeding), and the Consumers Union (which received $132,257 to participate in four separate rulemaking proceedings).[66]

Because the Federal Trade Commission was created during the progressive era as an independent regulatory commission, the judiciary was not the critical point of access to public participation in rulemaking procedures that it was at many other agencies charged with enhancing the quality of American life.[67] Yet, as noted in Chapter 7, many other agencies, particularly those created at the height of the "participatory revolution," were subjected to extensive judicial oversight, which played a significant part in expanding the regulatory activities in the areas of environmentalism as well as public health and safety. The alliance between citizen action and the judiciary is a rather strange one, inasmuch as the courts are organized within the American constitutional framework to be extensively independent of the public's views. The New Deal, however, redefined the meaning of the American constitutional order, paving the way for the judiciary to become an ally for "programmatic rights." During the 1970s, public participation in the administrative process became one of those central rights. In particular, lawsuits in the 1960s and early 1970s helped to establish the standing of citizen groups, which were then able to sue federal agencies for law enforcement. Moreover, many statutes, especially environmental laws, lent Congress's support to this development by granting automatic standing to sue and by establishing liberal provisions for class actions. As a result, the lawsuit, once considered the province of the privileged, became the principal tool during the 1970s for opening up the administrative process.[68]

Citizen Action and the Crisis of the Liberal Order

Although the consumer and environmental movements did gain substantial influence on the policy process by building elaborate organizational networks and making effective use of the media, this influence was never really solidified into an enduring political coalition. The emphasis of public-interest groups on single-issue advocacy and use of the media was characteristic of what James Q. Wilson refers to as "entrepreneurial politics"; in other words, consumer and environmental policy was dominated by a small number of Washington-based activists, who served as "vicarious representatives" of diffuse and poorly organized interests.[69] In a sense, this arrangement was necessary, for environmental, consumer, and health laws and regulations conferred general benefits on the public at a cost to small, albeit well-organized, segments of society. As the incentive to organize is relatively weak for beneficiaries but strong for opponents of such policies, it is perhaps necessary for public-interest advocates to position themselves in the regulatory process as representatives of the public interest. This stance puts environmental and consumer activists in a precarious position, however, because as defenders of general rather than specific concerns they are often without strong political allies.

The public-interest movement, then, while capable of eliciting popular support by dramatizing corporate abuse and defending unassailable values such as clean air and consumer rights, was, in fact, built upon a fragile institutional foundation. This institutional structure was well suited to the harnessing of symbolic political campaigns into regulatory programs, yet it was incapable of establishing deeply rooted political affiliations among the American public. In this sense, as Michael Pertschuk notes, public-interest advocacy was less a fundamental departure from the New Deal than a decrepit version of liberalism, which was all too tenuously linked with the American public:

> It might be said that we [public-interest advocates] represented the late New Deal liberal tradition. . . . We were disproportionately Ivy Leaguers, do-gooders, knee-jerk liberals, occupied with alleviating the hardships of others, fueled by faith in the capacity of government to represent the people against "private greed," so long as the government was peopled or stimulated by us. We defended ourselves against charges of elitism with the strong evidence that the principles we stood for and the causes we enlisted in enjoyed popular, if sometimes passive support. But if we were "for the people," for the most part we were not comfortably "of the people."[70]

This aspect of the public-interest movement was reinforced by its emphasis on administrative politics. The push for social regulation was motivated by the view that the bureaucracy created by the New Deal was unrepresentative. Yet, in the end, the advent of social regulation did not challenge the New Deal emphasis on public administration; nor did it lead to a fundamental reconsideration of the progressive tradition in American twentieth-century politics that lead to the displacement of the regular political process by executive administration. Rather, the public-interest movement embraced administrative politics while seeking to make it more accessible to direct political action. It is not surprising, therefore, that the culmination of liberalism was associated not with the renewal of party politics but with the rise of public-interest groups tailored to facilitate the direct participation of issue activists in the administrative process. As Richard Ayers, senior attorney for the National Resources Defense Council (NRDC), noted with respect to the creation of this environmental group:

> The motivating or animating idea of the NRDC was the realization that in the twentieth century and especially since the New Deal the executive branch is the most powerful of the three and the interests of the public get lost for lack of expertise and knowledge of the administrative process. In the past environmental or other citizen groups won victories in the legislative branch only to lose in the executive branch. It is clear that the administrative process is where the action is. . . . It is interesting that Labor which clearly challenged the political-economic establishment never learned how important the administrative arena was. . . . They haven't got, for all their legal expertise, an organization like the NRDC. They are involved in Congress and party politics which matter less and less.[71]

The institutional reforms of the 1960s and 1970s entailed a continuation not only of the New Deal emphasis on the executive branch but also of the recruitment of courts into administrative activity and the design of legislation to foster rigorous regulatory enforcement. As Dodd notes in Chapter 4, the institutional reforms in the Congress during the 1970s that devolved policy responsibility to subcommittees and increased the number of congressional support staff members were compatible with the attention being paid by legislators to policy specialization, which increased congressional oversight of the administrative state while making Congress more administrative in its structure and activities. Similarly, the judiciary's decreasing reliance on constitutional decisions in its rulings affecting the political economy and its emphasis on interpreting statutes to determine the responsibilities of executive agencies is symptomatic of its post–New Deal role as "managing partner of the administrative state."[72]

Thus, although the reformers of the 1960s and 1970s rejected as undemocratic the New Deal institutional forms which emphasized the president as the primary instrument of progressive government, they devolved public authority to a less visible institutional coalition of bureaucratic agencies, courts, congressional subcommittees, and public interest groups, thus defying meaningful public discourse and broad-based coalitions. Consequently, as Hugh Heclo has pointed out, with the most recent liberal innovations, American society has further "politicized itself" and at the same time "depoliticized government leadership."[73]

In important respects the roots of this problem can be attributed to the origins of programmatic liberalism. From its inception during the 1930s, modern liberalism was defined as a "second bill of rights" and, as such, was considered worthy of protection from the regular political process, party politics, and the vagaries of public opinion. Consequently, as noted, New Deal administrative reform was dedicated only in part to strengthening the presidency. Its more basic aim, in fact, was to establish a polity dedicated to programmatic rights that both presupposed a fundamental reconsideration of the purposes of American politics and laid the foundation for an administrative constitution, thereby giving institutional effect to this reformulated social contract.[74] The reformers of the 1960s and 1970s extended the institutional basis of the administrative state and greatly expanded the scope of programmatic rights. Thus, the economic constitutional order of the New Deal, as so clearly revealed in Chapter 7, was redefined to include "nondiscrimination rights," "collective rights" (associated with consumer and environmental protection), and "procedural rights." The focus of programmatic liberalism on rights facilitated acceptance of reform but, in the end, eroded the fabric of republican government. Just as the New Deal's focus on "rights" established a tenuous foundation for the steward of the economic constitutional order—the modern presidency—so the public-interest movement's commitment to extending rights circumscribed the participatory revolution of the late 1960s and 1970s. Consequently, the benefits of "procedural rights," designed to enhance the representation of the public in administrative politics, were limited to a rather small circle of program advocates.

The reforms of the late 1960s and 1970s, then, should perhaps be viewed as a natural extension of the philosophy of programmatic liberalism. That theory of governance required extensive and continuous administration of society; it also entailed an expansive understanding of rights, characterized by a relentless identification of new problems and the search for methods by which those problems might be solved. Although Roosevelt's commitment to "rational" planning was limited, he accepted and gave force to a new form of liberalism based on the understanding that the traditional emphasis in American politics on individual self-reliance was inadequate. As he noted during his Commonwealth Club address, in relation to the social contract established by the Declaration, "The task of statesmanship has always been the redefinition of these rights in terms of a changing and growing social order. New conditions impose new requirements upon government and those who conduct Government."[75]

Beginning with the Great Society, however, this task of "circumspect but intrepid social progress," as the Progressive reformer Herbert Croly put it, underwent an important change that deepened the administrative character of modern liberal politics. Implicit in the pursuit of "quality-of-life" issues was a rejection of those principles and practices at the core of a commercial republic. Whereas the New Deal emphasis on economic security essentially accepted commercial values as an inherent part of American life, the expressed aims of the Great Society rejected a view of the individual as most essentially defined by acquisitive desires.

The Johnson administration's indictment of material self-interest was for the most part restrained; for all his commitment to reform, Lyndon Johnson was a cautious leader. But such restraint was less evident in the rhetoric and political actions of citizen activists, who expressed a far less compromising commitment to addressing problems of the "spirit rather than the flesh." Although Roosevelt and Johnson sought to establish greater public direction over the economy, and in doing so fundamentally altered the decisionmaking process of the national government, they essentially sought to shore up rather than challenge the profit system.[76] In the view of the more ardent public-interest activists, however, the abuses of the market economy were sufficiently damaging and pervasive to justify a direct challenge to the basic principles and achievements of advanced capitalist societies. As Ralph Nader wrote in 1971:

This year the gross national product of the United States will exceed one trillion dollars, while the economy will fail to meet a great many urgent human needs. . . . Indeed, the quality of life is deteriorating in so many ways that the traditional statistical measurements of the "standard of living" according to personal income, housing, ownership of cars and appliances, etc., have come to sound increasingly phony.[77]

The moral basis of post–New Deal liberalism helps to explain its paradoxical relationship to democratic politics. If the frenetic materialism and conspicuous consumption of commercial republics could be attributed merely to the machinations of corporate capitalism, then direct and widespread citizen action might be consistent with the reform ambitions of public-interest advocates. To the degree that relentless materialism was deeply imbedded in the American way of life, however, "citizen" advocacy was in tension with a commitment to democratic politics. Widespread support could readily be obtained for many of the specific goals of social regulation, yet the principles underlying these specific programs were largely unacceptable in the context of American politics and, when unchecked, were capable of creating a strong backlash against the consumer and environmental movements. To be sure, these movements were not anticapitalist: There was no vision that conveyed an urgency to eliminate private property or to redistribute wealth. In fact, the advocates of social regulation defended values, such as clean air and product safety, that cut across traditional class conflicts, thus largely explaining their success in achieving broad, if not deeply rooted, support among the American people. Yet the emphasis on "quality-of-life" issues, the warning about resource limitations, and the criticism of consumer preference that characterize much public-interest advocacy collectively represent an indirect rejection of the foundation of a society dedicated to the pursuit of material satisfaction.

Thus, in seeking to depart from the New Deal's emphasis on economic security, contemporary social reformers were alienated from the values and institutions that earlier progressives had accepted as an inherent part of American life. It is not surprising, then, that the reformers of the 1960s and 1970s focused on administrative and legal channels that were far removed from the more democratic institutions in American politics. This institutional strategy was linked in part to the vision of liberal reform as an extension of rights, thus warranting protection from the regular political process. The focus on programmatic rights was reinforced, however, when the vision of liberalism was extended to "quality-of-life" issues. Administrative tribunals and the courts were certainly more appropriate forums than the strictly political institutions for the efforts being made to remake so substantially the character of the American political system. It is ironic and tragic that the resulting triumph of administrative politics, designed to strengthen citizen action, signified instead the deterioration of representative democracy.

CONCLUSION: THE LEGACY OF LIBERAL REFORM AND THE RISE OF THE NEW RIGHT

The development of programmatic rights during the New Deal promoted the expansion of national administrative authority at the expense of Congress, state governments, and especially political parties. The reforms of the 1960s and 1970s reinforced this development, deepening the commitment to programmatic rights. The expansion of the "administrative constitution" during this latter period limited the administrative power of the president, but involved Congress, the courts, and public-interest groups in the details of administration. In the final analysis, the institutional developments of the 1960s and 1970s not only fixed the business of government more on administration but also accelerated the decline of political parties. Thus, the rise of administrative politics created the conditions for the end of parties unless, or until, an anti-administration party would spring up. It is primarily in this capacity that the Republican party has provided loyal opposition to Democratic liberalism.

Yet the Republican party has provided an uncertain challenge to the institutional legacy of liberal reform. Since the New Deal and the extension of liberalism during the 1960s and 1970s greatly expanded the role of national administration, it is not surprising that the challenge to liberal reform in American politics was associated with the development of a conservative "administrative presidency." The advent of a conservative administrative presidency not only retarded the revival of party politics but also deepened the hostility generated by the Johnson administration to the exercise of presidential power.

Until the 1960s, opponents of programmatic liberalism had generally been opposed to the modern presidency, which had served as a fulcrum of progressive government. Nevertheless, by the end of the Johnson administration, it had become clear that a strong conservative movement would need to coalesce in order to counteract the developments instituted in American politics by the New Deal and the Great Society. Once opponents of liberal public policy, primarily based in the Republican party, recognized that the promotion of conservative politics would require an activist program of retrenchment, they looked to the possibility that the modern presidency could be characterized as a double-edged sword, which would cut in a conservative as well as a liberal direction.

Beginning with the Nixon presidency, a concerted effort was made to use the presidency as a lever of fundamental policy change in a rightward direction. Although Nixon emphasized a legislative rather than a managerial strategy to achieve policy goals during the first two years of his presidency, he later attempted to carry out his policies by executive administration. As Richard Nathan has noted, "Nixon came to the conclusion sometime in 1971 that in many areas of government, particularly domestic affairs, *operations is policy.* Many day-to-day management tasks for domestic programs—for example, regulation writing, grant approval, and budget apportionment—are substantive and therefore involve policy" (Nathan's emphasis).[78]

Nixon was responding to, and seeking to take advantage of, the administrative constitution spawned by liberal reform. His administrative presidency was not new, of course; indeed, it was reminiscent of a tendency that began with the creation of the modern presidency. The complete autonomy of the Committee to Reelect the President (CREEP) from the regular Republican organization was the final stage of an institutional development in which the White House continually preempted the political responsibilities of the national party committee. And the administrative reform program pursued after Nixon's reelection in 1972, in which executive authority was concentrated in the hands of White House operatives and four cabinet "supersecretaries," was the culmination of a long-standing tradition in the modern presidency of reconstructing the executive department as a more formidable and independent instrument of governance.[79] Ironically, the pursuit of policy goals with administrative capacities that were created for the most part by Democratic reform programs was considered especially suitable by a "minority" Republican president facing a hostile Congress and bureaucracy intent upon preserving those programs. Hence Nixon surpassed previous modern presidents in viewing the party system as an unwanted source of autonomous power and an obstacle to effective governance.

In many respects, however, the conservative administrative presidency was ill-conceived. The centralization of responsibility within the presidency was carried out to build a more liberal America. As a program of the Democratic party, the modern presidency depended upon a broad agreement among the Congress, the bureaucracy, and eventually the courts to expand programmatic rights; a formidable administrative presidency therefore depended upon a consensus committed to delegating powers to the executive department. As noted, by the time Lyndon Johnson left the White House, the political environment for presidents was becoming increasingly intractable. Nixon's presidency had the effect of strengthening the opposition to unilateral use of presidential power while further attenuating the bonds that linked presidents to the party system. The evolution of the modern presidency had left it in complete political isolation. This isolation continued during the Ford and Carter years—to such an extent that, by the end of the 1970s, statesmen and scholars were lamenting the demise of both the presidency and the party system.

It remains to be seen whether the reaction to this situation during the 1980s has restored presidential authority and ensured an enduring departure from programmatic liberalism. In the past, institutional and policy changes of the magnitude envisioned by the Reagan Administration have occurred periodically in American history as part of critical partisan realignments, characterized by massive shifts in party support and by revitalization of democratic politics. By the late 1970s, however, many observers believed that American government was stricken by a "dealignment," that is, by a disintegration rather than a renewal of party politics.[80] In a sense, the merging of politics and administration, and the concomitant decline of party, during the 1930s had set the stage for such a development. The reforms of the 1960s and 1970s extended and radicalized the institutional developments of the New Deal, hastening the decline of the party and further cementing the "administrative constitution" into the political system. Thus, although there has been much speculation that the 1980 and 1984 elections brought about another partisan realignment in American politics, working against such a possibility is the emergence of benign administration as the principal tool of governance since the 1930s. In the long-run, the prospects for such a realignment may depend not only on the success of the Reagan presidency, but also upon the revival of political parties, which in the past have been viewed as critical agents of reform, providing a focal point for the usually separated branches of the Constitution to combine and "find their vital contact with the people."[81]

There is some evidence that a revitalization of party politics is under way in the United States. In fact, the erosion of old-style partisan politics has opened up the possibility for the development of a more national and issue-oriented party system. The Republican party, in particular, has developed a strong organizational apparatus; indeed, its strength at the national level is unprecedented in American politics.[82] The evolution of the Republican party as a force against administration may complete the development of a "New American Party System." The nomination and election of Ronald Reagan, a far more ideological conservative than Richard Nixon, has galvanized the commitment of the GOP to such programs as "regulatory relief" and "new federalism," which have severely challenged the institutional legacy of liberal reform. These developments have contributed greatly to the revitalization of partisan conflict. If such a trend continues, the circumvention of the regular political process by administrative action could very well be displaced by the sort of full-scale debate about political questions usually associated with major political realignments in American history.

It is also significant that Ronald Reagan broke with the tradition of the modern presidency and identified closely with his party. Indeed, the president worked very hard at strengthening the organization and popular support of the GOP, surprising even his own political director with his "total readiness" to shoulder such partisan responsibilities as making numerous fundraising appearances for the GOP and its candidates.[83] After the 1984 election, Senator Robert Dole, who witnessed first-hand and participated in a variety of attempts at challenging the programmatic liberal tradition, noted that "Nixon thought he could build a conservative majority that was above party, and Ford tried to strengthen the traditional Republican party. Reagan is trying to expand the Republican party to include a majority."[84]

Yet the Democratic party's recapture of the Senate in 1986 and the devastation brought by the Iran-contra arms scandal soon thereafter has derailed, perhaps permanently, the resurgence of the Republican party that once was perceived by many as signaling a new political era in American politics. To be sure, the results of the 1986 elections and the Iran-contra affair can be explained in part by the "natural" rhythms of the electoral cycle and the "localized," if massive, mismanagement of policy, neither of which will necessarily thwart the future surge of the Republican party in American politics.[85] But these events are likely to have a profound and enduring influence, for they reflect the fact that the Reagan administration has been insufficiently attentive to the problematical political and constitutional effects of liberal reform.

The Reagan administration presents itself as committed to renewing the principles of the framers and restoring the vitality of limited constitutional government. Yet there are many supporters of the "New Right" (with whom that administration has frequently expressed common cause) who would prefer not so much to limit as to undertake new uses of the state. Accordingly, the administration has become committed to programmatic innovations in defense and foreign policy that have required the expanding, rather than the rolling back, of the national government's role. Furthermore, the moral imperatives of the modern conservative movement, which President Reagan has identified as that movement's most fundamental calling, are animated by a missionary zeal that seems intent upon abolishing, rather than restoring, the distinction between state and society. The supporters of this movement confuse persuasion with conversion in a way that belies an understanding of the appropriate relationship between the individual and community in a free, secular society. By the same token, the arguments brought to bear by moral conservatives to defend prayer in school suggest a mixing of church and state that would hardly challenge the political and constitutional failings of the administrative state. It may be significant, therefore, and not simply attributable to clumsiness, that conservatives have adapted the language of rights used by liberals (in referring, for example, to "the rights of the unborn") in the abortion dispute.[86]

Thus, Reagan's conservative Republican administration, while promising to bring about a "new federalism" and "regulatory relief," has been stalled in these tasks by the conception that a strong national state is needed to oppose communism and nurture "traditional" values. The Iran-contra scandal, for example, was not simply the result of a president being asleep at his watch. Rather, it was the unfortunate consequence of the Reagan administration's attempt to assume a forceful anti-Communist posture in Central America in the face of a recalcitrant bureaucracy and Congress.

The challenge to liberal reform, then, might end not in a challenge to the administrative state but in a battle for its services. In this regard, the legacy of the Reagan presidency will be an extension of the administrative Constitution brought by the New Deal. The "Reagan Revolution" has extended the support for this regime by demonstrating, or earnestly striving to demonstrate, that collectivism can serve the purposes of those who are opposed to the liberal welfare state. In the wake of this development, neither the current Democrats nor the Republicans respect principles that might provide the foundation for a revival of those political institutions, such as political parties and local governments, that nurture an active and competent citizenry. Rather, the current political debates tend to take place within bureaucratic agencies and courts in such a way that enervates representative democracy.

Such a tendency has been reinforced by practical necessity. The challenge to liberalism has been confined primarily to the presidency, thus encouraging the Reagan administration to pursue much of its program by means of administrative action. Hence the Reagan presidency has frequently eschewed efforts to modify the statutory basis of liberal reform, seeking instead to bring about fundamental policy departures through acts of administrative discretion. This pursuit of programmatic change has involved an attempt to centralize policy responsibility and personnel management in the White House—an attempt that marks the Reagan presidency as the most administratively ambitious one since the advent of the modern presidency. Especially in the area of social regulation, deregulation became the product not of legislative change but of administrative inaction, delay, and repeal. President Reagan's Executive Orders 12291 and 12498, which mandated a comprehensive review of existing and proposed agency regulations, respectively, and centralized that review in the Office of Management and Budget, demonstrated quite clearly the extent to which emphasis was placed on administrative regulatory relief.[87] Thus, the circumvention of the legislative process, existing statutes, and regular bureaucratic channels that came to light during the revelations of the Iran-contra scandal was not so much an aberration as an extreme example of the prevailing pattern of policymaking throughout the Reagan presidency.

The importance of presidential politics and executive administration in giving effect to the "Reagan Revolution" has weakened considerably the prospects for realignment. Although Ronald Reagan associated with his party enthusiasticlaly, he has, in the final analysis, continued and accelerated the decline of party. As Sidney Blumenthal notes, "[Reagan] did not reinvent the Republican party so much as transcend it. His primary political instrument was the conservative movement, which inhabited the party out of convenience."[88] The Reagan administration's devotion to certain conservative ideological tenets led to a reliance on public administration and conservative citizen groups that diminished the possibility that policy would emerge as a shared endeavor between different elements of the party. In this respect, the failure of the American people to heed the president's plea during the 1986 House and Senate campaigns to elect Republican majorities was in part an understandable response to Reagan's inattention to the deliberations necessary to make collective partisan responsibility meaningful.

That inattention does not necessarily point to the absence of fundamental and enduring policy change. The Progressive era, for example, entailed major shifts in public policy that were not directly attributable to a partisan realignment. Moreover, leading characteristics of the political landscape fashioned by liberal reform—the expansion of the nation's regulatory apparatus, the decline of parties, the growth of the media, and the enhancement of ideas and ideology—may increase the prospects of a major policy realignment without fundamental partisan change. Indeed, there were major departures from the New Deal during the 1960s and 1970s in the absence of fundamental partisan change. The reforms of the 1960s and 1970s, however, were the product of widespread legislative and institutional reform. In this sense, the interesting question about the "Reagan Revolution" may not be whether a partisan realignment has occurred but whether the evolution of an administrative constitution has advanced so far that a policy realignment can occur independent of both partisan swings and major legislative change.

A realignment of this sort would represent a remarkable triumph of the administrative presidency. Yet this triumph is not probable: Although forceful and centralized political administration may appear to be a logical and necessary response to the legacy of liberal reform, it is unlikely to nurture the substantial change in public values and institutions required to bring about a fundamental departure in the prevailing patterns of governance. Moreover, many of the reforms of the 1960s and 1970s in the areas of civil rights, consumer protection, environmentalism, and health and safety regulation are supported (as this and other chapters have taken pains to show) by an institutional coalition of courts, bureaucratic agencies, congressional subcommittees and staff, and public-interest groups that has established a formidable barrier between the presidency and public policy. Many of the recast institutional channels that now form the heart of the administrative constitution were created by statutes and cannot be transformed by executive actions alone. Rather, the institutional framework that was the product of the reforms of the 1960s and 1970s represents a form of post–New Deal administrative politics, which is based upon legal requirement rather than presidential and bureaucratic discretion. The limits of the administrative presidency—

even during the term of an incumbent with substantial political gifts and a clear agenda—were demonstrated rather dramatically by the ability of Congress and the courts to resist effectively Reagan's program of regulatory relief.[89]

In part, the failure of the Reagan presidency to bring about a new era of American politics is due to the enduring strength of the legacy of liberal reforms. Although those reforms led to troublesome political and constitutional consequences, they have effectively established liberal programs as rights—and these rights have elicited broad, if sometimes soft, support from the American people. Yet the Reagan presidency's failure also reflects the lack of a serious effort to reconsider the legacy of programmatic liberalism. Such a reconsideration of our inheritance from liberal reform should begin from the assumption that responsible political leadership presupposes a reasonably active and competent citizenry. And this assumption imposes on statesmen above all an obligation to recognize the limits and appropriate use of administrative power.

NOTES

The author thanks Richard Harris, R. Shep Melnick, and Abigail Thernstrom for their helpful comments on an earlier draft of this chapter.

1. Although many scholars have postulated the existence of an *administrative state* in American politics, the meaning of this term is rather obscure in the literature. John Rohr defines the administrative state as a situation signifying the empowering of bureaucratic agencies, staffed by unelected officials, to carry out important government functions. See his *To Run a Constitution: The Legitimacy of the Administrative State*, vol. 11 (Lawrence: University Press of Kansas, 1986), pp. xi and 217, n. 11. But the use of this term in this chapter signifies something broader than the emergence of a professional bureaucracy as an important institution of government. It refers to the development in American politics since the 1930s, whereby executive administration, centered in the presidency and administrative agencies, has become the dominant activity in carrying out the affairs of state. For a detailed discussion of the administrative state and its impact on the American political system, see Richard A. Harris and Sidney M. Milkis, "Programmatic Liberalism, the Administrative State, and the Constitution," paper prepared for delivery at the annual meeting of the American Political Science Association, Washington, D.C. (August 1986).

2. Harry McPherson, *A Political Education* (Boston: Little, Brown, 1972), p. 301.

3. Samuel Beer, "In Search of a New Public Philosophy," in Anthony King, ed., *The New American Political System* (Washington, D.C.: American Enterprise Institute, 1978), p. 26.

4. Anthony King, "The American Polity in the Late 1970's: Building Coalitions in the Sand," in King, ed., *The New American Political System*, pp. 372–373.

5. Samuel P. Huntington, "The Democratic Distemper," in Nathan Glazer and Irving Kristol, eds., *The American Commonwealth—1976* (New York: Basic Books, 1976).

6. Donald L. Horowitz, "Is the Presidency Failing?" *Public Interest*, vol. 88 (Summer 1987), p. 25.

7. Theodore J. Lowi, *The Personal President: Power Invested, Promise Unfulfilled* (Ithaca and London: Cornell University Press, 1985).

8. Huntington, "The Democratic Distemper"; see also his *American Politics: The Promise of Disharmony* (Cambridge, Mass.: Harvard University Press, 1981), pp. 167–220.

9. James MacGregor Burns, *The Lion and the Fox: 1882–1940* (New York: Harcourt, Brace and World, 1956), pp. 375–380.

10. Regarding the reconsideration of liberalism during the 1930s, see Harris and Milkis, "Programmatic Liberalism, the Administrative State, and the Constitution."

11. Franklin D. Roosevelt, *Public Papers and Addresses*, vol. 1 (of 13 vols.) (New York: Random House, 1938–1950), p. 756.

12. Roosevelt, *Public Papers and Addresses*, vol. 1, pp. 751–752.

13. Peri E. Arnold, *Making the Managerial Presidency: Comprehensive Reorganization Planning* (Princeton, N.J.: Princeton University Press, 1986), pp. 3–21.

14. For a discussion of the American party system's relationship to the Constitution and limited government, see James Piereson, "Party Government," *Political Science Reviewer*, vol. 12 (Fall 1982), pp. 27–53; see also James Ceaser, *Presidential Selection: Theory and Development* (Princeton, N.J.: Princeton University Press, 1979).

15. William E. Leuchtenburg, *Franklin D. Roosevelt and the New Deal: 1932–1940* (New York: Harper and Row, 1963), pp. 268–269.

16. For a discussion of presidential efforts to challenge recalcitrant party members in primary campaigns, see Sidney M. Milkis, "Presidents and Party Purges: With Special Emphasis on the Lessons of 1938," in Robert Harmel, ed., *Presidents and Their Parties: Leadership or Neglect?* (New York: Praeger Publishers, 1984).

17. Raymond Clapper, "Roosevelt Tries the Primaries," *Current History*, vol. 49 (October 1938), p. 16.

18. Of the dozen states within which the president acted against entrenched incumbents, he was successful in only two of them—Oregon and New York. Moreover, the purge campaign galvanized nationwide opposition, apparently contributing to the heavy losses that the Democrats sustained in the 1938 general elections.

19. The reference to the "second bill of rights" harks back to Roosevelt's 1944 State of the Union message, in which he gave clear expression to the vision of an "economic constitutional order." In that address, the president proclaimed that the government had the obligation to provide, among other

things, the right to a useful and remunerative job, the right to adequate medical care, the right to a decent home, and the right to a good education. See Roosevelt, *Public Papers and Addresses*, vol. 13, p. 41. See also Chapter 7 of this volume for further discussion of Roosevelt's speech.

20. It is interesting that Roosevelt chose a partisan event to herald the promise of a less partisan future. In his Jackson Day speech of 1940, he pointed to both the limited and declining significance of party politics in the United States. As he put it, "[T]he future lies with those wise political leaders who realize that the public is interested more in government than in politics; that the independent vote in this country has been steadily on the increase, at least for the past generation; that vast numbers of people consider themselves normally adherents of one party and still feel perfectly free to vote for one or more candidates of another party." See Roosevelt, *Public Papers and Addresses*, vol. 9, p. 28.

21. For a more detailed discussion of this point, see Sidney M. Milkis, "Franklin D. Roosevelt and the Transcendence of Partisan Politics," *Political Science Quarterly*, vol. 100 (Fall 1985), pp. 479–504, and "The New Deal, Administrative Reform, and the Transcendence of Partisan Politics," *Administration and Society*, vol. 18 (January 1987), pp. 433–472.

22. It is significant that the two Supreme Court cases that triggered the dispute between Roosevelt and the judiciary were *Humphrey's Executor* v. *U.S.* (295 U.S. 602, 1935) and *A.L.A. Schechter Poultry Corp. et al.* v. *United States* (295 U.S. 553, 1935), both of which imposed constraints on the executive authority of the president. William Leuchtenburg notes that the *Humphrey* decision, which denied Roosevelt's right to remove a commissioner from an independent regulatory agency, is misunderstood as an arbitrary act of retaliation in the face of a personal blow from the Supreme Court. In fact, it was "a rational attempt to enable the presidency to emerge as the central institution to cope with problems of the twentieth century world." See William E. Leuchtenburg, "The Case of the Contentious Commissioner: Humphrey's Executor *vs.* U.S.," in Harold M. Hyman and Leonard W. Levy, eds., *Freedom and Reform* (New York: Harper and Row, 1967), p. 312.

23. Fred I. Greenstein, "Nine Presidents in Search of a Modern Presidency," draft for King, ed., *The New American Political System*, 2nd ed.

24. The term *administrative presidency* comes from Richard Nathan's seminal work on the employment of executive action by modern presidents to pursue policy objectives. See Nathan, *The Administrative Presidency* (New York: John Wiley, 1985), which focuses on the Nixon and Reagan programs of presidential management.

25. The literature of party development has generally ignored the importance of presidential leadership and the evolution of the presidency, but there are important exceptions. See especially Lester Seligman, "The Presidential Office and the President as Party Leader (with a postscript on the Kennedy-Nixon Era)," in Jeff Fischel, ed., *Parties and Elections in an Anti-Party Age* (Bloomington: Indiana University Press, 1978); Harold F. Bass, "The President and the National Party Organization," in Harmel, *Presidents and Their Parties: Leadership or Neglect?*; and Lowi, *The Personal President: Power Invested and Promise Unfulfilled*, chs. 3 and 4.

26. Richard Polenberg, *Reorganizing Roosevelt's Government* (Cambridge, Mass.: Harvard University Press, 1966), pp. 23, 184; Civil Service Commission, "Statement Regarding Executive Order of June 24, 1938, Extending the Merit System," *Papers of the President's Committee on Administrative Management* (New York: Franklin D. Roosevelt Library, 1938).

27. The evolution of Social Security illustrates particularly well the process by which New Deal reforms were crafted through a merging of programmatic liberalism and administrative reform. The Social Security Agency was dominated by program advocates who quietly but effectively imbued the agency with the philosophy of liberalism. The selection and training of personnel were carried out in such a way that clerks, as well as higher-ups, were bound by a strong "client-serving ethic." The success of the Social Security program was largely attributable to its executive leaders' sophisticated circumvention of routine civil service procedures in order to assemble a staff whose members were exceptionally competent and "religiously" dedicated to the cause of reform. See Martha Derthick, *Policymaking for Social Security* (Washington, D.C.: Brookings Institution, 1983), especially pp. 17–37.

28. See the *Report of the President's Committee on Administrative Management* (Washington, D.C.: Government Printing Office, 1937), p. 53. The President's Committee on Administrative Management, headed by Louis Brownlow, played a central role in the planning and politics of executive reorganization from 1936 to 1940. For a full analysis of the background and impact of this committee, see Barry Karl, *Executive Reorganization and Reform in the New Deal* (Cambridge, Mass.: Harvard University Press, 1963).

29. See "Outline for the New York Conference" (April 8, 1936), *Papers of the President's Committee on Administrative Management*.

30. Interview with Harry McPherson (July 30, 1985).

31. *Public Papers of the Presidents*, 1963–1964, Volume 1, 704.

32. Richard A. Rovere, "A Man for this Age Too," *New York Times Magazine* (April 11, 1965).

33. See Roosevelt, *Public Papers and Addresses*, vol. 13, p. 41.

34. FDR did achieve substantial support among blacks by emphasizing the need to help those in economic distress. On the dramatic switch between 1932 and 1936 in black party loyalties from Republican to Democratic, see Nancy Weiss, *Farewell to the Party of Lincoln* (Princeton, N.J.: Princeton University Press, 1983). But according to Horace Busby, who served Johnson as a congressional and presidential aide, coming to terms with the race issue was viewed by the architects of the Great Society as the major challenge in completing the work left undone by Roosevelt: "Johnson essentially saw his role as completing the work the New Deal had to finish, e.g., Medicare, Civil Rights, which the New Deal did not start. . . . I remember being shocked in 1944 by Gunner Myrdal's book, *An American Dilemma*—there was a shock of recognition caused by his exposition of the contradiction between American democratic principles and the status of blacks in the United States. . . . This contradiction was not confronted by New Dealers" (interview with Horace Busby, June 25, 1987).

35. William E. Leuchtenburg, *In the Shadow of FDR: From Harry Truman to Ronald Reagan*, rev. ed. (Ithaca, N.Y.: Cornell University Press, 1983), pp. 142–143.

36. Larry O'Brien, Johnson's chief legislative aide, wrote an interesting report on one of the early strategy sessions that led to the Great Society in a November 1964 memo, in which he expressed surprise and concern about the ambitious program envisioned by the administration. See Larry O'Brien, Memorandum to Henry Wilson, *Henry Wilson Papers*, Box 4 (Austin: Lyndon Baines Johnson Library, November 24, 1964).

37. Douglas Cater, Memorandum to the President, *Office Files of Horace Busby*, Box 51 (Austin: Lyndon Baines Johnson Library, August 3, 1965); *Public Papers of the Presidents*, Volume 1 (1966), p. 6.

38. *Public Papers of the Presidents*, Volume 1 (1966), pp. 6–7.

39. Bill Moyers, Memorandum to the President, *Office Files of Bill Moyers*, Box 11 (Austin: Lyndon Baines Johnson Library, September 21, 1965).

40. See Milkis, "The New Deal, Administrative Reform, and the Transcendence of Partisan Politics," pp. 454–466.

41. William E. Leuchtenburg, "The Genesis of the Great Society," *Reporter* (April 21, 1966), p. 38.

42. James Gaither, *Oral History*, interviewed by Dorothy Pierce (Tape 1: November 19, 1968, p. 24; Tape 4, January 17, 1969, pp. 1–2) (Austin: Lyndon Baines Johnson Library, 1968 and 1970).

43. Alan Otten, "The Incumbents Edge," *Wall Street Journal* (December 28, 1967).

44. See David B. Truman, "Party Reform, Party Atrophy and Constitutional Change," *Political Science Quarterly*, vol. 99 (Winter 1984-1985), p. 639. See also Byron E. Shafer, *Quiet Revolution: The Struggle for the Democratic Party and the Shaping of Post-Reform Politics* (New York: Russell Sage Foundation, 1983).

45. R. Shep Melnick, "The Politics of Partnership," *Public Administration Review*, vol. 45 (November 1985), pp. 653–660.

46. Arthur M. Schlesinger, Jr., *The Imperial Presidency* (New York: Popular Library, 1973), p. 359.

47. To many liberal reformers, of course, the threat posed by the Vietnam War to the Great Society went well beyond the question of budgetary priorities. Leaders of the antiwar movement, including George McGovern, believed that the vision of the Great Society was desecrated by the Johnson administration's record in foreign affairs. Interestingly, the irreparable crack this record was to create in the Democratic party was foretold rather early on by the senator from South Dakota, who insisted in a private conversation with Johnson on March 26, 1965, that the president's "magnificent efforts to stop the injustice against Negroes" that had been "combined with the promise of a great society for all Americans" was an approach that needed to be applied in Asia as well, "even though the practical difficulties of carrying it out [were] great." See the statement of Senator George McGovern to President Johnson—Private Conversation at the White House, *Office Files of Horace Busby*, Box 6 (Austin: Lyndon Baines Johnson Library, 1965).

48. See Chapter 3 in this volume for a detailed discussion of the close connection between domestic reform aspirations during the late 1960s and 1970s and foreign policy issues.

49. Daniel P. Moynihan, *Maximum Feasible Misunderstanding* (New York: Free Press, 1970).

50. Beer, "In Search of a New Public Philosophy," pp. 16–17; see also Moynihan, *Maximum Feasible Misunderstanding*, pp. 61–101.

51. Peter Skerry, "The Charmed Life of Head Start," *Public Interest*, no. 73 (Fall 1983), p. 35.

52. For a discussion of the meaning and political significance of social regulation, see Richard A. Harris and Sidney M. Milkis, *Social Regulation, the Reagan Revolution, and Beyond: A Tale of Two Agencies* (New York: Oxford University Press, forthcoming).

53. Bernard Falk, quoted in Jeffrey M. Berry, *The Interest Group Society* (Boston: Little, Brown, 1984), p. 36.

54. Alexis de Tocqueville, *Democracy in America* (Garden City, N.Y.: Doubleday and Co., 1969), edited by J. P. Mayer, translated by George Lawrence, pp. 87–98.

55. Barry D. Karl, *The Uneasy State* (Chicago: University of Chicago Press, 1983).

56. Beer, "In Search of a New Public Philosophy," p. 27.

57. Karl, *The Uneasy State*, p. 236.

58. Berry, *The Interest Group Society*, p. 28.

59. Ralph Nader, "The Case for Federal Chartering," in Nader, ed., *The Consumer and Corporate Accountability* (New York: Harcourt Brace Jovanovitch, 1973), p. 365.

60. Beer, "In Search of a New Public Philosophy," pp. 27–28.

61. An interesting description of the "entrepreneurial coalition" that gave impetus to the expansion of consumer protection is given by Michael Pertschuk in his account of the "rise and pause" of the consumer movement. See Pertschuk, *Revolt Against Regulation: The Rise and Pause of the Consumer Movement* (Berkeley: University of California Press, 1982), pp. 13–36.

62. *National Petroleum Refiners Association* v. *FTC* (482 F 2d, 672, D.C. Cir., 1973).

63. Personal interview with Terry Latanich (December 17, 1982); Timothy J. Muris, "Statutory Powers," in Kenneth Clarkson and Timothy J. Muris, eds., *The Federal Trade Commission Since 1970: Economic Regulation and Bureaucratic Behavior* (Cambridge: Cambridge University Press, 1981), pp. 14–15.

64. American Bar Association, *Report on the Federal Trade Commission* (1969), p. 3.

65. Hearings, Subcommittee for Consumers, Committee on Commerce, 96th Cong., 1st Sess., "Oversight to Examine the Enforcement and Administrative Authority of the FTC to Regulate Unfair and Deceptive Trade Practices" (September 18, 19, 27, 28; October 4, 5, 10, 1979), p. 168.

66. For a list of the grants made under the FTC public-intervenor program, see ibid., pp. 158–160.

67. As an independent regulatory commission, the FTC was entitled to act as a court of equity in defining and enforcing public values. For example, in a 1972 decision involving alleged illegal trade practices by the company issuing S & H stamps, the Supreme Court ruled that "unfairness" for all intents and purposes meant what the commission said it did (*Federal Trade Commission* v. *Sperry & Hutchinson*, 405 U.S. 233, 1972). Public-interest groups, to be sure, pushed for mechanisms (such as automatic standing to sue) that made litigation a critical element of environmental regulation. The granting of these tools, however, would have required more radical surgery on the organic statute of the FTC than Congress was willing to undertake. The FTC, then, constitutes an interesting blend of principles and institutions crafted during different reform periods. But it has not been as consistently responsive to the reform impulse of the late 1960s and 1970s as have agencies created during the post–New Deal extension of liberalism. See the comparison between the FTC and the EPA in this regard in Harris and Milkis, *Social Regulation and the Reagan Revolution*, chs. 5 and 6.

68. Richard B. Stewart, "The Reformation of American Administrative Law," *Harvard Law Review*, vol. 88 (June 1975), pp. 1669–1813.

69. James Q. Wilson, ed., *The Politics of Regulation* (New York: Basic Books, 1980), pp. 370–371.

70. Pertschuk, *Revolt Against Regulation*, p. 130.

71. Interview with Richard Ayers, conducted by Richard A. Harris and Sidney M. Milkis (June 11, 1986).

72. Jeremy Rabkin, "The Judiciary in the Administrative State," *Public Interest*, vol. 71 (Spring 1983), pp. 62–84.

73. Hugh Heclo, "Issue Networks and the Executive Establishment," in King, ed., *The New American Political System*, p. 124.

74. E. Donald Elliott has suggested that the expansion of administrative power over the past century has created a "constitution of the administrative state" but that this expansion has not been accomplished by formally amending the Constitution. This "quasi-constitutional evolution," as Stewart notes, "is not a mere additive change to the structure of government. Inevitably it has transformed the nature and functions of existing institutions as well." See his "INS v. Chadha: The Administrative Constitution, the Constitution, and the Legislative Veto," *Supreme Court Review* (1983), p. 167.

75. Roosevelt, *Public Papers and Addresses*, vol. 1, p. 753.

76. As Roosevelt wrote in his letter of February 9, 1937, to Felix Frankfurter soon after announcing the Court-packing plan: "The return of prosperity at this moment may blunt our senses but under it all I am very certain that the maintenance of constitutional government in this nation still depends on action— but it is the same old story of those who have property to fail to realize that I am the best friend the profit system ever had, even though I add my denunciation of unconscionable profits." See *Felix Frankfurter Papers*, Microfilm Reel 60 (Washington, D.C.: Library of Congress, Manuscript Department, 1937).

77. Ralph Nader, "A Citizen's Guide to the American Economy," in Nader, ed., *The Consumer and Corporate Accountability*, p. 4. It is important to recognize,

of course, that not all of those active in the consumer movement endorse Nader's ardent criticism of the American political economy. Many consumer advocates, in fact, argue that the moral fervor that drives Ralph Nader and his associates is not particularly relevant to the protection of consumers. For example, influential organizations such as the Consumers Union have a primary interest in testing products and informing the consumer, which, from Nader's point of view, is too limited an agenda for the consumer movement. The consumer movement, and the public-interest movement in general, is a diverse one with varied philosophical understandings about the appropriate role of government and advocacy. But as the economic historian Lucy Black Creighton notes about consumerism, the public-interest movement has been dependent on activists like Nader for its continuing vitality: "Nader has been able to do what the consumer movement has not been able to do—he has raised money to support the cause and has brought about change. Probably even more important, Nader has been able to generate a level of enthusiasm and publicity for the consumer that is far greater than at any time before he came on the scene." See Creighton, *Pretenders to the Throne* (Lexington, Mass.: D. C. Heath, 1976), pp. 63–64.

78. Nathan, *The Administrative Presidency*, p. 45.

79. Ibid., pp. 43–56; see also The Ripon Society and Clifford Brown, *Jaws of Victory* (Boston: Little, Brown, 1973), pp. 226–242.

80. See especially Walter Dean Burnham, *Critical Elections and the Mainstream of American Politics* (New York: W. W. Norton, 1970); and Everitt Carl Ladd (with Charles D. Hadley), *Transformation of the American Party System*, 2nd ed. (New York: W. W. Norton, 1978).

81. Harry Jaffa, "A Phoenix from the Ashes: The Death of James Madison's Constitution (killed by James Madison) and the Birth of American Party Government," paper prepared for delivery at the annual meeting of the American Political Science Association, Washington, D.C. (1977), p. 43.

82. A. James Reichley, "The Rise of National Parties," in John E. Chubb and Paul E. Peterson, eds., *The New Direction in American Politics* (Washington, D.C.: Brookings Institution, 1985); Cornelius P. Cotter and John F. Bibby, "Institutionalization of Parties and the Thesis of Party Decline," *Political Science Quarterly*, vol. 95 (Spring 1980), pp. 1–27; Joseph A. Schlesinger, "The New American Party System," *American Political Science Review*, vol. 79 (December 1985), pp. 1152–1169; and Michael Nelson, "The Case for the Current Nominating Process," in George Grassmuck, ed., *Before Nomination* (Washington, D.C.: American Enterprise Institute, 1985).

83. David S. Broder, "A Party Leader Who Works at It," *Boston Globe* (October 21, 1985), p. 14; Interview with Mitchell E. Daniels, Assistant to the President for Political and Governmental Affairs (June 5, 1986).

84. Robert Dole, quoted in Reichley, "The Rise of National Parties," p. 176.

85. Most analyses of the 1986 elections focused almost exclusively on the national results, ignoring Republican gains in the states. The GOP gained control of eight additional governorships, giving them twenty-four, the most they have held in seventeen years. Moreover, in winning these gubernatorial contests, the Republicans picked up seats in the traditional Democratic strongholds of Alabama,

Florida, South Carolina, and Texas. These results, which may greatly strengthen the GOP's hand for the 1991 reapportionment, suggest that the view of the 1986 elections as a terrible defeat for the Republican party may be a shallow and short-sighted one. See Ronald Brownstein, "The Big Sweep," *National Journal* (November 8, 1986), pp. 2712–2718.

86. Harvey C. Mansfield, Jr., "The 1984 Americn Election: Entitlements Versus Opportunity," *Government and Opposition*, vol. 20 (Winter 1985), p. 17.

87. Michael Fix and George C. Eads, "The Prospects for Regulatory Realignment: The Legacy of Reagan's First Term," *Yale Journal on Regulation*, vol. 2, no. 2 (1985), pp. 293–318; and Harris and Milkis, *Social Regulation and the Reagan Revolution*, ch. 4.

88. Sidney Blumenthal, *The Rise of the Counter-Establishment: From Conservative Ideology to Political Power* (New York: New York Times Books, 1986), p. 9.

89. Harris and Milkis, *Social Regulation and the Reagan Revolution*, especially ch. 7; Merrick B. Garland, "Deregulation and Judicial Review," *Harvard Law Review*, vol. 98 (January 1985), pp. 507–591.

7

The Courts, Congress,
and Programmatic Rights

R. SHEP MELNICK

Without a doubt, among the most important political developments of the past quarter-century were the twin phenomena generally called "judicial activism" and the "rights revolution." The former refers to the federal courts' involvement in issues previously considered the domain of legislators and administrators. Today the judiciary helps shape policies on education, welfare, health and safety regulation, the conducting of elections, the treatment of the mentally ill, and the use of federal lands—to mention only a few. The "rights revolution" refers to the tendency to define nearly every public issue in terms of legally protected rights of individuals. Rights of the handicapped, rights of workers, rights of students, rights of racial, linguistic, and religious minorities, rights of women, rights of consumers, the right to a hearing, the right to know—these have become the stock and trade of American political discourse.

Although these two developments are clearly related, they are not identical. Courts, of course, make policy by defining and vindicating the rights of various parties. Interest groups state their causes in terms of rights to increase their chances of success in court. The courts, though, are not the only institution receptive to arguments about rights. One of the most important but least appreciated facts about the "rights revolution" is that most of these new rights are *statutory* rather than constitutional. They are not the product of unilateral judicial activism, but the handiwork of "separated institutions sharing power."

Consider some of the rights we hear about every day. Most employment discrimination cases arise under Title VII of the Civil Rights Act of 1964 rather than under the Fourteenth Amendment, which applies only to "state action." Most contemporary voting rights disputes involve the Voting Rights Act of 1965 rather than the Fourteenth or Fifteenth Amendment. What we commonly think of as the rights of women, the handicapped, and the elderly spring not from the Equal Protection Clause but from Title IX of the Education Amendments of 1972, section 504 of the Rehabilitation Act of 1973, the Education for All Handicapped Children Act of 1975, and the Age Discrimination Act of 1976. The right to participate in administrative rulemaking is based on the Administrative Procedures Act. All these statutes were passed by Congress, signed—and often proposed—by the president, and implemented by federal administrators.

If these rights are not constitutional in the ordinary meaning of that term, they are something more than statutory. The purpose of many of these acts is to define, expand, and protect constitutional rights. John F. Kennedy described the legislative proposal that eventually became the Civil Rights Act of 1964 as "sound constitutional policy." As Alexander Bickel pointed out at the time, Kennedy's phrase joined two previously distinct categories: constitutional law (the realm of the courts) and public policy (the realm of the legislative and executive branches).[1] Once an aberration, the Civil Rights Act has become a model for emulation.

Such "constitutional policymaking" involves new institutional patterns. The Civil Rights Act and similar statutes delegate tremendous authority to the courts. Federal judges, after all, are the "experts" on constitutional rights. The judiciary usually gives these statutes broad readings, interpreting the words of Congress in light of the constitutional "values" discovered by federal judges. On a few occasions Congress has pulled in the reins on the courts. But just as frequently Congress has criticized the courts for not being more aggressive. For example, when the Supreme Court narrowed its reading ot Title VII, the Voting Rights Act, and Title IX of the Education Amendments, large majorities in Congress voted to make evident its broader "intent."[2] The ongoing dispute between Democratic senators and the Reagan administration over judicial appointments (especially the nomination of Robert Bork) should remind us that many members of Congress fully support an active judiciary.

The central argument of this chapter is that a new institutional alliance coupled with a new understanding of individual rights has led to the unprecedented growth of what I will call "programmatic rights." Programmatic rights are the joint creation of the courts, Congress, and federal administrators. They fall within a gray area between what is purely statutory and what is overtly constitutional. Rather than creating expanded spheres of private autonomy, they increase the demands placed on the regulatory, welfare state. Although their proponents claim that these rights are somehow "above" politics, they are very much part of the daily lives of politicians in every branch of government.

AN INSTITUTIONAL MARRIAGE OF CONVENIENCE

The growth of programmatic rights is the result of two independent but intersecting institutional developments: judicial activism and the reassertion of power by a liberal, Democratic Congress. These two stories are familiar to all who study American politics. Yet surprisingly little attention has been paid to the manner in which each institution has reinforced the reformist impulses of the other.

Starting with its 1954 decision in *Brown* v. *Board of Education*, the Warren Court transformed the role of the federal judiciary. It sought to uproot segregation and other manifestations of racial prejudice, to protect a variety of "discrete and insular minorities," to broaden "freedom of expression," to reduce the autonomy of state and local governments, and to weaken entrenched political and economic elites. The Burger Court may have slowed the pace of judicially instigated change, but it neither shied away from its own form of activism nor seriously constrained the activism deeply embedded in the lower courts. Since 1969, the Supreme Court has issued key decisions on abortion, busing, capital punishment, and gender discrimination. The lower courts have effected a "reformation" of administrative law and restructured hundreds of prisons, mental hospitals, and state homes for the retarded—all without help from the Supreme Court.

The resurgence of Congress was both an attempt by the legislative branch to regain the many powers it had ceded to the president since 1932 and a partisan effort by the solidly Democratic Congress to reduce the power of Republicans in the White House. The most important change in Congress was the increase in the number, power, autonomy, and staff of its subcommittees. Already a decentralized institution, Congress became even more so. Only this time it was the younger, more entrepreneurial members, not their more conservative adversaries, who controlled the key units. Efforts to make these powerful subcommittees representative of Congress as a whole were abandoned as each member sought a piece of the action and was allowed to choose the type of action he or she favored. The influence of the more cautious and balanced "insider" committees (Appropriations, Rules, and Ways and Means) plummeted. Using subcommittee resources, members of Congress initiated new programs and revised old ones, challenging the president for the title of "chief legislator." No longer would Congress write vague legislation asking the executive to "do something." Now it was writing detailed statutes that frequently deviated significantly from the president's program.

Writing legislation is one thing; turning it into actual programs and policies is quite another. Program advocates on congressional subcommittees wanted administrators not just to comply with the letter of their newly minted statutes but to be guided by the "spirit" envisioned by the legislation's principal sponsors. Administrators are usually responsive to such congressional requests. But in the early 1970s, President Nixon began to construct what Richard Nathan has called the "administrative presidency," strengthening the Office of Management and Budget (OMB) and selecting subcabinet officials on the basis of ideological consistency with the administration. The purpose of these changes was clear: to ensure that the bureaucracy would take its orders from the White House, not subcommittees. Congress then scrambled to find new methods for ensuring agency fidelity to *congressional* intent.

At the same time, Supreme Court justices and lower court judges were discovering new reasons for using statutory interpretation rather than constitutional adjudication to achieve their policy goals. The frequently divided Supreme Court was constantly searching for narrow, ad hoc responses to the controversial issues it chose to address. Policy change without constitutional adventurism was a formula that could unite the Court's liberals and moderates. Even conservative justices preferred reading statutes broadly to confronting troublesome constitutional issues. Just as important, lower-court judges realized that the Supreme Court was much less likely to reprimand them for improperly interpreting statutes than for misreading the Constitution. The art of reading statutes "creatively" flourished. Some lower courts became specialists on particular statutes yet still managed to insulate themselves from effective Supreme Court review.

The interests and strategies of judges and members of Congress thus coincided. Federal courts would read congressional enactments broadly, relying heavily on the legislative records prepared by subcommittee chairs and their staff, preventing footdragging by OMB and political appointees within the bureaucracy, and forcing balky state and local officials to comply with congressional mandates and administrative rules. Ironically, the federal administrators who lost many of these cases soon came to appreciate the activities of the courts. They gained autonomy from the White House, greater control over state and local governments, and even more money and personnel. In many policy areas, relations among members of Congress, administrators, judges, and public-interest groups were much more amiable than our usual image of the separation of powers would lead us to believe.[3]

Perhaps the best example of the court-Congress alliance was the passage and implementation of the Education for All Handicapped Children Act. For many years subcommittees on education in both the House and the Senate had advocated increased federal guidance and funding for education of the handicapped. The Nixon and Ford administrations blocked legislation until 1975. Key to the eventual passage of the act in that year were two lower-court decisions ordering the District of Columbia and the State of Pennsylvania to provide an "appropriate" education for handicapped children. State and local educators demanded that Congress provide them with money to pay for these judicial mandates and with clearer policy guidelines. Even though one of these well-advertised court rulings was merely a consent decree and the other studiously avoided constitutional arguments, subcommittee advocates constantly maintained that their legislation was a necessary response to "landmark court decisions establishing the right to education for handicapped children."

Trusting neither the state and local educational systems, which in the past had excluded handicapped students, nor federal administrators accountable to presidents who had opposed federal legislation, the act's sponsors created elaborate hearing and appeals procedures for determining what constitutes a "free appropriate public education" for each handicapped child. The act also requires federal judges to make an "independent" evaluation of the adequacy of the "individual educational plans" brought before them. Over the past decade the federal courts have developed an extensive common law on this subject. Court decisions have helped push the cost of educating the handicapped to more than $10 billion annually—of which less than 10 percent comes from the federal government.

How typical is education of the handicapped? In the way its sponsors relied on tenuous judicial precedents, imposed expensive new duties on the states, and created convoluted procedures, it is extreme. But to the extent that legislators tried to build on constitutional litigation, to aid newly organized groups, and to use the courts to put teeth into federal regulations, it is paradigmatic. To paint a more accurate picture of both the extent and the variety of programmatic rights, I will divide these rights into four categories: nondiscrimination rights, procedural rights, entitlements, and collective rights. Though admittedly imprecise, these categories will allow us to discuss examples without becoming awash in a sea of detail and to probe the political dynamics of rights creation by the legislative, judicial, and executive branches.

Nondiscrimination Rights

The most important of all rights-creating statutes is the Civil Rights Act of 1964, which Alexander Bickel has described as "a fundamentally new departure in federal legislation."[4] The importance of the Civil Rights Act lies not just in its own reach—which is extensive—but also in the model it established for further legislation.

In passing the Civil Rights Act, Congress finally took a clear stand on the racial issues placed on the national agenda by *Brown* v. *Board of Education* and by the civil rights protest in the South. *Brown* had breathed life into the Equal Protection Clause of the Fourteenth Amendment by conceding the obvious: that *de jure* segregation is a form of racial discrimination. The act extended the nondiscrimination principle to private as well public establishments, forbidding discrimination in hotels, restaurants, and stores. It banned employment discrimination on the basis of gender as well as race. Equally important in the long run was the legislative mandate that the federal bureaucracy—meaning primarily the Department of Justice, the Department of Health, Education, and Welfare, and the newly formed Equal Employment Opportunity Commission— assist the courts and create parallel enforcement mechanisms. These proved to be potent weapons. Within four years the bureaucracy had accomplished what the courts acting alone had not done in the preceding fourteen: desegregation of the southern schools.

The Civil Rights Act is surprisingly silent on the meaning of the key term *discrimination*. The most common assumption of the bill's sponsors was "we mean what the courts have meant." Accordingly, no further explanation was needed. Congress clearly did not endorse the practice of inferring racial discrimination from nonproportional outcomes.[5] But it made no effort to put an end to the use of this inference by the courts and federal agencies in employment cases. Moreover, in some instances Congress has rejected as too weak-kneed the practice of requiring proof of discriminatory intent and has even endorsed the use of "benign" racial quotas.[6] Faced with the fundamental but difficult choice between a weak law that would punish only overt discrimination and a much stronger law that would ultimately require racial quotas, Congress chose to delegate.

The very ambiguity of the term *discrimination* constitutes a large portion of the political appeal of nondiscrimination statutes. Only a bigot would support discrimination in the abstract. Even the most fervent opponents of the 1964 act (many of whom, no doubt, *were* bigots) rested their case not on support for discrimination but on opposition to expansion of federal power over the states and private individuals. Once the civil rights "breakthrough" had legitimated such exercise of federal authority, opposition to nondiscrimination statutes became politically treacherous. Indeed, most nondiscrimination statutes—including section 504 of the Rehabilitation Act of 1973 (which prohibits discrimination on the basis of handicap), Title IX of the Education Amendments of 1972 (which prohibits discrimination on the basis of gender), and the Age Discrimination Act of 1975—engendered little debate despite their far-reaching consequences. Most were passed as small and seemingly insignificant sections of large omnibus bills.

This meant that courts and agencies would define *discrimination* for themselves. Far from limiting or guiding judicial activism, the afore-mentioned statutes expanded the courts' jurisdiction and made them more adventurous. Freed from the need to tie their rulings to the Equal Protection Clause, claiming to support rather than overturn the policies of elected officials, and at times using pieces of legislative history provided by allies in Congress, the courts have engaged in unembarrassed, often ad hoc policymaking. Judges and administrators have reinforced each others' activist impulses. Decisions by lower-court judges applying to particular defendants have been generalized and converted into regulations governing all school systems, all employers, or all recipients of federal funds. Conversely, judges have looked to the "remedial" regulations promulgated by "expert" agencies to aid them in the inter-pretation of statutes.[7]

Although Congress itself has generally avoided defining *discrimination*, it has occasionally followed the lead of judges and administrators in favoring a standard closely approximating proportional racial represen-tation. The leading example is voting rights. The Voting Rights Act of 1965 asserted extraordinary federal power to deal with the decades-old problem of disenfranchisement of southern blacks. The act not only barred the use of literacy tests in the South but also required that all changes in the voting laws of covered areas be "precleared" by the Department of Justice or the federal courts in order to prevent southern states from using clever new methods for achieving the old goal of preventing blacks from voting.

The courts first ruled that state laws which have an adverse *effect* on black registration violate the Voting Rights Act; then they applied preclearance to legislative and municipal redistricting. This meant that those districting plans that failed to give racial minorities their "proper" number of representatives violated the Act. When Congress extensively revised the act in 1975, it made no effort to overturn this policy. It did, however, add new groups to the list of those entitled to protection under the act. A form of rights-rolling emerged: Covered groups included not just Hispanics, but Aleuts, American Indians, and Asian-Americans as well. In 1982, Congress amended the act again. Despite the opposition of the Reagan administration, Congress rewrote a key section of the act to circumvent a Supreme Court decision that had pulled federal judges back toward an "intent" standard in redistricting cases. "The result of complex legislative, judicial, and administrative action," according to Abigail Thernstrom, "has been to establish the practice of creating as many safe minority seats as possible."[8]

One can offer many reasons why Congress was receptive to the proportional-representation approach to voting rights first championed by the courts. No one wants to oppose "voting rights," and civil rights groups were extraordinarily skillful in defining the pro-voting rights position. Black and Hispanic leaders supported this understanding of "nondiscrimination," and many members of Congress—Democrats and Republican alike—did not want to anger important constituencies. Subcommittee leaders and staff members in the House were adamant in their opposition to a simple "intent" standard. Some Republicans realized that districting plans that concentrate black voters in safe minority seats can improve the prospects of Republican candidates in the remaining white districts.

The moral is that groups generally viewed as "discrete and insular minorities" by constitutional law commentators have become—partly as a result of the success of the Voting Rights Act and the Civil Rights Act—much more politically powerful. They play coalition politics (with liberal Democrats, conservative Republicans, Hispanics, and even Aleuts) much as James Madison would have predicted. Civil rights politics has become a curious amalgam of high moral principle and politics-as-usual. Ironically, "rights politics" as now practiced has much in common with what Theodore Lowi has called "distributive" politics.[9] The language of rights serves to emphasize the benefits conferred on rights-holders while obscuring the nature, extent, and distribution of the program's costs. To say that rights must be protected regardless of cost is to say that even discussing who will suffer is of questionable propriety.

Procedural Rights

One of the chief characteristics of "nondiscrimination rights" is Congress's reluctance to define them with much clarity. As noted above, ambiguity is usually part of their political appeal; as such, it conforms to the conventional wisdom that Congress delegates power excessively, rarely writing detailed statutes. The conventional wisdom, however, is seriously deficient. Since 1970 congressional enactments have become increasingly lengthy and detailed. Sometimes Congress managed to be specific about substantive benefits and created entitlements. At other times the process of defining benefits proved more difficult, and Congress created elaborate, detailed procedures designed to help various groups procure benefits from various levels of government and the private sector.

The Education for All Handicapped Children Act offers a vivid illustration of congressionally created procedural rights. This act created not only hearing rights but also rights to both administrative and judicial appeals. Most housing and urban development programs contain some version of the original Community Action Program's "maximum feasible participation" requirement. Environmental and consumer protection statutes passed in the 1970s include elaborate hearing requirements and liberal citizen suit provisions designed to push laggard agencies into action. By one count there were approximately 225 citizen participation programs mandated by federal statutes by 1977.[10]

The courts have been vigilant in making sure that state and federal agencies adhere to the letter and the spirit of these participation requirements. Such statutory provisions have reinforced the courts' extensive efforts to expand participation by those claiming to speak for the poor, racial minorities, consumers, and environmentalists. Indeed, as Richard Stewart has shown, broadening political participation was the principal theme of the "reformation" of administrative law during the 1970s: "Courts have changed the focus of judicial review . . . so that its dominant purpose is no longer the prevention of unauthorized intrusions on private autonomy, but the assurance of fair representation for all affected interests in the exercise of the legislative power delegated to agencies."[11] With this goal in mind, judges put their own, sometimes tortured gloss on statutory provisions.[12] At the same time, Congress showed an inclination to write into law the procedures developed by the courts. What came from Congress and what came from the courts became increasingly difficult to discern.

Perhaps the best known of the new procedural rights are those that have grown up under the National Environmental Policy Act of 1969 (NEPA) and its environmental impact statement (EIS) mandate. When Congress passed NEPA, it gave very little attention to the question of how to enforce its command that federal agencies consider the environmental consequences of their actions. No one mentioned the courts or legal rights. Yet the courts quickly assumed this responsibility, enjoining scores of federal projects and developing an elaborate common law of NEPA requirements. Judges fastened on NEPA precisely because it provided a convenient justification for doctrines already developed unilaterally by the courts. In the mid-1960s, several appellate courts became convinced that federal agencies were not paying sufficient attention to the environment. They invented the "adequate consideration" requirement, which required agencies to convince reviewing judges that they have listened to all interested groups (environmentalists as well as developers) and considered all the consequences of their actions. NEPA, as Frederick Anderson points out, "was enacted at just the time the courts were generally tightening their review of agency decisionmaking. . . . They welcomed NEPA as an additional statutory basis for close judicial review."[13]

One might have expected Congress, which is reputedly wedded to pork-barrel projects, to react with hostility to court decisions blocking the construction of dams and highways. But in only a handful of cases did Congress limit the applicability of NEPA or overturn court rulings.[14] The right to participate in the NEPA process quickly become sacrosanct in a Congress newly committed to environmental protection.

Congress has not only tolerated, applauded, and strengthened the procedural innovations of the courts but has also made it easier for newly organized, nonbusiness groups to engage in litigation. Various authorizing statutes granted standing to all citizens, regardless of the nature of their injury. In 1980, Congress eliminated the $10,000 amount-in-controversy requirement for federal question jurisdiction. It also granted numerous exceptions to sovereign immunity. Reacting to a Supreme Court decision limiting the award of attorney's fees, Congress passed the Civil Rights Attorney's Fees Act of 1976, which authorized the courts to award attorneys' fees in a large number of cases. And much to the chagrin of Republican administrations, Congress protected the independence and the budget of the Legal Services Corporation, which brought a large number of the cases that had substantially altered federal welfare policy.[15] Litigation has become a normal part of the policymaking process, in part because Congress has been surprisingly eager to expand and protect the right to sue.

One way to explain Congress's attachment to procedural rights enforceable in court is to see them as methods for avoiding issues on which members of Congress receive conflicting pressure. Concerned about the safety of nuclear power plants but unwilling to rule out nuclear power as a source of electricity, members of Congress have insisted that the NRC follow ever-more elaborate licensing procedures. And unable to chose between endangered species and hydroelectric power, Congress has written "crosscutting mandates" resulting in extensive interagency negotiation as well as inevitable litigation.[16]

It would be wrong, however, to view these procedural rights simply as products of congressional issue avoidance. There was a strong anti-bureaucratic, anti-institutional ethos in Congress throughout the 1970s. Distrust of bureaucracy—a constant theme in American political culture—was nearly as common among liberal Democrats as among conservative Republicans. Republican control of the presidency made liberal Democrats even more wary of placing discretion in the hands of administrators. Encouraging greater participation by "public-interest" groups and by "average" citizens was an inviting solution to the problem of administrative discretion—especially for those members of Congress who had revolted against the "committee barons" and who claimed to support "participatory democracy" within Congress. Moreover, in some cases program advocates on congressional subcommittees, aided by sophisticated staff members and interest group leaders, wanted more than rhetoric. They gave a great deal of thought to the manner in which new procedures could be used to alter existing power relationships. Sometimes they succeeded.

Entitlements

In the second half of the 1960s, the federal courts announced sweeping changes in their treatment of entitlement statutes. In the legal literature these changes fall under the rubric of the "demise of the rights-privilege distinction" and are symbolized by the Supreme Court's decision in *Goldberg v. Kelly*.[17] In that 1970 case, the Court ruled that welfare benefits are "property rights" rather than mere "privileges" dispensed by generous legislators and administrators. Accordingly, they cannot be terminated in the absence of "due-process" hearings. Although legal scholars have devoted most of their attention to the procedures mandated by the courts, substantive judicial rulings have had a much greater effect on welfare policy. Before a judge can decide whether a plaintiff has been denied "property" without "due process of law," he must first define the property right created by the statute. Defining welfare entitlements had previously been considered the job of legislators and administrators, not judges. No longer. Since 1965, the federal judiciary has played a major role in shaping policy on Aid to Families with Dependent Children (AFDC), disability insurance, unemployment compensation, food stamps, Medicare, Medicaid, and housing programs. Court decisions have almost always expanded governmental benefits.[18]

These judicial developments coincided with important changes in Congress and the budgetary process. Before 1965, most federal spending (with the important exception of Social Security) was "controllable"—that is, subject to annual review by congressional appropriations committees and by the OMB. Since then, the percentage of the federal budget that is "uncontrollable"—based on long-term authorizations that mandate specific payments to individuals or subnational governments—has constantly increased. Northern liberal Democrats mounted a successful effort to strengthen the authorizing committees they controlled and to weaken the more conservative, tightfisted appropriations committees. The shift from discretionary to statutorily mandated spending not only altered the distribution of power within Congress; it also reduced the power of the OMB. For almost twenty years now, Congress has been seeking to increase domestic spending and has faced strenuous opposition from the White House.

The marked decline in the courts' willingness to accept administrators' interpretation of statutes was an outgrowth of both constitutional and political developments. Clearly worried about the "welfare crisis" of the mid- and late 1960s, the Warren Court in its twilight years started to find a "right to welfare" embedded in the Fourteenth Amendment. The Burger Court quickly put a stop to this development. In the meantime, however, first the Supreme Court and then the lower courts began to use statutory interpretation to achieve the welfare reforms urged by Legal Assistance attorneys. Relying primarily on vague statements of legislative "purpose"—and ignoring clear statutory language as well as years of administrative practice—the courts broadened eligibility, increased benefit levels, and reduced the discretion of state governments, which shared responsibility for running many welfare programs. These judicial developments started in cases involving Aid to Families with Dependent Children but soon spread far and wide.[19]

There can be little doubt but that the courts played fast and loose with congressional "intent" in order to give effect to a reform program of their own. Their goal was to make welfare programs more nationally uniform, more rule-bound, more generous, less punitive, and less categorical. They claimed that benefits should be based on need alone, not on race, family composition, state or length of residence, sexual behavior, or even willingness to accept employment. The courts, in short, were trying to remake AFDC and other means-tested programs, moving them closer to a guaranteed income.

Congress could—and at times did—overturn these court rulings. But on many issues, especially those related to AFDC, the legislative branch was hopelessly deadlocked. Conservatives denounced the court decisions. Liberals applauded and protected them. Given this alignment of political forces, revising the court-created status quo required both sustained political effort and unusual circumstances.[20] In other programs (such as the food stamp program), congressional committee leaders favored more uniform and generous benefits, and were happy to use the political leverage provided by the court decisions to make permanent changes in authorizing legislation.

Most members of Congress did not accept the need-only approach to welfare advocated by the courts. But a Congress dominated by the Democratic party and committed to extending income-maintenance programs found it very hard to reduce benefits already in place or to increase the authority of state governments, some of which had run harsh, racially discriminatory programs in the past. Thus the Congress of the 1970s provided the courts with a great deal of entitlement legislation to interpret and at times welcomed the judiciary as an ally in its battle with the president; it also proved reluctant to revise court rulings, however inconsistent with the original intentions of legislators.

Collective Rights

A key attribute of entitlement programs such as AFDC and Social Security is that they dispense "particularized" benefits to identifiable individuals. By contrast, some of the most important litigation and legislation of the past twenty years has dealt with collective benefits— in other words, benefits, such as environmental protection, that cannot be offered or withheld from one person without being granted or denied to many others. At first glance, one might expect the language of individual rights to be foreign to these programs. In no other advanced industrial democracy do courts or individual rights play a major role in policymaking for environmental or consumer protection.[21] Indeed, *collective rights* seems to be a contradiction in terms. How is it, then, that the courts have been so active in shaping programs providing collective benefits in the United States?

The answer has at least two parts. First, the courts have held, in effect, that each member of the public has a right to see federal laws carried out as Congress intended—that is, in a manner consistent with the courts' reading of congressional intent. Most legal challenges mounted by environmental groups are "private attorney general" cases: Plaintiffs claim that administrators have paid insufficient attention to statutory mandates or the public interest. If these plaintiffs suffer any concrete injury (a question most judges have long since stopped asking), then it is an injury suffered by many other citizens as well. In years past, the protection of such collective interests was seen as the job of elected officials rather than of judges.

In the late 1960s, though, judges began to question the adequacy of existing mechanisms for safeguarding the collective benefits established by federal statutes. Bureaucrats simply could not be trusted to follow congressional dictates, and Congress seemed incapable of sustained oversight. Especially with a president hostile to many new programs firmly ensconced in the White House, Congress needed judicial help. "Our duty," announced Judge Skelly Wright of the D.C. Circuit, "is to see that the legislative purposes heralded in the halls of Congress, are not lost in the vast halls of the federal bureaucracy."[22] To discover these "legislative purposes," judges looked primarily to the "legislative histories" created by subcommittee leaders and their enterprising staff.[23]

The second factor that helps explain the role of the courts in defining collective benefits is the tendency of congress members, public-interest groups, and judges to insist that health and safety legislation protect each and every citizen. According to several members of the National Commission on Air Quality, by passing the Clean Air Act "Congress recognized Americans' basic right to air that is fit to breathe."[24] If everyone has a right to "clean air" and if "clean" means harmless even to the most sensitive, then the government must insist that polluters do everything possible to clean up, regardless of cost. It is for this reason that the Environmental Protection Agency, its supporters in Congress, and environmental groups have persisted in arguing that the agency should not consider costs in setting air quality standards.[25]

Some federal judges have suggested that such rights to health and safety are ultimately grounded in the Constitution. In the case announcing the birth of the "new administrative law," Judge David Bazelon stated that "courts are increasingly asked to review administrative action that touches on fundamental personal interests in life, health, and liberty. These interests have always had a special claim to judicial protection."[26] The constitutional right to a "safe environment" had an intellectual life even shorter than that of the constitutional right to welfare. But this fact did not prevent judges from reading statutes in such a way as to favor the "health and safety of people" at the expense of owners of traditional private property. In this endeavor they have received considerable encouragement from congressional subcommittees, which have provided open-ended "citizen suit" provisions, created thousands of pages of legislative history, and ratified some of the courts' most audacious rulings. Few of the courts' decisions on collective rights have generated as much controversy as the welfare rights cases. This is so not because the courts have refrained from activism but, rather, because few members of Congress want to be perceived as opponents of environmental protection.

THE NEW RULES OF THE GAME

The Constitution lays out the separation of powers only in the broadest of terms. Ever since *Marbury* v. *Madison* and *McCulloch* v. *Maryland*, the federal courts have played an important role in defining the powers of the federal government, the states, Congress, the president, and the federal judiciary itself. Over the past twenty years, the courts have developed a number of doctrines that have profoundly affected the distribution of power between state and national governments and among the three branches of the federal government. Most of these doctrines— like programmatic rights themselves—are not constitutional in the conventional sense. Although they may at first seem to be merely technical, they have important (and unappreciated) political significance. Here I will focus on three changes that have contributed to the growth of programmatic rights.

Statutory Interpretation

The Constitution vests "all legislative powers" in the Congress of the United States—subject, of course, to presidential veto. But how do we know what Congress has decreed in its legislation? As Justice John Harlan so colorfully explained, many a statute "reveals little except that we have before us a child born of the silent union of legislative compromise." Congress "voice[s] its wishes in muted strains," leaving "the courts to discern the theme in the cacophony of political understanding."[27] One of the principal characteristics of American government, in contrast to parliamentary systems, is that the branch charged with "faithful execution of the laws" is electorally independent of the legislature and frequently espouses different policies. For this reason, the interpretation of statutes often requires the courts to arbitrate disputes between the legislative and executive branches.

The political consequences of statutory interpretation can be momentous. Take the maxim regularly cited by judges in the 1800s: "Statutes in derogation of the common law are to be strictly construed." This rule places a heavy burden on those who wish to revise the common law. They must dot every "i" and cross each "t," forsaking the ambiguity that greases compromise. To the extent that they fail, they must once more run the "obstacle course on Capitol Hill." At the other extreme one finds the maxim that "remedial legislation," especially when it seeks to protect the public health and safety, is to be "liberally construed." This can mean either that administrators have broad discretion to do whatever they deem appropriate for achieving the purposes of the statute, or that judges will arrogate to themselves similarly broad discretion.[28]

The past two decades have witnessed two important changes in statutory interpretation by federal judges. The first is heightened judicial attentiveness to legislative history; the second is increased reliance on brief statements of legislative purpose. In the United States as well as Britain and Canada, the usual rule of statutory construction is that judges should look to legislative history only when statutory language is ambiguous. Recent studies of the Supreme Court have shown that references to legislative history are frequent, increasing, and promiscuously employed. Some cynics have thus been led to claim that the actual American practice is to look to the statute only when the legislative history is ambiguous.[29]

Judge Harold Leventhal has likened the courts' use of legislative history to "looking over a crowd and picking out your friends." As in all crowds, some types of people manage to push their way toward the front. The most important piece of legislative history is the committee report, which today is usually written by subcommittee staff under the direction of the subcommittee chair. No vote is taken on the report once it leaves the committee. Indeed, given the length of many of these reports (the House reports on the 1977 amendments to the Clean Air Act and Food Stamp Acts were, respectively, 550 and 860 pages long), it is unlikely that even the most avid subcommittee members have read them with care. The next most important piece of legislative history is the floor statement of the bill's manager—which is usually addressed to a nearly vacant chamber. Here again it is the program advocate on the relevant subcommittee who constructs the legislative history. It should surprise no one that entrepreneurial subcommittee leaders and staff have used these advantages to achieve their policy goals.[30]

A related trend—one that has received less note—is the use of prefatory language and even the titles of acts to determine legislative purpose. Many federal laws grandiloquently proclaim that their purpose is "to protect and enhance the quality of the Nation's air resources" (Clean Air Act) or "to alleviate such hunger and malnutrition" (Food Stamp Act). Although canons of interpretation discourage judges from giving much weight to these broad statements, federal judges have often evaluated challenged policies by asking whether they further or retard these purposes.

As reasonable as this practice may seem at first, it is hard to deny that in passing most statutes Congress has many purposes in mind. Legislators want to help the needy but not spend too much money, encourage work yet provide aid to those who cannot, and protect the environment without hurting the economy. A bill's preface will usually trumpet the program's goals while ignoring its costs. When judges rely heavily on statements of purpose they, too, expand programs and downplay costs. The use of statutory "purpose," like the use of legislative history, thus strengthens the hand of program advocates within Congress. Instead of placing the burden on members of Congress and administrators to explain why the government should be allowed to displace private ordering, the burden is subtly shifted to those who oppose government expansion to explain why further action is not justified.

Nondiscretionary Duties

With its 1971 decision in *EDF* v. *Ruckelshaus,* the D.C. Circuit began an extensive restructuring of the rulemaking activities of federal agencies. Chief Judge David Bazelon marked the arrival of "a new era in the long and fruitful collaboration of administrative agencies and reviewing courts" by ordering recalcitrant administrators to initiate proceedings to ban the controversial pesticide DDT.[31] The court hoped to "open up" the administrative process, to put an end to the "capture" of agencies by regulated firms, and to make administrators more receptive to the concerns of "public-interest" groups. One way to accomplish these goals was to mandate elaborate new procedures that would broaden interest group representation. Another was to expand the category of "nondiscretionary duties."

In years past, judges were highly reluctant to order administrators to undertake new tasks. Their primary role, they claimed, was protecting private citizens from unauthorized government intrusion, not stimulating governmental expansion. They viewed the decision to issue an administrative rule as analogous to the decision to prosecute an alleged criminal: The latter was a matter of "prosecutorial discretion," the former, one of "administrative discretion." Judges questioned their competence to set reasonable administrative priorities and doubted their ability to write and enforce detailed affirmative injunctions.

Over the past fifteen years, though, the federal courts have issued hundreds of "action-forcing" decisions. Judges have not only ordered administrators to promulgate new rules but have even instructed them on how these rules must be enforced. Few areas of administrative discretion remain immune from judicial scrutiny.

Distrustful of the Nixon and Ford administrations and concerned about agency "capture," the Congress of the 1970s approved of many of these judicial developments. Although it made few changes in the generic Administrative Procedures Act, it included in authorizing statutes the elaborate rulemaking procedures devised by the courts. It also created "citizen suit provisions" allowing "any citizen" (not just those "adversely affected by agency action") to bring suit either against private parties violating the act or against administrators for failing "to perform any act or duty under this act which is not discretionary."[32]

This "new administrative law" has had two subtle but important implications for the role and structure of government. First, these court decisions nearly obliterated the distinction between public and private. "Public-interest" groups demanding increased regulatory activity were placed on equal footing with—or were even given preferential treatment over—traditional interest groups seeking to protect private property. Nonaction by an administrator became as serious a threat to individual rights as positive action. Indeed, in some instances the courts placed a "heavy burden" on administrators to explain why they did not issue the most stringent possible regulation. Within the past few years the courts have held that rescinding rules—and thus returning to private ordering—requires at least as much justification as promulgating a rule in the first place.[33]

Second, in applying these new doctrines, federal judges have strengthened the hand of the permanent bureaucracy and weakened the influence of political appointees and the Office of Management and Budget. Operating under the twin assumptions that on most issues one can ascertain a particular congressional intent and that policymaking should be based on "rational analysis" rather than on political negotiation, federal courts have frowned on the imposition of presidential priorities on "expert" agencies.

Private Rights of Action

Most statutes can be enforced in one of two ways: by giving administrative agencies authority to write regulations, issue orders, and file suit against those who fail to comply; or by authorizing private citizens to seek remedial action in the courts. In the antitrust field, for example, the Federal Trade Commission Act of 1914 adopted the former approach, and the 1890 Sherman Act the latter. For years, the federal courts had refused to recognize "private rights" of action"—that is, the rights of private citizens to bring suits against alleged violators of a federal statute—unless the statute clearly authorized such suits. Starting in 1964, though, the Supreme Court changed direction. It first encouraged judges to find private rights of action "implicit" in federal statutes, and then to read 42 USC 1983—originally passed as part of the Civil Rights Act of 1870 and all but forgotten for nearly a century—as creating a generic private right of action applicable to nearly all federal laws.[34]

The expansion of private rights of action has had two important political consequences. First, as enforcing a law nearly always involves interpreting it, the recognition of private rights of action transfers substantial policymaking power from administrators to judges. Unlike administrators, judges are not subject to presidential directives; nor do they need to pay attention to the budgetary, economic, or political consequences of their policies. Moreover, private rights of action allow plaintiffs to "forum shop" to find the most hospitable environment for pressing their claims.

Second, private rights of action carry surprising consequences for federalism. A large number of national programs, ranging from AFDC to interstate highways, from disability insurance to urban renewal, are run jointly by state and federal governments. Usually the federal government provides both money and "strings" (i.e., conditions on how this money can be used). For many years the only way federal administrators could enforce these "strings" was to cut off funding, a drastic action they were seldom willing to take. Thus the federal government was limited in its ability to establish policy for these programs.

From 1935 to 1965, the courts decided very few cases involving federal grants-in-aid. Funding decisions were left to the executive branch.

This arrangement changed quickly in the mid-1960s. Without explanation, the courts began to hear cases brought by plaintiffs claiming that states had denied them benefits promised by federal statutes. If the courts had recognized "implied private rights of action" but had ruled that the penalty for failure to comply with federal rules was denial of federal funding (surely the most obvious conclusion), then the list of such cases would be a short one. An AFDC beneficiary receiving $60 per month from the state of Mississippi would not go to court to claim that this figure should be $100 if the consequence of winning would be to reduce it to zero. What plaintiffs asked for and expeditiously received were *injunctions* ordering state officials to comply with all federal requirements. To mix metaphors, this put new teeth into federal strings. Once a state accepted federal funding, it was obliged to obey all requirements found to be contained in federal laws. And the courts did not hesitate to use creative interpretation to add requirements not evident on the face of the statute.

These judicial practices troubled many state officials but pleased those federal administrators and members of Congress who understood what was going on. Officials at HEW were particularly eager to take advantage of these new institutional arrangements. Soon after approving and funding state plans, they would appear in court to announce their agreement with plaintiffs challenging state programs. Few judges asked why these administrators had approved inadequate plans. The Democratic Congress, which had repeatedly repulsed Republican efforts to replace categorical grants with block grants, likewise welcomed these judicial developments.

The combination of private rights of action, ready use of injunctions, and heavy reliance on legislative history has proved explosive. States receiving small amounts of money from the federal government found themselves under court order to follow extensive, detailed requirements spelled out in House and Senate reports and in agency regulations. In one instance the Third Circuit relied on an ambiguously worded "Bill of Rights for the Institutionalized" to impose on state institutions for retarded people 4,000 pages of regulations included in the legislative history of the Developmental Disabilities Act. The cost of complying with these rules would have far exceeded the funding available from the federal government. The court went so far as to claim that, in passing the Developmental Disability Act, Congress had exercised its authority under the Fourteenth Amendment and thus could force states to comply whether or not they chose to participate in the federal program. This was too much for the Supreme Court, which overturned the circuit court decision.[35] But it remains a graphic illustration of the lower courts' use of statutory interpretation to effect major political change.

CONCLUSION: BEYOND THE NEW DEAL?

Judicial activism constitutes the clearest evidence that American policymaking today no longer follows the New Deal model that prevailed
from the mid-1930s to the late 1960s. New Deal jurisprudence could
be distilled into one word: deference. As Martin Shapiro has explained,
according to the New Deal view of the political world, "courts should
defer to Congress, Congress should defer to the President. So courts
really were to defer to the Executive." Deference was the rule of thumb
not just in constitutional law but in administrative law as well. Judges
were to defer to administrators largely because administrators were to
share the progressive liberalism of popularly elected presidents. "Put
all together," these institutional norms "spelled Roosevelt."[36]

Roosevelt, of course, was not immortal; nor was the Democratic party
invincible. In fact, twenty-four years' worth of Republican presidents
since 1952 have led some political scientists to suggest that the nation
has undergone a "split-level realignment" with normally Republican
presidents and a predictably Democratic Congress.[37] This realignment
by itself was enough to throw the New Deal model of policymaking
into disarray. But there was much more. Three important congressional
elections—in 1958, 1964, and 1974—created a more liberal Congress
than FDR had ever seen. The civil rights movement (which, ironically,
had loosened the Democratic party's control over the presidency by
alienating the Solid South) strengthened liberal northern Democrats and
reduced the power of conservative southern members of Congress.
Moreover, landmark decisions of the Warren Court, especially *Brown* v.
Board of Education and *Reynolds* v. *Sims,* opened up new frontiers of
constitutional law, convinced judges that they could spearhead political
reform, and encouraged the development of new forms of public-interest
groups. To New Dealers the president and the bureaucracy were the
engines of progress, and Congress and the courts were parochial and
anachronistic brakes. For today's progressives, the opposite is more nearly
true. Changing political necessities and opportunities were the mother
of institutional invention.

One should not overlook, however, the deeper historical roots of
judicial activism, congressional entrepreneurship, and programmatic rights.
One of the strongest and most persistent elements of American political
culture is hostility to governmental authority in general and to bureaucratic
authority in particular. Faith in administration was one element of the
New Deal program that never took firm hold. The American left has
proved to be at least as distrustful of bureaucracy as the right; it remains
far more populist and individualistic than the left in other Western
democracies. One consequence of this situation is that liberal Democrats

have been more comfortable exercising power through the courts and congressional subcommittees (institutions that play essentially critical, oppositional roles in government) than through the executive branch, which governs more openly and directly.[38]

Despite the fact that the growth of programmatic rights reveals the extent to which American politics has been "remade" and New Deal institutional norms reversed, in substance these rights bear a striking resemblance to the long-term policy goals of Roosevelt and his supporters. Roosevelt may have sought a rubber-stamp Congress, attacked the "nine Old Men" on the Supreme Court, and sponsored a Court-packing plan, but he also announced an "Economic Bill of Rights" to supplement the "sacred Bill of Rights of our Constitution." This "Second Bill of Rights" reads like a catalogue of contemporary programmatic rights: "the right to earn enough to provide adequate food and clothing and recreation"; "the right of every family to a decent home"; "the right to adequate medical care"; "the right to adequate protection from the economic fears of old age, sickness, accident and unemployment"; "the right to a good education." Each of these rights, moreover, "must be applied to all our citizens, irrespective of race, creed or color."[39] Some of Roosevelt's appointments of the bench—most notably, Supreme Court Justice Felix Frankfurter—loyally adhered to the institutional norm of judicial deference. But others, especially Justice William O. Douglas, advanced from the bench the New Deal's more forceful substantive vision of the good society.

"What all these rights spell," President Roosevelt explained in 1944, is "security." Eighteenth-century liberalism promised security from civil war, anarchy, and arbitrary government action. Its cornerstone was the protection of a realm of private autonomy—especially private property—from government intervention. Contemporary liberalism promises a broader security—a security against the vagaries of the business cycle, against the multiple unintended hazards created by a dynamic capitalism against the prejudices of private citizens and the consequences of three centuries of racism, against the risks of congenital handicaps and inevitable old age, and against the consequences of poverty and of family decomposition. It is no coincidence that the largest of all our federal programs is not called "superannuation" or even "old-age pensions" as in Europe, but Social Security. The cornerstone of this form of liberalism is the right to enlist the government's support in the battle against the many sources of human insecurity.

Protecting traditional rights required the courts to restrain the growth of government—especially centralized, bureaucratic government. The new understanding of rights, in contrast, has led the judiciary to expand and centralize government, both by putting new issues on the public agenda and by magnifying the initiatives of others. No longer just another "veto point," the courts have become an unexpected source of political energy, showing the American political system to be more flexible and less hostile to the welfare state than most observers have realized.

NOTES

1. Alexander Bickel, "The Civil Rights Act of 1964," *Commentary*, vol. 33 (August 1964), p. 30.

2. In 1978, Congress added section 701(k) to the Civil Rights Act, overturning the Supreme Court's decision in *General Electric* v. *Gilbert* (429 U.S. 125, 1976), which had allowed employers to distinguish pregnancy from other forms of disability. In 1982, Congress amended the Voting Rights Act to overturn *Mobile* v. *Bolden* (446 U.S. 55, 1980), which had made it more difficult to prove racial discrimination in voting rights cases. Congress is in the process of overturning the Supreme Court's decision in *Grove City College* v. *Bell* (79 L.Ed.2d 516, 1984), which narrowed the reach of Title IX of the Education Amendments and, by implication, Title VI of the Civil Rights Act and section 504 of the Rehabilitation Act.

3. R. Shep Melnick, "The Politics of Partnership," *Public Administration Review*, vol. 45 (1985), p. 653.

4. Bickel, "The Civil Rights Act of 1964."

5. See section 703(j) of this act; *United Steelworkers of America* v. *Weber* (443 U.S. 193, 1979); and Nathan Glazer, *Affirmative Discrimination: Ethnic Inequality and Public Policy* (New York: Basic Books, 1978), pp. 43ff.

6. See Gary Bryner, "Congress, Courts, and Agencies: Equal Employment and the Limits of Policy Implementation," *Political Science Quarterly*, vol. 93 (1981), p. 411; and the discussion of the Voting Rights Act below.

7. Jeremy Rabkin, "Office of Civil Rights," in James Q. Wilson, ed., *The Politics of Regulation* (New York: Basic Books, 1980); Robert Katzmann, *Institutional Disability: The Saga of Transportation Policy for the Disabled* (Washington, D.C.: Brookings Institution, 1986); and Peter Schuck, "The Graying of Civil Rights Law: The Age Discrimination Act of 1975," *Yale Law Journal*, vol. 89 (1979), p. 27.

8. Abigail Thernstrom, "The 'Voting Rights' Trap," *New Republic* (September 2, 1985), p. 22. This discussion of voting rights is based primarily on the work of Thernstrom, especially "The Odd Evolution of the Voting Rights Act," *The Public Interest* (Spring 1979), p. 49, and *Whose Votes Count? Affirmative Action and Minority Voting Rights* (Cambridge, Mass.: Harvard University Press, 1987).

9. Theodore Lowi, "American Business, Public Policy, Case Studies, and Political Theory," *World Politics*, vol. 16 (1964), p. 27.

10. Jeffrey Berry, *The Interest Group Society* (Boston: Little, Brown, 1984), p. 32, citing work by Walter Rosenbaum.

11. Richard Stewart, "The Reformation of American Administrative Law," *Harvard Law Review*, vol. 88 (1975), p. 1712.

12. Donald Horowitz provides an interesting example of this in *The Courts and Social Policy* (Washington, D.C.: Brookings Institution, 1977), ch. 3. Another example is the Food Stamp Program "outreach" decision of district court Judge Miles Lord, *Bennett* v. *Butz* (386 F. Supp. 1059, D. Minn., 1974).

13. Frederick Anderson, "The National Environmental Policy Act," in Erica Dolgin and Thomas Guilbert, eds., *Federal Environmental Law* (St. Paul, Minn.: West, 1974), p. 412. The key cases were *Scenic Hudson* v. *FPC* (354 F.2d 608, 2nd Cir., 1965) and *Citizens to Preserve Overton Park* v. *Volpe* (401 U.S. 402, 1971).

14. Serge Taylor, *Making Bureaucracies Think: The Environmental Impact Statement Strategy of Administrative Reform* (Stanford, Calif.: Stanford University Press, 1984), Appendix F.

15. Warren E. George, "Development of the Legal Services Corporation," *Cornell Law Review*, vol. 61 (1976), p. 681.

16. For an example of Congress's use of procedures for citizen participation to sidestep difficult issues, see Pietro Nivola's discussion of the Public Utilities Regulatory Policy Act in *The Politics of Energy Conservation* (Washington, D.C.: Brookings Institution, 1986), pp. 178–184.

17. *Goldberg* v. *Kelly* (397 U.S. 254, 1970).

18. See, for example, Deborah Stone, *The Disabled State* (Philadelphia: Temple, 1984); Jeffrey Berry, *Feeding Hungry People* (New Brunswick, N.J.: Rutgers, 1986); Frank Block, "Cooperative Federalism and the Role of Litigation in the Development of Federal AFDC Policy," *Wisconsin Law Review*, vol. 1979, p. 1; Rand Rosenblatt, "Health Care Reform and Administrative Law: A Structural Approach," *Yale Law Journal*, vol. 88 (1978), p. 243; and Frank Michelman, "The Right to Housing," in Norman Dorsen, ed., *The Rights of Americans* (New York: Pantheon, 1971).

19. Samuel Krislov reviews the constitutional developments in "The OEO Lawyers Fail to Constitutionalize a Right to Welfare: A Study of the Uses and Limits of the Judicial Process," *Minnesota Law Review*, vol. 58 (1973), p. 211. For a detailed analysis of statutory interpretation, see Fred C. Doolittle, "State-Imposed Nonfinancial Eligibility Conditions on AFDC: Confusion in Supreme Court Decisions and the Need for Congressional Clarification," *Harvard Journal on Legislation*, vol. 19 (1982), p. 1; and Melnick, "The Politics of Statutory Interpretation: Courts, Congress, and Welfare Rights," paper prepared for delivery at the annual meeting of the American Political Science Association, Washington, D.C. (1986).

20. In 1981 and 1982, the Reagan administration and the Senate Finance Committee used omnibus reconciliation bills to overturn a number of court decisions, many of which were more than a decade old.

21. David Vogel, *National Styles of Regulation: Environmental Protection in Great Britain and the United States* (Ithaca, N.Y.: Cornell, 1986); and Ronald Brickman, Sheila Jasanoff, and Thomas Ilgen, *Controlling Chemicals: The Politics of Regulation in Europe and the United States* (Ithaca, N.Y.: Cornell, 1985).

22. *Calvert Cliffs Coordinating Committee* v. *AEC* (449 F.2d) at 1111.

23. I explain these developments in much greater detail in *Regulation and the Courts: The Case of the Clean Air Act* (Washington, D.C.: Brookings Institution, 1983), especially ch. 10; and in "The Politics of Partnership."

24. National Commission on Air Quality, *To Breathe Clean Air* (Washington, D.C.: Government Printing Office, 1981), pp. 5–32.

25. Melnick, *Regulation and the Courts*, ch. 8.

26. *EDF* v. *Ruckelshaus* (439 F.2d 584, 1971) at 598.

27. *Rosado* v. *Wyman* (397 U.S. 397, 1970) at 412.

28. J. G. Sutherland, *Statutes and Statutory Construction*, 4th ed. (Chicago: Callaghan Press, 1973), ch. 58.

29. Jorge L. Carro and Andrew R. Brann, "The U.S. Supreme Court and the Use of Legislative History: A Statistical Analysis," *Jurimetrics Journal*, vol. 22 (1982), p. 294; Patricia Wald, "Some Observations on the Use of Legislative History in the 1981 Supreme Court Term," *Iowa Law Review*, vol. 68 (1983), p. 195; and Reed Dickerson, *The Interpretation and Application of Statutes* (Boston: Little, Brown, 1975), p. 164. While on the D.C. Circuit, Antonin Scalia announced, "I think it is time for courts to become concerned about the fact that routine deference to the detail of committee reports . . . [is] converting a system of judicial construction into a system of committee-staff prescription." See *Hirschey* v. *FERC* (777 F.2d 1, 1985) at 7–8.

30. Examples abound. See Melnick, *Regulation and the Courts*, pp. 252–255, 340–342, and 373–379; Bruce Ackerman and Andrew Hassler, *Clean Coal/Dirty Air* (New Haven, Conn.: Yale University Press, 1981), pp. 48–54; Katzmann, *Institutional Disability*, pp. 52–54; and Michael Malbin, *Unelected Representatives* (New York: Basic Books, 1980), p. 30 and ch. 5.

31. *EDF* v. *Ruckelshaus* (439 F.2d 589, 1971) at 597.

32. The quotes come from the Clean Air Act, section 304. The citizen suit provision was included despite—indeed, partly because of—opposition from the Nixon administration. See *A Legislative History of the Clean Air Act Amendments of 1970* (Washington, D.C.: Government Printing Office, 1974), pp. 436–439.

33. See *Motor Vehicle Manufacturers Association* v. *State Farm Mutual* (103 S.Ct. 2856, 1983); *Chevron* v. *NRDC* (104 S.Ct. 2778, 1984); and other cases cited in Merritt Garland, "Deregulation and Judicial Review," *Harvard Law Review*, vol. 98 (1986), p. 505, notes 185 and 186.

34. *J. I. Case* v. *Borak* (377 U.S. 426, 1964) and *Maine* v. *Thiboutot* (448 U.S. 1, 1980). The many twists and turns of court action on section 1983 and private rights of action are admittedly difficult to follow. The stout-hearted can consult Richard Stewart and Cass Sunstein, "Public Programs and Private Rights," *Harvard Law Review*, vol. 95 (1982), p. 1195; and Theodore Eisenbert, *Civil Rights Legislation* (Charlottesville, Va.: Bobbs Merrill, 1981), ch. 2.

35. *Pennhurst State School and Hospital* v. *Halderman* (612 F.2d 84, 3rd Cir., 1977, and 451 U.S. 1, 1981).

36. Martin Shapiro, "APA: Past, Present, Future," *Virginia Law Review*, vol. 72 (1986), p. 451. This article is the best short discussion of the difference between contemporary administrative law and New Deal administrative law. For an illuminating illustration, see Ackerman and Hassler, *Clean Coal/Dirty Air*, especially the first chapter ("Beyond the New Deal").

37. D. Ronald Kiewiet and Douglas Rivers, "The Economic Basis of Reagan's Appeal," in John Chubb and Paul Peterson, eds., *The New Direction in American Politics* (Washington, D.C.: Brookings Institution, 1985).

38. In the words of Samuel Huntington, "During the 1960s the balance of power between government and opposition shifted significantly. The central governing institution in the political system, the presidency, declined in power; institutions playing oppositional roles in the system, most notably the national media and Congress, significantly increased their power." See Huntington, "The United States," in Michael Crozier, Samuel Huntington, and Joji Watanuki, eds., *The Crisis of Democracy* (New York: New York University Press, 1975), p. 92. For a discussion of the "adversarial" nature of the American Left, see Aaron Wildavsky, "The Three Cultures: Explaining Anomolies in the American Welfare State," *The Public Interest* (Fall 1982), p. 45.

39. See Roosevelt's State of the Union Address of 1944 and his campaign address on October 28, 1944.

PART III

Nongovernmental Institutions

8

Candidate-Centered Parties: Politics Without Intermediaries

STEPHEN A. SALMORE
BARBARA G. SALMORE

The theme of this volume—reform in the United States—is likely always to be a timely one. The American polity was conceived as an exercise in reform. The Constitution was a reform of the Articles of Confederation, and Americans have engaged in repeated political reforms ever since. The latest burst of political reform—of presidential nomination procedures and campaign finance in the 1970s—reinforced and accelerated changes in the role of political parties that had begun in the Progressive Era. These reforms, combined with technological changes, fully realized the Progressive agenda of breaking the power of party leaders. The end result is the voter- and candidate-centered political system that the Progressives desired but that was not technologically possible to achieve at the time.

In a larger sense, however, the reforms of the 1970s made little difference; with or without them, we would have had a candidate-centered system. The reforms made the emergence of a candidate-dominated rather than party-dominated presidential contest a bit easier, and more significantly, they gave institutional shape to the current political system by encouraging the emergence of political-action committees and the decline of parties. The seeds of this system were sown at the turn of the century, but more than fifty years passed before they emerged full-blown, when social and technological conditions were finally appropriate. Those who argue that the decline of the parties was due primarily to the reforms vent their dismay at a convenient scapegoat but miss the larger picture: The reforms reflect fundamental social shifts of which they are as much a consequence as a cause.

After more fully developing this historical analysis and elaborating on how changes in presidential nominations and campaign finance reinforced the decline of the party's role in elections, this chapter will consider the nature of the current political system and its consequences for public policy. The major impact of weakened parties is the increased reluctance of elected officials to tackle divisive issues that might jeopardize their success at the polls. Without the assurance that a party organization and the party label can produce electoral majorities, politicians increasingly cope with substantive issues by inventing devices that require neither the adoption of explicit positions nor recorded votes. Thus they turn to "Gramm-Rudman"–type bills, entitlement programs, catch-all continuing resolutions, and omnibus reconciliation bills instead of requiring up or down votes on specific issues. Extraparliamentary devices such as the initiative and referendum, balanced-budget amendments, and expenditure caps are more attractive to both legislators and their constituents as means of forcing government action on troublesome issues. Although many observers have predicted that weakened parties necessarily lead to political immobilism, we believe that new policy processes are emerging to cope with a new alignment of political forces.

AMERICAN PARTY ORGANIZATIONS:
A BRIEF HISTORICAL SUMMARY

American parties as organizational entities have undergone four phases, each conditioned by the prevailing "rules of the game."[1] In the first phase, through the mid-1820s, party organizations were purely legislative caucuses or parliamentary parties. Legislators, self-nominated or chosen in caucuses of local notables, sought direction and information from other members of their state delegations rather than from the weak and undeveloped institutional leadership. Party lines and even membership were amorphous, and fluid and shifting coalitions were typical. Antipathy to partisan politics was as pervasive among officials as it was among the public. Presidents, nominated by factional congressional party caucuses, were forced to construct personal coalitions, all the while regarding nominal partisan majorities, in Jefferson's words, as "a rope of sand."[2]

In the second phase, from roughly 1830 to the turn of the century, the parties evolved into elaborate extragovernmental organizations whose chief purposes were to choose nominees for office at all levels and to campaign for their election. Rooted in sectional and religious division, sustained by patronage and particularistic, distributive policy, supported by strong partisan voting, and concentrated at the state and local level, the extragovernmental organizations came to be the meaning of "party" in common speech. As the period progressed and legislative service became more demanding, complex, and materially rewarding, professional politicians replaced the reluctant amateurs of the first phase. At the presidential level, as the pro- and anti-Jacksonian factions coalesced into national parties, both decided that national conventions would be the best way to choose a standard-bearer and plan a national campaign. These conventions were dominated by the state parties, which found them a convenient way to gather every four years for the purpose of presidential selection. Politics was ideological and vituperative—a matter of "preaching to the choir" and mobilizing a partisan base rather than of attempting to persuade or convert.[3]

A third (transitional) phase began at the end of the nineteenth century and lasted through approximately 1960. Locally based extragovernmental organizations and strong partisan identification continued in many areas of the country. But socioeconomic upheaval spawned the Populist and Progressive movements, which in turn generated political reforms that made primary challenges and split-ticket voting feasible for the first time since 1830. The predominantly lower-class and agrarian Populists provided the initial emotional public reaction against concentrations of economic and political power, but it was the predominantly middle-class and urban Progressives who eventually enacted the legislation that began the next transformation of American parties.

The establishment of the direct primary was the key reform, potentially removing nominating powers from the party organizations and subjecting the parties, previously "unknown to law," to massive public regulation.[4] The adoption of government-prepared secret ballots, the direct election of U.S. senators, the elimination of much federal patronage, and the imposition of registration laws were also important. In addition, the Progressives provided for methods to bypass parties altogether, by means of nonpartisan local elections and the initiative, referendum, and recall.

The reformers did not entirely eliminate or even weaken the stranglehold of party organizations on nominations and campaigns in those areas where they were well established before the Populist and Progressive onslaught. But they made serious inroads into the hegemony of the southern Bourbons (large landowners) and the minions of the mining companies, banks, and railroads in the west.[5] Thus the first half of the twentieth century was characterized by a mixed system of traditional and weak extragovernmental party organizations. The electoral realignment of 1932 gave new life to the development of strong psychological party identification, which had waned during the Populist and Progressive Eras, and the patronage opportunities of New Deal programs gave a lift to traditional party organizations as well.[6]

The Progressive reforms had the least effect on presidential nominations. Many states that chose all other major officeholders in the primaries still used state party caucuses and conventions to select delegates to the national party conventions that named presidential candidates. Congress rejected the national presidential primary initially proposed by Woodrow Wilson in 1913. The alternative route—whereby convention delegates were chosen in individual state primaries—did make some headway, reaching a high-water mark of 26 in 1916. This total would not be reached, much less exceeded, for another fifty years. In the interim, presidential primaries, unlike those for other offices, increasingly fell into disuse, dropping back to 16 by 1936.

James Ceaser cites a number of reasons why a presidential primary system failed to take hold.[7] Short-term political factors in 1916 worked against it. The Democrats had in Wilson a popular incumbent who did not draw primary opponents, and attractive "popular hero" figures did not emerge on the Republican side. Many states had complex laws requiring early filing dates and large numbers of petition signatures. In some, the delegates selected in the primaries were not legally bound to particular candidates. The Democrats' "two-thirds rule"—requiring that the nominee win the support of that proportion of delegates—made it impossible to win their nomination mostly by primary victories. When no candidate pursuing a dominant primary-based "outside strategy" succeeded between 1916 and 1924, presidential hopefuls increasingly abandoned the primary route.

Hence, after the early 1920s many states abandoned their presidential primaries, negated their intent by passing laws barring delegates from publicizing which candidates they favored, or developed a tradition of entering "favorite son" candidates for bargaining purposes at the national conventions. Primary results could still make a difference when combined with significant organizational support. For example, Franklin Roosevelt's strong primary showings against Al Smith in 1932 made it easier for party leaders to deny Smith's renomination and to turn to New York's current governor instead. John Kennedy's 1960 primary victory in over-whelmingly Protestant West Virginia diminished fears about the electoral effect of his Catholicism. On the other hand, Estes Kefauver's string of 1952 primary victories could not overcome the party leaders' distaste for the Tennessean. In general, however, this transitional period did prompt party leaders to give more consideration to public opinion as they made their presidential choices.

Though not completely successful from the reformers' point of view, the third phase of party development did set the stage for the fourth and current epoch. Richard Jensen calls this epoch, which began in the 1960s, "the last party system."[8] Social and geographic mobility, television, computers, and the development of the private political-consulting in-dustry finally freed almost all candidates from the need to rely primarily on an extragovernmental party organization. Political consultants did not arise to fill the gap caused by disintegrating party organizations;

rather, as is true of markets generally, they were competitors to the party organizations, and they grew as they became able to offer the same services more efficiently and effectively.[9] The increasing loss of confidence in all public institutions during the 1960s and 1970s, including the political parties, certainly helped the candidate-centered process along, but it is unlikely that it was causal. The traditional subnational extragovernmental parties had previously survived the larger crises of the Civil War and the Great Depression.

Insurgents of the third phase still thought in terms of party organizations as the vehicle for electoral success. The Progressives and Populists *were* parties that ran candidates for many offices and sought to control government. They had before them a recent historical example of a third or "minor" party—the Republicans—that had become the majority party. Yet the Progressives' legacy of legal regulation of the parties set the stage for the institutionalization of the two party system. With the third party option virtually ruled out, the "reformers" of the 1950s set up "shadow" political clubs that aimed to "take over" the "regular" party organizations.[10] By the fourth phase, however, entrepreneurial candidates had found the major parties' primaries so permeable that organizations beyond their own personal followings were largely unnecessary. Classic "third party type candidates"—such as 1980 presidential contestant John Anderson and major gubernatorial candidates in Maine and Arizona in the late 1970s and 1980s—did not have to maintain even the pretense of running as "party" candidates.

Congressional candidates in the fourth phase who constructed their own electoral coalitions and worked ceaselessly to maintain them created the "incumbency effect" that political scientists first noted in the early 1970s. On the macro level, the power of presidential coattails diminished and the average number of congressional districts with split partisan results increased markedly.[11] So did the interelection swing in individual House districts.[12] On the micro level, straight-ticket voting by partisan identifiers decreased and independent voters heavily favored incumbents.[13] The proportion of voters citing personality characteristics and attentiveness to constituents as reasons for positively evaluating incumbents increased and references to party, experience, and record declined. Yet the voters' increasingly individual judgments also carried dangers; credible challengers could threaten all but the safest incumbents, and the margin required to maintain a "safe" seat also widened.[14] Though studied most intensively in relation to House elections, the incumbency effect, the increase in split-ticket voting, and the importance of challenger quality also play significant roles in elections for the U.S. Senate, governorships, and the state legislatures.[15]

The last bastion to fall completely was the presidential nomination; the reforms of the 1970s finally ended the dominance of the party organizations in that venue as well. The mixed system ended, as presidential candidates became essentially self-nominated, and the state parties were swept aside. These reforms fall into two basic categories: changes in the delegate-selection process for the parties' quadrennial presidential nominating conventions, and changes in the campaign finance rules for both presidential and nonpresidential federal elections.

CHANGES IN THE PRESIDENTIAL
NOMINATION RULES

The occasion for major changes in the presidential nominating process was the stormy Democratic convention of 1968. Activists opposing the Vietnam War had managed to drive President Johnson out of the contest and succeeded in bringing to the forefront two anti-war candidates, Eugene McCarthy and Robert Kennedy, who between them garnered more than 75 percent of the votes cast in the seventeen primaries that year. Yet, despite their strong showing and the tragedy of Kennedy's assassination on the final night of the primary season, the Democratic regulars who still controlled the majority of convention delegates were able to write a more or less pro-war platform for the party and nominate Vice-President Hubert Humphrey, who had not contested a single primary following Johnson's withdrawal. Both inside and outside the Chicago convention hall, frustrated opponents expressed their rage. After Humphrey's general election loss, the splintered Democratic party appointed a commission headed by South Dakota Senator George McGovern and Minnesota Representative Donald Fraser to consider what could be done to avoid a replay of 1968.

Austin Ranney provides a convenient summary of the extensive literature on the Democratic party delegate-selection reforms enacted by the McGovern-Fraser Commission between 1968 and 1972 and only marginally altered by the succeeding Mikulski and Winograd Commissions that set the rules for the 1976 and 1980 conventions.[16] Ranney notes that the reformers had three basic goals: increased participation for issue and candidate proponents, proportional representation for selected demographic groups, and "fair reflection" of candidates' support.

A number of rule changes were directed at increased convention participation by those mobilized by a particular candidate or issue in any given year. Simply put, state parties were required to adopt a uniform set of rules for delegate selection all over the state and to make those rules easily available. A number of other practices that had benefited party regulars—such as beginning the delegate-selection process before all candidates were declared or at least known, proxy voting, and the unit rule—were abolished.

Proportional representation of certain demographic groups was another device intended to ensure representation at the nominating convention by groups that were important supporters of Democratic candidates but had not been well represented in traditional party organizations. It was political scientist Austin Ranney, as a member of the McGovern-Fraser Commission, who originally suggested that blacks should enjoy an affirmative action provision;[17] other members quickly added women and young people to the list. The outcome was that, by 1980, representation of all these groups at Democratic conventions had more than tripled relative to 1968.[18]

Finally, "fair reflection" of candidate strength resulted in the outlawing of winner-take-all primaries such as those in California, where all of the state's delegates were given to the candidate who was "first past the post"—even if that candidate garnered only a narrow victory over the competition. The new system, approaching proportional representation, would likely benefit candidates other than the favorite of the regulars.[19]

Most of the reformers' wishes were fulfilled. As a result of their efforts, conventions were now increasingly populated by first-time attenders, non-regulars, and non-officeholders—devotees of quintessentially "outside" candidates such as George McGovern and George Wallace in 1972 and Jimmy Carter in 1976. Much of the middle-aged, white male backbone of the party organization was replaced at the convention by blacks, women, and young people. Because many of the party officeholders supported "regular" candidates who did not fare that well in the new delegate-selection procedures, the number of officeholders attending the convention as delegates plummeted. For example, whereas almost two-thirds of all Democratic senators and one-third of the party's House members had been convention delegates in 1968, less than one-fifth of both groups were represented in the 1976 and 1980 party gatherings.[20] Proportional representation kept the candidacies of insurgents alive long after they would have faded away under the old system.

Perhaps the only unexpected result of the reformers' efforts was one that the 1920s Progressives, had they been watching, would have heartily approved. The members of the McGovern-Fraser Commission had no desire to substitute a large number of primaries for the dominant state caucus-convention mode. Their wish, seen in the provisions for regularizing and publicizing the holding of local caucuses and conventions, was that issue and candidate activists would be able to join traditional party leaders in choosing delegates at party caucuses. They hoped that if they "made the party's nonprimary delegate selection processes more open and fair, participation in them would increase greatly and consequently the demand for more primaries would fade away."[21] However, fearful of running afoul of the complex rules for holding caucuses, many state parties chose to hold primaries instead. The number of primaries rose from 17 in 1968 to 31 in 1980. By 1976, the presidential candidates' own organizations had completely asserted their primacy over the state parties. The quadrennial party conventions became shows run by the winning candidates' organizations.

The number of primary voters was on average only about half the general election turnout, but still more than four times the participation in a well-attended state caucus. Thus, although the primary voters were better educated, wealthier, and otherwise different from the general electorate, it would be difficult to claim that they were less representative than the party regulars participating in caucuses who had preceded them. As Willilam Crotty has written, "If popular involvement is the objective of the reformers, and to a large extent it is, then primaries quite clearly appear to be the best mechanism available."[22]

Three Democratic nominating cycles—those in 1972, 1976, and 1980—operated under a fairly pure version of the McGovern-Fraser rules. A number of observers argued that their effects were deleterious to the party; they pointed out that the first beneficiary, George McGovern, was swept away in one of the largest landslides in American history, and that the failed presidency of the 1976 "outsider," Jimmy Carter, was responsible for an even more widespread party defeat in 1980. Consequently, after the 1980 election, a kind of reform "counter-revolution" set in as yet another party commission, the Hunt Commission, chaired by the then-governor of North Carolina attempted to "reform the reforms."[23]

In actuality, the goals of the Hunt Commission were relatively modest and did little in either theory or practice to tamper with the main thrusts of the McGovern-Fraser Commission's work. The two principal goals of this latest commission were, first, to make it somewhat easier for a single candidate to build up an early lead and limit the possibility of a brokered and factionalized convention that would not play well on television; and, second, to restore the opportunity for officeholder-delegates and other party professionals to play a restraining role at the convention in their efforts to ensure that both the candidate and the platform were widely acceptable.[24] The first goal was to be achieved by allowing each state to raise its "threshold"—that is, the proportion of votes a candidate had to garner in a primary to be awarded any delegates. Although statewide winner-take-all primaries were not reinstated, in addition to pure proportional representation, states were permitted to use the winner-take-all system on the basis of electoral districts, or to award a "bonus delegate" to the leading candidate in a district, in what might be called "winner-take-more" system. The second goal was to be met by creating the "superdelegate" category, which entailed the awarding of additional convention seats to states and the distribution of these seats only to officeholders (especially members of the congressional delegation and governors) and party leaders. As a result, the representation of senators at the 1984 convention returned to the 1968 level, and House members more than doubled their 1968 participation rates.[25] Most superdelegates, unlike other convention participants, were not legally bound to any candidate.

It can be argued not only that the Hunt Commission reforms largely failed to achieve their stated goals[26] but also that the problems they addressed had no empirical basis. Beginning in 1972, fears were expressed in every election cycle that proportional representation would lead at worst to a brokered convention and at best to a late decision on a nominee who would then have little time to heal party wounds. In fact, after the McGovern debacle, the likely nominee was evident fairly early in the primary season, as a combination of media "winnowing" and voter judgments quickly reduced the number of active candidates. The 1988 nomination contest, when Michael Dukakis broke from the pack of candidates (uncharitably and unfairly known as the "Seven Dwarfs") following the early April Wisconsin primary, provided the acid test of the ability of a system based heavily on proportional representation to "winnow": Here was a lame-duck Republican president enmeshed in scandal as the primary season opened, and an open race in both parties.[27]

Nor did the superdelegates play their appointed role as disengaged or unpledged observers who could weigh in on the side of pragmatism if the primary season ended with an unsettled or unsatisfactory result. In 1984, a large number of superdelegates declared for Mondale before the primary season had even started, and the cushion they provided the former vice-president likely salvaged Mondale's candidacy. Ironically, they also ensured the defeat of Gary Hart, who was, throughout most of the race, running much better in the polls against President Reagan than was the establishment favorite. Moreover, the rules aimed at helping "insider" candidates did not prevent consummate outsiders Hart and Jesse Jackson from together garnering more primary votes than Mondale. In 1988, Jackson did even better; and the closest thing to an "insider," House leader Richard Gephardt, was driven out of the race after Super Tuesday. This time, most of the superdelegates waited until the primary contests were over and then declared for the obvious frontrunner, Dukakis.

On the other hand, the Hunt Commission may have had an impact on the popular view of the Democratic party. It was no accident that it was headed by a governor from the South—that region of the country whose changing allegiances contributed so much to the Democrats' downfall after 1968. Paul Kirk, the new party chair after 1984, also moved to reinforce the moderate image that the Hunt Commission projected by dismantling all the "special group" demographic caucuses attached to the Democratic National Committee and substituting in their place a more conventional geographic organization. Dukakis's choices of Texans Ann Richardson and Lloyd Bentsen as the 1988 convention keynote speaker and vice-presidential candidate, respectively, continued the Hunt Commission's image thrust.

A major point to note about the work of the Democratic rules commissions since McGovern-Fraser is that they have essentially operated in the short-term tactical interests of the leading candidates. The Winograd Commission changed the 1980 rules to favor the renomination of the incumbent, Jimmy Carter. At the 1984 convention, the Mondale forces, in an effort to promote harmony, agreed to yet another "Fairness Commission" to set the rules for 1988. The task of this last commission was to deal with complaints by the Hart and Jackson forces about the changes the Hunt Commission had made in delegate allocation and the role of the superdelegates. In fact, the commission left the rules basically unchanged, except for slightly *increasing* the number of superdelegates. In 1988, Jackson once again brought up the same issues, and the 1988 Convention Rules Committee, controlled by Michael Dukakis, agreed that the 1992 convention will have fewer superdelegates and will require all states to use only proportional representation to allocate delegates. If the agreement holds, the work of the Hunt Commission would, in considerable measure, be eradicated. Commenting on these changes, David E. Price (a political scientist elected to the House in 1986, who was in 1980 staff director of the Hunt Commission) observed with dismay, "it is a familiar path that we see. Candidates meet their short-term needs but sell out the long-term interests of the party." Alluding specifically to the cutback in superdelegates, Price continued, "It's just a terrible idea. It goes another step toward making the national committee candidate-dominated."[28]

THE PRESIDENTIAL NOMINATING REFORMS— CAUSE OR EFFECT?

Ironically enough, despite the enormous amount of both favorable and unfavorable commentary about the reforms of the 1970s, the massive changes in presidential nomination procedures called for by these reforms were, to the extent that anything is, virtually inevitable. The reforms themselves were merely part of these inevitable changes.

The democratization (with a small "d") of the presidential nomination process was the end of a process that was set in motion by the Progressives at the turn of the century—one that had already substantially affected the contests for every other visible political office in the country. Its spread to the presidency awaited only widespread, reliable jet air travel and the television networks that would make of the country one media market. We could advance this assertion with considerable confidence if there were an example of another major political party that did not suffer the events of 1968, and made no significant attempts to "reform" itself, but ended up with a nomination process similar to that of the Democrats. Fortunately, we do have such an example—the Republicans.

The Republican party did not adopt any of the McGovern-Fraser Commission's major goals. Nor did it not impose any delegate-selection procedures on its state parties. In 1988, many Republican proceedings, particularly in the smaller states, were the same informal caucuses organized by "regulars" that they had been twenty years ago. There were no calls for "proportional representation"; even women did not achieve near-parity until the Republican convention of 1984. "Fair reflection" of candidate showings was a rarity; most of the large states holding Republican primaries clung to the statewide winner-take-all model. The fact that the Democrats controlled the majority of state legislatures during the reform period and state laws governed some aspects of the presidential selection process (such as the dates of primaries for state offices) meant that the Republicans would be dragged along by the Democratic tide to some extent. But these effects were fairly minimal, inasmuch as numerous Republican state parties chose a selection procedure different from that of their Democratic counterparts or held their events on a different day.

Despite its "unreformed" nature, however, the Republican selection process came to mirror that of the Democrats in many ways. Opponents of reform who point to the McGovern-Fraser dicta as the reason for insurgent George McGovern's success in 1972 do not explain how insurgent Barry Goldwater gained the Republican nomination in 1964 under the "old rules." The 1976 election is remarkable not just because a Democratic challenger unseated an incumbent Republican president, but because Republican challenger Ronald Reagan garnered almost half the primary and convention vote in the incumbent president's own party—a far more impressive performance than Edward Kennedy's challenge to his party's incumbent president four years later. Just as former Democratic Vice-President Walter Mondale had to contend with an initially large field in 1984, so too did Republican Vice-President George Bush in 1988. Mondale's principal opponent, Gary Hart, failed in 1984 in large measure because he had not constructed a personal organization to turn out for caucuses and fill delegate slots in the South. An almost identical problem bedeviled Bush's chief rival, Senator Robert Dole, in the South on Super Tuesday, 1988.

Hence, if there is a "culprit" in the current presidential selection process, the evidence points not to the reformers of the 1970s but, rather, to the technology that permitted the Progressives' dream of a half-century ago to finally come true. A number of the harshest critics of the reforms reluctantly acknowledge the role of technology (particularly television). Jeane Kirkpatrick, who wrote a well-known critique of party reform in the midst of the 1970s reform era, in fact lays the blame for contemporary conditions squarely at the feet of both the Progressives *and* technology: "It is the use of television in direct primaries and other open contests which enables would-be candidates to develop with voters relations that are not mediated by the parties."[29] She adds that although advocates of the direct primary may have wished to return power to the people, "presumably they did not intend to vest power in Walter Cronkite and other media moguls or to speed the development of a personalist politics with standards and practices more relevant to entertainment than to public affairs."[30] In so critiquing the alleged impacts of the reforms, she attributes a type of influence to the press that systematic analysis does not find,[31] and she attributes to participants in torchlight parades and smoke-filled rooms a more serious concern with public affairs than that of the issue-oriented activists of the television era.

The recent presidential nomination reforms may have changed the odds for certain candidates, but there is no evidence that in the absence of these reforms, we would not have the present candidate-dominated presidential nomination system. The reforms were more consequence than cause. The televised debates of 1960 were widely considered a major reason for John Kennedy's victory, and the powerful television images of the events surrounding his assassination drew the nation together. His successor, Lyndon Johnson, pioneered television advertising by political consultants, was brought down by the first televised war, and used a televised speech to withdraw from the presidential contest in 1968. Moreover, the television images of the 1968 Democratic convention were a major factor in generating the presidential nomination reforms that followed it, as anti-party activists chanted, "The whole world is watching."[32]

The reformers of the 1970s deliberately used television as a major weapon to overwhelm the party regulars. As Crotty notes, the McGovern-Fraser Commission skillfully used the media to gain support for its efforts:

The commission leaders and staff made every effort to cultivate the press. . . . It hoped to pressure party leaders on the state and national level toward a more receptive stance on reform questions by nurturing as pro-reform a media orientation as it could. . . . The burden was placed on those against reform to explain themselves to a public and press generally favorable to what the McGovern-Fraser Commission was trying to do. The anti-reformers never effectively dealt with this handicap.[33]

Television, which first reached a majority of American households in 1960, thus made the wider public feel they were players, and it was the characters in the play—the candidates and other personalities—to whom they reacted.

This is not to say that the political reforms of the 1970s failed to exert a powerful and independent influence on politics. They did have this effect—particularly to the extent that they dealt with campaign money, the "mother's milk of politics." It is to this second set of reforms that we now turn.

CAMPAIGN FINANCE REFORMS IN THE 1970S

Long experience with campaign finance legislation shows that the amount of money flowing into politics cannot be stopped or even notably diminished but only to some extent directed. The presidential nomination reforms could not alter the ultimate shape of the process; they could only benefit certain types of candidates. But the campaign finance reforms, whether intentionally or not, exerted a much more powerful independent influence on the trend toward candidate-centered rather than party-centered campaigns.

The public financing of presidential elections contributed to the candidate-centered trend in a number of ways. First, and most important, the legislation specified that money would flow through candidate rather than party committees. The success of candidates in the nomination phase thus became dependent on their individual abilities to raise the money needed for high media visibility and construction of a national organization. Second, the limits placed on the size of individual con-tributions meant that a few party "fat cats" could not provide most of the funds for a particular candidate as they often had done in the past. Candidates had to demonstrate an ability to attract relatively small sums from a large number of people all over the country—an estimated 30 million in 1988. Third, once the major party candidates were chosen and had accepted public funding, they could no longer accept new contributions or spend any leftover money from the primary season.[34]

The strictures placed on spending in the general election—that is, the strictures on both the absolute amounts and the legitimate purposes—made candidates extremely leery of cooperative ventures with fellow partisans running in other contests.[35] Amendments to the rules in 1979, permitting so-called soft-money expenditures by state and local parties for "party-building" and such items as buttons and bumper stickers, had only minor effects on the amount of overt cooperation between presidential and other campaigns; as the soft money accounts grew, so too did criticism of them and demands for public disclosure of these contributions and expenditures.

The major reason why the campaign finance reforms of this period were much more far-reaching than the more intensively studied presidential nomination reforms is that they affected aspirants for almost every other office as well. Public financing of the presidential race had the clear effect of directing money that would have been spent on that contest to legislative candidates instead. Even though the presidential spending limits were breeched by soft money and independent expenditures and were greatly in excess of the nominal public funding limits, Alexander and Haggerty estimate that when adjusted for inflation, the amount spent on the 1972 election (the last without public funding and spending limits) was still slightly more than the total amount spent in 1984.[36]

In contrast, congressional spending, controlled for inflation, more than doubled between 1974 and 1986. Much of the money came from business-related PAC contributors whose political spending was both regularized and legitimized by the new finance laws. Since the PAC contribution limit of $5,000 per candidate per election applied to presidential as well as legislative candidates, and since there were so many more legislative candidates, PAC money was insignificant in presidential elections but increasingly significant in legislative contests. The PAC portion of legislative warchests spiraled upward in each succeeding election cycle, constituting 34 percent of all House candidates' campaign spending in 1986. Another sizable chunk came from the only individual expenditures that were not limited by law—spending by individual candidates. In the landmark *Buckley* v. *Valeo* decision, the Supreme Court ruled that in the absence of public funding, limiting personal expenditures by candidates constitutes abridgement of the freedom of speech. In practice, therefore, only presidential candidates are limited (to $75,000) in the spending of their own money. Individual personal expenditures of more than $1 million by federal legislative candidates are increasingly common.[37]

The decision to channel the vast majority of PAC spending through individual candidate campaign committees was a decisive blow to party-centered campaigning at the legislative level. Although individual PACs were much more limited than the party organizations in the amounts they could donate to individual candidates, there was no ceiling on the total amount of PAC money a candidate could accept, and the number of PACs proliferated to more than 4,000 by the 1988 election cycle. As a result, the absolute maximum all party organizations could contribute in a hotly contested legislative race was approximately 10–15 percent of a candidate's warchest, whereas the average PAC portion was more like half of the total. Over time, therefore, the PAC to party ratio of campaign money increased from 3:2 in 1978 to 5:2 in 1986.

Although FECA (the major federal campaign finance law) does not apply to state-level candidates, it had a noticeable effect at that level. This effect was in contrast to the presidential selection changes, inasmuch as the direct primary and television had made media and candidate-centered executive campaigns common in gubernatorial races by the late 1960s, when they propelled insurgents such as Nelson Rockefeller in New York and Milton Shapp in Pennsylvania to victory.

The FECA reforms also had notable repercussions, however. First, beginning in the 1970s, the wealthy national Republican party, legally barred from spending all it had raised in the federal races, increasingly channeled money to state parties, particularly those otherwise feeble and bankrupt, such as in the South. These state Republican parties, facing the same or greater deficits of party identifiers as at the national level, saw that the key to electing more state legislators and governors was an essentially nonpartisan appeal to independents and weak Democrats—based not on party but on issues or candidate personality. Thus party money was directed to boosting the campaigns of individual legislators by means of expensive high-tech tactics such as polling, direct mail, and media advertising. Aside from brief verbal or small-print "disclaimers" giving the required notice of who paid for the message, it was almost impossible to determine the candidate's party.

Second, in the wake of the national mood of reform in the 1970s, many states enacted campaign finance laws with significant similarities to FECA. In a few, such as New Jersey and Michigan (and, to a lesser extent, Wisconsin and Minnesota), public financing was provided for governors' races, with contribution and expenditure limits closely modeled on FECA. In almost all states, however, legislation was passed that established state-level PACs. Curiously enough, PACs were set up and became widely used campaign-contribution vehicles, even in states that placed no limits on the size or role of corporate contributions in legislative campaigns. Perhaps concern about their image in a moralistic era led businesses in these states to establish political action committees and to use them as their primary contribution channel.

This newly available party and PAC money had the same effect in the larger states that it did at the federal level: increasingly expensive, media-based, and candidate-centered campaigns. By the 1980s, in such states as New Jersey, New York, Ohio, Pennsylvania, and Illinois, hotly contested legislative races were regularly costing $300,000 and up. In California, where state senate districts are larger than federal congressional districts, warchests for competitive races consistently exceeded $1 million.

A device that became particularly common at the state level was the amassing of large sums controlled by the legislative leadership and donated primarily by PACs. At the federal level, corporate PACs directed their contributions heavily to relevant committee and subcommittee chairs, and to incumbents far more than to challengers. Each congressional campaign was of sufficient size to operate as an individual "enterprise."[38] However, most state legislative candidates, while requiring many of the same campaign services as U.S. legislators, did not have the same resource base or economies of scale. In addition, greater legislative turnover in some states and a tradition of rotating committee leadership rather than honoring seniority made it more "rational" for contributors seeking favors and access to give their contributions to the party leaders in the legislature who often appointed committee chairs and were responsible for posting and scheduling bills. Most leaders did not dole out these contributions on the basis of party fealty; rather they selected recipients who could be counted on to support the leaders' own tenure in office.[39]

In sum, the campaign finance reforms—unlike those of the presidential nomination process—cannot be seen simply as a reflection or culmination of a trend that was inevitable. Intentionally or not, they contributed much more directly and massively to the spread of the candidate-centered style to virtually every level of the system.

THE REFORMS OF THE 1970S
AND THEIR IMPACT ON THE POLICY PROCESS

The major policy impact of the most recent political reforms is that it is now more difficult for presidents to assemble policy coalitions; in addition, legislators are even more sensitive than before to prospects of electoral retribution resulting from the policy positions they take. In the past, stronger party identification and more coat-tail voting made presidents' jobs easier. A victorious presidential candidate could assume a partisan majority in both houses of the legislature: Not once in the twentieth century until Eisenhower's second election did the president's party fail to carry the House and Senate.

Although coalitions on major pieces of legislation were not identical, presidents could assume some stability in the patterns of support and, except in the case of the southern Democrats, some measure of party loyalty. Party voting in the House peaked around 1910 but returned to levels almost as high in the early Roosevelt and Eisenhower years. The oft-noted party voting of the Reagan era was notable only by comparison with the recent past; it never reached the peaks that Roosevelt or Eisenhower had scored.[40] Even the popular Reagan could not carry the House in 1980, and his strong first-term staff had to choose its policy shots carefully in order to succeed.

From the standpoint of federal legislators throughout the 1960s, there was (for most members) much to be gained from going along with the president or party leadership on major votes, and little to be lost. Close to half of all members came from marginal districts (getting less than 60 percent of the vote), and the fortunes of a substantial number were pinned to the president's success or failure. As party identification and its impact on the vote declined throughout the 1970s and 1980s, however, legislators' party labels became significantly less important and their records became more so.[41] Going along with the president or the party leadership on a tough vote now had to be considered in the light of how the vote could be used in an opponent's negative television commercial or direct-mail piece.

There were many institutional manifestations of legislators' electoral calculations. The total number of bills introduced, the roll calls, the substantive votes on authorizations and appropriations, and the ratio of items passed to those introduced all dropped dramatically after the mid-1970s, as legislators sought to protect their electoral flanks.[42] As Mayhew and Fiorina had predicted, position-taking, advertising, credit-taking, and constituency service came to be seen as more rewarding, or at least safer, ways to spend one's time than legislating.[43]

In addition to Congress lowering its electoral exposure by legislating less, the nature of legislation changed. Particularly in the Reagan years, statutes increasingly dealt with decremental matters—never a happy prospect for a politician. The response was to make such pieces of legislation as few and as invisible as possible. Changes—especially cuts— were folded into single budget resolutions and massive continuing resolutions (CRs). Legislators had to vote only once on the CRs and the budget resolutions. Even better, from their point of view, was the Deficit Reduction Act of 1986, popularly known as Gramm-Rudman-Hollings for its chief sponsors. This act absolved Congress of the need to vote on budget cuts at all by specifying that cuts would occur automatically across the board if Congress failed to cut the budget by a specified amount each year into the 1990s. Moreover, supporters of Gramm-Rudman-Hollings could claim that they had voted for strong action against the spiraling budget deficit; but they could also argue, with technical correctness, that they had not personally voted to cut any particular programs popular with constituents. Finally, legislators in many of the states could increasingly leave contentious issues to be dealt with as initiative or referendum questions rather than taking them on themselves.[44]

Perhaps most remarkable in this situation is the fact that the candidate-centered period saw the passage of a number of pieces of genuinely landmark legislation. At the same time that many members of Congress were viewing a low profile and ombudsmanship as the ticket to reelection, other policy entrepreneurs were taking advantage of their relative freedom from a president's agenda and an era of a feisty legislative branch to push important measures. Certainly included in this category would be recent immigration legislation and the tax cut and tax reform acts that more or less bracket the beginning and end of the Reagan presidency.

Two similarities in all of these Reagan-era landmarks bear mention. First, all are familiarly known by the names of the members of Congress who pushed them, and a number were bipartisan efforts. (The Simpson-Mazzoli bipartisan immigration duo; the Kemp-Roth tax-cut alliance; the leadership group that offered the Bradley-Gephardt and Kemp-Kasten tax reform measures come to mind.) The nomenclature of these far-reaching pieces of legislation is a nontrivial reminder of a member-centered legislature's current role vis-à-vis a president twice elected in landslides. In the mid-1900s, the practice of identifying major bills by their sponsors had pretty much died out. Major Nixon-era measures, for example, such as the War Powers Act and the Budget Act, are not known by the names of their chief advocates. But the practice of attaching such names has returned in the 1980s.

Second, many of these legislative entrepreneurs were able to eventually carry the day for their innovations—but not because they were committee chairs or even senior members. Indeed, at the time that Kemp-Roth and Gramm-Rudman-Hollings passed, none of the officeholders most visibly associated with the bills (Kemp, Gramm, and Rudman) had served on a tax-writing committee. Rather, they were skilled at interacting with the Washington policy communities and issue networks, and at public and media relations. Their audience was made up of issue and media elites, not party elites. Students of Congress increasingly note a new pattern of legislative activity, in which collegiality counts more than hierarchy and entrepreneurship counts more than formal leadership roles.[45]

CAN THE REFORMS BE REFORMED?

When Jeane Kirkpatrick argued that of all the factors that contribute to the decline of parties' abilities to perform their traditional functions reforms are the most important, she and likeminded critics presumably meant that further reforms could improve the situation for the parties.[46] Indeed, as discussed earlier, both the actions taken during Paul Kirk's chairmanship of the Democratic party and the work of the Hunt Commission were perceived as constituting a certain amount of "counter-reform." Yet all of the most important outlines of the McGovern-Fraser rules remain intact. Although the tinkering with the length of the primary "window," thresholds, and proportional representation may offer minor advantages to certain types of candidates, it has had virtually no affect on the basic candidate-centered process—as the "unreformed" Republican experience shows. The one set of reforms that could actually strengthen parties—giving parties control over most campaign money—is seriously discussed by no one but a handful of political scientists.[47]

A number of fundamental American cultural characteristics contribute both to the inability of any "pro-party" reform to make a notable dent in the candidate-centered nature of American politics and to the continuing hope, mostly on the part of political scientists, that some set of new changes will re-empower the parties. Let us begin with the proponents of parties. As Harris indicates in his introductory essay in this volume, Americans have held to the metaphor of the body politic as a machine that can be "fixed" or "adjusted" if we simply modify or change some parts. This thinking is reflected clearly in many of the writings of scholars associated with the Committee for Party Renewal.[48] Sabato, for example, advances a typical set of "reforms" that would strengthen the parties, and then immediately reports the results of a specially commissioned poll indicating that the public opposition to every single one of them is so great that passage of any is virtually impossible.

These poll results point to a second fundamental characteristic of American culture—the historical strain of anti-partyism that stretches back to the Federalist Papers and Washington's Farewell Address. It was precisely the anti-party nature of the Progressive reforms, and not certain technicalities in their drafting, that enabled them to achieve as many of their objectives as rapidly as they did.

Kirkpatrick and others[49] recognize the organic rather than mechanistic or rational nature of politics, but they err in thinking that if only the reformers of the 1970s had never existed, the parties could have been significantly revived or at least would not have disintegrated further. As argued earlier, however, the cultural dynamics appear inexorable. Ceaser notes that four basic factors affect party strength: prevailing public opinion, social change and communications technology, realigning issues, and legal rules.[50] Looking at these factors over time, one can argue, as Epstein does, that only the last keeps the parties from becoming nothing more than what Arterton[51] calls "super-PACs":

The electoral looseness of the established major parties, especially as it is legally institutionalized, acts as a preservative. But like a preservative in food processing, or perhaps an embalming fluid, it also changes the nature and quality of what is being preserved. In the case of the parties, the end product may be little more than an electoral label whose value or meaningfulness beyond election day is often questioned.[52]

Public opinion toward the parties may have become somewhat less hostile and simply more neutral in recent years,[53] but it is certainly not supportive. The overdue realignment, suspected since 1964, has been incomplete at best or buried by a concurrent dealignment at worst.[54] Social change and communications technology have been the key factors in substantially shaping public opinion and the issue climate in a way unconducive to party-centered politics. The only force moving in the opposite direction are the laws and court decisions that institutionalize the parties in the electoral process. Among the most important are those giving parties control over who may vote in their primaries.[55] Interestingly, however, the state parties involved in the most notable of these decisions— in Wisconsin and Connecticut—were determined to use this right to weaken and not strengthen the definition of party membership, specifically by permitting independents to vote in their primaries. Also notable are the provisions in the presidential public financing law that essentially guarantee continued full funding only to the two major party candidates, and make it difficult for third parties or candidates to quality—and then only after they have demonstrated significant public support. However, the provisions channeling money through candidate committees make the parties merely "public utilities," to use Epstein's phrase.

Critics of party reform correctly point out that it always has unintended consequences—in their view, overwhelmingly bad ones. They argue that weak parties make for rule by "fads," "manias," and "crazes."[56] Candidate-centered politics, they assert, encourages fringe movements and removes structure and meaning from politics.[57] Yet, more than a half-century after the Progressive victories and following almost two decades of experience with the latest reform movement, there is little evidence to suggest that these critics are correct. It is clear that "more democracy" does not benefit any particular set of policy positions. In recent years, the conservative advocates of tax-cutting measures such as California's Proposition Thirteen and the liberal champions of the nuclear freeze movement have both used the initiative and referendum—the purest instruments of direct democracy. Curiously, the critics have accused the reforms of producing antithetical outcomes—on the one hand, hasty ill-considered schemes resulting from policy "fads" and, on the other hand, stasis and gridlock produced by a lack of leadership accountability and parochial interests. Yet neither outcome has occurred. In the absence of strong parties (at least in the American context), the constitutional separation of powers does indeed seem to work, as Madison hoped it would, to "cure the mischief" of the special-interest groups we now understand to be "factions." In the absence of party leadership, entrepreneurial leaders can emerge, as they did in the first party system, to put together policy realignments rather than partisan ones.[58] The "politics without intermediaries" of the founding era is recreated in a postindustrial mass democracy by the instruments of television and computerized direct mail. As Crotty has noted, "The maturation process a mass democracy undergoes is not necessarily a pleasant sight."[59]

NOTES

1. Richard McCormick, *The Party Period and Public Policy* (New York: Oxford University Press, 1986).

2. See, for example, J. S. Young, *The Washington Community: 1800–1828* (New York: Harcourt, Brace and World, 1966); P. Kleppner, *The Evolution of American Electoral Systems* (Westport, Conn.: Greenwood Press, 1981); W. N. Chambers and W. D. Burnham, eds., *The American Party Systems: Stages of Political Development* (New York: Oxford University Press, 1967); and S. M. Lipset, *The First New Nation* (New York: Basic Books, 1963).

3. See, for example, R. L. McCormick, *The Second American Party System* (Chapel Hill: University of North Carolina Press, 1966); W. G. Shade, "Political Pluralism and Party Development: The Creation of a Modern Party System: 1815–1852," in P. E. Kleppner, ed., *The Evolution of American Electoral Systems* (Westport, Conn.: Greenwood Press, 1982), pp. 77–111; S. J. Kernell, "Toward Understanding Nineteenth-Century Congressional Careers: Ambition, Competition and Rotation," *American Journal of Political Science*, vol. 21 (1977), pp. 669–694; and H. D. Price, "Congress and the Evolution of Legislative 'Professionalism,'" in N. J. Orenstein, ed., *Congress in Change* (New York: Praeger, 1975).

4. A. Ranney, *Curing the Mischiefs of Faction* (Berkeley: University of California Press, 1975), pp. 75–81.

5. V. O. Key, Jr., *Southern Politics in State and Nation* (New York: Alfred A. Knopf, 1949); M. Shefter, "Regional Receptivity to Reform: The Legacy of the Progressive Era," *Political Science Quarterly*, vol. 98 (1983), pp. 459–483.

6. D. R. Mayhew, *Placing Parties in American Politics* (Princeton: Princeton University Press, 1986).

7. J. W. Ceaser, *Reforming the Reforms: A Critical Analysis of the Presidential Selection Process* (Cambridge, Mass.: Ballinger, 1982), pp. 23–25.

8. R. Jensen, "The Last Party System," in P. Kleppner, ed., *The Evolution of American Electoral Systems* (Westport, Conn.: Greenwood Press, 1982), pp. 202–235.

9. A. Ware, *The Breakdown of Democratic Party Organization: 1940–1980* (Oxford: Clarendon Press, 1985).

10. J. Q. Wilson, *The Amateur Democrat* (Chicago: University of Chicago Press, 1962).

11. R. L. Calvert and J. A. Ferejohn, "Coattail Voting in Recent Presidential Elections," *American Political Science Review*, vol. 77 (1983), pp. 407–419; J. E. Campbell, "Predicting Seat Gains from Presidential Coattails," *American Journal of Political Science*, vol. 30 (1986), pp. 165–183.

12. G. C. Jacobson, *The Politics of Congressional Elections* (Boston: Little, Brown, 1987).

13. T. E. Mann and R. Wolfinger, "Candidates and Parties in Congressional Elections," *American Political Science Review*, vol. 74 (1980), pp. 617–632; P. R. Abramson, J. H. Aldrich, and D. W. Rohde, *Change and Continuity in the 1984 Elections* (Washington, D.C.: Congressional Quarterly Press, 1985).

14. G. C. Jacobson and S. J. Kernell, *Strategy and Choice in Congressional Elections* (New Haven: Yale University Press, 1981); Jacobson, *The Politics of Congressional Elections*; B. E. Cain, J. Ferejohn, and M. P. Fiorina, *The Personal Vote: Constituency Service and Electoral Independence* (Cambridge: Harvard University Press, 1987).

15. M. E. Jewell and D. Olson, *American State Political Parties and Elections*, 3rd ed. (Homewood, Ill.: Dorsey Press, 1988); S. A. Salmore and B. G. Salmore, *Candidates, Parties and Campaigns: Electoral Politics in America* (Washington, D.C.: Congressional Quarterly Press, 1985); S. A. Salmore and B. G. Salmore, "The Congressionalization of State Legislative Politics: The Case of New Jersey," paper presented to the Annual Meeting of the American Political Science Association, Chicago, Ill. (September 1987); A. I. Abramowitz, "Explaining Senate Election Outcomes," *American Political Science Review*, vol. 82 (1988), pp. 385–404.

16. A. Ranney, "Farewell to Reform—Almost," in K. L. Schlozman, ed., *Elections in America* (Boston: Allen and Unwin, 1985). See, for example, Ceaser, *Reforming the Reforms*; W. J. Crotty, *Political Reform and the American Experiment* (New York: Thomas Y. Crowell, 1977); W. J. Crotty, *Decision for the Democrats* (Baltimore, Johns Hopkins University Press, 1978); W. J. Crotty, *Party Reform* (New York: Longman, 1983); J. J. Kirkpatrick, *Dismantling the Parties: Reflections on Party Reform and Decomposition* (Washington, D.C.: American Enterprise Institute, 1978); N. Polsby, *The Consequences of Party Reform* (New York: Oxford University Press, 1983); D. E. Price, *Bringing Back the Parties* (Washington, D.C.: Congressional Quarterly Press, 1984); Ranney, *Curing the Mischiefs of Faction*; and B. E. Shafer, *The Quiet Revolution: Reform Politics in the Democratic Party, 1968–72* (New York: Russell Sage Foundation, 1984).

17. Ranney, *Curing the Mischiefs of Faction*, p. 188.

18. Ranney, "Farewell to Reform—Almost," p. 95.

19. W. Cavala, "Changing the Rules of the Game: Party Reform and the 1972 California Delegation to the Democratic National Convention," *American Political Science Review*, vol. 68 (1974), pp. 27–42.

20. T. E. Mann, "Elected Officials and the Politics of Presidential Selection," in A. Ranney, ed., *The American Elections of 1984* (Durham, N.C.: Duke University Press, 1985).

21. Ranney, *Curing the Mischiefs of Faction,* p. 206.

22. Crotty, *Political Reform and the American Experiment,* p. 228.

23. Ceaser, *Reforming the Reforms.*

24. Ranney, "Farewell to Reform—Almost," pp. 103–104.

25. Mann, "Elected Officials and the Politics of Presidential Selection."

26. Ibid.

27. In 1988, 47 percent of the delegates to the Democratic National Convention were chosen by proportional representation, 23 percent by the "winner-take-more" system, and 14 percent by the district winner-take-all system. The remaining 16 percent were superdelegates. See *Congressional Quarterly Weekly Report* (July 2, 1988), p. 1801.

28. *Congressional Quarterly Weekly Report* (July 2, 1988), p. 1799.

29. Kirkpatrick, *Dismantling the Parties,* p. 20.

30. Ibid., p. 22.

31. See, for example, M. Clancy and M. Robinson, *Over the Wire and on TV* (New York: Russell Sage, 1984); and M. J. Robinson, "News Media Myths and Realities: What Network News Did and Didn't Do in the 1984 General Campaign," in K. L. Schlozman, ed., *Elections in America* (Boston: Allen and Unwin, 1985).

32. The best discussion of the role of television in the nomination and election of the president is Theodore White, *America in Search of Itself: The Making of the President 1956–1980* (New York: Harper & Row, 1982).

33. Crotty, *Party Reform,* pp. 58–59.

34. Since the establishment of public funding in 1976, only one major-party candidate, John Connolly, has declined public funding. His experience (spending $11 million to win one delegate in the brief period before he dropped out of the 1976 race) was not calculated to encourage future candidates to take this route.

Leftover presidential campaign money is now often deposited into personal candidate PACs, which have been set up by numerous presidential candidates since 1980, including Ronald Reagan, Walter Mondale, Edward Kennedy, George Bush, Robert Dole, Jack Kemp, Joe Biden, Paul Simon, Richard Gephardt, and Jesse Jackson. Although used principally to support candidate travel and organization prior to formal announcement of candidacy, these PACs also contribute sizable amounts to other candidates during the presidential selection process.

35. R. B. Cheney, "The Law's Impact on Presidential and Congressional Election Campaigns," in M. J. Malbin, ed., *Parties, Interest Groups, and Campaign Finance Laws* (Washington, D.C.: American Enterprise Institute, 1980).

36. H. E. Alexander and B. A. Haggerty, *Financing the 1984 Election* (Lexington, Mass.: D. C. Heath, 1987), p. 84. However, in July 1988, Alexander estimated a sharp increase in spending in the 1988 contests—in real dollars, from $325 million in 1984 to $500 million four years later. See Charles Babcock, *Washington Post National Weekly Edition* (July 4–10, 1988), p. 11.

37. F. J. Sorauf, *Money in American Politics* (Glenview, Ill.: Scott, Foresman, 1988).

38. R. H. Salisbury and K. A. Shepsle, "Congressman as Enterprise," *Legislative Studies Quarterly,* vol. 6 (1981), pp. 559–576.

39. Tom Loftus, "The New 'Political Parties' in State Legislatures," *State Government*, vol. 58 (1985), pp. 109–110.

40. H. W. Stanley and R. G. Niemi, *Vital Statistics on American Politics* (Washington, D.C.: Congressional Quarterly Press, 1988), p. 172.

41. B. E. Cain, J. Ferejohn, and M. P. Fiorina, *The Personal Vote: Constituency Service and Electoral Independence* (Cambridge: Harvard University Press, 1987).

42. Stanely and Niemi, *Vital Statistics on American Politics.*

43. D. R. Mayhew, *Congress: The Electoral Connection* (New Haven, Conn.: Yale, 1974); M. P. Fiorina, *Congress: Keystone of the Washington Establishment* (New Haven, Conn.: Yale University Press, 1977).

44. D. B. Maglesby, *Direct Legislation: Voting on Ballot Propositions in the United States* (Baltimore: Johns Hopkins, 1984).

45. See, for example, S. S. Smith, "New Patterns of Decision-Making in Congress," in J. E. Chubb and P. E. Peterson, eds., *The New Direction in American Politics* (Washington, D.C.: Brookings, 1985); and B. Sinclair, "Senate Styles and Senate Decision-Making, 1955–1980," *Journal of Politics*, vol. 48 (1986), pp. 877–908.

46. Kirkpatrick, *Dismantling the Parties*, p. 20.

47. Members of the Committee for Party Renewal regularly make this suggestion. The failure of the Byrd-Boren legislation in the 100th Congress shows how difficult it will be to pass further campaign finance legislation of any sort. However, even Byrd-Boren had no provision for decreasing candidates' control over their own campaign money. It is difficult to imagine a scenario whereby officeholders would be willing to hand over such control to parties.

48. See, for example, G. Pomper, *Party Renewal in America* (New York: Praeger, 1980); and L. J. Sabato, *The Party's Just Begun* (Glenview, Ill.: Scott, Foresman, 1988).

49. For example, Polsby, *The Consequences of Party Reform.*

50. Ceaser, *Reforming the Reforms*, pp. 157–160.

51. F. C. Arterton, "Political Money and Party Strength," in J. L. Fleishman, ed., *The Future of American Political Parties* (Englewood Cliffs, N.J.: Prentice-Hall, 1982).

52. L. Epstein, *Political Parties in the American Mold* (Madison: University of Wisconsin Press, 1986), p. 245.

53. M. P. Wattenberg, *The Decline of American Political Parties, 1952–1984* (Cambridge: Harvard University Press, 1986); M. P. Wattenberg, "The Reagan Polarization Phenomenon and the Continued Downslide in Presidential Candidate Popularity," *American Politics Quarterly*, vol. 14 (1986), pp. 219–246; T. M. Konda and L. Sigelman, "Public Evaluations of the American Parties, 1952–1984," *Journal of Politics*, vol. 49 (1987), pp. 814–829.

54. Everett C. Ladd, "On Mandates, Realignments and the 1984 Election," *Political Science Quarterly*, vol. 100 (1985), pp. 1–25.

55. Epstein, *Political Parties in the American Mold.*

56. Polsby, *The Consequences of Party Reform.*

57. Ranney, *Curing the Mischiefs of Faction.*

58. Everett C. Ladd, "Party Reform and the Public Interest," in A. James Reichley, ed., *Elections American Style* (Washington, D.C.: Brookings, 1987).

59. Crotty, *Political Reform and the American Experiment*, p. 202.

9

Subgovernments, Issue Networks, and Political Conflict

JEFFREY M. BERRY

Few approaches for analyzing the American political system have endured as long or as well as that of the policy subgovernment. In simple terms—and its simplicity is part of its attraction—a subgovernment consists primarily of a limited number of interest group advocates, legislators and their aides, and key agency administrators who interact on a stable, ongoing basis and dominate policymaking in a particular area. Its central belief seems indisputable: Policymaking takes place across institutions. Thus government decisionmaking can best be understood by looking at how key actors from different institutions and organizations relate to each other.

Although this model of policymaking has evolved over time, it has never been subjected to a great deal of critical scrutiny. Many scholars have used it to illuminate policymaking without rigorously evaluating its fundamental assumptions. As Hugh Heclo has noted, the widespread acceptance of the early work in this area led to a view that "is not so much wrong as it is disastrously incomplete."[1]

Our understanding of policy communities is still incomplete. Although the subgovernment model remains popular, this chapter suggests that it is no longer descriptive of most policy communities. Fundamental changes have altered the nature of policymaking in Washington in ways that work against the operation of a subgovernment. Chief among these has been the growth in the number of interest groups. The lobbying explosion has eroded the closed policymaking arrangements that characterize subgovernments. More interest groups do not simply mean bigger subgovernments. Bargaining becomes more complex, control and coordination by key actors becomes more difficult, boundaries become harder to define, and the likelihood of conflict between competing coalitions increases.

Change on the interest group side of the equation has been accompanied by changes in the Congress and in administrative agencies. Both institutional reforms and changing norms have affected the way legislators, administrators, and lobbyists interact with each other. In Congress the growth in the number of subcommittees is just one factor that has affected classic subgovernment politics. Another important development has been the effort of the White House to exert greater control over the bureaucracy, which in turn has worked to diminish the autonomy of subgovernments.

Despite the changes that have taken place, the subgovernment model maintains a tenacious hold in political science. The model has some critics, but reports of its death are greatly exaggerated. An alternative model, that of "issue networks," is a much more accurate representation of contemporary policymaking, even though it is not yet widely utilized by political scientists. One of the arguments here is that political scientists have had difficulty abandoning subgovernments because they fit so well within a dominant paradigm of interest group politics. Subgovernments are said to preserve the status quo of dominant groups in each policy area. The cooperative relationship that exists between these groups and key policymakers perpetuates a biased system of representation. In short, the subgovernment model validates existing theory by showing how the imbalance in interest group politics is maintained.

These points will be taken up more fully in the remainder of this chapter. First, we will evaluate both the subgovernment and the issue network approaches in light of recent research. Second, we will focus in turn on the Congress, administrative agencies, and interest groups. Our analysis will concentrate on the political and institutional changes that have altered the nature of policymaking in Washington. We will also examine the incentive systems that guide the behavior of legislators, administrators, and lobbyists, with specific attention paid to the goals, norms, and constraints that drive these actors toward cooperation, independence, or conflict. Third, we will analyze the implications of these patterns of behavior and institutional practices for interest group theory.

SUBGOVERNMENTS VERSUS ISSUE NETWORKS

The subgovernment model can be traced back to Ernest Griffth's description of policy whirlpools in *Impasse of Democracy*.[2] Although the term *Whirlpools* had little staying power, other terms did gain currency, including *iron triangles, triple alliances, cozy little triangles,* and *subgovernments*. Whatever the label, the basic idea has been the same: (1) A small group of actors plays a dominant role in developing policy in a particular field; (2) policymaking is consensual, with quiet bargaining producing agreements among affected parties; and (3) partisan politics does little to disturb these relatively autonomous and stable arrangements. Douglass Cater's description of the sugar subgovernment is instructive:

> Political power within the sugar subgovernment is largely vested in the Chairman of the House Agriculture Committee who works out the schedule of quotas. It is shared by a veteran civil servant, the director of the Sugar Division in the U.S. Department of Agriculture, who provides the necessary "expert" advice for such a complex marketing arrangement. Further advice is provided by Washington representatives of the domestic beet and cane sugar growers, the sugar refineries, and the foreign producers.[3]

The subgovernment model proved popular with political scientists for a number of reasons. First, it provided a means of escaping the confines of institutional analysis. Research on the Congress or the bureaucracy could not capture the full nature of the policymaking process unless it went well beyond the boundaries of those institutions. Second, a great deal of scholarship in political science focuses on an individual policy area. To those who wanted to study the evolution of a particular program or set of policies, subgovernments offered a conceptual framework to guide their research. Third, the subgovernment idea could be communicated easily to students and scholars alike. The model was based on some rather straightforward and convincing case studies, and those who read the relevant works were not required to make any leaps of faith or to agree to any problematic assumptions. Fourth, subgovernments offered a critical perspective on the performance of American government. The closed nature of the policymaking system and the critical role played by key interest grouups in each area made subgovernments an inviting target for those who found fault with the direction of public policy. A central charge was that the public interest was not served because not all important interests were represented at the bargaining table.

Despite the model's utility, many interest group scholars were quick to embrace Hugh Heclo's well-reasoned contention that the image of the narrow, stable, tightly controlled subgovernment was an anachronism. If we look "for the closed triangles of control," says Heclo, "we tend to miss the fairly open networks of people that increasingly impinge upon government."[4] Criticism also mounted from those who analyzed policymaking in particular fields. After he and his colleagues examined a number of different regulatory agencies, James Q. Wilson concluded that "there is supposed to be an 'iron triangle' of influence linking each agency, congressional committee, and interest group into a tight and predictable pattern of action, but we have not seen many of these triangles. Those we have seen appear to be made of metal far more malleable than iron."[5]

Heclo suggests that subgovernment politics has evolved largely into issue network politics. "An issue network is a shared knowledge group" that ties together large numbers of participants with common technical expertise.[6] Unlike the simple and clearly defined nature of subgovernments, issue networks are rather sloppy and ill-defined. Participants move in and out easily, and it is "almost impossible to say where a network leaves off and its environment begins."[7] Boundaries are sloppy because issue areas overlap extensively; moreover, as an issue develops, new coalitions often form. Yet issue networks are not amorphous blobs; they are shaped in two major ways. First, within a network some groups are more central players than others and are involved in a wide range of issues. Such groups, like large trade associations, may act as "brokers" of information and have the most lines of communication with other network members.[8] Second, there are frequently clusters of groups that have a good deal in common and are likely coalition partners.[9] For example, in the telecommunications network, the seven regional phone companies ("Baby Bells") form one cluster. In agricultural policymaking, the various commodity groups will often be found working together.

Networks are not radically different from subgovernments in terms of membership: Lobbyists, legislators, legislative aides, and agency administrators still constitute the vast majority of actors. White House aides, consultants, and prominent, knowledgeable individuals can also be found in their midst, though. Issue networks are more distinctive in terms of their size and accessibility to new participants. A large network can be made up of scores of interest groups, a number of executive branch offices, and various congressional committees and subcommittees. Even a smaller network allows for broader and more open participation than a subgovernment.

The exchange of information is what makes individuals who share expertise part of a network. But this exchange does not make allies out of all participants within a network. Lobbyists have a strong incentive to become highly expert because such expertise adds to their credibility with policymakers and their staffers. The lobbyists' goal is to become a trusted source of information and to have their data and views solicited by those writing statutes and regulations. Their expertise also becomes a resource for other sympathetic interest groups within a network.

Issue network politics can become highly conflictual when coalitions form to represent diverse viewpoints on emerging issues. Networks lack the stable set of relationships that characterize subgovernments as well as the commitment of participants to work together through compromise to control policy development. Thus coordination becomes difficult, and decisions are made and remade at different stages in the policymaking process. Deals become harder to "cut," and losers quickly move to the next stage of the process to appeal the previous decision.

Despite its descriptive and analytical value, the issue network approach has not been widely utilized by political scientists. In many ways, subgovernments still remain the dominant model of how policymaking is conducted across institutions. Freshman American government textbooks, a rough indicator of the conventional wisdom in our discipline, commonly describe iron triangles and subgovernments as being typical in our policymaking process. Students are frequently told that subgovernments are highly autonomous and that the president of the United States has trouble breaking their powerful hold over policy decisions.

More sophisticated works also use the subgovernment model to analyze the policymaking process. Randall Ripley and Grace Franklin's *Congress, the Bureaucracy, and Public Policy*[10] carefully examines different types of issues and shows how the degree of subgovernment dominance varies among them. Brinton Milward and Gary Wamsley go so far as to reject Heclo's argument that we should move beyond the policy subsystem model. They respond that suggestions for the "abandonment" of the policy subsystem model "have emerged without any additional knowledge being added to the rather shaky base that originally undergirded its enshrinement in conventional wisdom." Of greater use, they contend, would be a more rigorous, more theoretically developed policy subsystem concept. "The policy sybsystem, we argue, is *the* unit of analysis with the greatest potential leverage for understanding this polity of interest group liberalism."[11] Subgovernments receive emphasis not only for their value as a tool for understanding the policymaking process but also because of the normative issues they raise. Jack Knott and Gary Miller note that majoritarian politics can sometimes challenge subgovernments, but that "the effect of majoritarian politics on public policy, therefore, is probably more volatile and erratic than subgovernment politics. It often possesses a 'flash-in-the-pan' character with no lasting, major changes in outcomes."[12]

UNTANGLING THE CONTRADICTIONS

Clearly, there are two very distinct and contradictory views regarding what kinds of policy communities are most descriptive of modern Washington politics. No one argues that there are only issue networks or only subgovernments active in policymaking. Rather, the argument is over what is most typical and most descriptive of the political process.

Which should serve as our framework for analyzing how laws and regulations are made?

A first step in evaluating these two conflicting perspectives is to see how strong the support is for each in the empirical literature. Recent research reveals the emergence of some strong patterns. One important finding is that the interest groups in Washington are commonly in open and protracted conflict with other lobbies working in their policy area. This is antithetical to the notion of the subgovernment, in which policy is made in a quiet, consensual manner. The typical interest group views itself as having adversaries in the interest group community. Robert Salisbury and his colleagues found that in four different policy domains, between approximately 65 and 85 percent of the groups surveyed cited adversary groups in Washington.[13]

One major reason for this high degree of conflict is the expanding universe of interest groups in Washington. The explosion of interest-group activity has brought a large number of new participants who aggressively seek to influence legislators and agency officials. For example, the Department of Agriculture, long the bureaucratic center of many subgovernments, has been transformed by this "proliferation of groups," which "has destabilized the agricultural subsystem." William Browne has identified more than 200 lobbies concerned with farm, agribusiness, or rural interests.[14]

Of particular note is the growth in the number of citizen groups. These organizations represent those who have been chronically under-represented in Washington interest group politics. The surge of liberal groups in the late 1960s and 1970s was followed by an increasing number of conservative groups. And, as Thomas Gais, Mark Peterson, and Jack Walker note, "Once these new groups of the Left and Right became permanent fixtures in Washington, the conditions that had nurtured the decentralized system of subgovernments were fundamentally altered."[15]

Business lobbying has grown, too, partly in response to the expanding numbers of liberal citizen-advocacy groups. Antagonism between business and citizen groups is now a greater source of conflict than the traditional antipathy between business and labor.[16] Another cause of increased business lobbying was the growth in regulation that came with the new agencies and new programs of the late 1960s and early 1970s. The new "social regulation" cut across industry sectors, creating diverse and often conflicting clienteles for agency administrators. Business lobbying expanded also because of growing competitive pressures within the business community.

Finally, conflict comes not only the from other interest groups but from broader social forces as well. Martha Derthick and Paul Quirk document how the intellectual force of scholarly analyses of regulatory practices eventually led to recent moves toward deregulation. The hold of the trucking, airline, and telecommunications industry over regulatory policy was shattered by the intellectual appeal of deregulation proposals, nurtured first in academe and in think tanks, and then pushed by sympathetic figures in the legislative and executive branches.[17]

Recent research has also demonstrated the critical influence that partisan change has on interest group access to policymakers. Subgovernments are held to be relatively autonomous from the electoral process: Presidents come and go, but subgovernments live on forever. This, however, is not what Mark Peterson and Jack Walker found in their surveys of interest groups in 1980 and 1985:

> When Reagan replaced Carter in the White House, there was a virtual revolution in the access enjoyed by interest groups in Washington. In the past, many groups have been able to maintain their contacts with the bureaucratic agencies of the federal government through politically isolated subgovernments or iron triangles, no matter what the outcome of the election, but it was difficult to build such safe enclaves around a group's favorite programs during the 1980s.[18]

Clearly the Reagan administration profoundly affected the Washington interest group community with its highly ideological agenda and its successful effort to cut many budgetary sacred cows. The election of Jimmy Carter in 1976 also had a significant impact on policy subgovernments in Washington. The large number of liberal public-interest groups that arrived in Washington before Carter were a major beneficiary of his administration. Activists from these organizations, such as Naderite Joan Claybrook and environmentalist David Hawkins, filled important administrative positions and gave generous access to public interest lobbyists. The same groups had found the door to the Nixon administration tightly shut. Some sectors of the interest group community took a hit from both the Republican and Democratic administrations. One study found that the Carter administration first began the process of breaking up the "cozy relationships" of the intergovernmental lobby. The trend was then "accelerated" during the Reagan administration.[19]

There is also research that finds subgovernments still dominating a policy area. In his thorough study of energy policymaking, John Chubb determined that "strong energy subsystems continue to thrive."[20] An examination of the Sea Grant program, a small source of funds for colleges, concluded that it is best described as a traditional subgovernment.[21] Nevertheless, the majority of recent empirical studies are critical of the traditional subgovernment thesis. A study of the food stamp program found a pattern of behavior that conformed much more closely to an issue network than to a subgovernment.[22] William Browne's study of the Agriculture Department reached the same conclusion.[23] Sociologists Edward Laumann, David Knoke, and Yong-Hak Kim used network theory from their discipline to explain national policymaking in the broad areas of energy and health.[24]

Although they do not adopt an issue network framework, many other studies document the transformation of a subgovernment into a more conflictual pattern of interaction. Christine Campos describes the "decline" and "fragmentation" of traditional subgovernments in the aging field.[25] Tim Miller found that water subgovernments "have declined considerably since the late 1970s," although they are still surviving.[26] Another line of research focuses on conflict between interest groups so enduring and frustrating that the opposing parties have turned to direct mediation and negotiation. Christopher Bosso details how chemical manufacturers and environmentalists found negotiations fruitful after years of legislative gridlock.[27] Andrew McFarland's analysis of mediation between coal producers and environmentalists shows that the initial agreements could not be sustained because the government failed to play an active role, thus allowing new conflict to sink the mediation effort.[28]

A number of conclusions can be drawn from the recent literature. First, significant conflict among interest groups is characteristic of policymaking. Such conflict is not an anomalous condition found only in some areas where subgovernments have deteriorated or have been subjected to some unusual circumstances. Second, presidential elections significantly influence the access to policymakers for large numbers of interest groups. Third, the subgovernment model has become an increasing target of criticism by scholars working in the interest group area. Generally, they have not tried to repair or adapt it. Fourth, although there is no unanimity regarding which new approach to use, some scholars have found the issue network model to be useful in explaining Washington policymaking for a particular program or broader policy domain.

In light of these conclusions, what direction should future work in this area take? As there are some subgovernments still operating in particular areas, and as this model has such a strong following in political science, does it make sense to try to integrate it with the issue network model? Would blending subgovernments and issue networks into a broad framework that would account for both types of policy communities offer a useful means of reconciling these two schools of thought?

A way of integrating these two models would be to focus on issue areas and the types and range of interest groups they attract. Work could build on efforts already undertaken to identify the predictable patterns of autonomy, conflict, and participation that characterize different policy areas. Yet there is good reason to question whether trying to integrate issue networks with subgovernments is the best path to take. Although they both describe relationships among lobbies, agencies, and Congress, the fact remains that the two models are fundamentally at odds with each other. Issue networks are not just a different kind of policy community in which there is more conflict and more open participation than in a traditional subgovernment. Rather, a fully developed issue network model makes assumptions about political behavior that are much different from those underlying the subgovernment model.

Principally, there are different assumptions in the two models about the incentives and constraints that lead lobbyists, legislators, and administrators toward cooperative behavior. First, in an issue network there is often much to be gained by pursuing a strategy in conflict with other actors. The goal orientation of subgovernment participants is complementary; this is not usually the case for those in an issue network. Issue network participants are guided by a different set of expectations about how the policymaking process works, and they make different strategic calculations in trying to reach their objectives. Subgovernments and issue networks also suggest different pathologies in our political system. Different diseases require different cures.

Beyond the contradictions of issue networks and subgovernments, there is still the matter of the recent literature that is so critical of the subgovernmental model. After distilling the central propositions of subgovernments and evaluating them in light of two major surveys of interest groups, John Tierney found all of those propositions to be of questionable validity.[29] If the subgovernment model is not generally applicable, it makes little sense to build a broader theory of policymaking upon it.

In short, the differences between subgovernments and issue networks are highly significant. They are not merely two terms used to describe slightly different forms of the same phenomenon. Instead of refining existing work on subgovernments by incorporating issue networks into them, political scientists need to push forward with developing the issue network model or some other alternative, free of the assumptions that guide the subgovernment model. One way of proceeding with this task is to ask two central questions about the principal actors within a policy community. First, what are the incentives that influence the behavior of each set of actors within a policy community and affect their relationships with one another? Second, how have structural changes altered the rules, norms, and expectations of these actors within their policy community?

LEGISLATORS: CREDIT CLAIMERS
OR POLICY ACTIVISTS?

Substantial as it is, the literature on Congress does not provide an unequivocal view on the incentives underlying legislative behavior. Probably the most influential work is David Mayhew's *Congress: The Electoral Connection.* Members of Congress are described by Mayhew as "single-minded reelection seekers," and all other goals are regarded as subservient to that of reelection.[30] As a result, legislators are less interested in developing good public policy than in being able to claim credit for providing particularized benefits to constituents.

Contrasting perspectives are offered by Richard Fenno and Lawrence Dodd. Fenno argues that representatives have three basic goals: reelection, influence within the House, and good public policy. He goes on to say, "All congressmen probably hold all three goals. But each congressman has his own mix of priorities and intensities—a mix which may, of course, change over time."[31] Dodd takes issue with Mayhew, suggesting that members tend not to be "solely preoccupied with reelection." Rather, members "are preoccupied with power considerations," and each wants "to make the key policy decisions."[32]

In fashioning an explanation of how a policy community operates, we find that it makes a critical difference if legislators are held to be preeminently concerned with reelection or held to be highly concerned with other goals, too. If members of Congress are preoccupied with reelection, they are going to be much less interested in the nuts and bolts of policy formulation. They will be highly selective in choosing issues to be active on so as to maximize the credit they get for the time they put in, and they will be particularly uninterested in oversight, which is not as routinely newsworthy as other activities.

Assume instead that members of Congress are highly interested in good public policy, that they can pursue policy interests without seriously damaging their chances for reelection, and that spending time on mastering the complexities of policy questions can complement the desire to maximize power within the House or Senate. If this portrayal is correct, then a policy community takes on a different complexion. Under this assumption, members of Congress are more willing to devote considerable time to the long-term evolution of legislation, to choose issues to work on with eye toward doing much more than maximizing credit, and to expend time on oversight.

The argument here is that members of Congress *can have it all.* They each have a mix of goals that they want to achieve, but they can choose routes to those goals that allow them to pursue the goals in tandem. A member of Congress who spends a lot of time working on a policy area for reasons of ideology or personal interest (rather than out of a need to please the home constituency) can help himself or herself electorally. Real influence and effort exerted are important to interest groups and political action committees (PACs). The reputation of being a workhorse rather than a showhorse is helpful at election time, just as is the ability to deliver particularized benefits to the constituency. In terms of building a career within the House or Senate, the expertise that comes from issue work is invaluable. Sam Nunn (D.-Ga.) is a case in point. Upon entering the Congress, he devoted himself to pursuing his interest in defense policy; his continuing work in that area soon brought the respect of his peers. He was widely consulted on defense policy by other members and was probably the most influential member in this area even before he became chairman of the Senate Armed Services Committee in 1987. But his becoming known as a great expert on defense policy and his being very powerful in the Congress in this area have not meant that he is perceived in Georgia as being unconcerned about casework or about bringing home the bacon.

Nunn may be an unusually successful member of Congress in developing a national reputation for his expertise, but the pattern is a common one nevertheless. Expertise, not just seniority and political skill, is frequently seen as a factor in explaining the power of an individual member of Congress over policy formulation in a particular area. That expertise helps to build power in the Congress and to attract political support from interest groups and constituents.

How does this view affect the relationship between legislators and other actors in a policy community? The area of oversight is instructive. If legislators place a great deal of value on both achieving good public-policy outcomes and building a strong base of power within their house, they will then place far greater emphasis on oversight than a legislator who is a single-minded seeker of reelection. If a legislator is to maximize influence over policy formation, he or she must be concerned about agency rulemaking and implementation practices. Important decisions are frequently made at the administrative level, and legislators can often influence those decisions through aggressive and persistent efforts at intervention. Legislators help to build a reputation for influence, and thus increase their power position within their chamber, by being perceived as individuals who are successful at affecting administrative decisions.

If Congress has numerous members willing to devote time to oversight, the equation changes within a policy community. In a traditional subgovernment, quiet negotiation between a key committee chair, an agency administrator, and representatives of the major client groups can resolve policy questions facing an administrator. But in a broader, more conflictual issue network, lobbyists will appeal to sympathetic legislators to intervene in agency policymaking. When legislators are willing to spend time intervening, administrators can find themselves facing different coalitions trying to influence rulemaking decisions.

Having said this, I must acknowledge that Congress does not have a reputation for aggressive oversight. It is true, of course, that Congress is generally given poor marks for the way it carries out its oversight responsibilities, although it's not clear that its reputation in this regard is entirely deserved. Two points should be made. First, recent research studies focusing on legislative oversight are few and far between. We really do not know how much oversight is being done, although it is surely safe to fall back on the old cliché that Congress ought to do more. We do know that institutional changes have given the Congress a greater capability to monitor agency behavior. The tremendous growth in staffs and the creation of specialized staff units have given the legislators great resources to help them oversee agencies if they so choose.

Second, oversight is often assumed to take the form of committee review of agency actions. By that standard, the conventional wisdom probably isn't far from the truth. But when we take into account the broader array of efforts to influence agency administrators to follow the policy goals of Congress, a much more positive picture emerges. In an earlier study of the food stamp program, I found that the agriculture committees did little formal oversight of the Department of Agriculture's administration of the program. Yet throughout the program's history, oversight came from legislators outside the committee who paid exceptionally close attention to rulemaking and implementation. Over the years such legislators as Leonor Sullivan (D.-Missouri), Robert Kennedy (D.-N.Y.), Robert Michel (R.-Ill.), George McGovern (D.-S.D.), and Jesse Helms (R.-N.C.) made concerted and repeated efforts to get administrators to shape agency rules according to what those legislators perceived to be the will of Congress. Through informal meetings, written comments on proposed rules, and hearings before committees that had some interest in nutrition or welfare, these legislators frequently influenced the content of administrative regulations. These regulations were not just the unfinished details of legislation, but significant policy decisions concerning the level of benefits for participants.[33]

A common pattern in the food stamp issue network was for lobbyists representing poor people to work with congressional allies to influence uncooperative administrators. Intervention into rulemaking usually came at the behest of the hunger lobby. Another example of aggressive legislative review of administrative policymaking comes from Bosso's study of chemical-pesticide legislation. He describes the period between 1972 and

1980 as a time of "endless oversight."[34] This was hardly a highly visible policy issue back in the district or state, and yet there was continuous conflict as various members of Congress tried to work their will with the Environmental Protection Agency (EPA).

The conflict in legislative-administrative relations that comes about from the legislators' incentives to intervene into agency policymaking has been complemented by changes in the structure and norms governing the congressional process. In particular, the growth of subcommittee government has meant more overlapping jurisdictions.[35] As Steven Smith points out, decentralization means that "the scope of conflict changes continually, usually expanding, as legislation passes from one stage to the next. Deals and accommodations devised at one stage cannot be adhered to later because negotiations must be reopened at each stage."[36] Changes have also occurred in legislators' behavior in terms of activism outside their areas of specialization. A recent study shows that senators offer more floor amendments and offer more amendments to bills from committees on which they do not serve, and that, overall, "specialization has declined; more and more senators have become generalists."[37] As a result, the Senate is characterized by "unrestrained activism."[38] Two other important changes have already been mentioned. First, there has been a significant growth in the number of congressional staffers, thus helping legislators become active in a wider variety of policy areas. Second, the growing numbers of interest groups have broadened the support that a legislator can find for any policy position he or she might want to pursue. By the same token, there are more interest gropus requesting members of Congress to work on legislation or to intervene in the administrative process.

ADMINISTRATORS: CONFLICTING PRESSURES

Change has also come to the administrator's world. For many administrators, like committee chairs, the quiet bargaining of the subgovernment has been replaced by a much more complex and conflictual environment. Although some administrators may have to deal with only a limited number of client groups and legislators, it is common today for an administrative agency to find itself with more than one House and one Senate subcommittee asserting some interest in its policymaking, and a large number of interest groups who compete against each other for the agency's favors.

A strong rationale underlies the administrators' willingness to participate in subgovernments. Interest groups provide political support for agencies. They can be counted on to help win higher appropriations from the Congress and to defeat executive branch reorganization plans unpopular with agency administrators. They might even provide support for policy proposals initiated by agency administrators. Good relations with congressional committee chairs offer significant benefits as well.

Even so, there are a number of reasons why many administrators' relations with legislators and lobbyists no longer resemble the stable predictable world of the subgovernment. As previously noted, the growing number of interest groups changed the nature of the clientele that many agencies must now deal with. It is not just that there are more groups, but that there are more groups in conflict with each other. This conflict, in turn, gets played out in the administrative rulemaking process. Citizens groups upset the equilibrium at many agencies. The access of these groups depends greatly on who controls the White House, but lack of access does not mean that they are removed from the decisionmaking environment. Even the EPA's antagonism toward environmental groups during the Reagan administration did not erase their influence over programs administered by that agency. By relying on allies in Congress and on an aggressive litigation strategy, environmental groups have affected policy decisions.

Another source of conflict is the growing competition in various sectors of the American economy. The Comptroller of the Currency's clientele is composed of an array of financial services institutions, each trying to gain entry into new markets while not permitting new competitors in their own traditional markets. Banks and securities firms represent one basic division, with each side willing to challenge the Comptroller's decisions by appealing to sympathetic legislators or going to court to try to overturn unfriendly decisions.

Conflicting pressures on administrators have come not only from interest groups and members of Congress but also from the White House. As the bureaucracy has expanded, the White House has tried to centralize control over it. Various steps have been taken by many different presidents to try to assert greater control over bureaucratic policymaking. Indeed, the power of subgovernments has been a main reason why presidents have tried to centralize control in the White House. Although the process of centralization and greater White House control has been an incremental process, Ronald Reagan has been unusually successful at it. He has skillfully used the OMB to ride herd on the bureaucracy, entrusting it to protect his policy preferences against undue agency compromises with legislators or lobbyists. As Terry Moe notes, the OMB's regulatory review process allows it "to venture into territory long regarded as the rightful domain of the established bureaucracy and to act as the president's agent in screening and shaping decisions that would otherwise be lost to the permanent government."[39]

Finally, it should be noted that administrators' relations with legislators and lobbyists may differ from those in a subgovernment because of their own personal preferences. First, administrators value autonomy. That is, all things considered, they would rather make rulemaking decisions themselves. Frequently they are not able to do this, but they can easily create barriers to participation by outsiders and make them expend political capital to become involved. Administrators running the food stamp program often avoided efforts to build alliances with sympathetic legislators and lobbyists, even though such alliances would have made their lives easier. They saw themselves as experts who were better able to run the program without the interference of outsiders.[40]

Second, administrators, like members of Congress, want to make good public policy. To do that, they will risk coming into conflict with legislators and lobbies that have a different conception of what good public policy is. Many agency decisions that promoted deregulation have come from administrators committed to an appealing economic theory rather than to a particular political coalition.

Administrators are thus pulled in different directions. Many have large and diverse clienteles. Enduring conflict among their clients is also common. Differing committees or subcommittees may actively try to influence an agency rulemaking decision. The OMB may exert a strong hand over policy development. Finally, administrators may have ideas of their own (as do others in the agency with whom they must work) as to what course the agency should pursue. None of this turns administrators into helpless, pitiful giants ground into inaction by political conflict. What it does mean, however, is that administrators are often in the position of choosing sides between competing coalitions of their issue network, while at the same time endeavoring to put their own mark on agency policymaking.

INTEREST GROUPS: APPEALS COURT LOBBYING

Although participation in a classic subgovernment may not appeal to all administrators, it is an ideal policymaking arrangement for an interest group—ideal, that is, so long as the group holds a dominant position in it rather than being on the outside looking in. Among the thousands of interest groups in Washington today, only a small percentage enjoy this privilege. Still, there is great value in participating in an issue network. To begin with, such participation enhances an interest group's ability to monitor rapidly changing events in a large, complex policymaking arena. Information may be gathered quickly and inexpensively through informal interaction with other actors in the network. As Edward Laumann, David Knoke, and Yong-Hak Kim suggest, interest groups are faced with great uncertainties about how policy events will develop. "In trying to manage these uncertainties, an organization attempts to establish predictable, stable relationships of interorganizational information and resource exchanges that permit it better to negotiate its external environments."[41]

Issue networks are not unified bodies that place cooperation and internal agreement above the individual goals of participants. In large and potentially conflictual domains, groups are constantly aligning and realigning themselves with other organizations. One study concludes that "persistent cleavages appear very much to be the exception to the rule."[42] Even within a smaller subnetwork of usual allies, participants may place little value on keeping the peace by moderating their stances so as to achieve compromise. Principle easily divides the best of friends.

Policymakers can, of course, pressure a factionalized network into putting a premium on unity. While serving as chairman of the Banking Committee, Senator Jake Garn (R.-Utah) told industry groups to agree on legislation before they brought it to him. Despite the incentive to compromise, banking and other financial groups were unable to agree on policy proposals and no major legislation emerged from the committee between 1982 and 1986. A member of the House Banking Committee blames the expanding nature of this issue network as the reason. "When I first came to Congress," says Chalmers Wylie (R.-Ohio), "there were five major financial trade groups, but now there are at least five times that. Now if you're trying to satisfy all the trade groups, it's pretty hard to do."[43]

The growth in the number of lobbying groups has led not only to larger networks but also to more possibilities for coalitions within a network. New groups entering a network are not carbon copies of the old; rather, they represent either new, previously unrepresented interests or constituents who have some allegiance to existing groups but do not feel that all their concerns win sufficient attention from these organizations. A smaller group that might previously have compromised its differences with a large peak association within its policy area, or hesitated to take it on when they differed, might instead coalesce with other smaller groups within an expanded network to do advocacy independent of the larger organization.

With incentives both to work cooperatively with other groups and to seek a visible and independent presence, part of the everyday management function in a lobbying organization is to decide how much time and resources should be committed to coalitions. Issue networks facilitate the small, informal coalitions that are unlikely to gain such public visibility that they will badly overshadow the efforts of the contributing groups. They also promote turn-taking in leadership roles:

No group is interested in always being the caddy. An organization will easily assent to joining a coalition that is simply a more formalized and routinized way of exchanging information than phone calls and chance interactions with other network members. Routinized information exchange may evolve into a division of labor; for example, various groups may agree to lobby particular members of Congress. As more resources must be committed, however, the level of cooperation by groups becomes more problematic. The propensity to expend resources on coalition efforts is related, of course, to the importance of the issue to the group. Still, groups prefer to keep arrangements informal and flexible so that scarce resources remain available for rapidly changing issue needs.[44]

The logic of how a group chooses to expend its lobbying resources on issues of importance is driven not by the needs of potential coalition partners but by the structure of opportunity that it perceives. That is, an interest group scans the political horizon and decides where it has the greatest opportunity to influence policy at the time. As policymaking takes place incrementally at so many different stages and institutional settings, interest groups find themselves moving from one target to another as developments unfold. Over time, their efforts become a matter of "appeals court lobbying" as they try to improve upon one decision (or "nondecision") by going to another set of policymakers. For instance, at various times while fighting the government's effort to break up the Bell system, AT&T lobbied the House, the Senate, the Defense Communications Agency, the Justice Department, the Commerce Department, the Federal Communications Commission, the White House, and the federal courts.[45]

Given the nature of our policymaking system, it is not surprising that interest groups keep shopping around for a better deal when they are dissatisfied. When the American Medical Association could not halt the changes in Medicare payment provisions in a 1986 budget bill, they tried to persuade the Department of Health and Human Services to modify them. When that failed, they sued in federal court. Although interest groups still try to establish ongoing, working relationships with policymakers, the more competitive interest group environment creates a different set of expectations about the security of those arrangements. Appeals court lobbying is the logical consequence of the decline of subgovernments.

The norms of interest group behavior fit well into issue network politics. Groups easily move in out of coalitions, sometimes leaving past friends behind as new combinations and recombinations of lobbies form. Little premium is placed on being friends forever. Groups expect that new policy issues will cause new divisions and alliances within their policy arena. As the number of groups within a network grows, relationships become even more fluid. In short, although interest groups are not unconcerned with building long-term relationships, their alliances with other interest groups are strongly guided by the pragmatic needs of the here and now.

POLITICAL SCIENCE AND POLITICAL CONFLICT

The subgovernment perspective continues to thrive in spite of growing evidence that it is not adequately descriptive of a large number of policy areas. Numerous studiees of individual issue areas reveal the absence of the essential characteristics of a subgovernment. And analysis of the political behavior of legislators, administrators, and lobbyists casts further doubt on the utility of the subgovernment model.

The charmed life of subgovernments in political science can be explained by a number of factors. First, the conventional wisdom in any field is always slow to change as it takes time for new evidence to build and become widely known. As more studies are completed, published, and digested, opinion will change (or be reinforced). Second, the central argument is not that subgovernments have disappeared altogether. Rather, it is more subtle. American politics is said to have changed in such a way that many subgovernments have lost their dominance. Broader, more conflictual issue networks exist in many policy areas now, although subgovernments rein in others. The question that must be asked, then, is what is the prevailing model of policymaking that ought to be transmitted to students? Third, issue networks are elusive phenomena; just trying to describe one is a difficult task.

A final reason is that subgovernments fit so well into a dominant, if not fully articulated, paradigm in political science. Our view of interest groups tends to be one of "antipluralism." Since the publication of *Who Governs?* considerable effort has been devoted to disproving its pluralist argument that democratic ends are reached through the bargaining and compromise of affected interests in an open political system.[46] Scholars such as Theodore Lowi and Grant McConnell made persuasive arguments that interest groups inhibited rather than facilitated democratic policy-making.[47] Political power was unjustly delegated to groups, and the autonomy they enjoyed closed off policymaking from conflicting interests. The consequence of this restricted participation was that policy outcomes did not represent the public interest. Subgovernments offer an image that fits exceedingly well within this broad indictment of interest group politics in America. Subgovernments represent agency capture, highly restricted participation, and stability that preserves the status quo.

Although the extensive attack on pluralism may seem part of our past, an important legacy of that fight is this critical view of interest group politics. The sophisticated and powerful arguments that were made concerning the bias of the interest group system remain at the heart of contemporary thinking about the relationship of groups to government. No new school of thought has replaced this broad theorizing, and it continues to be logically connected to subgovernment politics.

Issue networks do not fit as easily into prevailing interest group theory. Issue networks suggest that the policymaking process is more open, more conflictual, more dynamic, and more broadly participatory than the pluralist critics believed. In short, issue networks show more potential for fulfilling the pluralist prescription for democratic politics than do subgovernments. How close they come to promoting true pluralist democracy is not yet known. Despite their expanded participation, issue networks do nothing to ensure that all affected interests are represented at the bargaining table. With its lack of a centralized decisionmaking process, issue network politics may also favor the status quo by increasing the difficulty of achieving compromise when sharply divergent views emerge. There are surely different kinds of networks, and some may lead to more democratic processes and fairer outcomes than others. Clearly, more research is needed to understand how policy decisions are affected by contemporary issue network politics.

As research is undertaken, it should be free of the assumption that key actors in a policy community can easily find ways of producing optimal solutions whereby everybody wins. The subgovernment model removes political conflict from political science. Recent scholarship, however, shows that conflict and competition among interest groups is characteristic of our policymaking system. The subgovernment model was also built on an overly simplistic view of the incentive systems that drive the behavior of participants. As this chapter was demonstrated, the incentive systems are more complex and can push individuals in a policy community toward goals that vary widely. The growth of interest group politics and various institutional changes have significantly changed the policymaking environment for many policy communities. Thus, our task as political scientists is to develop models of policy communities that are grounded on a realistic assessment of participant goals, institutional constraints, and political conflict.

NOTES

The author wishes to thank Chris Bosso, John Tierney, and the editors of this volume for their helpful comments on an earlier draft of this chapter. Sections of the chapter appear in a somewhat altered form in *The Interest Group Society*, 2nd ed. (Glenview, Ill.: Scott, Foresman/Little, Brown, forthcoming).

1. Hugh Heclo, "Issue Networks and the Executive Establishment," in Anthony King, ed., *The New American Political System* (Washington, D.C.: American Enterprise Institute, 1978), p. 88.

2. Ernest Griffith, *Impasse of Democracy* (New York: Harrison-Hilton Books, 1939); and John T. Tierney, "Subgovernments and Issue Networks," paper presented at the annual meeting of the American Political Science Association, New Orleans (1985), p. 28.

3. Douglass Cater, *Power in Washington* (New York: Vintage Books, 1964), p. 18.

4. Heclo, "Issue Networks and the Executive Establishment," p. 88.

5. James Q. Wilson, "The Politics of Regulation," in James Q. Wilson, ed., *The Politics of Regulation* (New York: Basic Books, 1980), p. 391.

6. Heclo, "Issue Networks and the Executive Establishment," p. 103.

7. Ibid., p. 102.

8. David Knoke and Edward O. Laumann, "The Social Organization of National Policy Domains," in Peter V. Marsden and Nan Lin, eds., *Social Structure and Network Analysis* (Beverly Hills, Calif.: Sage, 1982).

9. Robert H. Salisbury, John P. Heinz, Edward O. Laumann, and Robert L. Nelson, "Who Works with Whom? Patterns of Interest Group Alliance and Opposition," paper presented at the annual meeting of the American Political Science Association, Washington, D.C. (1986); and Edward O. Laumann, John P. Heinz, Robert Nelson, and Robert Salisbury, "Organizations in Political Action: Representing Interests in National Policy-Making," paper presented at the annual meeting of the American Sociological Convention, New York (1986).

10. Randall B. Ripley and Grace A. Franklin, *Congress, the Bureaucracy, and Public Policy*, 4th ed. (Chicago: Dorsey Press, 1987).

11. H. Brinton Milward and Gary L. Wamsley, "Policy Subsystems, Networks and the Tools of Public Management," in Robert Eyestone, ed., *Public Policy Formation* (Greenwich, Conn.: JAI Press, 1984), p. 4.

12. Jack H. Knott and Gary J. Miller, *Reforming Bureaucracy* (Englewood Cliffs, N.J.: Prentice-Hall, 1987), p. 143.

13. Salisbury, et al., "Who Works with Whom?" p. 17.

14. William P. Browne, "Policy and Interests: Instability and Change in a Classic Issue Subsystem," in Allan J. Ciglar and Burdett A. Loomis, eds., *Interest Group Politics*, 2nd ed. (Washington, D.C.: Congressional Quarterly, 1986), p. 187.

15. Thomas L. Gais, Mark A. Peterson, and Jack L. Walker, "Interest Groups, Iron Triangles and Representative Institutions in American National Government," *British Journal of Political Science*, vol. 14 (1984), p. 166.

16. Key Lehman Schlozman and John T. Tierney, *Organized Interests and American Democracy* (New York: Harper & Row, 1986), pp. 283–287.

17. Martha Derthick and Paul J. Quirk, *The Politics of Deregulation* (Washington, D.C.: Brookings Institution, 1985).

18. Mark A. Peterson and Jack L. Walker, "Interest Group Response to Partisan Change," in Cigler and Loomis, eds., *Interest Group Politics*, p. 172.

19. Charles H. Levine and James A. Thurber, "Reagan and the Intergovernmental Lobby: Iron Triangles, Cozy Subsystems, and Political Conflict," in Cigler and Loomis, eds., *Interest Group Politics*, p. 211.

20. John E. Chubb, *Interest Groups and the Bureaucracy* (Stanford, Calif.: Stanford University Press, 1983), p. 251.

21. Lauriston R. King and W. Wayne Shannon, "Political Networks in the Policy Process: The Case of the National Sea Grant Program," *Polity*, vol. 19 (1986), pp. 213–231.

22. Jeffrey M. Berry, *Feeding Hungry People* (New Brunswick, N.J.: Rutgers University Press, 1984).

23. Browne, "Policy and Interests."

24. Edward O. Laumann, David Knoke, and Yong-Hak Kim, "An Organizational Approach to State Policy Formation: A Comparative Study of Energy and Health Domains," *American Sociological Review*, vol. 50 (1985), pp. 1–19.

25. Christine Day Campos, "Interest Groups and Aging Policy in the 1980s," paper delivered at the annual meeting of the American Political Science Association, New Orleans (1985).

26. Tim R. Miller, "Recent Trends in Federal Water Resource Management: Are the 'Iron Triangles' in Retreat?" *Policy Studies Review*, vol. 5 (1985), pp. 395–412.

27. Christopher Bosso, "Transforming Adversaries into Collaborators: Interest Groups and the Regulation of Chemical Pesticides," paper delivered at the annual meeting of the American Political Science Association, Washington, D.C. (1986).

28. Andrew S. McFarland, "Groups Without Government: The Politics of Mediation," in Cigler and Loomis, eds., *Interest Group Politics*.

29. Tierney, "Subgovernments and Issue Networks."

30. David R. Mayhew, *Congress: The Electoral Connection* (New Haven, Conn.: Yale University Press, 1974), p. 17.

31. Richard F. Fenno, *Congressmen in Committees* (Boston: Little, Brown, 1973), p. 1.

32. Lawrence C. Dodd, "Congress and the Quest for Power," in Glenn R. Parker, ed., *Studies of Congress* (Washington, D.C.: Congressional Quarterly, 1985), p. 491.

33. Berry, *Feeding Hungry People*.

34. Bosso, "Transforming Adversaries into Collaborators," p. 4.

35. Lawrence C. Dodd and Richard L. Schott, *Congress and the Administrative State* (New York: Wiley, 1979).

36. Steven S. Smith, "New Patterns of Decisionmaking in Congress," in John E. Chubb and Paul E. Peterson, eds., *The New Direction in American Politics* (Washington, D.C.: Brookings Institution, 1985), p. 221.

37. Barbara Sinclair, "Senate Styles and Senate Decision Making," *Journal of Politics*, vol. 48 (1986), p. 895.

38. Ibid., p. 898.

39. Terry M. Moe, "The Politicized Presidency," in Chubb and Peterson, eds., *The New Direction in American Politics*, p. 262.

40. Berry, *Feeding Hungry People.*

41. Laumann et al., "An Organizational Approach to State Policy Formation," p. 3.

42. Laumann et al., "Organizations in Political Action," p. 21.

43. Monica Langley, "Feuding Lobbies Hinder Push to Write Comprehensive Legislation," *Wall Street Journal,* March 24, 1986.

44. Jeffrey M. Berry, *The Interest Group Society* (Boston: Little, Brown, 1984), pp. 202–205.

45. Steve Coll, *Deal of the Century* (New York: Atheneum, 1986).

46. Robert A. Dahl, *Who Governs?* (New Haven, Conn.: Yale University Press, 1961).

47. Theodore Lowi, *The End of Liberalism* (New York: Norton, 1979); and Grant McConnell, *Private Power and American Democracy* (New York: Vintage, 1966).

10

Politicized Management:
The Changing Face of Business
in American Politics

RICHARD A. HARRIS

AMERICAN BUSINESS AND THE
NEW SOCIAL REGULATION

Of all the institutional changes that took place in American politics during the 1970s, the most widespread and dramatic occurred in the realm of regulatory politics and policy. The enactment and implementation of the so-called new social regulation[1]—that is, regulation dealing with public health, worker safety, consumer affairs, and the environment—transformed the institutions of regulatory policymaking. That transformation, in turn, fundamentally redefined the relationship between government and business in the United States. On one level, this is hardly surprising: Influenced by the New Left critique of the "establishment"[2] and mobilized by the antiwar movement of the 1960s,[3] the public lobbyists who advocated the new social regulation wanted to reshape government-business relations. They demanded that American businesses, especially major corporations, exhibit a sense of "social responsibility" in their behavior;[4] government action, of course, was deemed necessary to ensure such behavior. In addition, they sought to open up the subgovernmental networks of regulatory policy, to inject a perspective other than the business point of view, and to break what they perceived to be business's stranglehold on the administration of regulatory policy. Thus, those who brought the new social regulation into being *intended* to change regulatory politics as well as regulatory policy.

The new social regulation, however, also transformed regulatory institutions in ways not anticipated by public lobbyists or their political allies. Very often these *unintended* consequences of changes in institutions are as significant as the intended consequences: Such is the case with the new social regulation. Arguably, the institutional changes accompanying these new policies did evoke more socially responsible corporate behavior, and they did compel business men and women to deal with public lobbyists on a regular basis. Yet, an equally important, though unintended, result was the *politicization of management* in American business.

Politicization means (1) a growing awareness of government and its relevance to the activities of one's daily life; (2) a rising concern about politics; and (3) increased political participation and attempts to influence policymakers. The new social regulation is responsible, to a great extent, for the development of these attitudes and behaviors among corporate managers. The nature of managerial decisionmaking has changed, therefore, and this change has important implications not only for American business but also for American politics.

Thus far, the politicization of management has attracted the interest primarily of management scientists, who, quite naturally, have concentrated their attention on the new social regulation's impact on corporate structure and performance.[5] Although management scientists concerned with the new social regulation had to consider the political process and business's role in it, politics was not their focus. From their organizational-theory vantage point, politics was simply another "environmental variable," albeit a very important one, with which corporate managers had to cope in running a business. Therefore, although they have much to tell us about the politicization of management, they offer little insight into the reciprocal effects that politicized management might have on the institutions and processes of regulatory politics.

This chapter takes up both the response of business to the new social regulation and the question of how that response has affected regulatory politics. In doing so, it blends the contributions of management science with those of political science to arrive at a better understanding of the causes and consequences of politicized management.

THE EMERGENCE OF THE
NEW SOCIAL REGULATION

As its name implies, the new social regulation constituted a shift in the substance of regulatory policy, a shift away from the regulators' traditional focus on prices and competition in the marketplace. Thus, the new social regulation has been contrasted with older "economic" regulation associated with the Progressive Era and the New Deal. The earlier brand of regulatory policy reflected the economic security issues of an industrial society, whereas the newer variety reflected the "quality-of-life" issues typical of a postindustrial society. This sharp historical contrast between economic and social regulation can be misleading in particular instances; a regulatory concern with consumer welfare, for example, can be discerned as early as the Progressive era, and this concern was rooted as much in social as in economic affairs. Still, the new terminology does accurately call our attention to an overall reorientation in the substance of federal regulation.

The substantive shift in policy is readily seen in the creation of new regulatory programs during the late 1960s and the 1970s. Between 1965 and 1977, forty-four major social regulatory laws were enacted (See Chapter 1, Table 1.1): The policy problems encompassed in those laws ranged from cigarette advertising to toxic waste management. The new regulatory programs also brought into being new bureaucratic agencies (See Chapter 1, Table 1.2) to administer the laws and write the accompanying regulations. Some of the most highly visible and important of these were the Environmental Protection Agency (EPA), the Occupational Safety and Health Administration (OSHA), the National Highway Traffic Safety Administration (NHTSA), and the Consumer Product Safety Commission (CPSC). Moreover, the implementation activities of these new bureaucracies touched the daily operations of American businesses as economic regulation never had.

The two most obvious ways in which the new social regulation intruded on business were the introduction of significant costs associated with compliance and the establishment of administrative procedures that occupied the time and energy of business men and women. Compliance costs confronting business managers included not only the expenditures on plant and capital required to meet regulatory performance standards but also considerable "front-end costs" imposed by statutory requirements for environmental impact statements, design plans for new projects, and other information necessary in advance of new business ventures. These front-end costs, especially those required under environmental statutes, could run into millions of dollars and generate expensive delays. In addition, the creation of elaborate reporting procedures and requirements for public hearings on new regulations or proposed changes in existing rules added to the costs of doing business. These administrative procedures seemed particularly burdensome in light of the apparent inflexibility, sometimes written into statutes, of bureaucrats responsible for implementing the new social regulation.[6] For example, environmental statutes sometimes required that regulations be written to attain a "no-effect level" of pollution or that cost considerations be specifically discounted. Similarly, consumer and worker safety laws often specified in great detail not only what business should do but also how bureaucrats were to enforce the relevant laws and regulations.

This enumeration of the problems confronting business under the new social regulation is intended not as an indictment but as an indication of the extent to which this shift in policy affected business. The new social regulation clearly presented American business with a new and serious challenge. Businesses were on the defensive in the early 1970s as they scrambled to adjust to new laws, new agencies, and new compliance problems—in short, to a new regulatory environment. It is important to recognize, however, that the need for adjustment was brought about as much by a change in the nature of regulatory politics as by a change in the substance of regulatory policy. The new social regulation not only altered the substance of federal regulation, it also introduced new regulatory institutions; and much less has been written about these changes and their impact than about the substantive ones.

As Donald Brand and Robert Eden have shown (see Chapters 2 and 3, respectively), the reforms of the 1970s sprang from the radical social, political, and intellectual milieu of the 1960s. The implication of these origins is that the reforms were predicated on a deep suspicion of establishment institutions and the channels of mainstream American politics such as the electoral process and the two-party system: Big government and big business were seen as oppressing the individual in society and undermining democracy in the political processes. Perhaps more than any other set of reforms, the new social regulation embodied an attempt to restructure existing institutions.

Mistrustful of the subgovernments that decided important questions of regulatory policy, public lobbyists sought to establish mechanisms of participatory democracy, mechanisms that would ensure a role for themselves in the implementation as well as the enactment of regulatory policy. The specific purpose of these mechanisms was to create regulatory institutions that business would find difficult to manipulate. As Joan Claybrook, president of Public Citizen, explained,

> Social regulation took decisionmaking out of the hands of corporate managers and socialized it. Now public interest groups and government regulators influence product design or performance. There were a whole number of changes in the way business did business, but decisionmaking was the key issue. Public interest groups essentially democratized the decision process and put something other than profit into the equation.[7]

This effort to remake regulatory politics, however, was based on more than a mistrust of big government and big business. It also grew out of a particular interpretation of how American politics had evolved. Reformers felt that since the New Deal the focus of activity in American politics had shifted dramatically from the legislative arena to the administrative arena. In a sense, they were simply assimilating the conclusions of political scientists.[8]

In response to the shift in focus of political activity, public-lobby groups sought to acquire a permanent presence in Washington, D.C.[9] Only in that way, they felt, could they compete effectively. Yet their organizational resources paled in comparison to those of business. The answer was to restructure the administrative institutions and processes to redress this imbalance. Thus the laws of the new social regulation placed a great deal of emphasis on participation and procedure. Douglas Costle, the Environmental Protection Agency administrator under Jimmy Carter, noted that "public interest lobbyists were more interested in the process of regulation than the substance."[10] Even more concretely, Bruce Ackerman and Andrew Hassler argue that environmental regulation "represents part of a complex effort by which the present generation is *revising the system of administrative law inherited from the New Deal*" (emphasis added).[11]

The institutions of regulatory politics were changed in a number of ways, all of which meant that subgovernmental decisionmaking would force business lobbyists to deal with public lobbyists. One of the most important changes in the administration of regulatory policy was the introduction of citizen law suits. In particular, many regulatory statutes of the 1970s granted automatic standing to sue to "interested parties" in civil cases. In some instances, interested parties also could initiate regulatory enforcement action at federal agencies.[12] Ordinarily an "interest" was defined as an economic interest, without which no standing to sue existed. However, in the case *Sierra Club* v. *Morton*,[13] the Supreme Court established that interest could be defined more broadly; specifically, environmentalists with an "aesthetic" interest in natural scenery could sue to prevent business ventures that might affect that scenery. The use of class-action suits under these provisions became a potent weapon in the arsenal of environmentalists and consumer advocates. They were employed to promote an adversarial kind of regulatory politics in which courts served as both an arena and a model of competition.[14] The idea behind this model was that adversarial proceedings were the only way to ensure justice in regulatory policy, although as Eden has noted in Chapter 3, it also represented a basic institutional departure. The courts thus became pivotal players in regulatory oversight and enforcement, and assured public lobbyists an access point to those administrative activities.[15]

An institutional change related to citizen law suits was the mandating of *public procedures* in granting permits or licenses under the new social regulation. These innovations appeared in a number of different guises: as requirements for environmental or social-impact statements; as statutory provisions spelling out in detail how agencies and businesses should publicize hearings on proposed new products or construction; and as specific provisions for public participation in administrative rulemakings. By opening up administration, public lobbyists achieved a double victory. On the one hand, they assured themselves a role in business decisions that have broad social implications; in Joan Claybrook's words, they "socialized" business decisionmaking. These public proceedings, however, provided them with a paper trail to follow into court if they felt business was not complying with regulatory standards: Businesses had to go on the record in these proceedings.

Among the most controversial of the measures to open up administration to effective public lobby participation was the *intervenor funding program* at the Federal Trade Commission (FTC) (see Chapter 6). Under this initiative, the federal government subsidized public lobby participation in rulemakings, thereby ensuring a regular channel of input for consumer interests. Similar programs were tried in other social regulatory settings. This type of activity has been all but eliminated under the Reagan administration. Nevertheless, the expertise and experience acquired by public lobbyists in the 1970s endowed them with a certain legitimacy that has ensured their continued access to rulemakings. Even under the Reagan administration, regulatory agencies must consult with public lobbyists.

The ideas and demands underlying the new social regulation were brought largely to fruition. After more than a decade of experience with the new social regulation, in both the public and private sectors, William Ruckleshaus recognized that:

> Today the debate on public participation is over, The new regulatory process reflects the public take-back of delegated power following Vietnam . . . this led to the War Powers Act . . . on the domestic side there was a similar phenomenon reflecting a lack of faith and trust in the executive branch . . . There must be guarantees for citizen participation. The question is how to make it work?[16]

Such an assertion from a member of the Nixon and Reagan administrations and a chief executive of the Weyerhaeuser Corporation suggests the success that advocates of the new social regulation have enjoyed in remaking the institutions of regulatory politics. Of course, this success has come at the expense of business interests; and so we now turn to a consideration of how business responded to this new, more open, and more competitive regulatory environment.

THE POLITICIZATION OF MANAGEMENT

Initially it may seem odd to proclaim the politicization of management in the second half of the twentieth century. Business leaders, after all, have long played a prominent role in American politics, especially regulatory politics. After some thought, however, one might be led to see the proliferation of corporate political action committees (PACs) and their ever-increasing involvement in congressional campaigns[17] as indicative of the trend toward politicization. Although the development of PACs is surely related to the reform environment of the 1970s, the politicization of management refers to more than just the involvement of business interests in the councils of government and the electoral process. Under the new social regulation, business participation in politics has not only increased; it has taken on a much different character.[18] Under the new social regulation hardly any business enterprise can avoid dealing with federal regulatory bureaucracies on a regular basis. These dealings, moreover, tend to center on the details of how businesses are operated. It is, indeed, this regularized contact about the day-to-day operations of a business firm that has politicized management.

Because the new social regulation insinuated regulators into firm operations, middle as well as upper management was politicized. Politicized management, then, refers to changes in the attitudes and behaviors of middle-level decisionmakers at individual firms: That is what is new. It is not that business generally is affected by decisions taken in the arenas of regulatory politics but, rather, that the activity of management itself has been colored by those decisions.

In an important article published in the *Harvard Business Review*, Richard Leone has claimed that "the fact of the matter is that the indirect influence of government action on the competitive and *institutional environment* in which business operates directly influences the kinds and mix of skills one needs to succeed as a manager" (emphasis added).[19] According to Leone, the chief cause of this new environment was the new social regulation, and the chief asset new managers needed was "political savvy." It is not sufficient, though, simply to observe that the politicization of management coincided with the emergence of the new social regulation. The linkages between the two must be demonstrated. In other words, how did the new social regulation politicize management?

One way to approach this question is to ask why trade associations and other business lobby organizations, the institutions that historically had served the regulatory interests of business, no longer sufficed in the 1970s. What was it about the new social regulation that made these older institutions inadequate and involved management directly in regulatory affairs?

A signal feature of the new social regulation is the develoment of uniform *performance standards*, regulatory criteria that govern plant design, product quality, and business operations and are applied in exactly the same way to all industries or firms within an industry regardless of their geographic, economic, or financial circumstances. Such regulation cuts across individual firms, systematically imposing costs and benefits depending on the particular characteristics of individual firms. Consequently, many firms or industries that are advantaged by the imposition of these standards will support the new social regulation, while others will oppose it. Under these "competitive" circumstances, corporate management is not likely to see a compelling case for coordinating regulatory action with other firms. Thus, trade associations face a severe collective-action problem: Their objections have become muted since some of their members will strongly oppose the new social regulation, others will support it because they have ventures under way and simply want to get on with them, and still other members will tacitly support it because they see a long-term strategic advantage in "playing ball" with federal regulators and public lobbyists. In fact, some individual firms have discovered that it could be advantageous to portray themselves as reasonable participants in regulatory politics by contrasting themselves with hardline trade associations. They have been able, in this way, to use the trade associations as lightning rods for criticism of business generally while privately cutting deals with regulatory agencies on matters of specific importance to them.

In addition, the front-end and capital costs imposed by the new social regulation politicize management because they, too, present opportunities to some firms and penalties for others. Most obviously, larger firms in general will be able to absorb compliance costs more easily than smaller competitors, a situation that holds out the prospect of picking up market shares if those smaller firms are forced out of business by increased costs. Similarly, capital-intensive firms may find it easier than labor-intensive firms to afford the new social regulation. These possibilities, in turn, lead top management to think more carefully and analytically about the long-term costs and benefits of the new social regulation. The new regulation, then, has destabilized the competitive forces in the marketplace.

Finally, the new social regulation's restructuring of regulatory institutions has helped to politicize management and undermine the role of trade associations in the political process. Public hearings, citizen suits, intervenor funding, and other measures to ensure the full participation of public lobbyists in the implementation of regulatory policy all required businesses to adapt to a new decisionmaking environment. The tight subgovernments of regulatory policy were, as Jeffrey Berry has noted in the preceding chapter, converted to relatively open "issue networks."[20] The emergence of such issue networks has required businesses to interact with new actors and in new ways. They have had to deal not only with public lobbyists but also with bureaucrats zealously committed to the missions of the new regulatory agencies and with federal courts, which played an active oversight function, often dictating specific, operational instructions to corporate managers.

In this kind of issue network, business organizations had to, in the words of Peter Drucker, "think through and develop concepts, policies, rules and then have to take the lead in educating lawmakers, bureaucrats, their own industry and public opinion."[21] Traditionally, these kinds of activities were performed by trade associations rather than by individual firms and managers within those firms. Under the new social regulation, then, firms more and more frequently established or upgraded their own Washington offices. According to Robert Reich, in the 1970s, the number of firms with Washington offices doubled, and we now have more than 500 such outposts of corporate management.[22] The role of these offices is to gather political information, to deal regularly with legislators and public-lobby groups within issue networks, and to interact with federal regulators on matters of specific relevance to the management and operation of firms.

In addition to setting up their own Washington offices to interact more effectively with their external environment, corporations responded to the new social regulation by altering their internal organizations. These internal changes included the increase of resources for political and regulatory analysis as well as the reallocation of existing resources.

Finally, it is important to note that at exactly the time firms were responding individually to the new social regulation, they were also seeking to react collectively when possible. David Vogel, in fact, argues that in the late 1970s the business community acquired a "class consciousness." Citing the creation of the Business Roundtable (an organization of corporate CEOs committed to working out common positions on political affairs) and the formation of numerous ad hoc business coalitions on specific issues such as labor law reform and tax policy, Vogel asserts:

> In essence, during the 1970's the fight over government regulation became the focus of class conflict for the first time in American history: it pitted the interests of business as a whole against the public interest movement and organized labor. The nature of the conflict over regulation became analagous to the struggle over the adoption of the welfare state.[23]

Although accuracy demands that we acknowledge these broad efforts at coordination, the fact remains that they were limited in scope. There are outstanding examples of businesses forming coalitions with unions or public lobbyists; business class-consciousness had its limits. Even Vogel is quick to point out that "companies remained more likely to become concerned with those issues that promised to affect their own operations."[24] In sum, many farsighted business leaders have vigorously pursued a collective response to the new social regulation, but individual firm responses remain a central concern.

Unfortunately, political scientists have had little to say about the behavior of individual firms, let alone the internal reorganizations they may undertake in response to the new social regulation. Generally, political scientists have viewed institutions as either a *consequence* of political behavior or simply a *context* within which that behavior takes place.[25] The politicization of management, however, demonstrates that institutional change such as that evoked by the new social regulation can also *cause* political behavior—in this case, business's response. Business firms, moreover, may be considered institutions or organizations in their own right. Accordingly, we must rely on the work of organization theorists to gain additional insight into politicized management.

POLITICIZED MANAGEMENT AS AN ORGANIZATIONAL RESPONSE

Classical organizational analysis rests on the assumption that a firm is a coalition. As R. Cyert and J. March have noted, "In a business organization, the coalition members include managers, workers, stockholders, suppliers, customers, lawyers, tax collectors, regulatory agencies, etc."[26]

Although a distinction is drawn between primary and secondary members of the organizational coalition (the former being the managers and workers of the firm proper), all members play a role in the life of the business organization. This conception of the firm leads to two important conclusions, both of which are helpful in understanding the politicization of management. First, goal formation—that is, the process of deciding on organizational objectives—is an important activity within the firm. If the firm is a coalition rather than a hierarchy, goals and objectives are negotiated among key members of the coalition rather than simply decreed by top management and executed by subordinates. This portrait of the firm contrasts sharply with the traditional microeconomic view, which holds that firms behave like individual decision-makers or, if a coalition exists, that the "side payments" or concessions by top management necessary to maintain the coalition are simply an expense of doing business. An organizational analysis, on the other hand, examines how decisions are reached among the firm's managerial subunits, such as finance, marketing, accounting, governmental affairs, legal affairs, and production, as well as among the various secondary actors in the organizational coalition.

In addition to emphasizing the centrality of goal formation as an organizational process, conceptualizing a business organization as a coalition suggests that maintenance of the coalition is a fundamental goal. Indeed, the goal of coalition maintenance is at the heart of business response to the new social regulation. Maintaining the coalition may be equated with ensuring the survival of the business organization, and survival may be challenged if major shifts occur in the political-economic environment of the organization—shifts such as the enactment and implementation of the new social regulation. In the parlance of organization theorists, such major changes characterize a *turbulent* organizational environment.[27] Business response to the new social regulation, then, may be seen as an effort to maintain the organizational coalition in the face of a turbulent environment. Organization theory also has some more specific hypotheses about how firms adjust to turbulence, and these hypotheses seem to fit the case of the new social regulation almost perfectly.

In a turbulent environment, organizations must reassess their goals and objectives, or at least the priorities among them, in order to serve the overarching goal of organizational maintenance. That reassessment, however, fosters competition among the managerial subunits of the organization as they vie for influence and input in the process of goal formation. Turbulence presents some subunits with advantages and others with disadvantages as the organization seeks to adapt its internal structure and behavior to the changing political-economic environment: "Organizational subunits have a dynamics of their own; they act to enhance their power and prestige relative to other departments in the organization."[28]

In particular, the new social regulation, through its success in changing institutions of regulatory decisionmaking, in challenging the "establishment," and in imposing performance standards on business, has put a premium on expertise in governmental and legal affairs, scientific analysis, engineering, and public relations. Top management at firms, then, is drawn into closer and more frequent interactions with subunits displaying such expertise. Indeed, these subunits may develop a vested interest in the new social regulation, inasmuch as its continuation and expansion enhance their position within the organizational coalition. They can help to maintain the organization in the new political-economic environment by (1) developing political intelligence and interpreting the new regulatory setting; (2) establishing relations with regulators and winning their confidence, or at least avoiding their suspicions; (3) responding effectively to technical and scientific issues raised by the new social regulation; and (4) achieving amendments to laws or variances in regulations that bear directly on the firm's objectives.

In sum, the new social regulation elevates organizational subunits within the firm that have political and technical expertise. The prominence of these subunits is a critical element in the politicization of management; not only does top management occupy itself more and more with matters of political interaction and regulatory compliance, but the subunits with a permanent interest in these affairs acquire a greater influence in making decisions and policy within the firm.

Another hypothesis organizational theory contributes to our understanding of business response to the new social regulation is that a turbulent political-economic environment will transform the organizational coalition.[29] Specifically, the new social regulation has injected public lobbyists, new regulatory institutions, congressional subcommittees, and federal courts into coalitions. This analysis bears a striking resemblance to the political science argument that the new social regulation has transformed issue networks. The main difference between these two approaches is that political scientists see regulatory agencies as the focal point of issue network affairs, whereas organization theorists obviously view the firm in that light. The concept of an issue network directs our attention to the fact that the new social regulation has drawn business managers directly into regulatory politics. The concept of an organizational coalition, on the other hand, raises the question of how admitting new and often hostile members to the coalition has affected the management and operations of the firm. Both perspectives are necessary if we are to arrive at an accurate understanding of politicized management and its implications.

Although organizational theory stresses the importance of looking at the interactions *within* organizational coalitions to understand the business response to environmental changes, it also suggests that, when threatened by external forces, businesses will participate more regularly in the political process. This hypothesis accords with the establishment of corporate offices in Washington, D.C., and with the develoment of in-house expertise in political affairs. One major chemical manufacturer, for example, recently established a policy of identifying executives likely to advance rapidly in the firm and assigning them to the Washington office for a two-year period. The justification for this policy was that successful managers had to have a working knowledge of Washington politics not only to make intelligent corporate decisions, but also to know how to participate effectively.[30]

This sort of policy clearly supports Richard Leone's claim that political savvy has become an indispensable managerial resource. As James Post, a leading organizational theorist, points out, "In a world where political decisions are made about more and more things, it is inevitable that the greater the interpenetration between enterprise and society, the more likely it [the firm] is to be embroiled in political decisions."[31]

The new social regulation, though, does more than politicize business decisions and promote participation in regulatory politics; it also challenges the legitimacy of corporate enterprise itself.[32] In this sense, the new social regulation calls for a more programmatic response by businesses. Individual firms must engage in political activities more broadly conceived in order to defend their legitimacy. Thus it is not coincidental that, beginning in the late 1970s, we have witnessed individual corporations advertising in newspapers and on television not to promote their products or services but, rather, to extol the virtues of a private enterprise—exactly the kind of adversarial response David Vogel argues is emerging. However, firms also use these media channels to demonstrate their social responsibility and to claim that they are good citizens. Thus, management in a corporation becomes as much a political as an economic or financial activity.

POLITICIZED MANAGEMENT AND THE POLITICS OF REGULATION

The politicization of management is a significant development in its own right, but it also has a broader implication: It is a cause as well as a consequence of institutional shifts in regulatory politics. In the first instance, as we have seen, the new social regulation politicized management by changing the institutional environment of government-business relations. The emergence of politicized management, however, has also had a reciprocal impact on regulatory institutions by altering the composition, structure, and behavior of issue networks established by the new social regulation. Thus our understanding of contemporary regulatory politics depends not only on an appreciation of how changes in regulatory institutions during the 1970s affected business but also on an appreciation of how business's response, which we have described as politicized management, affected those regulatory institutions in turn.

Delineation of the impact of business's response on regulatory politics is a complex matter. In some respects, politicized management has hindered or even halted the development of the new social regulation. In other important respects, though, it has reinforced or even legitimized the institutions and policies of the new social regulation. Politicized management, then, appears to have had contradictory or crosscutting effects, on the one hand arresting and on the other abetting the new social regulation. Yet viewed from another perspective, politicized management seems to have combined with the new social regulation to lead us toward a new politics of regulation, a politics characterized neither by the pluralistic competition applauded by mainstream political scientists nor by the adversarial competition that advocates of the new social regulation sought to institutionalize, but rather by a fairly insulated, though not narrowly restrictive, system of consultation and collaboration set within the various issue networks of social regulation.

Turning first to the ways in which the development of the new social regulation was arrested, we find that, beginning in the late 1970s, economic criteria were successfully reintroduced in regulatory decision-making. We also find an erosion of the bureaucratic inflexibility decried by many critics of the new social regulation. Under President Jimmy Carter, questions of regulatory cost and economic efficiency were slowly woven back into social regulation. In particular, a Regulatory Analysis and Review Group (RARG) was established in the White House, and its linkage with the Council of Wage and Price Stability (COWPS) ensured that its decisions would not be made in an economic vacuum. Although this step was a small one dealing with social regulation on a selective rather than a wholesale basis, it did signal that the days of such concepts as "no-effect level" and of such practices as disallowing cost considerations were ending. Slowly, federal agencies such as the Environmental Protection Agency and the Federal Trade Commission began to experiment with ways of making social regulation cost-effective, and these regulatory reforms required the participation of corporate management.

Businesses also achieved some success in easing the inflexibility with which the new social regulation was implemented. These successes were for the most part achieved on a case-by-case basis; there was no general redirection of the new social regulation. Nevertheless, the fact that many firms received variances or waivers from environmental and consumer regulations indicated a mellowing in the approach of federal agencies and, to some extent, even in the views of public lobbyists.

Neither in the reintroduction of economic criteria nor in the easing of bureaucratic inflexibility did the emergence of politicized management alone impose limitations on the new social regulation. Much of the pressure for the reforms of the late 1970s came from the combination of a relentless attack by economists or other policy analysts on the inefficiency of the new social regulation and the dismal state of the American economy at that time.[33] Politicized management did, however, contribute significantly in both cases.

In particular, politicized management provided businesses with a voice in the social regulatory issue networks that was not automatically suspect. To the extent that individual firms were able to dissociate themselves from business in general and older trade associations in particular, they acquired a certain credibility among federal regulators and advocates of the new social regulation. This credibility was predicated on corporate management's acceptance, in principle, of the new social regulation and the institutions associated with it. If businesses were not perceived as a threat to the fundamentals of the new social regulation, they could argue more effectively for modifications that would benefit them. Thus, politicized management helped to moderate some of the worst impacts of the new social regulation, but the price of this moderation was acceptance of its general institutional and policy aims. The new social regulation remade regulatory politics, and the politicization of management did not undo that.

On the contrary, politicized management helped to solidify the changes brought about in regulatory politics during the 1970s. Precisely because the price of adjusting the new social regulation on the margins was acceptance of its broad principles, the tendency was to legitimize the regulatory politics rather than to challenge it. In a sense, corporate managers and social regulators shared a common objective—to increase certainty in the regulatory environment. As compliance costs did not threaten the existence of large corporations, many managers wanted above all to know what the rules governing regulatory policy were so they could get on with their activities. And in their turn, advocates of the new social regulation wanted to ensure that performance standards would be applied uniformly to American business. By the 1980s, this common interest led to a more cooperative posture on the part of many corporations and public lobby groups. It may be a supreme irony that what David Vogel and others saw as an emergent class consciousness in American business ultimately had the effect of embroiling corporations ever deeper in regulatory politics, thereby socializing business to the ways of Washington and to the aims of the public lobbyists.

When Ronald Reagan took office, his administration adopted a strong stance in favor of deregulation, the major thrust of which was directed at the new social regulation.[34] However, the administration's understanding of deregulation differed from that which emerged in the late 1970s. Rather than adjusting the new social regulation on the margins, it raised fundamental questions not only about policy aims but also about key institutional principles such as public participation and extensive use of the courts in oversight and enforcement. Instead of accepting the view of many corporations that, as William Ruckleshaus stated, the debate on participation was over and the only issue was how to implement it effectively, deregulators in the Reagan administration challenged the institutions as well as the policies of the new social regulation. They attempted to do this by seizing control of the regulatory process, cutting back sharply on enforcement budgets and actions, and undermining the participation of public-lobby groups in that process.

This frontal assault on the new social regulation angered corporate managers as well as public lobbyists. The latter may actually have felt somewhat ambivalent about the Reagan deregulation; although it attacked policies and institutions they had struggled to put in place, it also generated public indignation and mobilized support for the new social regulation. In fact, public participation and use of the federal courts in enforcement proved effective in blocking many ambitious deregulatory initiatives. The opposition of business men and women, of course, is even more surprising when one considers that the deregulators intended to help, not harm, private enterprise.

From the standpoint of organizational theory, though, this opposition appears perfectly reasonable. Many business organizations had spent the better part of the 1970s coming to terms with the environmental turbulence imposed by the new social regulation; and just when there appeared to be hope of increased certainty as well as more flexibility in the administration of that regulation, the Reagan administration introduced another large dose of turbulence into regulatory politics. In the 1980s, the idea of increased uncertainty in regulatory politics appealed to neither businesses nor public lobbyists. Also, it is useful to recall that the new social regulation benefited some organizational subunits over others, and those advantaged subunits were wedded to the new social regulation; their missions and enhanced position depended on the continued importance of that regulation. Thus, there were forces within business organizations that would have reacted negatively to regulatory relief.

In addition, many corporations that had acted in good faith and spent millions of dollars to comply with the new social regulation objected to the Reagan deregulation on the grounds that it rewarded their competitors, who had adopted a defiant stance. Moreover, politicized managers feared that heavyhanded deregulation could fuel a backlash that would jeopardize the regulatory reform efforts begun in the late 1970s or, worse still, rekindle the anti-business sentiment of the early 1970s that gave rise to stringent social regulation. Businesses, as a result, sought to distance themselves from outspoken deregulators in the Reagan administration, especially from Secretary of Interior James Watt and Environmental Protection Agency Administrator Ann Burford, who spearheaded the attack on environmental regulation.[35] In doing so, businesses intended to reassure both the public and, perhaps more important, other members of issue networks that there was no general business conspiracy afoot to gut the new social regulation. In fact, during the early years of the Reagan administration, politicized management helped sustain the new social regulation by publicly opposing deregulators in many instances and by according it legitimacy through continued participation in its institutions. The Reagan administration did successfully rein in the new social regulation, but only temporarily through the exercise of administrative control: All of the laws that had established the new social regulation remained intact.[36]

Although politicized management bolstered the new social regulation in the 1980s, it also caused adjustments in regulatory institutions. In particular, politicized management's acceptance of new social regulations in principle, as well as its integration into regulatory decisionmaking, diminished the confrontational character of regulatory politics that had characterized the early 1970s. This is not to suggest that a clear and durable consensus on the new social regulation has arisen. On the contrary, business men and women still have serious objections to the new social regulation, and they would like to see more of the kinds of regulatory reforms that were begun in the late 1970s. Public lobbyists, for their part, remain suspicious of private enterprise. Of necessity, though, a *modus vivendi* between business and public lobby groups is emerging.

Public lobbyists, as well as their supporters in Congress and the bureaucracy, have had to adapt to the reality that the politicization of management has brought about a more sophisticated and more effective business participation in the issue networks of the new social regulation. No longer are they pitted against a hidebound business community content to let trade associations or "hired gun" lawyers represent their interests. Nowadays, business managers at the firm level keep abreast of regulatory politics, think strategically about regulatory impacts, and are often willing to seek common ground with their opponents, or at least to engage in dialogue. Interactions between business and public-lobby participants, therefore, have become both deeper and more frequent: A certain level of empathy, even mutual respect, has developed between the two.[37]

Although this scenario does not apply universally to the new social regulation, it is readily identifiable and provides an alternative model of regulatory politics—a model that, in its broad outline, is *neocorporatist*. The prefix *neo* is intended to distinguish such policymaking systems from the European fascist regimes of the 1930s that portrayed themselves as corporatist. The basic feature of any corporatist arrangement, though, is that it brings competing interests into more or less formal relationships through which policy conflict can be managed.[38]

Neocorporatism refers to a system of "interest intermediation"—that is, to an institutional arrangement through which conflict between competing interests is managed.[39] Neocorporatist arrangements need not be established by legislative action or executive fiat; they usually evolve in a sui generis way from political interaction and pragmatic attempts to resolve policy disagreements rather than from any forceful and coherent ideology.[40] But they must be ongoing, and they must be recognized as legitimate by both constituencies and governmental authorities in the policy process.

These arrangements have been studied primarily in the context of advanced capitalist societies' efforts at resolving class conflict over economic policy.[41] Naturally, therefore, neocorporatist scholars have focused their attention on Western Europe.[42] Nevertheless, the concept of neocorporatism can help in interpreting regulatory politics in the United States. Fundamentally, neocorporatism describes a political approach to managing conflict, not an approach to economic policymaking. If the substance of central policy conflicts differs from one capitalist society to another, so too should the focus of analysis; neocorporatist institutions can mediate conflict over regulatory policy as well as over economic policy.

The concept of neocorporatism can be applied to a variety of nations; its use is also varied among political theorists. In addition to defining the concept, then, we must be clear about its theoretical scope. For our purposes, neocorporatism is not employed normatively as a prescription for conflict management, although numerous scholars have used it in precisely that manner.[43] Rather, the concept is meant to be descriptive; it aids us in our understanding of the regulatory institutions that already exist. Second, the concept is not employed as a comprehensive description of a political system, although, again, it has been used that way. For our purposes, neocorporatism describes an emergent set of institutional relations specific to the realm of regulatory policy and, even more particularly, to the realm of the new social regulation. Indeed, neocorporatism is an intriguing concept precisely because it offers an alternative model of general conflict management. For the present, though, its applicability appears to be rather narrowly circumscribed. Neocorporatist institutions have developed unevenly in the United States and elsewhere.[44] And where they have developed, they do not stand completely apart from more traditional institutions of consensus building. As Leo Panitch notes in his critique of neocorporatist studies, they are interwoven in complex ways with preexisting institutions: "These [neocorporatist] structures developed on a 'pragmatic' basis and were by no means self-avowedly corporatist; they grew up alongside and in conjunction with the dominant representative systems of parliamentarianism and interest group lobbying."[45]

Finally, neocorporatism refers to more than just an arrangement in which conflicting interests consult and confer. It is genuinely collaborative. Gerhard Lehmbruch has gone so far as to argue that neocorporatism involves the "collusion of administrative authorities with the large interest associations" in the making of public policy.[46] Without the added dimension of collaboration in policymaking, the concept of an issue network would be an adequate representation of interest interaction. Neocorporatist institutions promote a less combative posture among competing interests—a case not of complete harmony but of collective action in concern. Many political scientists agree that the new social regulation opened up subgovernmental politics and institutionalized participation of all interested parties. The argument here is that politicized management has begun to push issue networks beyond consultation and participation to actual collaboration. It is in this sense that neocorporatism is a concept appropriate to the politics of the new social regulation.

Evidence of the emergence of neocorporatist institutions is fragmentary and anecdotal thus far. Still, it is difficult to ignore. Indeed, business leaders and public lobbyists have acknowledged a degree of collaboration in certain instances and wondered about its implications. Their self-conscious appraisal of the costs and benefits of collaborative policymaking is in itself strong evidence. More concretely, though, in the last five to ten years, business leaders and public-lobby groups have participated in numerous conferences and ongoing dialogues about the new social regulation and its impact. These experiences are directed toward a seeking out of common ground regarding both contemporary issues and the question of which issues should be included on the national agenda. More important, the writing and contesting of rules to implement the new social regulation takes place with the regularized interaction of public lobbyists and affected businesses. It is at this level of administration and implementation that neocorporatist institutions emerge most clearly.

Perhaps the most striking evidence of neocorporatism has been the development of regulatory negotiation, or "regnegs." Traditionally, the process through which federal agencies wrote regulations to implement social regulatory laws was characterized by formal administrative rulemaking. The agency would work out a proposed regulation, allow for a specified period of comment by interested parties (ordinarily, organized interest), hold an administrative hearing, and finally decide whether to issue, amend, or table the rule under consideration. Parties unhappy with the outcome of the rulemaking could pursue their dissent through the courts, and often did. This process resulted in extraordinary delays and in almost inevitable litigation in which federal Appeals Courts were transformed into quasi-administrative agencies (see Chapter 7). According to the *National Journal,* 80 percent of the 300 rules issued by the EPA annually end up in federal court.[47] Regnegs were born of the dissatisfaction with this process.

Quite simply, regnegs entailed the bringing together of bureaucrats and competing interests behind closed doors to informally work out an acceptable policy before initiating the formal rulemaking. In that way, all interests would be party to the making of regulatory policy. No one interest is likely to predominate all the time, and all are apt to achieve some measure of success. David Doniger, an attorney for the Natural Resources Defense Council, called regnegs "a ripple of the future—but an important ripple." Gail Bingham, another public lobbyist working for the Conservation Foundation, argued that "what you're doing is shifting from an adversarial taking of positions to a problem-solving process. . . . You are going deeper than the position to the underlying interests, and you attempt to reach agreements that reach those underlying interests."[48] These regnegs are the clearest example yet of neocorporatists institutions. Moreover, they have set a precedent that has carried over into the legislative arena. Business and environmentalists, for example, worked out an accord on pesticide law language in advance of the introduction of a bill.

Another kind of collaborative effort between businesses and public lobbyists is the joint commission or study group established to grapple with policy problems. The classic, and possibly best-known, example of such an enterprise is the Citizens' Coal Project, a commission designed to study the best ways to tap America's abundant coal resources in an efficient and socially responsible manner. The Project's membership include key representatives of regulatory bureaucracies, public-lobby groups, business organizations, individual firms, and the scientific community. Jointly, they explore alternative formulations of a national policy on coal development.

To be sure, public lobbyists and business managers worry about the implications of this kind of collaboration. Public lobbyists fear that they may be co-opted and become too "establishment"; even worse, by forsaking an adversarial posture, they might hurt their fundraising efforts. Firm managers always risk the possibility that they may be giving up too much. Yet both sides recognize the advantages of the more manageable and efficient policymaking sytsem that such neocorporatists institutions seem to promise.

CONCLUSION

The argument developed in this chapter is that the new social regulation politicized management and that the politicization of management in turn reshaped the policymaking institutions put in place by the new social regulation. It further suggests that the concept of neocorporatism aptly describes the new regulatory politics. Although politicized management means that individual firms rather than business associations are key actors, and although neocorporatism usually refers to the institutionalization of interest groups in the policy process, the critical point is that corporations are organizations in themselves. Neocorporatism is predicated on policymaking relations among competing organized interests; hence the crucial fact is that the interests are embodied in organizations, not that they are groups. Politicized management, therefore, has combined with the new social regulation to generate neocorporatist policymaking arrangements.

Neocorporatist institutions also hold broad implications for American politics. In considering these wider implications, we must understand that the scope of neocorporatist institutions is still narrow in the context of American politics as a whole. Nevertheless, such institutions do offer an example of an alternative way to make policy, a way that entails neither the benign vision of pluralist competition nor the openly adversarial vision of the new social regulation. In addition, if neocorporatism describes a significant proportion of social regulatory decisionmaking, it does have an impact on current policy affecting millions of citizens, both individual and corporate. Therefore, it is important to ask what neocorporatist politics is like and how it fits into American political culture.

It seems clear that neocorporatism promotes efficiency in decision-making, understanding and consensus among competing interests, and, ultimately, improved governance in the complex issue areas of the modern state. Neocorporatist institutions reduce the time and money that competing interests must commit to policymaking, especially to the implementation and administration of policy. Policy negotiations among a small cast of characters, outside the glare of the media and public scrutiny, can minimize delay and cost. In addition, negotiation is an educational and socializing experience for business and public-lobby groups. The suspicions and negativism each side tends to harbor toward the other could be tempered by successful policy collaboration.

Neocorporatist institutions also hold the promise of improved governance—not simply more efficient, but also more effective and more legitimate, public policy. As neocorporate researchers have pointed out, in the late 1960s and early 1970s many capitalist democracies were consumed in political turmoil and policy disarray.[49] As socioeconomic differences became open, visceral, and ideological, traditional pluralist institutions geared toward bargaining and compromise were increasingly challenged, rejected, and weakened to the point that political competition gave way to conflict and protest. Where successful, neocorporatist arrangements evolved as pragmatic efforts to manage such conflict, to reassert the authority of government in what appeared to be a crisis of legitimacy. In this sense, neocorporatism can be seen as a fresh approach to policymaking, developed in response to the acrimony of the 1960s and 1970s—that is, as an effort to reestablish politics as the societal pursuit of the public good rather than the particularistic pursuit of public goodies or a narrow ideological vision.

All of the serious criticisms of neocorporatism revolve around the allegation that the price of increased efficiency and governance is a policy system that runs counter to pluralism and democracy. Pluralism is usually understood as a politics of coalition building in which various groups in society have more or less stable interests and make demands on government based on those interests. Politics in a pluralist system, then, is all about generating policy to satisfy the demands of competing interests; it is a *demand-side* politics. Neocorporatist institutions, on the other hand, provide the opportunity to shape or reshape, through negotiation, the interests expressed by political competitors.[50] Neocorporatist politics is about containing the political conflict by changing policymaking institutions; it is a *supply-side* politics. In this sense, neocorporatism does mean a change in basic American conceptions of politics. It makes specific the emphasis on organized interest representation and administrative politics that were begun in earnest during the New Deal, extended during the Great Society, and refined with the new social regulation.

The emphasis on administrative decisionmaking and collaboration among organized interests naturally leads to a collapsing of the arena and the participants in policymaking. It is in this respect that neocorporatism seems to undermine democracy, at least the traditional American pluralist conception of it. It not only attenuates democracy by restricting meaningful participation to organized interest, as Theodore Lowi has argued;[51] it also establishes an institutional framework of interest "intermediation" rather than interest "representation." Intermediation means that government becomes a forum for managing conflict rather than for satisfying interests.[52] As Claus Offe puts it, politics becomes a matter of keeping policy output "at levels that are considered reasonable or affordable, while channeling demand inputs in a way that appears compatible with available resources. The variable to be manipulated and balanced . . . is not policy outputs, but *the system of interest representation and the modes of resolution of conflict*" (emphasis added).[53] This description seems to fit almost exactly the kinds of negotiations that have been observed in the realm of environmental and consumer regulation.

Perhaps the most serious questions about the long-range implications of neocorporatism, especially in the American context, have been raised by Philippe Schmitter. He suggests that neocorporatist institutions reflect an organizational revolution and, hence, that traditional political associations and mechanisms of representation have been supplanted. Historically, American democracy has been characterized by the free and unstructured competition of socioeconomic interests. James Madison, in fact, argued that such groupings were the most durable and significant,[54] although he did not foresee the rise of an administrative state that could dwarf in power and subjugate these factional interests. Later, Alexis de Tocqueville expressed deep concern over the democratic tendency toward centralization of authority. His hope was that the informal and unstructured "art of association" in American democracy would limit this threat in two ways: first by fostering competition for control of government (much as Madison had envisioned) and, second, by performing social functions so that government would not be called upon to do so. Although Tocqueville recognized the threat of coalescing political authority, he did not foresee the development of bureaucratic forms of organization. The response to the rise of a "bureaucratic state"[55] was the replacement of classical interest groups by more sophisticated organizations that not only represented interests but also participated in shaping interests through negotiation. In Schmitter's words, "What Tocqueville could not anticipate and what his pluralist epigones failed to recognize is that the development of permanent, specialized, and professionalized intermediaries between citizen and state might transform the 'art of association' into a 'science of organization.'"[56]

In a way, the reference to Tocqueville is ironic because he had maintained that a signal difference between America and Europe was that the latter was characterized by intermediary institutions that buffered the citizen from the state. Perhaps the rise of a stronger state in America has given rise to intermediary institutions here, though not ones rooted in class distinctions as the historical European ones were. The problem is that even if neocorporatism institutionalizes access to policymaking for many key interests, it does so by restricting it to organizations only— and, in this sense, it threatens to bring about, as Schmitter puts it, a "vicarious democracy" that in the short run widens participation to include, for example, public lobbyists but in the long run may turn out to be a less-than-acceptable form of democracy.

NOTES

1. W. Lilley and J. Miller, "The New Social Regulation," *The Public Interest*, vol. 47 (1977), pp. 49–62; and D. Vogel, "The Public Interest Movement and the American Reform Tradition," *Political Science Quarterly* (Winter 1980-1981), pp. 607–627.

2. S. Beer, "In Search of a New Public Philosophy," in A. King, ed., *The New American Political System* (Washington, D.C.: American Enterprise Institute,

1978); and S. Rothman and R. Lichter, "Elite Ideology and Risk Perception in Nuclear Energy Policy," *American Political Science Review* (June 1987).

3. E. Haefele, "Shifts in Business-Government Interactions," paper presented to the National Chamber of Commerce, Washington, D.C. (1978).

4. M. Anshen, *Corporate Strategies for Social Performance* (New York: Macmillan, 1980); and R. Nader, "The Case for Federal Chartering," in R. Nader, ed., *The Consumer and Corporate Accountability* (New York: Harcourt Brace Jovanovich, 1973).

5. B. Baysinger, "Domain Maintenance as an Objective of Business Political Activity: An Expanded Technology," *Academy of Management Review* (April 1984), pp. 249–258; R. Miles, *Coffin Nails and Corporate Strategies* (Englewood Cliffs, N.J.: Prentice-Hall, 1982); J. Pfeffer and G. Salancik, *The External Control of Organizations* (New York: Harper and Row, 1978); and J. Post, *Corporate Behavior and Social Change* (Reston, Va.: Reston Publishing Company, 1978).

6. E. Bardach and R. Kagan, *The Problem of Regulatory Unreasonableness* (Philadelphia: Temple University Press, 1982); and G. Eads and M. Fix, *Relief or Reform? Reagan's Regulatory Dilemma* (Washington, D.C.: Urban Institute, 1984).

7. Joan Claybrook, personal interview (June 11, 1986).

8. See especially T. Lowi, *The End of Liberalism: The Second Republic of the United States*, 2nd ed. (New York: W. W. Norton, 1979).

9. See especially J. Berry, *Lobbying for the People* (Princeton, N.J.: Princeton University Press, 1978).

10. Douglas Costle, personal interview (April 8, 1985).

11. B. Ackerman and W. Hassler, *Clean Coal/Dirty Air* (New Haven, Conn.: Yale University Press, 1981), p. 5. Emphasis added.

12. L. Galloway and T. Fitzgerald, "The Surface Mining Control and Reclamation Act of 1977: The Citizen's Ace-in-the-Hole," *Northern Kentucky Law Review* (1981); and R. Harris, *Coal Firms Under the New Social Regulation* (Durham, N.C.: Duke University Press, 1985).

13. *Sierra Club v. Morton* (405 U.S. 727, 1972).

14. Joan Claybrook, personal interview (June 11, 1986).

15. R. S. Melnick, "The Politics of Partnership: Institutional Coalitions and Statutory Rights," Occasional Paper No. 84-3, Center for American Political Studies, Harvard University (1985).

16. William Ruckleshaus, personal interview (June 5, 1985).

17. See J. Perham, "A Big Year for Political Action," *Dunn's Review* (March 1978), pp. 100–102; and M. Malbin, ed., *Money & Politics in the United States: Financing Elections in the 1980's* (Chatham, N.J.: Chatham House, 1984).

18. C. Bagge, "The Changing Regulatory Scene," in D. P. Moynihan, ed., *Business and Society in Change* (Washington, D.C.: American Telephone and Telegraph, 1975); and J. Q. Wilson, ed., *The Politics of Regulation* (New York: Basic Books, 1980).

19. R. Leone, "The Real Costs of Regulation," *Harvard Business Review* (November-December, 1979), p. 64. Emphasis added.

20. H. Heclo, "Issue Networks and the Executive Establishment," in A. King, ed., *The New American Political System* (Washington, D.C.: American Enterprise Institute, 1978), p. 57.

21. *Wall Street Journal,* (June 17, 1978), p. 32.

22. R. Reich, "Corporate Lobbying," *Harvard Business Review* (November-December 1977), pp. 83–96.

23. D. Vogel, "The Power of Business in America: A Reappraisal," *British Journal of Political Science* (January 1983), p. 36.

24. Ibid., p. 34.

25. J. March and J. Olsen, "The New Institutionalism: Organizational Factors in Political Life," *American Political Science Review* (September 1984), pp. 134–149.

26. R. Cyert and J. March, *A Behavioral Theory of the Firm* (Englewood Cliffs, N.J.: Prentice-Hall, 1963), p. 27.

27. F. Emery and E. Trist, *Towards a Social Ecology* (New York: Plenum Publishers, 1976); and Pfeffer and Salancik, *The External Control of Organizations,* 1978.

28. Pfeffer and Salancik, *The External Control of Organizations,* p. 77.

29. Cyert and March, *A Behavioral Theory of the Firm.*

30. Lee F. Nute, personal interview (March 7, 1985).

31. Post, *Corporate Behavior and Social Change,* p. 6.

32. See Beer, "In Search of a New Public Policy"; Ackerman and Hassler, *Clean Coal/Dirty Air;* and Miles, *Coffin Nails and Corporate Strategy.*

33. Eads and Fix, *Relief or Reform?*

34. Ibid.; see also M. Kraft and N. Vig, "Environmental Policy in the Reagan Presidency," *Political Science Quarterly* (Fall 1984): 415–439.

35. Kraft and Vig, "Environmental Policy."

36. Kraft and Vig, "Environmental Policy."

37. Harris, *Coal Firms Under the New Social Regulation.*

38. G. Lehmbruch, "Liberal Corporation and Party Government," *Comparative Political Studies* (April 1977), pp. 91–126; P. Schmitter, "Interest Intermediation and Regime Governability in Contemporary Western Europe and North America," in S. Berger, ed., *Organizing Interests in Western Europe* (New York: Cambridge University Press, 1981); and P. Schmitter, "Democratic Theory and Neocorporatist Practice," *Social Research* (Winter 1983), pp. 885–928.

39. Schmitter, "Democratic Theory and Neocorporatist Practice"; and L. Panitch, "Recent Theoretizations of Corporatism: Reflections on a Growth Industry," *British Journal of Sociology* (June 1980), pp. 159–187.

40. Schmitter, "Democratic Theory and Neocorporatist Practice."

41. Lehmbruch, "Liberal Corporation and Party Government"; and C. Offe, "The Attribution of Public Status to Interest Groups: Observations on the West German Case," in S. Berger, ed., *Organizing Interests in Western Europe: Pluralism, Corporatism, and the Transformation of Politics* (New York: Cambridge University Press, 1981).

42. S. Berger, ed., *Organizing Interests in Western Europe.*

43. Panitch, "Recent Theorizations of Corporatism."

44. F. Wilson, "Interest Groups and Politics in Western Europe: The Neo-Corporatist Approach," *Comparative Politics* (October 1983), pp. 105–123.

45. Panitch, "Recent Theoretizations of Corporatism," pp. 160–161.

46. Lehmbruch, "Liberal Corporation and Party Government," p. 99.

47. *National Journal* (November 15, 1986), p. 2764-b.

48. Ibid., p. 2765.

49. Offe, "The Attribution of Public Status"; and Wilson, "Interest Groups and Politics in Western Europe."

50. March and Olsen, "The New Institutionalism"; Offe, "The Attribution of Public Status"; and Wilson, "Interest Groups and Politics in Western Europe."

51. Lowi, *The End of Liberalism.*

52. Schmitter, "Democratic Theory and Neocorporatist Practice."

53. Offe, "The Attribution of Public Status," p. 126. Emphasis added.

54. A. Hamilton, J. Madison, and J. Jay, in C. Rossiter, ed., *The Federalist Papers*, no. 10, (New York: New American Library, 1961).

55. J. Wilson, "The Rise of the Bureaucratic State," *The Public Interest*, vol. 42, pp. 77–103.

56. Schmitter, "Democratic Theory and Neocorporatist Practice," p. 912.

Conclusion

11

The Emerging Regime

HUGH HECLO

The end of the Reagan administration offers a fitting occasion on which to draw some conclusions about the state of our political order. As the dust begins settling on what will undoubtedly be known as "the Reagan years," a chapter in our political history is surely closing. Opponents of many of the reforms put in place during the 1960s and 1970s have enjoyed their turn at bat in the 1980s. Now that reform and counter-reformation have both had their innings, we should be in a better position to judge what it was in the political upheavals of the pre-Reagan years that proved enduring or transient. In the process we may also begin discerning some early clues about the political meaning of the 1980s.

Of course, it can be objected that the Reagan counterreformation never really got its full turn at the plate. The House of Representatives has remained firmly under Democratic control. Only gradually did judicial vacancies occur, allowing conservatives to put their stamp on the federal courts (President Carter made no Supreme Court nominations, but he did fill more than one-third of all federal judgeships with lifetime appointees).[1] Loss of Republican control of the Senate in 1986 spelled still more trouble for critics of earlier liberal reforms.

All these caveats are true, but they really serve to help make the point. The past eight years have been a kind of ongoing "referendum" on what was put in place in the pre-Reagan years. The fact that Republicans could not wrest control of the House, maintain control of the Senate, or readily prevail in attempts to rein in an activist judiciary is indicative of the mixed verdict emerging from that "referendum"— my shorthand term for the thousands of budget battles, court cases, election contests, and other controversies that have taken place in the political trenches since 1980.

Careful readers will notice that I have already managed to mix three metaphors: baseball, a public referendum, and trench warfare. Perhaps that betrays nothing more than my own personal confusion, but I would like to think that it might have something to do with the different features coexisting in our present state of affairs.

Baseball, as George Will keeps reminding us, is an apt metaphor for the civil, often Fate-driven game of politics—a game that cannot be played (or watched) well with clenched teeth. We would do well to take a slow, long-term—that is to say, baseball-esque—view of any assertions about the "New American Political System," the "New American State," the "New Direction in American Politics,"[2] or even the "Remaking of American Politics." *Mea culpa.* Having written about "new" issue networks, I find that I cannot improve much on Pendleton Herring's 1940 (ouch) description of party decline vis-à-vis looser group attachments: "This development has reached vast proportions today. It presents a vascular politics with an infinite number of arteries penetrating down into the community. Self-government demands free circulation of individuals' impulses. This calls for a varied network throughout the social structure."[3]

The baseball metaphor captures something of the familiar and little-changing routines of our politics: the cycles of activism and lethargy, the endless extra-innings of executive/legislative competition decreed by constitutional structure, the advantages brought to the playing field by the privileges of money, and so on.

There is also something to be said for the referendum metaphor. Whatever else one thinks about the reformers' intentions in the 1960s and 1970s, they certainly had to do with "opening up the system," as the phrase went. It is difficult to think of any aspect of our political life that is not more open now to public scrutiny and outside influence than it was at the beginning of the reform era. More on this later. The important point for our present purposes is that this greater openness—in everything from congressional processes and executive branch leakiness to public-interest group access to the courts and black access to the ballot box—ensured a spirited public contest over any Reagan effort to roll back pre-Reagan reforms. The effect truly has been an ongoing, de facto referendum.

At the same time, it is difficult to avoid the feeling that a good deal of ideological warfare and general nastiness has become the political norm. Groups on both the left and the right have become accustomed to seeing themselves in conflict with enemies—not simply with opponents. New? Perhaps not if we think back, for example, to the bitter domestic fights of the late 1940s. But a working tradition of bipartisanship (embodied in an Arthur Vandenburg or a George Marshall) was also a part of the scene. In fact, we seem much better at fighting among ourselves than at struggling against foreign economic and political threats.

Other presidential nominees for the Supreme Court have been turned down, but never in modern times has one been worked over the way Robert Bork was. Other postwar Republican presidents have annoyed conservative opinion, but never were they turned on as Ronald Reagan, the most conservative of all modern presidents, has been. These are only two examples of the war of ideas as well as interests that has been going on in the political trenches.

But I am getting ahead of myself. Resorting to mixed metaphors as a point of departure helps suggest that our political system has been changing in a complex way. No single, neat formula will capture it. In thinking over what has been said in earlier chapters, I am reinforced in that observation. At first glance it might seem that not everyone writing in this book can be right. Let us review the bidding, going from the general to the more specific.

It would appear a simple matter to decide whether developments during the 1960s and 1970s represented a major break with the preceding political order. Not so. In Chapter 2, Donald Brand paints a picture of fundamental discontinuity—so fundamental, in fact, that we must look back to the eighteenth-century Anti-Federalists to find a full-fledged counterpart. In both cases we see a drive hostile to capitalism and fervently in favor of participatory democracy, a rejection of interest group politics, and a yearning for formal, "ruleful" standards for governing. Although he acknowledges worthwhile accomplishments in particular areas, Brand characterizes the overall reform era as a radical project undermining our political institutions for the sake of a romantic and anachronistic ideal.

In Chapter 3, Robert Eden offers us a rather different view of the world. Here the reforms of the 1960s and 1970s are presented as an opposite sort of discontinuity. Whereas Brand sees the reform Democrats as hostile to interest group politics, Eden sees them as enshrining a group politics of organized minorities. And whereas Chapter 2 sees a hopeless reform effort to recreate the earlier standards of civic virtue in a small republic, Chapter 3 decries the reformers' attempts to obliterate civic virtue—that is, a shared ethic of the common good (or what Eden terms the New Deal concept of democratic "honor"). In this sense, Brand is critical of reform Democrats for trying to create what Eden criticizes them for destroying.

And yet subsequent chapters dealing with specific institutional reforms often point us toward continuity rather than discontinuity between the preexisting New Deal design and the underlying thrust of the 1960s and 1970s. To be sure, in Chapter 6 Sidney Milkis notes a number of departures between the two periods. He contends that reform Democrats elevated quality-of-life issues over meat-and-potatoes New Deal security issues. They also demonstrated little of the New Dealers' trust in the presidency and executive bureaucracy to sustain their agenda. But when all is said and done, Milkis portrays an underlying continuity. The recent reforms are seen as representing the culmination of developments begun in the 1930s. Like the New Dealers, modern reformers sought to protect their programs and agenda from political parties. This time, however, reformers had learned that they had to insulate their regime of administrative politics from the discretion of presidents and bureaucrats as well. The result has been that the New Deal-ish preference for administrative government has been carried still further by replacing faith in the executive branch with faith in judicial interventions and interested citizen activity.

In Chapter 7, R. Shep Melnick discusses an even more fundamental continuity. Like Milkis he argues that the means of the New Deal model were changed. Although New Dealers sought through methods of executive administration to avoid the parochial obstruction of courts and Congress, modern reformers forged new alliances among these institutions. Interacting with administrators, the reforming impulses of Democratic Congresses and activist courts have reinforced each other. But unlike Milkis, who sees a drastic change from a quantitative to a quality-of-life agenda, Melnick observes a striking similarity between the ends of the New Deal and those of the reforms of the 1960s and 1970s. Roosevelt's vision of security and of an economic bill of rights reads, as Melnick puts it, "like a catalogue of contemporary programmatic rights."

Descending from levels of public philosophy and policy visions, we find additional divergences in the chapters regarding particular institutions. Both Lawrence Dodd and Edward Weisband agree that reforms have produced a more technocratic orientation in Congress, that they have enhanced representative openness, and that the resulting fragmentation poses severe challenges to central leadership for governing Congress as a whole. However, the differences in interpretation between the two authors are at least as important as the similarities. Dodd sees an institution divided by the incentives facing careerist legislators. Congress is said to be so deeply divided that only the adversarial tension between a Republican White House and a Democratic Congress has prevented the centrifugal pressures from wreaking havoc on Congress's governing mechanisms. Weisband examines arms-control policy, an area in which one would think executive prerogatives in national security and foreign affairs would be most hostile to the new congressional assertiveness. And yet the story he tells is less one of adversarial politics than one of codetermination. Dodd worries that if the power pendulum swings back so that Congress does not feel itself threatened as an institution by the executive, legislative chaos will result. Weisband takes a different and more optimistic view. He argues that codetermination and the reforms of the 1970s have curtailed such swings in the pendulum and have actually improved the capacity of Congress to perform.

The chapters on interest groups present another study in contrasts. Despite a good many overlapping observations by Jeffrey Berry and Richard Harris (i.e., that interest groups have been growing in number, are more prone to open conflict, are less stable in their alliances, and so on), the bottom-line judgments of the two authors differ substantially. Berry offers a number of reasons for thinking that issue networks represent something much more permanent than simply a temporary opening up and proliferation of subgovernments. Harris argues more or less the opposite. He contends that, at least in the realm of social regulation, the institutionalization of participatory democracy has changed the system of the 1960s and 1970s in such a way as to force business to consider a more collaborative strategy. Roughly speaking, neocorporatism is the new collective noun for the old system of subgovernments.

Given that a concluding chapter is supposed to reach conclusions, I have necessarily had to omit many details in trying to draw comparisons among the earlier chapters. However, I think my general characterizations of the different positions are fair. Some of these differences have arisen because the authors are looking at different pieces of the picture. Some are derived from putting different interpretations on the same events. The contrasts I have drawn are not meant to be critical. Even if the authors are looking at the same piece of the picture and simultaneously making incompatible observations, this does not mean that one writer must be right and the other wrong. Contradictory processes may actually be at work in the political order. To accept that fact is to acknowledge complexity in the situation—a view I find more persuasive than the notion of unidirectional change and unambiguous outcomes. In other words, we should be open to the idea that trends in our political life appear contradictory and confused because they really *are* contradictory and confused.

As a practical matter, then, it may be correct to say both that reform Democrats were hostile to interest group politics and that they enshrined a system of minority-group politics—they simply did not regard "their" groups as interests. Milkis may be correct in saying that reform Democrats were like New Dealers in circumscribing the reach of partisan politics, and Eden and Berry may be correct in saying that policy decisionmaking has become much more extensively politicized and conflictual. In short, some authors may be as justified in talking about certain continuities as others are in talking about discontinuities.

TAKING STOCK

To give an account of such a complex situation, we might try to think about the changes that have occurred or not occurred in terms of four basic categories:

1. Changes that were intended in the reforms of the 1960s and 1970s and that have survived the test of the 1980s.
2. Changes that were intended but seem to have faded during the Reagan era.
3. Important changes that were unintentionally set in motion by reformers and that have endured.
4. Unintended changes that have not survived the passage of time.

As the last category is more a task of footnoting history than anything else, the following discussion will concentrate on the first three aspects of political development. Such a survey must not only take account of what has been said in earlier chapters but also acknowledge other important influences shaping our politics. The latter category would have to include questions regarding federalism, public attitudes, and especially America's changing economic situation. Institutional developments are of course affected by larger changes in the economy and society, just as institutions do much to shape our responses to such changes.

Intentions Realized

In an imperfect world we should probably not set too high a standard; no one ever fully realizes their intentions, especially when it comes to political reform. At most, we should expect to see outcomes that bear some reasonable resemblance to what the reformers had in mind. By that criterion, there are areas of enduring change that do stand out.

In terms of public policy we can note the obvious: Just about all of the basic enabling legislation enacted during the reform era of the 1960s and 1970s remains in force at the end of the 1980s. This applies to the Civil Rights Acts of 1964 and 1968 and the Voting Rights Act of 1965 (extended for another seven years in 1982). It holds for the Freedom of Information Act, the Privacy Act, and the 1978 Ethics in Government Act. In fact, the same applies to all of the statutorily established rights discussed in Chapter 7.

Legislation that established the "new social regulation" is also part of this story of endurance. It is true that in the implementation of this legislation, greater attention than originally intended is now being paid to the economic implications of such regulation—a shift that was well under way before Ronald Reagan took office. It is also true that conservative and some business interests have been able to prevent the adoption of new programs (acid rain initiatives being a good example). The fact remains that the basic structure of social regulation—the authorizing legislation, administering agencies, and body of rules—has withstood challenge and remains intact. The Environmental Protection Agency (EPA) under Anne Burford and the Interior Department under James Watt were important test cases. No less important was the attempt to amend the 1970 Clean Air Act during the 97th Congress (1981–1983). Despite an intense lobbying effort by industry groups and the Reagan administration, environmentalists allied with Democrats and a number of Republican (even in the Republican-controlled Senate) repeatedly defeated attempts to weaken the act's requirements. The very public and decisive nature of the outcome probably helped deter similar frontal assaults on other acts. In this and other instances, supporters of the earlier reforms needed only to block action in order to maintain the pre-Reagan regulatory system; their reforms had become part of the status quo. Thus the operative presumption at the end of the 1980s remains one of expecting government to regulate the social impact of business for purposes of environmental and consumer protection, worker safety, and public health.[4]

As earlier chapters suggest, reformed processes did much to ensure the durability of reformed policies. Legislation was designed not only to create environmental, consumer, occupational safety, and other programs but also to change the rules of the game so as to protect the purposes of those programs. As these techniques have already been discussed in other chapters, we need only summarize them here. Public-interest groups backing such legislation gained new legal standing to help ensure its enforcement. Courts acquired more statutory rules to interpret and greater scope in which to intervene in administrative decisions. Administrators were put under new pressure to open hearings, produce studies and impact statements, entertain challenges, and otherwise justify their actions. Congress composed itself into more specialized subcommittees and staffs watching over the continued implementation of reform legislation. Generally speaking, all of these procedural changes remain in place today.

It was not this or that isolated change in procedures but their interconnected, mutually reinforcing pattern that really helped institutionalize the crusades of the 1960s and 1970s. The more specialized subcommittee policy shops of Congress self-consciously provided material (rules, language on congressional intent, etc.) for activist courts and new points of access for interested groups. The courts and subcommittees in turn provided a workable arena (more manageable than election contests, party battles in Congress, or presidential agendas) to do combat for their causes—and help mobilize members and contributions in the process. The groups' causes helped members of Congress establish reputations as policymakers and organize election support. Administrators had strong incentives to pay special attention to the relevant subcommittees, courts, and public lobbies. And, as Chapter 10 shows, even business interests themselves were divided and selectively co-opted by the diverse impacts of this complex system.

A number of early Reagan appointees to government thought that their main problem was to get bureaucrats to do what they were told. Their *real* problem was to change a regime, and this proved very difficult to do. To be sure, process reforms that seemed to be pushing to extremes were reined in. The reactions against the Federal Trade Commission and its intervenor fund are an example. Likewise, highly expansive interpretations of standing to sue were deflated (although only in the absence of statutory language granting such standing).[5] On the whole, however, the main body of reform processes thus far mentioned has remained intact.

Civil rights reforms are another area of enduring change, even though the results undoubtedly fall short of what minority leaders and others might have hoped for. In this case the supporting linkage between policy purposes and reformed processes was especially direct; that is, the enhancement of the political rights of minorities created an enlarged constituency to defend other policies for racial justice. In the 1960s, 29 percent of Southern blacks were registered to vote (compared to 61 percent of whites); by 1984, 66 percent of blacks in the South were registered (compared to 75 percent of whites). During that time the total number of blacks in elective office more than quadrupled to 6,000. This increased political presence of blacks has been a powerful force for protecting gains in other areas such as fair housing, educational programs, and employment policies. These gains are nowhere more obvious than in the changed sensitivities of white politicians, not least of all Southern Democratic senators who once spearheaded the drive to block federal integration initiatives. It is not too far-fetched to say that Robert Bork began losing his chance for a seat on the Supreme Court with the passage of the 1965 Voting Rights Act.

The result for civil rights reforms resembles that for social regulation. Opposition forces have been strong enough to block new initiatives and—where there was a broadly shared feeling that things had gone too far—strong enough to trim back some of the designs inherited from the 1970s. Federal enforcement efforts in equal opportunity programs have been reduced administratively but by no means eliminated, especially when the courts have intervened. Affirmative Action, perhaps the most controversial inheritance, represents another example. Through a series of court cases, the role of racial quotas (the most extreme form of Affirmative Action) has gradually if tortuously been circumscribed, but it has by no means been abolished.[6] These qualifications notwithstanding, this essential point should not be overlooked: Our current civil rights policies and processes are not really very far removed from the reform era enactments of some twenty years or so ago. By comparison, the state of affairs in "Negro policies" twenty years prior to the reforms of the 1960s and 1970s seems like ancient history. In political time, we have not moved nearly so far from the 1960s and 1970s as those years have distanced themselves from the 1940s and 1950s.

There is another area in which what we now take for granted tends to obscure the enduring changes created by reform. The 1960s and 1970s embodied an essentially questioning and skeptical approach to all forms of organized authority. This movement of social criticism eventually found expression in efforts to prescribe and enforce higher standards of conduct on those in positions of public and private authority. The creation of new procedures to oversee bureaucrats or new regulations to hold private business accountable for the social side-effects of their activity was only one part of this larger picture. That picture included campaign finance rules, the 1978 Ethics in Government Act, a new system of inspectors general for each federal department, a permanent procedure for special-prosecutor appointments, a new Office of Government Ethics, stricter financial reporting requirements, greater oversight of executive intelligence activities, and, one could add, legitimization of a much more adversarial brand of investigative journalism.

Of course, it would be naive to contend that such reforms purified our politics. However, politics in the 1980s did bear the imprint of these critical forces set in motion during the 1960s and 1970s. The feel-good mood of the Reagan years seemed to smother a good deal of social criticism, but it could not eliminate the pre-Reagan laws or the media incentives to investigate. Between 1981 and April 1986, 110 senior Reagan administration officials stood accused of unethical or illegal conduct. Has the 1980s level of veniality been greater than that in other administrations? Perhaps not; the point is, as former White House Counsel Fred Fielding put it, "There's a heck of a lot more scrutiny by the press and the laws are tighter now."[7] The same doubting, critical perspective dogs the footsteps of presidential candidates, White House spokespersons, members of Congress, Wall Street operators, and television evangelists. It *is* harder for those in positions of authority to get away with funny business, and that is just the way the reformers in the 1960s and 1970s wanted it to be.

If we had to choose one word to summarize the enduring legacy of the pre-Reagan reforms, it should probably be *openness*. Earlier chapters demonstrate that reasonable people may disagree about the reformers' ultimate motives or goals, but there can be little doubt about their preferred means to those ends. Their method was to "open the system." Opening the system could mean anything from direct action in the streets to complicated changes in administrative law. It entailed making political processes and institutions accessible to those with a stake in their decisions. Today, at the end of the 1980s, our political life bears the unmistakable imprint of that drive for openness. There are examples not just in this book but all around us. Consider just a few.

1. The nightly news carries a steady stream of stories about groups, some national and other local, protesting against one thing or another. We take the reports for granted. And yet "protesting" (especially in front of the electronic media) has become a routine political practice only in our own time—a soft version of direct action that has come to be accepted as a regular part of the decisionmaking process. Before the 1960s, protests were a nonroutine phenomenon watched on newsreels, usually with some alarm, usually having to do with union activities, and often intimating political subversion. Today there are probably many people who would be suspicious if a major decision in the public or private sectors occurred and did *not* spark some form of protest.

2. Greater openness in political parties and the electoral process was clearly the intention and the result of reforms in the 1960s and 1970s. Women and minority candidates now routinely appear on political tickets to an extent unknown twenty-five years ago. The extreme form of the 1971 McGovern-Fraser rules has clearly been modified by Democratic party leaders. And party and elected officials' entitlement to a modest number of delegate seats in the nomination process has been restored.[8] However, both Democratic and Republican parties now seem to have accepted the fundamental shift from a presidential nominating system based on state and local party leaders in brokered conventions to one based on rank-and-file party voters participating in primaries and caucuses. In 1959, Vice-President Nixon ran for the presidency by conferring with party chieftains and touring foreign countries; in 1987, Vice-President Bush had to run by participating in candidate debates and touring Iowa.

3. Openness in Congress has taken a variety of forms. As described in Chapter 4, the legislature is a more accessible institution than it was twenty years ago in terms of its more public voting record and deliberations, the reining in of seniority as an automatic source of power, and the diaspora of influence from committee chairs to far-flung subcommittees, to mention only the most obvious developments. As noted, the reforms of the earlier years have been somewhat temporized in the

1980s, but nothing has happened to reverse the fundamental shift from the prereform cozy clubbiness to today's more open and frantic congressional system.

These examples of a more open politics could easily be expanded with material from earlier chapters. Our system of pressure-group politics, like the work of administrative agencies and courts, has become more accessible to new groups—not always to every group, not always on the terms they might like, but more open than in the pre-Kennedy years of national politics. This accessibility is precisely one of the important goals the reforms of ten and twenty years ago aimed to accomplish.

Faded Hopes

Being an optimistic people, we tend to sentimentalize politics and resist acknowledging failures. But, of course, political life is not a Frank Capra movie, and struggling valiantly and losing is part of the story. Certainly there are important areas in which efforts to remake American policy and politics have not stood the test of time.

No one living through the 1980s can doubt that reform of the national budget process represents one such monument of faded hope. In the beginning—that is, with the passage of the 1974 Budget Reform and Impoundment Control Act—there were high hopes of bringing greater rationality to the process of setting national priorities and coordinating longer-run decisions on spending and taxation. That has not happened. The reformed process gave Congress a tool for making tough choices that too many legislators did not want to make, especially as economic growth slowed. In the 1980s it soon became clear that the reformed process was also a tool a president could alternately exploit and disregard to his own political advantage. While President Reagan continued to propose an executive budget promising only more domestic spending cuts and no tax increases, and while Congress annually tied itself up in knots trying to arrive at an alternative, responsible management of the nation's finances became as rare as love beads. Budgeting occurred through stopgap continuing resolutions, periodic threats to close down the government, and omnibus spending bills that almost no one liked. In the meantime, the national debt tripled in the 1980s, and the amount owed to foreigners to finance the deficit approached $1 trillion. In a historically brief period, the United States had reversed roles from being the largest net creditor to being the largest net debtor in the world.

Another area of disappointed hopes had to do with the attempt to impose strict, rights-based standards on public policy outcomes. The same underlying logic appeared in one area after another in the 1960s and 1970s, and it went something like this. (1) Core policy issues are essentially a question of protecting certain rights; (2) rights set absolute standards that, when subject to compromise and half-measures, cease to be rights; (3) established authority cannot be trusted to protect such rights; and, therefore, (4) it follows that policy must spell out in fine print and uncompromisable terms the results to be achieved.

I doubt that we have to search into abstract matters of political theory or public philosophy to understand the effective sources of this logic. The one source that stands out lay within the civil rights movement, and understandably so. For decades the political rights that blacks enjoyed in the abstract had been subverted by a white system's maneuverings— a polite term for lies, tricks, threats, violence, and various administrative manipulations of the law. The more powerful and self-conscious civil rights movement of the 1960s would have none of it. What the leaders of this movement wanted and often got was precise legislation and overt rulings specifying in detail what could and could not be done and what results were to be achieved.[9] Security lay in making it as difficult as possible to evade agreements embodying rights.

The lesson was not so much deliberately learned as indirectly absorbed by others. The results were embedded in legislation, court rulings, agency regulations, and other policy prescriptions. The right to a healthy environment meant clean air, which meant air-quality standards set at precisely that threshold where concentrations of a pollutant became a health threat. The right to consuming safe products referred to products with never more than a zero level of carcinogens in them. The rights of the handicapped meant specific standards of access to buses, multi-storied buildings, and so on. The rights of poor persons meant ever more detailed, uniform standards to remove discretion in the granting of relief. Protecting our resources meant never doing anything that would endanger any animal species with extinction.

Of course, a host of specific standards still dots the policy landscape. However, I think it is fair to say that the original intention of driving major public policies along tracks laid out by strict, rights-based standards and mandated outcomes has failed. The policy absolutes have in practice become contingent. This result has had less to do with the political and ideological counterattack of conservatives in the late 1970s and 1980s than with the particular realities that such policies have had to confront from their beginning.

One such reality has simply been technical feasibility. Regarding standards of air quality, for example, it has not been scientifically possible to identify thresholds beyond which there are no adverse health effects for some people; the absence of sharp dividing lines between what is safe and unsafe has forced policymakers into the much messier business of debating acceptable risks. Similar practical difficulties have accompanied efforts to draw black and white pictures of carcinogens (at what dosage? for how long? on what test animals? and so on) and to reduce their levels to zero in the products we consume (given the widespread existence of potential carcinogens even in the natural environment). Likewise, the zero-option in species extinction has encountered immense practical problems, including the ambiguity in a workable definition of species and the frequency with which Nature itself routinely blots out species of animal life.[10] In general, science has hindered rather than helped to set the clear, unambiguous standards that reformers wanted.

A second reality is the changing economic environment. Beginning with the OPEC oil price increase of 1973 (though by no means solely caused by that), the U.S. economy set out on a long period of sluggish growth, diminished productivity, and relative decline in its position in the international trading order. Well before the arrival of huge budget deficits in the 1980s, there were strong reasons for asking, again, a question that was often forgotten in the earlier years of affluence and confidence in economists' ability to manage the economy. The question was, Can we afford it? Asking it introduced an inherent tone of contingency into the reform language of rights and strict standards to be obtained at any cost. As discussed in Chapter 10, the latter half of the 1970s witnessed a gradual reintroduction of economic criteria and bureaucratic flexibility into the new social regulation. Similar developments occurred in other policy areas, as well as in the course of implementation by state and local governments.

As always, questions of sheer political power were another important reality. For example, in the 1960s and early 1970s there was much talk of welfare rights and "the new property" represented by social entitlements. Reformed procedures (intended to provide administrative due process, to reduce residency requirements for public relief, and so on) were important and have remained in force. However, claims of more substantive rights—say, to a basic minimum level of income support—proved entirely rhetorical. In practice, welfare or new property rights extended no further than the political power of claimant groups in question. The elderly and the handicapped did better in advancing their agenda and in later resisting budget cuts largely because they were better mobilized and more popularly acceptable than poor people generally. The latter watched more or less passively as the real value of AFDC welfare benefits declined, food stamp eligibility was curtailed (mainly for the working poor), and medical and nutritional programs for poor women with infants were weakened. Such was the enduring status of *their* welfare "rights."

Those seeking to remake American politics had not intended this traditional powerlessness to persist into the nation's future. This brings us to the third and final entry in the catalogue of dashed hopes—the hope of producing a fundamental, bottom-up reorientation of political forces in America. On this point the distance in political time seems very great indeed, for it is difficult today to recall the fervor behind this project of creating a "New Politics."

What exactly this might mean depended of course upon who among the reformers was doing the shouting.[11] Certainly there was a vivid streak of romanticism within the political movements of the 1960s and 1970s. For many younger Americans a new politics meant the fundamental transformation of established authority into a truly participatory democracy. According to the New Left's Port Huron statement, such a return to original ideals would help reverse the "loneliness, estrangement (and) isolation that describe the distance between man and man today."

In our more cynical times such student philosophizing is likely to be dismissed, but we would do well to recall the sincere energy poured into efforts to give concrete expression to related ideals. Community Action Programs (CAPs), for example, encouraged grass-roots participation by many persons who had never been involved in social programs in any capacity other than as passive recipients. Another strand of reform was devoted to workplace democracy. For example, in matters of worker health and safety—the "indoor environment," as it became known— the discontent of certain rank-and-file workers was used by a small group of labor activists, public health experts, and other reformers to challenge the existing system.[12] To the consternation of employers and their safety experts, the Occupational Safety and Health Act of 1970 not only codified a radical vision of all workers' rights to a minimum level of well-being in the workplace; it also established workers' rights to participate in worksite inspections, gain access to findings, and appeal agency actions.

For still others, a "new politics" had less to do with a revival of local community power or workplace democracy than with reconstituting the democratic base of existing political forms. Thus an influential figure like Ralph Nader emphasized active involvement in much more aggressive consumer groups (preferably within his organizational network) rather than mass consumer action such as product boycotts or individual griping. Likewise, the Democratic party reformers on the McGovern-Fraser Commission quickly rejected the idea of a national presidential primary. What they sought was not increased direct mass participation but increased participation and control by issue and candidate activists, the kind of enthusiasts who had created Eugene McCarthy's 1968 candidacy.[13] They would be the vanguard of—yes, of what?

For anyone familiar with only European politics, the natural answer would be cast in class terms. But neither the members of the New Left nor other reformers really operated from a perspective of working-class mobilization. Theirs was a thoroughly American vision of a broad, good-government, citizens' movement led by outsiders who were uncorrupted by established authority. It was to be a new politics embracing the young, workers, minorities, consumers, ordinary people worried about the environment—not just the downtrodden but everyone who was not one of the bosses—and giving them a say in the issues affecting their lives.

We are overlooking something important if we see only the particular pieces of legislation and miss the inspiration behind the reform movements, or if we dismiss that inspiration as so much "creedal passion" (to use Samuel Huntington's phrase). One does not have to be seized by a fit of moral passion to become fed up with presidents who lie, business practices that threaten peoples' health, products that do not work, bureaucracies that do not protect, and rules of the game that benefit the already privileged. Advocates of a new politics hoped for an enduring transformation in political life that would respond decisively to the sources of such concerns.

That did not happen. To be sure, incremental steps have continued, even in the Reagan years; local citizen groups that did not exist before can now apply for $50,000 federal grants to hire consultants who will help them understand environmental-impact statements that did not have to be made before. However, the larger hopes of recasting the structures of power over peoples' lives seem a misty dream. Some of the reasons may be obvious; others are less so.

Clearly there was an inherent practical problem in the more romantic aspirations to rebuild community through participatory democracy. Rhetoric side, such participation attracts only the minority of people who like to spend their evenings out; and, in any event, bonds of fellow citizenship are not so easily forged in modern society. However, as noted above, it would be wrong to exaggerate the naiveté of all reformers; their usual strategy was to construct reform measures of countervailing power, not direct democracy.

Another obvious factor lay in the changing economic context. Some argue that reformism was a kind of luxury good, something that is easier to sell in good times than in periods (as after 1973) when people have to worry about their jobs, inflation, and other meat-and-potato economic issues. As we observed with respect to the renewed salience of costs versus rights, this economic interpretation contains a portion of the truth, but it, too, is an explanation that should not be pushed too far. A sense of personal economic vulnerability and heightened uncertainty may also make people more susceptible to calls for reconstituting the bases of political power. Thus the hard times of the 1930s, and not the booming 1920s, presented the real opportunity for reform.

Day-to-day experience with participatory reforms also played a part in fostering disillusionment. For example, the experiment with maximum feasible participation in Community Action Programs exploded amid a series of controversies with established local power structures and horror stories of gross mismanagement. Aspirations for workplace democracy quickly receded in face of the realities of legislating in Washington; union leaders and other policymakers had little interest in challenging the established system of employer/employee relations. Finally, of course, the McGovern presidential campaign of 1972 disillusioned many reformers.

Perhaps most important, there was an inherent contradiction between the aspirations of a new politics distrustful of organized political authority and the organizational means necessary to achieve any major reorientation of political forces. To sustain reform hopes for a new politics it would have been necessary to create a political mechanism capable of penetrating deeply and broadly into American society—into its interest group structure, voluntary associations, town halls, statehouses, and community activities. The necessary thing would have been not merely to recast Democratic party procedures but to rebuild the party into something more like a mass-based Social Democratic movement or, if one prefers an American analogy, a counterpart to the creation of the Republican party in the mid-nineteenth century.

However, the reformers of the 1960s and 1970s were institution challengers, not institution builders. With the major exception of the civil rights movement, their work remained generally detached from the political lives and affiliations of ordinary Americans, as Sidney Milkis suggests in Chapter 6. Procedural rights of participation were a reality for only small circles of activists. Their efforts penetrated the arcane world of administrative law and legal maneuverings but not street-level politics. The reformers could capture media attention, but they were much less interested in the mundane work of grass-roots organizing and precinct politicking. Their proliferating groups became expert in the pursuit of particular issues, but no one was interested in subordinating their cause to the needs of a permanent coalition or party movement. The new politics enlisted enthusiasts, Washington operators, and advocates of all sorts. Through an advancing technology of mass communications they could appeal, sometimes successfully, to the worries of average citizens. But they could never institutionalize a new politics because they deeply distrusted both institutions and leaders.

Surprising Legacies

Our final category concerns enduring changes that were unintentionally set in motion by the efforts to remake American policy and politics. Tracing the unforeseen consequences of well-intentioned reforms has become a favored subject in political studies, and the melancholy examples are legion (so much so that one writer has recently been driven to write a book asking if reform is possible. He concludes that it is).[14] Space limitations here permit me to mention only some of the more important spillovers unintentionally bequeathed by the reform period and persisting through the 1980s.

Virtually everyone agrees that in creating a more open, democratically organized Congress, the reformers also produced a more fragmented legislative body that is much more difficult to manage as a whole. The authors of earlier chapters agree, too, that the reformed Congress has become a more technocratic institution—a place where policy expertise and specialized staffs play a much more prominent role, and where elected bureaucrats struggle ceaselessly with more complex budget issues and program details. Such changes have in turn produced more work for interest groups and more points of access in the legislature through which to do it.[15]

Such changes were not generally what reformers had in mind in the 1970s. What many of them did want was a Congress that could more effectively check the power of the executive. Toward that end a host of externally oriented changes were introduced while Congress was simultaneously engaged in reforming itself internally. A War Powers Act sought to circumscribe presidential power to commit U.S. forces to military action. A new Budget Act attempted to reduce executive discretion in spending and reallocating funds. Defense and intelligence budgets were cut, and for the first time in the postwar period Congress refused funds for major weapons programs. Covert operations extending beyond intelligence gathering were prohibited without the express approval of the president as reported to congressional foreign relations committees. More provisions for legislative veto and oversight of executive actions were enacted; and the list goes on.

The conventional question then becomes, Who's winning? Has the balance of power shifted in favor of Congress or the president? It is a poor question because what has happened is more complicated than a game of passing the power beanbag between the two branches. If Congress had remained in an internally unreformed state—as a carryover, say, from the 1950s with strong central leaders, unquestioned seniority rules, a handful of powerful committee chairs, more private deliberations—*and* it had passed the measures we have noted for checking the executive, then the verdict would clearly have been a power shift in favor of Capitol Hill. The reverse would be true if Congress had reformed itself to be more fragmented, open, and democratic but had not also initiated its external reforms aiming to check the executive. But of course Congress did both, and the result adds up to an unexpected legacy.

It is a legacy whereby the various pieces of Congress have enhanced their capacity to delve into details and micro-manage executive branch activities, while Congress as a whole is less able to assemble agreed positions with which to face the President. The odd result is to strengthen the incentives for the postreform presidency to go its own way, detached from the work of others in the governing community. This result is not as paradoxical as it sounds. The "regular government"—Congress, executive departments, regulatory agencies—grinds its way through the labyrinthine legislative, oversight, and budgeting processes. And agency heads struggle on a dozen fronts with the strict scrutiny of their work demanded by the congressional reforms in place. All of this dispersed congressional checking of executive power has rendered the president a more detached figure, a figure freer to enunciate general policy but with no playing partners either on the Hill (which is too fragmented to bargain over broad, enforceable, presidential-level deals) or in the rest of the executive branch (where the need to respond to congressional scrutiny often means unreliability from a White House perspective).

Thus the president at the end of the 1980s stands freer to expound a budget policy that is largely detached from the product that emerges from the agonies of the congressional budget process. His ultimate threat at the end of each year is to reject that product and close down the government, almost as if he were an outsider looking in on Washington rather than one of the jointly responsible parties to governing. A similar tendency has been at work in foreign affairs. Because Congress can continually micro-manage and harass—but is reluctant to risk a public backlash and constitutional crisis by invoking its ultimate weapon, the War Powers Act—the president can pursue his foreign policy while various parts of Congress pursue theirs. Often there need be little connection between the two. Hence, despite the War Powers Act, Congress was largely an onlooker to President Reagan's military moves in Lebanon, Grenada, Libya, and the Gulf region. And when strict scrutiny threatened presidential preferences in supporting the contras, the White House/ NSC complex became an even more irregular government unto itself in the Iran-contra affair.

By making Congress a more aggressive critic and a more diffuse bargaining partner, reformers also made go-it-alone strategies look more attractive to people in the White House. There were many other examples of the tendency for reform to provoke unexpected reactions. The causes of "interest group liberalism" in the 1960s helped mobilize the "interest group conservatism" that bore fruit in Ronald Reagan's election. Advocates of a more open, participatory democracy eventually found the referendum and initiative devices they favored being used by opponents to cut taxes and spending. The attacks on military spending and intelligence agencies helped spawn by the end of the 1970s a vigorous counterattack by those decrying the neglect of national security interests and the decline of American power. As Chapter 10 shows, previously quiet business groups were given new cause to mobilize and meet their challengers. Campaign finance reforms at first seemed to facilitate citizen fundraising for liberal causes; soon the law as interpreted by the Supreme Court was doing much more to boost conservative causes and the power of incumbents.

The results of this challenge/response dynamic have hardly ended there, of course. If the Reagan administration symbolized a reaction to many of the initiatives of the 1960s and 1970s, it provoked its own counterreaction in turn. There were few more effective fundraisers for the environmental cause than James Watt and Ann Gorsuch (Burford), and few activists doing more to keep civil rights groups alive than Edwin Meese and Bradford Reynolds. The post-1980 proliferation of court challenges to agency action and inction, the intensity of bureaucratic infighting between departments and congressional subunits, the defensive escalation of fundraising and public campaigns among competing single-issue groups—these and more are also part of the legacy. The rather "soft" personal images of the Ford, Carter, and Reagan presidencies should not deceive us. Behind the scenes, in the policy trenches, ideological struggles at least as intense as anything happening in the Johnson/ Nixon years have been going on. Activists of different persuasions in the 1980s will tell you they are facing not just opponents, but a war with real, live domestic enemies.

To be honest, much of this conflict passes right by ordinary citizens. Only activists have cause to try and understand the complex rules of candidate selection, the intricate legislative struggles, rulemaking procedures, or legal maneuvers. The policy contenders (like electoral candidates) know that public support depends upon maintaining a critical mass of favorable media attention. It is the media that will usually interpret the meaning of results and declare winners and losers. They and not the parties, groups, PACs, and all the rest will be the primary means of teaching people what they should be worrying about. Thus another important objective that was unintentionally accomplished in the reform era and that has persisted through the 1980s was the indirect increase in the role of the media in our political affairs (although just about everything one can think of seems to have that effect). Protesters clashing with police outside the 1968 Democratic convention in Chicago had chanted "the whole world is watching." Everyone may not be watching, but today much of our public affairs is conducted through made-for-television politics.

REFORM, REAGANISM, AND BEYOND

Remaking American politics—it is a fit subject for participles. Americans have always been in the business of remaking their politics, never reaching and resting at a point of politics remade. The question of remaking is not whether but how. And always, too, the new or at least changing politics has overlaid a largely unchanging state. Our politics— its style, content, techniques—would astonish the founding fathers. Our state in the sense of the underlying constitutional order would (with the exception of the courts' policy role) be quite familiar to them.

We come then to an interim report on a subject for which there are only interim reports: What does the legacy of the latest reform era, with its successes, failures, and surprises, add up to when we try to characterize the regime as a whole at the end of the 1980s? Trying to answer that question is also a first step to putting the Reagan years in perspective, although as I suggested at the outset, to judge Reaganism with confidence we will need to skip a beat historically; only at the end of the next administration will we be in a good position to gain a clear idea of the Reagan legacy.

One way to gain perspective on the present state of our political system might be to perform a mental experiment. Imagine being carried back thirty years in time as, say, a newly elected senator in the aggressive incoming class of 1958.[16] As you look at the surrounding political world with 1988 eyes and try to do business in that world, what would strike you as particularly different and remarkable? It is not good enough to say that the deficit problem, economic conditions, or international order were completely different. True, the deficit then was tiny by present standards, but balancing the budget was a preoccupation on all sides in 1958. There was also a pervasive fear of slipping into another recession. All that plus a tight-fisted if genial president would have posed a major barrier to any bold new initiatives you might have had in mind. Then, too, people were intensely worried about the nuclear threat and America's relative power vis-à-vis the Russians; Atoms for Peace, People to People programs, and the need to defend ourselves against the Sputnik challenge were much in the air.

The essential differences a time-traveler would notice would not lie so much in the content of the problems as in the political architecture of the world in which one moved. Your contemporaries might not perceive it, but from a 1988 perspective the truly striking thing would be that you must navigate in a regime of establishments. There was a congressional establishment in 1958, and your pet projects and advancement would have depended on the goodwill of that inner circle, which included not only the Johnson/Rayburn axis but also senior senators such as Walter George, Richard Russell, and James Eastland and Congressmen such as Howard Smith at the Rules Committee. Foreign policy is something you would have been expected to leave for a few national leaders in the executive, Congress, and beyond.[17] You might not have heard of the incoming Secretary of State Christian Herter, but the east coast foreign policy establishment had. In domestic affairs the picture was more complex but fairly well structured. You would have had to deal with an establishment of recognized labor leaders regarding workers' legislation. There was also a Negro establishment centered on the NAACP with whom you would have consulted, more or less quietly, on civil rights matters; a Social Security establishment for social insurance matters; a social services profession that dominated welfare legislation; a self-contained business/government complex that presided over nuclear energy policy; a public works subgovernment for conservation; another one for highways; and on and on.[18] If you were a new senator in 1958 you might have found a young colleague named Kennedy making plans in his inner office to run in a small number of presidential primaries— not really to win delegates but to impress an establishment of state Democratic party leaders who could deliver the convention.[19] And there was a press establishment that was not telling everything it knew about John Kennedy's private life, much less investigating it.

This is not the political world we live in today. The chapters in this book describe a different regime that is much more open, fragmented, self-critical, nondeferential, and fluid in its attachments. But anyone observing Washington over the intervening years does not need a book to tell them that. The same features have been increasingly true of Congress internally, of presidential relations with Congress, of interest groups and their coalitions, of parties, political campaigns, and of voters' reactions to this passing parade.

It is not clear how we should label this altered political regime that overlays our 200-year old constitutional state order. *Pluralism* comes to mind, of course, but then there was also a plurality of establishments in the world we have lost. In describing the "new political system," some favor the term *atomistic*.[20] And yet what we see around us is not a myriad of isolated atoms bumping in random profusion. There are lines of force and counterforce composing themselves, not in one unchanging pattern but in shifting assemblies of political interaction. Still others seem to have given up the descriptive struggle and refer simply to "the glob," a semipermanent, semisovereign, semiprofessional crowd of Washingtonians and would-be Washingtonians.[21]

I suspect that we are struggling too hard to coin a new term when a very old term—*factionalism*—will do well enough. Our contemporary version may be somewhat less geographically based than the factionalism James Madison tried to design against and George Washington warned us about, but both versions embody a rich and complex variety of economic interests and ideological commitments. The main difference is that our factionalism has shaped itself around a governmental presence that is doing so much more in so many different areas of life. The factions that once sprang up around a few problems (foreign trade, internal improvements, disposition of public lands, etc.) now come to life across a huge spectrum of government activities touching almost everything about ourselves as a society. It is the factional creation of and response to that reality that invites one to speak of a politicizing of society.

Might this regime simply be a transitional phase, a hangover from the unsettling changes introduced in the 1960s and 1970s? From what can now be gleaned about developments in the Reagan years, that seems unlikely. The most aggressive conservative challenge in our modern history has yielded, not greater order and stability in our political affairs, not presidential government or congressional government or party government, not a decisive conservative agenda for the nation (unless one makes the dubious assumption that deficit reduction is an inherently conservative exercise) nor a liberal counteragenda. It has yielded more factionalism. The world of establishments has been lost, and it will not soon reappear. Why not?

One reason is that once openness, access, and skepticism of institutional authority have become the norm, it is difficult to put the genie back in the bottle. Who will stand up to demand less openness and a more exclusionary politics? Who will contend that those in authority know better how to look after other peoples' rights than they do themselves? Who will argue for a more cramped view of what Melnick calls programmatic rights? As he points out, elected politicians today are adept at preventing such scalebacks. To observe former segregationist politicians seeking black votes or a once self-contained nuclear power industry courting public opinion in media ads is to realize that "the people, no" is an unworkable proposition in contemporary America.

A second reason we may expect modern factionalism to endure is that too many thresholds legitimating government activity—and thus also indirectly legitimating factional struggles for shaping such activity—have been breached. There was a time when political policy struggles could be contained by a far simpler cleavage: the division between those who thought various spheres of social activity were or were not any of the federal government's business. This division of opinion applied at one time or another to such questions as primary and secondary education, pension insurance, health care, basic science research, consumer protection, worker safety, family issues (contraception, abortion, child support, day care), private-sector racial, age, or gender discrimination, and many other areas. Once this boundary question was overcome, and it was overcome in all of these areas, policy conflict had to take a more diffuse and complicated form. The line of scrimmage disappears, so to speak, and the struggle takes on more of the quality of continuous broken field running. Once the question of government action per se becomes a non-issue, the contending sides necessarily subdivide over questions of means, extent, modifications, exceptions, cost-shifting, and so on. What seemed monolithic blocs—for instance, the people opposed to "socialized medicine"—become decomposed groups of insurers, co-insurers, doctors, providers (i.e., hospitals) for profit and not for profit, employers with and those without health benefit programs, and so on. Without the fictive boundary between public and private, rule rescinding becomes as controversial and politically demanding as rulemaking, doing nothing is seen to be as much a policy as is doing something.

Third, the modern factional regime represents what Marxists like to call an objectification of hegemony: Its operations generate the concrete forces necessary to sustain it. One does not need to dream up a cause or ideological stance to activate factional activity. The normal workings of the system continually do that automatically. It is an accessible system that invites its actions to be challenged; hence losing groups are faced with the constant incentive to mobilize and challenge—what Jeffrey Berry calls "appeals court shopping." It is a system that clasps an inherently disruptive player to its bosom; public-interest groups, as Donald Brand points out, have one foot inside and one foot outside the interest group system. If such groups become too accommodative or too satisfied, they jeopardize their very existence. It is an interactive system of courts, group advocates, congressional subunits and staffers, governmental agencies, and media events. As U.S. business corporations soon learned, one becomes a permanent and adaptive player or one gets left behind (and, of course, by mobilizing to fight the system, the corporations, too, became part of the system). New members of Congress, Hill staff, disgruntled interests, bureaucratic entrepreneurs, and (dare we say) new judges learn the same lesson. The activism of each feeds on that of the other.

We cannot, therefore, expect the decomposition of establishment politics to reverse itself soon. Modern factionalism is a system of the activists, by the activists, and for the activists. Formally speaking, the United

States may have two political parties, but the operating reality is that it now also has a multiparty system of policy parties—a churning collection of the "involved" variously competing and cooperating with one another to influence the multiple levers and vast activities of government. Some of the issues are technical (e.g., a quiet but ongoing little struggle to influence what questions to ask on the next census); some are ideologically charged (e.g., abortion policy); many are both (e.g., SDI, welfare reform, trade policy, toxic dump site cleanup, and so on). There are corners of the realm in which corporatist-style consultation persists. But there is too much variation, conflict, and unpredictability to use the term *corporatism* to characterize the system as a whole or even its program sectors over time.

Modern factionalism reflects an activist elite that has become broader in membership and more deeply divided against itself in many different directions over the past thirty years. A previously existing elite consensus on free trade and foreign policy has been replaced by sharp disagreement. A once-unified upper-middle class of white Northern Protestants has by some accounts become the most polarized class in the country.[22] The black community has fractionalized into a growing middle class that has made it and a growing underclass that has not.[23] Arbitrary and exclusionary as the older postwar consensus might have been, it did reflect a society that was once more sure of itself and where it wanted to go. In its place today we have the multiple advocacy of policy activists who must struggle to marshal broader support on one issue after another.

How does that larger public and its potential support fit into this fluid regime of factionalism we have been describing? Certainly there is a structural similarity with the world of activists in this sense: Ordinary citizens' political attachments have become more volatile and disorganized. The older building blocks of party loyalty and regional, ethnic, and class identity have tended to decompose into a more fluid style of independence, issue voting, and shifting allegiances to the political personalities of the moment.

What the public does not share with the activists and policy parties is a strong sense of policy and political involvement that is in turn related to underlying ideological divisions and commitments. Surveys of general predispositions as well as of quite specific policy issues continue to reveal the public's ambivalence about government as either simply the solution or the problem.[24] At the same time, a large and growing proportion of "all Americans" are reporting that government and politics have become so complex that they cannot understand what is going on, that decisionmaking is in the hands of interests outside their control.[25] Without trying to exaggerate their importance, one can view such polls as tapping an increasing sense of distance between average Americans and a political realm they feel unable to comprehend or influence.

Political parties have been conventionally assigned the task of making such linkages, but they too seem to have decomposed amid modern factionalism. As discussed in chapter 8, Democratic and Republican parties have recently revived as national organizations. But in their struggle against each other and in the ideas of their activists, neither party seems to have touched ordinary citizens' allegiences in such a way as to help them make sense of and attach their active consent to what is going on in the political world. In the test between 1960s liberalism and 1980s conservatism, pragmatic disbelief won as far as the general public was concerned. Each side seemed to follow a law of wretched excess that ended by undermining public credibility of the vision being advocated.

For Liberals the excesses in question accumulated slowly but with seeming inexorability. Appalled by the Vietnam War, abuses by intelligence agencies, and dangers of the nuclear arms race, they automatically opposed military spending and became embarrassed by talk of national patriotism or anti-communism. Shocked by the intolerance of racism, fundamentalist religion, and establishment authorities, Liberals began separating themselves from concerns for religious values and moral discipline. To be seriously concerned about crime and violence, one had to concentrate on ways of changing the social system—but not on ways of catching and punishing criminals. To be seriously concerned about welfare, one had to be worried about getting people above a poverty income line but not, for fear of being called punitive, about getting welfare recipients into the workforce. To *do something* about America's problems one had to think about new government programs but not— for fear of being labelled pro-business—about tax burdens or economic competitiveness. As one of the leaders of the previously confident New Left put it following Ronald Reagan's first inauguration in 1981: "Having thus lost God, the flag, national defense, tax relief, personal safety and traditional family values to the conservatives, it became more than a little difficult for these liberals to explain why they should be entrusted with the authority to govern."[26]

For the conservative political vision in the 1980s the troubles had been building for some time but they seemed to come with a rush following the Republicans' loss of control in the Senate in 1986. Fate, in the form of wretched excesses no less wretched than those of the Liberals, seemed to be taking direct aim at the central tenets of Reaganism. Faith in the market and free enterprise begot speculative bubbles, junk bonds, Ivan Boesky and sleaze capitalism. Faith in "traditional values" begot squelched administration initiatives (on pornography, parental notification of birth control counseling, etc.), Jim and Tammy Bakker, and sleaze evangelism. Militant anti-communism brought the scandals of Iran/contra and its sleaze diplomacy of trading with terrorists. The good-news message of national economic strength acquired merely through cutting our own taxes produced an America in hock to foreigners.

Is it any wonder that the parties, as vehicles for linking ordinary citizens with political happenings, have achieved a state of virtual stalemate? The proportion of Americans identifying themselves with the Republican party has drawn roughly even with the share claiming to be Independents and slightly behind the proportion of Democratic party identifiers; Republicans do better among the youngest current age group, but this is an extremely volatile group to be making long-range predictions about. The more fundamental point is that the personal political meaning of such party identifications has become rather empty for many people. And in looking over the events and disillusionments of the past thirty years, one might well wonder why anyone *should* feel inclined to become deeply committed to either partisan persuasion. The political world of the Inner Beltway has become a sort of black hole sucking in funds, manpower, and public hopes—a whirlpool in which activists expend huge amounts of political and technocratic energy flailing at the state's structural obstacles to governing and from which little enlightment emerges for average citizens trying to make sense of their political choices.

If nothing else, some of the apparently contradictory observations with which this chapter began may now be less puzzling. Some see a changing system in which partisan politics has become less pervasive, and some see a system increasingly permeated by partisan politics. Both views may be correct depending on how and where we look. There has surely been a decline in the capacity of party politics to organize political choices within government (where the technocratic, administrative quality of policymaking has grown within Congress and the executive branch) and within the general public (where allegiances have become more fluid and policy struggles less understandable). But it is also accurate to say that modern factionalism has inundated society with the struggles of policy partisans mobilized amid a never-ending stream of issues for political choice.

Another puzzle has to do with the question of how the nation could have moved toward a series of realignments in public policy over the last thirty years in the apparent absence of a major electoral realignment. The answer may have to do with the detached quality of modern factionalism, whereby it is possible for activists to win and lose in their struggles over the levers of government without really engaging the general public in a decisive argument about the choices. If so, it is a tendency that should worry anyone seriously concerned about the democratic quality of our political life.

But should we worry? I am inclined to think we should. There seems to be an important mismatch between the direction of our politics and the requirements of our state. It is widely acknowledged that, if nothing else, the Reagan years have restored a sense of confidence and power in the presidency. That is probably true and desirable as far as it goes. The more troubling fact is that this restoration of presidential prestige adds to an already persistent tendency to pin excessive hopes on the presidency to solve our problems of self-government. With factional advocacy on all sides, the president becomes almost "the sole source of whatever concept of the general welfare receives attention" (to use Pendleton Herring's phrase). We derive false comfort by concentrating so much on the restored faith in the presidency. The important question is whether at the end of the Reagan years our institutions of government *as a whole* are more or less able to perform their appropriate governing duties. It was part of the founding fathers' wisdom to see governance as a holistic enterprise. Never did they argue that any one institution in their design was a fully satisfactory instrument of government; it was the joint workings of the different parts that would constitute effective government and safeguard liberty.

As activists struggle against one another to shape institutions and policies, modern factionalism has the tendency to try and make each part into the whole of government; it seeks to prevail on one's chosen issue by turning courts into little legislatures and executive agencies as well, by turning congressional committees and subcommittees into little management bureaus and offices for shaping judicial interpretation. Nor is the presidency immune. In the long clawing of one's way toward the White House, factional obligations are accumulated and promises made that make it seem as if there are powers of legislation, adjudication, and implementation in the White House. But of course there are not. Once in office, the president faces outward to a public expecting him to solve problems for the general welfare and inward to the black hole where the policy parties in his entourage engage, and by doing so reinforce, the factional system.

First we shape our institutions, and then our institutions shape us. Both by design and accident we have created in the past thirty years a regime that keeps pushing the conduct of public affairs in a certain direction, regardless of the ideological content of the factions involved. A strategy of reform for openness, distrust of authority, and inclusiveness has reverberated throughout the development of political institutions, and the institutional developments have produced an incentive structure in which some strategies subsequently make sense and others do not.

One way to think about the interaction of ideas and institutions is to say that strategy tells structure how to grow and structure tells strategy how to conform. There is little point in exhorting new members of Congress to support stronger, more integrative congressional leadership because it will be in the long-term interests of Congress as a whole. There is little point in exhorting new presidents to behave in ways that will shore up party government among the branches, the congressional budget process, or other forms of integrative leadership that could serve as more coherent and useful bargaining partners concerning the general welfare. And there is little point in urging activists to submerge their causes into a broader, permanent coalition that could eventually involve the informed consent of average citizens to the policy choices being made.

Why not? It is easy to become too abstract in talking about institutions, strategies, and so on. The points can be made by becoming more personal.

Suppose you are a new member of Congress elected in 1988. As a result of the reforms and changes that have taken place over the last thirty years, you have probably been elected as a kind of political entrepreneur, running your own campaign, owing little in your career to a political party, knowing very well that your reelection chances will depend on your going into business for yourself with your local constituents. You enter an institutional structure on Capitol Hill that facilitates such entrepreneurship. If you are not inclined to work too hard at it personally, there are rafts of staff at hand to work at entrepreneurship for you. You now are one of the many scattered targets offering opportunities for interest groups to pursue their causes and influence executive agency actions. The courts may be more willing to take action on issues of importance to your agenda; if not, interest groups and staff will help your subcommittee write language in legislation and reports that will encourage them to do so. All this busyness gives advocacy groups work to claim credit for, which aids the fund-raising available through PACs, which in turn provides resources for you to run an election campaign as a political entrepreneur—and so the loop is closed.

Or suppose you were a new president facing today's regime. What would you do: Attempt to sustain other, integrative leadership structures that might be in place by the time your successor takes office? I think I would attempt to exploit modern factionalism—to expound positions without really taking responsibility, to try and further divide and conquer, to cut my deals wherever and whenever I could find them, to build ad hoc coalitions and let tomorrow take care of itself. If a modern president chooses to hunker in the shelter rather than behave like a vulnerable partner in the governing process, and if he refrains from sustaining longer-term institutional processes to integrate policy choices, it is not because he is willful or uninformed. It is because he is politically smart, given the context.

Thus prospects for discovering a politics of the general welfare are not bright. However, it is a good idea to be a little skeptical even about one's own doubts, and so let me offer a concluding speculation on the other side. Tocqueville argued that America's local, participatory politics would counter the country's otherwise narrow individualism and yield a larger view of self-interest. Obviously our emerging regime is far removed from that era of town meetings, just as it has left behind the world of establishments. And yet it is at least possible to imagine that a similar effect might be produced by other contemporary tendencies at work so that, in Tocqueville's words, "there should be an infinite number of occasions for the citizens to act together and so that every day they should feel that they depended on one another."[27] These tendencies have to do with the changing ways in which Americans derive a sense of psychological well-being from their social environment. To judge from the available evidence, Americans since the late 1950s have tended to become less dependent on formal social organizations and more involved in creating and nurturing their own networks of social support.[28] There has been a shift from more socially fixed, formal anchors to more personally defined conceptions of well-being. It is not that marriage, jobs, neighborhood concerns, ethnic identities, and so on have become less important, but that they have remained important in a changing way—less as formal roles carrying inherent value assigned by society and more as settings for interpersonal relationships to be embraced or dropped as they are felt to contribute to personal fulfillment.

In an admittedly limited way, many of our modern political inventions—media-saturated coverage of politics, hyperactive polling and reports on public responses to poll reports, talk shows and their semi-interactive public conversations about things political, public-interest groups and direct-mail "cause" campaigning with its outreach efforts—these are really devices by which ordinary people can share feelings and more fluidly get into and out of political involvements. Such substitutes just might help fulfill the broadening, empathetic function that Tocqueville had in mind.

Traditionalists will argue with cause that these modern contrivances are pale imitations of genuine citizen involvement in public affairs. Perhaps. The fact is, however, that our emerging regime truly does challenge our older ways of thinking about politics to catch up with reality. In the past we have believed in the necessity of more or less permanent building blocks of political allegiance, but it may be that more changeable, plastic attachments will do. We may be like the aging rock-and-roll fan who thinks that to maintain its integrity a group has to be like the Beach Boys and stay together permanently. Yet contemporary groups seem to do well with more fluid attachments. Might Genesis be a more appropriate model for our political future?

NOTES

1. Jimmy Carter appointed 258 federal judges during his four years. Ronald Reagan surpassed this number in 1986 and will have appointed well over half of the 729 federal judges by the end of his second term.

2. Anthony King, ed., *The New American Political System* (Washington: American Enterprise Institute, 1978); John E. Chubb and Paul E. Peterson, eds., *The New Direction in American Politics* (Washington, D.C.: Brookings Institution, 1985); and Louis Galambos, *The New American State* (Baltimore: Johns Hopkins University Press, 1987). Interesting comparisons can be drawn with Walter Edward Weyl, *The New Democracy* (New York: Macmillan, 1912), or Arthur Holcombe's *The New Party Politics* (New York: W. W. Norton, 1933).

3. Pendleton Herring, *Politics of Democracy* (W. W. Norton, 1940), p. 110. I am grateful to John Kessel for bringing the quotation to my attention.

4. Richard Harris and Sidney M. Milkis, *Social Regulation and the Reagan Revolution* (New York: Oxford University Press, forthcoming).

5. In a pivotal Supreme Court case, Justice William Rehnquist in 1982 wrote for the majority, "Standing is not measured by the intensity of the litigant's interest or the fervor of his advocacy." See *Valley Forge Christian College* v. *Americans United For Separation of Church and State* (454 U.S. 464, 1982).

6. Thus race may not be used as the sole criterion for selection of students in a university where there is no history of racial prejudice, but it may be one among other criteria used for selecting applicants. See *University of California* v. *Bakke* (98 S. Crt. 2733, 1978). Racial quotas are said to be constitutional for union admission, training, and job promotion where there has been an active record of racial discrimination in the past. See *United States Steelworkers* v. *Weber* (443 U.S. 197, 1979) and *Local 28 of the Sheet Metal Workers International* v. *Equal Employment Opportunity Commission* (54 U.S.L.W. 4984, 1986). However, minority preferences in hiring cannot be used to prevent racial imbalances in dismissal through the routine operation of a seniority (i.e., last-hired/first-fired) system. See *Firefighters Local Union No. 1784* v. *Stotts* (104 S. Crt. 2576, 1984).

7. *Washington Post* (April 27, 1987), p. A-11.

8. Thus, for 1988, the number of delegate seats reserved for party officials was raised from 550 to 650, out of a total of 4,158 convention delegates. However, the drive for openness was hardly moribund. Rules changes for 1988 also relaxed requirements for Democratic party membership with respect to participation in primaries and caucuses, and lowered the qualifying percentage to win convention delegates from 30 percent to 15 percent of the primary or caucus vote.

9. Charles V. Hamilton, "New Elites and Pluralism," in Richard M. Pious, ed., *The Power to Govern*, vol. 34, no. 2 (New York: Proceedings of the Academy of Political Science, 1981).

10. Nature seemed to target the luckless Carter administration. In 1978, the Supreme Court ruled that under the Endangered Species Act the snail darter, a three-inch fish, had a right to absolute protection against the threat posed to its existence by completion of the Tellico Dam in Tennessee. The Carter administration vigorously and unsuccessfully opposed legislation pushed by Tennessee Senator Howard Baker to overturn the Court's decision by exempting the dam from the act. Having expended significant political capital in the fight, officials were astonished to read a year later that environmentalists desperately seeking a new home for the snail darter had accidentally discovered another 1,000 or more of the species inhabiting one of the most polluted rivers in eastern Tennessee.

11. Space limitations preclude further details, but it is worth emphasizing that, when referring to "the reformers," one is really talking about a diverse collection of people and ideas. The "counterculture" of hippies, Yippies, flower children, and so on, pushed—when they were not dropping out in the 1950s style of the "beats"—for changes having mainly to do with freedom of expression. The "New Left" embodied in the SDS, Black Panthers, and so on, sought a radical transformation in social power relations through confrontation and direct action. The "Old Left" was composed of remnants from various Marxist and socialist factions who, having seen the power of U.S. anti-communism, urged greater caution in attacking "the system." Of far greater consequence for the reforms discussed in this book were the civil rights activists, the liberal descendants of New Deal Democrats, and other critics of the status quo interested in particular causes. The conservative reaction that began with Young Americans for Freedom and Goldwater's and Wallace's challenges in the 1960s eventually succeeded in unifying these elements in the minds of many people. This was a unity that "liberalism" could never achieve in practice. Useful recent historical accounts are James Miller, *Democracy Is in the Streets* (New York: Simon & Schuster, 1987); Maurice Isserman, *If I Had a Hammer* (New York: Basic Books, 1987); and Todd Gitlin, *The Sixties* (New York: Bantam, 1987).

12. Charles Noble, *Liberalism at Work* (Philadelphia: Temple University Press, 1986).

13. Austin Ranney, "Farewell to Reform—Almost," in Kay Lehman Schlozman, ed., *Elections in America* (Boston: Allen and Unwin, 1987).

14. Stein Ringen, *The Possibility of Politics* (Oxford: Oxford University Press, 1987).

15. Kay Lehman Schlozman and John T. Tierney, "More of the Same: Washington Pressure Group Activity in a Decade of Change," *Journal of Politics*, no. 45 (1983).

16. In 1958, the country was in the midst of a recession. Proposals for new spending were being routinely defeated in the Democratically controlled Congress for fear of further unbalancing the budget, and efforts by liberal Senator Paul Douglas to enact a tax cut to stimulate the economy were being overwhelmingly

defeated. Congressional elections that year produced a Democratic landslide and the arrival of fifteen new Democratic senators, including such liberals as Philip Hart, Eugene McCarthy, and Edmund Muskie.

17. The problems created by the loss of such an establishment seem to lie at the heart of much criticism concerning America's foreign policy process. See Leslie Gelb and I. M. Destler, *Our Own Worst Enemy*, 2nd ed. (New York: Simon & Schuster, 1985).

18. A fuller study would show that 1958 was, in fact, a year in which the challenge to establishment politics was beginning to intensify, especially under the prodding of an activist bloc in Congress and its outside allies. An excellent account is James L. Sundquist's *Politics and Policy* (Washington, D.C.: Brookings Institution, 1968). Even so, in reading the detailed cases of policy innovation and reform prior to the 1960s (e.g., the Civil Rights Act of 1957 or the National Defense Education Act of 1958), one is struck by what a tidy and disciplined political process it was compared to today.

19. Theodore H. White, *The Making of the President, 1960* (New York: Atheneum, 1961).

20. King, *The New American Political System*, p. 391.

21. Richard E. Neustadt, *Presidential Power* (New York: John Wiley, 1980), p. 214.

22. James Q. Wilson, "American Politics, Then and Now," *Commentary* (February 1979); Everett Carll Ladd and Karlyn H. Keene, *The Ladd Report #6* (New York: W. W. Norton, 1987).

23. William J. Wilson, *The Declining Significance of Race*, 2nd ed. (Chicago: University of Chicago Press, 1980); and *The Truly Disadvantaged* (Chicago: University of Chicago Press, 1987).

24. Attitudes toward government are reported in *Public Opinion*, March-April, 1987. More in-depth studies of public views on particular policy issues can be found in the publications of the Public Agenda Foundation. See, for example, Keith Melville and John Doble, *The Public's Perspective on Social Welfare Reform* (New York: Public Agenda Foundation, January 1988).

25. See the results of the 1984 election surveys reported by the Center for Political Studies at the University of Michigan.

26. Tom Hayden, "The Future Politics of Liberalism," *The Nation* (February 21, 1981), p. 209.

27. Alexis de Tocqueville, *Democracy in America*, edited by J. P. Meyer and Max Lerner (New York: Harper and Row, 1966), p. 482.

28. See Joseph Veross, *The Inner American: A Self-Portrait 1957–76* (New York: Basic Books, 1981). See also Ralph H. Turner, "The Real Self: From Institution to Impulse," *American Journal of Sociology*, vol. 81, no. 5 (1974); and Theodore Caplow et al., *Middletown Families: Fifty Years of Change and Continuity* (Minneapolis: University of Minnesota Press, 1982).

About the Contributors

Jeffrey M. Berry is professor of political science at Tufts University. His works include *Feeding Hungry People: Rulemaking in the Food Stamp Program, The Interest Group Society,* and *Lobbying for the People.*

Donald R. Brand teaches American politics at the University of Pennsylvania. He is the author of *Corporatism and the Rule of Law: A Study of the National Recovery Administration* (forthcoming).

Lawrence C. Dodd is professor of political science and director of the Center for the Study of American Politics at the University of Colorado, Boulder. He is the author of *Coalitions in Parliamentary Government* (1976), coauthor of *Congress and the Administrative State* (1979), and coeditor of *Congress Reconsidered* (1977, 1981, 1985) and *Congress and Policy Change* (1986).

Robert Eden is professor of political philosophy, American government, and constitutional law in the Department of History and Political Science at Hillsdale College in Hillsdale, Michigan. He is the author of *Political Leadership and Nihilism: A Study of Weber and Nietzsche* (1984) and is currently writing a second book, on constitutionalism and political realignment in the United States.

Richard A. Harris is associate professor of political science and public policy at Rutgers University–Camden. He is the author of *Coal Firms Under the New Social Regulation* (1985) and of articles on regulatory affairs. He is also coauthor, with Sidney M. Milkis, of *Social Regulation and the Reagan Revolution: A Tale of Two Agencies* (forthcoming).

Hugh Heclo is Robinson Professor of Public Affairs at George Mason University in Virginia. He is currently working on a book concerning social welfare issues in America.

R. Shep Melnick is associate professor of politics at Brandeis University and a member of the associated staff at the Brookings Institution. He is the author of *Regulation and the Courts: The Case of the Clean Air Act* and is currently finishing a book on the courts, Congress, and welfare policy.

Sidney M. Milkis teaches politics and is a research associate with the Gordon Public Policy Center at Brandeis University. His articles on the presidency have appeared in the *Political Science Quarterly*, *Administration and Society*, and *PS*, as well as in several edited volumes. He is coauthor, with Richard A. Harris, of *Social Regulation and the Reagan Revolution: A Tale of Two Agencies*. At present, he is completing a book on the modern presidency and the American party system.

Barbara G. Salmore is professor of political science at Drew University and a past president of the Northeastern Political Science Association. She is the coauthor of *Candidates, Parties and Campaigns* (1985) and has written several articles on American political campaigns and their broader effects on politics.

Stephen A. Salmore is professor of political science at the Eagleton Institute of Politics, Rutgers University, and a past director of the Eagleton Poll, a regular public opinion survey on New Jersey politics. He has served as a polling consultant for many candidates in federal and state elections and has written numerous articles about political campaigns and state politics.

Edward Weisband is Distinguished Teaching Professor in the Department of Political Science, University Center at Binghamton, State University of New York. He is the coauthor, with Thomas Franck, of *Foreign Policy by Congress* (1979), *Secrecy and Foreign Policy* (1974), and *Word Politics* (1971) and is the author of *Poverty Amidst Plenty* (Westview, forthcoming).

Index

Action for Children's Television, 167

Activism, 4, 12, 14, 245, 295, 304, 319(n11)
  and factionalism, 311–312
  judicial, 207–208
  nomination process, 307–308
  social activism, 55–56, 57–58, 310–312

Administration, 124, 149, 179, 190–191, 263. *See also* Administrators; Management

Administrative Procedures Act, 35, 189

Administrators
  conflicting pressures, 251–253
  See also Administration

Advocacy groups. *See* Interest groups; Public-interest groups

AFDC. *See* Aid to Families with Dependent Children

Affirmative Action, 5, 297

Age discrimination, 193

Age Discrimination Act (1976), 189

Agencies, 35, 164, 165, 250, 274
  regulatory, 7(table), 241–242, 263
  See also individual agencies

Aid to Families with Dependent Children (AFDC), 67, 198, 199, 200

Alien and Sedition Acts, 42

American Medical Association, 255

Americans for Democratic Action, 167

Anderson, John, 219

Anti-Federalists, 28–29, 46, 47, 291
  democracy, 39–42, 43–44
  legislature, 40–41
  liberalism, 41–42

Anti-poverty programs, 161–162. *See also* Great Society; Welfare

Anti-satellite device (ASAT), 137–138, 141

Arms control, 112, 127
  codetermination, 113, 121–122, 130–131
  Congress, 131, 132–143, 144(n29)
  Reagan administration, 131, 138–139

Articles of Confederation, 29, 215

ASAT. *See* Anti-satellite device

Aspin, Les, 132, 133

Bailyn, Bernard, 29

Baker, Howard, 133, 137, 319(n10)

Baker v. *Carr*, 30

Bedell, Berkley, 136

Bell system, 255

Bentsen, Lloyd, 224

Bolling, Richard, 99

Bolling Committee, 99, 105–106

Bork, Robert, 291

Brandeis, Louis, 9

Brezhnev, Leonid, 131

Brown, George E., 138

Brownlow Committee, 10–11, 154–155

Brown v. *Board of Education*, 34, 190, 193, 207

Buckley v. *Valeo*, 228

Budget, 301, 306
  congressional process, 102–104, 107–108

control, 161, 198
Reagan administration, 21, 231–232, 299
Budget Control Act (1974). *See* Budget Reform and Impoundment Control Act
Budget Reform and Impoundment Control Act, 161, 299
Bumpers, Dale L., 134
Bureaucracy
discretion in, 34–36
strengthening, 204–205
Burford, Ann, 276, 295, 307
Burger Court, 199
Bush, George, 237(n34), 298
Business, 9, 13, 14, 272–273, 280
coalitions, 270–271
deregulation, 275–276
issue networks, 268–269
lobbying, 244, 265
performance standards, 267–268
public policy, 15–16
social regulation, 163, 263–264, 265, 269–270
social responsibility, 261–262, 266
Business Roundtable, 269
Byrd, Robert C., 135

Campaign finance, 5, 215, 237(n34), 238(n47)
1970s reforms, 227–230
Campaign Finance Act (1974), 38
Cannon, Joseph, 93
CAP. *See* Community Action Program
Capitalism, 27–28, 29, 36, 40, 49(n33)
Carter, Jimmy, 56, 166, 174, 224, 245, 274, 307, 318(n1), 319(n10)
arms control, 113, 131
nomination, 84(n81), 221, 222
Central Intelligence Agency (CIA), 116
CIA. *See* Central Intelligence Agency
Citizens, 20, 45, 164, 298
activism, 70–71

government participation of, 31–33, 106–107, 197, 244, 266, 302
rights of action, 205–206
Citizen's Coal Project, 280
Civil Aeronautics Board, 14
Civil rights, 8, 67, 82–84(nn 70, 80), 157, 178, 309, 319(n11)
promoting, 65–66
reform, 296–297
voting, 194–195
See also Civil Rights Act (1870, 1964); Civil rights movement
Civil Rights Act (1870), 205
Civil Rights Act (1964), 65, 188, 189, 209(n2), 294
implementation, 192–195
Civil Rights Attorney's Fees Act (1976), 197
Civil rights movement, 30, 33–34, 300. *See also* Civil rights; Civil Rights Act (1964)
Civil service, 56, 154
Claybrook, Joan, 245
Clean Air Act, 200, 295
Clean Air Act Amendments, 35
Coalitions, 195
businesses as, 270–271
Congress and, 45–46, 48–49(n31)
legislative, 230–231, 239, 255
public-interest, 169–170
Codetermination, 127, 292–293
arms control, 121–122, 136–138, 140–143
foreign policy, 112–114
Iran-contra affair, 114–117
reform, 120, 124–125
specialization, 125–126
Cohen, William S., 132, 133
Committee for Party Renewal, 233, 238(n47)
Committee on Committees, 105
Committees, 90, 100, 161
congressional, 91–92, 93–96, 190
House of Representatives, 98–99
jurisdiction, 126–127
representation, 96–97
See also Subcommittees

Committee to Reelect the President (CREEP), 173–174
Common Cause, 38
Common Law, 43
Community Action Program (CAP), 31–32, 161–162, 196, 302, 304
Comprehensive Nuclear Test Ban Treaty (CTBT), 136
Congress, 16, 31, 46, 120, 207, 212(n38), 230, 298–299
  arms control, 121–122, 131–133, 140–143
  authority, 124–125, 127
  autonomy, 122–123
  budgetary process, 102–104, 231–232
  career legislators, 89–90, 91–92, 95–96
  committees, 90, 91–92, 93–94, 190
  and courts, 191–192
  Democratic party, 97–99
  democratization, 45, 100–101
  environmentalism, 197–201
  and executive branch, 105–106, 107
  foreign policy, 62–63, 112–113, 114
  founding, 90–91
  functions, 117–120
  governing structure, 92–93, 109
  leadership, 127–128, 316
  oversight, 15, 119, 129, 250, 305
  policymaking, 89, 94–95, 106, 112, 121, 123–124, 248–251
  power, 50(n49), 101, 305
  procedural rights, 195–196
  representation, 92, 96–97, 118
  speakership, 104–105
  specialization, 125–126
  See also House of Representatives; Senate
Congress for Peace Through Law, 128
Congressional Budget Office, 103, 105, 106, 119
Congressional Research Service, 106, 119
Conservatism, 175, 176–177, 313–314

Constitution, 42
  Anti-Federalists, 28–29, 39, 41, 46
Consumer Product Safety Commission (CPSC), 45, 263
Consumers, 5, 34, 168, 178, 302
  Federal Trade Commission, 165–166, 167, 185(n67)
  protection, 8, 15, 16, 163
  regulation for, 3, 45
Consumers Union, 167
Continuing resolutions (CRs), 231
Costle, Douglas, 265
Council of Wage and Price Stability (COWPS), 274
Courts. *See* Federal courts; Judiciary; Supreme Court
COWPS. *See* Council of Wage and Price Stability
CPSC. *See* Consumer Product Safety Commission
CREEP. *See* Committee to Reelect the President
Croly, Herbert, 12
CRs. *See* Continuing resolutions
CTBT. *See* Comprehensive Nuclear Test Ban Treaty

Dahl, Robert, 28
Daley, Richard, 67
Defense Appropriations Act (1984), 138
Defense Authorization Act (1983), 139
Defense Authorization Act (1986), 134
Democracy, 54
  Jacksonian, 53–54
  participatory, 27, 31, 82–83(n70), 147, 162, 303–307
Democratic Caucus, 129
Democratic Convention (1968), 159–160, 220–221
Democratic honor, 60–61, 68–70
  consensus politics, 71–73
  New Deal, 54–55, 59–61
  Tocqueville's definition, 53–54, 58–59, 78(n32)

Democratic party, 61, 66, 79(n44),
    82–83(n70), 96, 181(n20), 207,
    218, 289, 304, 314, 319–320(n19)
  delegate representation, 222–223,
    318(n8)
  foreign policy, 62–65
  House of Representatives, 97, 105
  liberalism, 57, 160
  machinery, 159–160
  participation, 67–68
  and presidency, 82(n68), 174
  primary system, 221–222
  reform, 30–31, 63, 69–70, 98–99,
    291, 293
  Roosevelt, Franklin D., 54, 55, 56–
    57, 151–152, 153–154
  Senate, 100, 176
Democratic Study Group (DSG)
  reform, 97–99
Democratization, 30–33, 225
  Congress, 45, 100–101
  political parties, 44–45
Department of Defense Authorization
  Act, 134, 138
Department of Health, Education,
  and Welfare, 193
Depression, 67
Deregulation, 245
  under Reagan, 177, 275–277
Developmental Disability Act, 205
Dicks, Norman D., 132
Dole, Robert J., 135, 175, 226,
  237(n34)
Domestic policy
  McGovern reforms, 65–67
Douglas, William O., 208
DSG. See Democratic Study Group
Dukakis, Michael, 223, 224
Dworkin, Ronald, 28

Eastland, James, 309
Eccles, Marriner, 12
Eckhardt, Bob, 48
Economic Opportunity Act, 32
Economy, 9, 19, 171, 185–186(n77),
  208, 274, 301, 319–320(n16)

Great Society, 156–157
  New Deal, 146, 180–181(n19)
  security, 156–157
EDF v. Ruckelshaus, 203
Education, 191–192
Education Amendments (1972), 182,
  193
Education for All Handicapped
  Children Act (1975), 189, 191–
  192, 195–196
EIS. See Environmental impact
  statement
Elections, 30, 226, 298
  candidate-centered, 218–220
  financing, 227–230, 237(n34)
  policymaking, 248, 249
  political party roles, 215–216
  state finances, 229–230
Electoral districts, 41
Ely, John Hart, 28
End of Liberalism, The (Lowi), 28, 43
Entitlements, 198–199, 200
Environment, 3, 5, 8, 19–20, 164,
  168, 300, 301. See also
  Environmental impact statement;
  Environmentalism; Environmental
  Protection Agency; National
  Environmental Policy Act
Environmental impact statement
  (EIS), 196, 303
Environmentalism, 34, 36, 178, 201,
  265, 319(n10)
  procedural rights, 196–197
  Reagan administration, 252, 307
  See also Environment;
  Environmental impact statement;
  Environmental Protection
  Agency; National Environmental
  Policy Act
Environmental Protection Agency
  (EPA), 15, 45, 165, 201, 251,
  252, 263, 265, 274
EPA. See Environmental Protection
  Agency
Equal Employment Opportunity
  Commission, 193
Equal Protection Clause, 193, 194

Ethics in Government Act, 294, 297
Executive branch, 42, 112, 148
  budget, 102–103
  congressional oversight, 105–106,
    107, 119–120, 305
  control, 252–253
  grants-in-aid, 205–206
  independence, 10–11
  New Deal reorganization, 153–155
  policymaking, 89, 152–153
  power, 50(n49), 101, 156, 163–164
  Roosevelt's reforms, 10–11
  Virginia resolutions, 42–43
  See also Presidency
Executive Office of the President, 158
Executive Reorganization Act (1939),
    153, 154, 155

Factionalism, 315
  social issues, 310–312
Fascell, Dante B., 129
FBI. *See* Federal Bureau of
    Investigation
FECA, 229
Federal Bureau of Investigation (FBI),
    116
Federal Communications
    Commission, 14
Federal courts, 22, 191, 197, 210(n20)
  collective rights, 200–201
  entitlement statutes, 198–199
  legislative history, 202–203
  private rights of action, 205–206
  rulemaking, 203, 204
Federalism, 47(n8), 84–85(n92), 205–
    206
Federalist, The, 39–40, 72
Federalists, 28, 39, 42, 43, 46, 47
Federal Trade Act, 5
Federal Trade Commission (FTC), 14,
    37
  consumer advocacy, 165–166, 167,
    185(n67)
  Magnuson-Moss Act, 32–33
Federal Trade Commission Act
    (1914), 205, 266, 274, 296

Finance. *See* Budget; Campaign
    finance
Food stamps, 245–246, 260
Ford, Gerald, 174, 191–192, 307
Foreign policy, 67, 75(n19), 81–
    82(n64), 306, 309
  accountability, 115–116
  codetermination, 112–114
  Congress, 112–113
  Democratic party, 61–65
  Johnson administration, 80(n48),
    161
Fourteenth Amendment, 193
Frankfurter, Felix, 208
Fraser, Donald, 220
Fraser Commission, 63, 67
Freedom of Information Act, 294
Frye, Alton, 130
FTC. *See* Federal Trade Commission
Fulbright, William, 62

GAO. *See* General Accounting Office
Gardner, John, 12
Garn, Jake, 254
General Accounting Office (GAO),
    106, 119
George, Walter, 309
Gephardt, Richard, 223, 237(n34)
Goldberg v. *Kelly*, 198
Goldwater, Barry, 225
GOP. *See* Republican party
Gorbachev, Mikhail, 139
Gore, Albert, 132, 133
Government Operations Committee,
    106
Gramm-Rudman-Hollings legislation,
    107, 231
Grants-in-aid, 205–206, 303
Great Society, 156, 171, 183(nn 36,
    47)
  goals, 157–158, 162

Hansen Committee, 98, 99, 104, 106
Harris, Joseph, 155
Hart, Gary, 223, 224, 225–226
Hawkins, David, 245

Head Start, 162
Health, 178, 255, 300–301
  public, 5, 15–16
Heclo, Hugh, 241–242
Helms, Jesse, 250
Herter, Christian, 309
Hoover, Herbert, 75(n21), 78(n35)
House Committee on Foreign Affairs, 136
House of Representatives, 41, 106, 107, 129, 132
  committees, 10, 93–94, 98–99
  Democrats, 97–98
  representation, 96–97, 99
  speakership, 104–105
  See also Congress
House Revolt (1910), 10, 11
House Rules Committee, 105
Hughes Commission, 67
Humphrey, Hubert, 220
Hunt Commission, 223–224, 233
Huntington, Samuel, 52–53
  American honor, 54–55
  consensus politics, 71–72

Immigration Act (1965), 83(n71)
Industrialism, 93
Information, 5, 106. *See also* Telecommunications
Institutionalism, 18–19
Interest group liberalism, 13–14, 16, 307
Interest groups, 164, 165, 244, 245, 249
  issue networks, 253–254, 257
  leadership, 254–255
  policymaking, 239, 240
  regulatory negotiation, 280–281
  subgovernments, 251–252
  See also Interest group liberalism; Public-interest groups
Intervenor funding program, 266
Iran-contra affair
  accountability, 116–117
  conservative government, 176–177
  hearings, 115–116

Issue networks
  business, 268–269
  defined, 240, 242
  interest groups, 253–254, 257
  policymaking, 246, 247
  politics of, 242–243

Jackson, Jesse, 63, 223, 224, 237(n34)
Jeffersonians, 42–43
Johnson, Lyndon B., 80(n48), 171, 226
  Great Society, 157, 158
  political power, 61–62, 67, 155–156
  presidency, 79–80(nn 45, 47), 158–159, 161–162
Johnson, Norma, 138
Judges, 56, 291. *See also* Federal courts; Judiciary; Supreme Court
Judiciary, 29, 33, 295–296, 318(n1)
  activism, 207–208
  collective rights, 200–201
  entitlements, 198–199
  legislative implementation, 190–191
  lobbying, 255–256
  power, 43, 188
  procedural rights, 195–196
  Roosevelt, Franklin D., 56, 76–77(nn 26, 27, 28)
  See also Federal courts; Supreme Court
Juries, 41

Kefauver, Estes, 218
Kemp, Jack, 237(n34)
Kemp-Roth Bill, 232
Kennedy, Edward M., 132, 135, 225, 237(n34)
Kennedy, John F., 189, 218, 226, 309
Kennedy, Robert, 220, 250
Kirk, Paul, 224, 233

LaFollette, Robert, 12
Leach, Jim, 136
Leadership, 316
  arms control, 132–133
  Democratic party, 153–154

foreign policy, 114–115
interest groups, 254–255
legislative, 127–128
presidency, 101, 147–148
See also Speaker of the House
Legal Services Corporation, 197
Legislation, 83–84(n80), 107, 120,
122, 248, 280
aggressive, 250–251
anti-discrimination, 193–194
coalitions, 230–231
implementation, 190–192
interpretation, 202–203
Reagan era, 231–232
social regulation, 294–295
See also Legislators
Legislative Reorganization Act (1946),
95–96
Legislative Reorganization Act
(1970s), 98
Legislators
career, 89–90, 91–92, 93–94, 96,
108–109
policymaking, 248–251
Liberal formalism, 27, 28, 45
Liberalism, 177, 313
Anti-Federalists, 41–42
civil rights, 33–34
Democratic party, 57, 160
Great Society, 156, 157, 171
interest groups, 13, 16
New Deal, 146–147, 148–149, 171–
172
programmatic, 149–150, 157, 161,
170–171, 173
public-interest groups, 168, 169,
245
security, 208–209
Lindblom, Charles, 28
Litigation, 197
Lobbying, 1, 99, 239, 244, 254
aggressive, 250–251
appeals courts, 255–256
business, 265, 266
pressure, 252–253
public, 16, 261, 265, 277
regulatory negotiations, 264, 280

Lowi, Theodore, 12–13, 20, 28, 43,
256

McCarthy, Eugene, 56, 220, 302
McGovern, George, 56, 63, 65, 220,
221, 222, 225, 250
McGovern-Fraser Commission, 22,
30, 158, 302
Democratic party reform, 159–160
media support, 226–227
rule changes, 220, 221–222, 233,
298
McGovern reforms
domestic policy, 65–67
foreign policy, 63, 64
goals, 62, 68, 69–70
McHugh, Matthew F., 138
Madison, James, 18, 39–40, 42–43,
72, 283
Magnuson-Moss Act, 32–33, 48(n22),
166–167
Management
politicization, 262, 266–267, 273–
275, 281
Markey, Edward J., 136
Marshall, John, 29
Meany, George, 67
Medicare, 255
Michel, Robert, 250
Mikulski Commission, 220
Minorities, 8, 55, 182(n34), 296,
318(n6)
civil rights, 65–66
Democratic party, 82–83(n70), 221
political organization, 21, 61
voting rights, 194–195
Missiles
deployment, 133–134, 135, 141
Moakley, Joe, 138
Mondale, Walter, 84(n81), 100, 223,
224, 237(n34)
MX missiles, 132, 133–134, 141

Nader, Ralph, 12, 48(n22), 185–
186(n77), 302
National Commission on Air Quality,
200

National Environmental Policy Act (NEPA), 196–197
National Highway Traffic Safety Administration (NHTSA), 263
National Resources Defense Council (NRDC), 169
Nature
conquest of, 59–60
Neoconservatives, 49(n33)
Neocorporatism, 283, 293
application, 277–279
interest groups, 280–281
policymaking, 281–282
regulatory negotiations, 279–280
NEPA. *See* National Environmental Policy Act
New Deal, 5, 9, 12, 13, 20, 54, 55, 57, 169, 170, 207, 291–292, 293
administrative reorganization, 153–155
democratic honor, 59–61, 68–69
Great Society, 156–157
liberalism, 146–147, 148–149, 171–172
party politics, 152–153
policy reform, 10, 11
work ethic, 66–67
New Left, 4, 8, 12, 164–165, 319(n11)
"New Nationalism," 9
NHTSA. *See* National Highway Traffic Safety Administration
Nicaragua, 108. *See also* Iran-contra affair
Nixon, Richard, 32, 166, 298
administrative presidency, 173–174
education legislation, 191–192
presidential power, 102, 160–161, 173, 174, 191
Nomination procedures
activism, 307–308
changes in, 220–227, 298
political parties, 216–217, 219
presidential, 4, 16, 79–80(n45), 84(n81), 215, 217–218, 220
NRC. *See* Nuclear Regulatory Commission

NRDC. *See* National Resources Defense Council
Nuclear Regulatory Commission (NRC), 197
Nuclear test ban treaties, 135–137
Nunn, Sam, 132, 136, 138, 139, 249

Occupational Safety and Health Act, 302
Occupational Safety and Health Administration (OSHA), 263
Office of Communication of the United Church of Christ v. FCC, 33
Office of Economic Opportunity, 32
Office of Government Ethics, 297
Office of Management and Budget (OMB), 103, 177, 191, 198, 205, 252–253
Office of Technology Assessment, 106, 119
"Old Guard," 10
Olson, Mancur, 28
OMB. *See* Office of Management and Budget
O'Neill, Thomas P., Jr., 133, 137
OSHA. *See* Occupational Safety and Health Administration

PAC. *See* Political Action Committee
Party whips, 128–129
Patronage, 10, 92, 217
Peaceful Nuclear Explosion Treaty (PNET), 136
Percy, Charles H., 132
Pertchuk, Michael, 37
Pesticides
legislation, 250–251, 280
Pluralism, 8, 27, 50(n40), 309–310
attack on, 12–13, 28, 256–257
basic values, 52–53
Madison's views, 39–40
neocorporatism, 281–282
PNET. *See* Peaceful Nuclear Explosion Treaty
Pocock, J.G.A., 29
Policy, 79(n44), 178

business, 272–273
executive branch, 152–153
fads, 234–235
models, 246–247
process, 13–14
protection of rights, 299–300
regulatory, 262–264
shifts in, 11–12
See also Policymaking
Policymaking, 89, 90, 93, 239, 254, 255, 261
aggressive, 250–251
by Congress, 94–95, 96, 106, 112, 121, 123–124
constitutional, 188–189
goals, 248–249
issue networks, 242–243, 246
legislators, 248–251
neocorporatists, 281–282
organization, 18–19
politics of, 17–18
subgovernment, 240–241, 243, 245–246
See also Policy
Political Action Committee (PAC), 38, 237(n34), 249, 267
campaign contributions, 228–230
political parties and, 233–234
Political parties, 151, 173, 175, 298, 312, 313
Congress, 104–105
delegate selection, 220–221
democratization, 30–31, 44–45
election roles, 215–216, 298
formation, 216–217
leadership, 63–64
organization, 218–219
public attitudes, 233–234
realignments, 174, 178
See also Democratic party; Republican party
Political science, 256–257
Politics, 17, 18, 78(n35), 92, 242, 267, 290, 300, 302, 308–309, 317
consensus, 53–55, 58, 71–73
ethical reforms, 297–298
partisan, 151, 152

power, 155–156
Politics and Markets (Lindblom), 28
Poll tax, 30
Pollution, 5, 15–16
Populist movement, 217, 219
Poverty, 32
Power, 67, 73(n7), 191, 198, 201
administrative, 172–173
citizen's, 303–304
of Congress, 50(n49), 91, 92, 93, 101, 106, 107–108
Democratic party, 97–99, 105
executive branch, 42, 50(n49), 160–161, 163–165
Johnson, Lyndon, 61–62
party whips, 128–129
presidential, 95, 101–102, 108
Presidency, 60, 82(n68), 95, 113, 119, 148, 158, 170, 207, 215, 306
administrative policy, 149, 153, 172–174, 178–179, 191
campaign financing, 227–229
leadership, 101, 114–115, 147–148
legislative coalitions, 230–231
nominating process, 5, 16, 79–80(n45), 84(n81), 216–218, 220–227
power, 101–102, 160–161, 181(n22), 305
Reagan, 174–175, 177–178, 179
See also Executive branch
Primaries, 45, 217–218, 221–222, 223
Privacy Act, 294
Private rights of action, 205–206
Procedural rights
education, 195–196
environmental concerns, 196–197
Progressive Era, 5, 9–10, 11, 12, 215, 217, 219, 233, 263
Public-interest groups, 165, 167, 185(n67), 197, 200, 245, 265, 295
Magnuson-Moss Act, 166–167
reform initiatives, 37–38
social regulation, 168–169
See also Interest groups

"Quality-of-life," 5
  Great Society, 157–158, 162, 171

Ranney, Austin, 221
RARG. *See* Regulatory Analysis and
  Review Group
Rawls, John, 28
Reagan, Ronald, 19, 225, 231,
  237(n34), 295, 296, 318(n1)
  arms control, 136, 138–139
  election, 8, 9
  presidency, 175, 179
  See also Reagan administration;
  "Reagan Revolution"
Reagan administration, 108, 109, 149,
  245, 266, 289
  arms control, 113, 131, 132, 134,
  135
  budget, 21, 299
  bureaucratic control, 252–253
  chemical weapons, 139–140
  congressional codetermination,
  130–131
  conservative movement, 176, 177–
  178
  deregulation, 275–277
  Iran-contra affair, 116–117
  Republican party, 177–178
  See also Reagan, Ronald
"Reagan Revolution," 177–178
Regnegs. *See* Regulatory negotiation
Regulations, 6(table), 16, 274
  citizen participation, 32–33
  neocorporatist, 277–278
  performance standards, 267–268
  social, 261–262
  See also Social regulation
Regulatory Analysis and Review
  Group (RARG), 274
Regulatory negotiation
  interest groups, 280–281
  neocorporatism, 279–280
Regulatory programs, 274
  restructuring, 268–269
  social, 163, 177, 262–263
  See also individual programs

Rehabilitation Act (1973), 193
Reorganization Act (1939), 11
Republic, 44, 49(n37)
Republicanism, 29–30, 49(n37),
  50(n40)
Republican party, 10, 31, 98, 173,
  207, 219, 229, 314
  nomination process, 218, 225–227
  power, 176, 186–187(n85)
  Reagan administration, 177–178
Residency requirements, 30
Reynolds v. *Sims*, 30, 207
Richardson, Ann, 224
Roosevelt, Franklin D., 21, 67, 75(nn
  19, 21), 76–77(nn 26, 27, 28),
  78–79(n36), 101, 154, 182(n34),
  218
  American honor, 54, 59–60
  consensus politics, 71–73
  court-packing, 10, 185(n76)
  Democratic party reform, 55, 56–
  57, 151–152, 153–154, 181(n20)
  economic rights, 180–181(n19), 208,
  292
  liberalism, 149–150, 151, 170–171
  social activism, 55–56
  See also New Deal
Roosevelt, Theodore, 9
Rousseau, Jean-Jacques, 39, 40,
  49(n37)
Rulemaking, 35, 45, 81(n55), 166,
  252, 266
  Democratic party, 67–68, 222–224
  federal courts, 203, 204
  New Deal, 57–58
  nomination procedures, 220–224
  regulatory negotiation, 279–280
  restructuring, 203–204
Russell, Richard, 309

Safety, 178
  health regulations, 300–301
  workplace, 5, 15, 34
SALT II, 130, 131, 134–135
Schmitter, Philippe, 282
Scowcroft Commission, 133

SDI. *See* Strategic Defense Initiative
Security, 138
  economic, 156–157, 172, 292
  liberalism, 208–209
Seiberling, John F., 138
Senate, 106, 107, 135, 176
  committees, 93–94
  reform, 99–100
  representation, 96–97
  See also Congress
Senate Armed Services Committee,
  129–130
Senate Arms Control Observer
  Group, 135
Senate Foreign Relations Committee,
  62
Sherman Act (1890), 205
Sierra Club v. *Morton*, 265
Smith, Al, 218
Smith, Howard, 309
Social Contract, The (Rousseau), 39
Social programs, 163
  anti-poverty, 161–162
  public interest, 168–169
Social regulation
  business, 261–262, 267, 276
  costs, 268, 274
  legislation, 294–295
  organizational units, 271–272
  public procedures, 265–266
  shifts in, 262–266
Social Security, 182(n27), 200, 208
Social Security Agency, 182(n27)
Soviet Union
  arms control, 132, 134, 136, 139
Speaker of the House, 107
  power, 93, 104–105, 106
Special interests, 37. *See also* Interest
  groups; Public-interest groups
START. *See* Strategic Arms Reduction
  Talks
States rights. *See* Federalism
Statutes. *See* Legislation
Steering and Policy Committee, 104–
  105
Steering Committee, 104
Stevenson, Adlai, 100

Stevenson Committee, 100
Strategic Arms Reduction Talks
  (START), 130, 132–133, 135
Strategic Defense Initiative (SDI),
  131–132, 141
Subcommittees, 126, 190, 240, 295–
  296
Subgovernments, 230, 242
  administrators, 251–252
  interest groups, 251–252
  negotiation, 249–250
  policymaking, 240–241, 245–246,
  247
  political science, 256–257
Submarines, 134
Sullivan, Leonor, 250
Superdelegates, 223, 224
Supreme Court, 30, 181(n22), 189,
  191, 265, 291, 318(n5)
  court-packing, 56, 185(n76)
  legislative history, 202–203
  New Deal legislation, 10, 76(n26)
  rights to welfare, 198, 199

Task forces
  Johnson administration, 158–159
Tax reform, 232
Telecommunications
  and arms control, 138–139
  in Congress, 106–107
Television
  power of, 226–227
Threshold Test Ban Treaty (TTBT),
  136
Tocqueville, Alexis de, 51(n58), 283,
  317
  honor, 53–54, 58–59, 68, 69, 70,
  78(n32)
  reform, 46–47
Trade associations, 16, 267–268
Treaties
  nuclear test ban, 135–137
  See also SALT II
TTBT. *See* Threshold Test Ban Treaty
Tugwell, Rexford, 12
24th Amendment, 30

26th Amendment, 30

United States Department of the
  Interior, 295

Values, 164
  consensus, 52–55
Vietnam War, 8, 112, 116, 183(n47)
  Democratic party, 61–65
Virginia Resolutions, 42–43
Voting age, 30
Voting Rights Act (1965), 65, 188,
  189, 194, 209(n2), 294, 296

Wallace, George, 221
Warner, John, 138, 139
War on Poverty, 32
War Powers Act. *See* War Powers
  Resolution (1973)
War Powers Resolution (1973), 105,
  107, 161, 266, 305, 306
Warren Court, 190, 199, 207

Washington, George, 42
Watergate, 160–161
Water pollution, 5
Watt, James, 276, 295, 307
Weapons
  chemical and biological, 139–140
  freeze proposal, 131–132
  nuclear, 131–132, 133–135,
    144(n29)
Weinberger, Caspar, 129–130, 138
Welfare, 67
  rights of, 34, 180–181(n19), 198,
    199, 301
Wheeler-Lea Act, 5, 165
White House Office, 158
Wilson, Woodrow, 218
Winograd Commission, 220, 224
Wood, Gordon, 29
Work ethic, 66–67, 68
Working Group on Nuclear Risk
  Reduction, 139
Workplace
  safety in, 5, 34, 302